"An inflection point in history occurred when Dennis Archer was elected mayor. It was clearly an election about turning the page to project hope on the future while attacking the problems that had beset the city. We wanted to make voting for Dennis Archer a vote for what the future could be. So, when we said, 'Let the Future Begin!' it was really not about him. It was about Detroit. And it was about what the city and community could do together to build a better future. Now the future has truly begun in Detroit, and it's an exciting story!"

— DAVID AXELROD
CNN COMMENTATOR
FORMER SENIOR ADVISOR TO PRESIDENT BARACK OBAMA AND
CAMPAIGN STRATEGIST AND ADVISOR FOR FORMER DETROIT MAYOR DENNIS ARCHER

"Dennis Archer turned Detroit around. In my judgment — I really say this sincerely — I know of no other person, black or white, who laid the foundation for what Detroit is now, or who has done as much to keep this city where it is now."

— JUDGE DAMON J. KEITH
U.S. COURT OF APPEALS, SIXTH CIRCUIT

"Booker T. Washington, in his book *Up From Slavery* said, 'To be successful, grow to the point where one completely forgets himself — that is, to lose himself in a great cause.' I stand before you today, the son of a lost man… lost in the dreams and aspirations of our children, lost in the despair and plight of our homeless and disenfranchised, and lost in the possibilities and potential of the city he now leads. While he is lost, Detroit has made a great find. You have found a man who will dedicate his life to you. You have found a man who will relate to all of you, who will listen to all of you, and who will include all of you. I know this to be true because he has been a remarkable father."

— DENNIS WAYNE ARCHER JR.
SPEAKING AT MAYORAL INAUGURAL CEREMONY
JANUARY 3, 1994

"Most of you know him for his vision. I know him for helping me create my vision. Most of you know him for his dream for our city. I know him for showing me how to dream. Most of you know him for the goals he has set for our community. I know him for helping me reach my goals. The

man you call Mayor — my father, my friend. As mayor, he has the baton
that Mayor Coleman Alexander Young received when he became mayor,
and Dad has run with it. As mayor, his administration has brought businesses into Detroit to invest in our city, and to invest in our people. As
mayor, he has helped break ground on more new developments than our
city has seen in past decades. As mayor, he has instilled within us a new
hope and desire for Detroit to be the world class city of the new millennium. The man you call mayor — my father, my friend."

— VINCENT DUNCOMBE ARCHER
SPEAKING AT MAYORAL INAUGURAL CEREMONY
JANUARY 3, 1998

"Because he's a good lawyer, Dennis Archer is a very collegial person to
work with. You could discuss all topics. He appointed good people to run
agencies and departments. He worked hard on improving the administration and performance of government. There were a number of things we
were able to get done."

— JOHN ENGLER
FORMER GOVERNOR OF MICHIGAN
PRESIDENT, THE BUSINESS ROUNDTABLE

"Dennis represented a symbol of African American lawyers bridging that
gap between what traditionally was the white mainstream and the parallel
universe of minorities. Without his work, a lot would not be happening
as quickly as it is now. Obviously, I applaud mega investment in the city,
but we must give credit where credit is due, which is Dennis Archer's
compassion and tireless commitment to get the job done by surrounding
himself with brilliant people to transform the city of Detroit with innovation and excellence."

— PHYLLIS JAMES
FORMER CORPORATION COUNSEL, CITY OF DETROIT
EXECUTIVE VICE PRESIDENT AND CHIEF DIVERSITY & CORPORATE RESPONSIBILITY
OFFICER FOR MGM RESORTS INTERNATIONAL

"Dennis was not only the mayor of Detroit; he was a considerable national
figure. Dennis delivered tough messages in diplomatic terms. He had a
judicial temperament; he was assertive and measured at the same time.
You never saw him hesitate to take the initiative to speak on what was
best for the residents and city of Detroit. That passion came through."

— MARC MORIAL
FORMER MAYOR OF NEW ORLEANS
PRESIDENT OF THE NATIONAL URBAN LEAGUE

LET THE FUTURE BEGIN

Dennis W. Archer
Elizabeth Ann Atkins

For information about this title or to order other books and/or electronic media,
contact the publisher:
Atkins & Greenspan Writing
18530 Mack Avenue, Suite 166
Grosse Pointe Farms, MI 48236
www.atkinsgreenspan.com
atkinsgreenspan@gmail.com

ISBNs:
    978-1-945875-13-7 (Hardcover)
    978-1-945875-12-0 (Paperback)
    978-1-945875-11-3 (eBook)

Printed in the United States of America

Cover and Interior design: 1106design.com

Cover portrait © Patricia Hill Burnett

All photographs used with permission. All uncredited photographs courtesy of
the Archer Family Collection.

Dedication

This book is dedicated to:

My Parents, Ernest James Archer and Frances Marie Carroll Archer; Grandmother, Letitia "Lettie" Carroll Garner; Aunt, Josephine Lombardo; and Uncles, James, Warren, and Ronald Garner for my start in life.

To my wife, Trudy DunCombe Archer, for the help and guidance that led to my accomplishments. For the future, I entrust to our sons, Dennis Wayne Archer Jr. and Vincent DunCombe Archer; our grandsons, Dennis Wayne Archer III (Trey) and Chase Alexander Archer, and future generations of our family.

CONTENTS

ACKNOWLEDGEMENTS

FIRST AND FOREMOST, acknowledgement goes to my wife, Trudy DunCombe Archer, for encouraging me to put pen to paper and compose this memoir. In fact, she set me on a lifetime course to LET THE FUTURE BEGIN by encouraging me to attend law school more than a half century ago.

That's why it's fitting to release this book during the year that we celebrated our 50th wedding anniversary on June 17, 2017.

Also instrumental in bringing this book to fruition has been the support of our sons, Dennis Wayne Archer Jr., and Vincent DunCombe Archer, as well as my sister-in-law, Beth DunCombe Brown, who was influential in my Michigan Supreme Court retention election and my mayoral campaign

Trudy and I walk down the aisle after exchanging wedding vows on June 17, 1967 at Blessed Sacrament Cathedral in Detroit.

and for the city. In addition, I draw the most inspiration today from our grandsons, Dennis Wayne Archer III (Trey) and Chase Alexander Archer.

Immense gratitude rests with my parents, Ernest James Archer and Frances Marie Carroll Archer; my grandmother, Letitia "Lettie" Carroll Garner; my aunt, Josephine Lombardo; and my uncles, James, Warren, and Ronald Garner. Together they laid a foundation of character, respect, education, and an impeccable work ethic upon which my adult future could begin.

Very importantly, I must thank Elizabeth Ann Atkins for helping to compose this book, and Catherine M. Greenspan of Atkins & Greenspan Writing for publishing this autobiography. At my request, Elizabeth interviewed dozens of people and wove their recollections into the tapestry of my life story.

Likewise, I am extremely grateful for each of those individuals who were interviewed for generously giving their time and expertise. I especially appreciate those who contributed to the hard work and accomplishments of our mayoral administration that LET THE FUTURE BEGIN to elevate Detroit to the city that it is today.

My utmost appreciation goes to my mentor and friend, Judge Damon J. Keith, Senior Judge for the United States Court of Appeals for the Sixth Circuit, for blessing this book with his poignant message in the Foreword.

My many lifelong friends deserve credit for always supporting me, personally and professionally, and for providing time and space for me to relax and enjoy life.

The people, organizations, and educational institutions that have touched and shaped my life are too numerous to name. However, I am especially thankful for Cassopolis, Michigan; Western Michigan University; the Detroit College of Law, now Michigan State University School of Law; the American Bar Association; the National Bar Association; the State Bar of Michigan; the Wolverine Bar Association; the law firms of Dickinson Wright, Charfoos and Christensen, and Hall, Stone, Allen and Archer; the Michigan Supreme Court; the citizens of Detroit, its regional communities, and the state of Michigan; the Detroit Regional Chamber; as well as former President Bill Clinton, Vice President Al Gore, President Barack Obama, and Vice President Joe Biden; the corporations whose public and for-profit and advisory boards of directors of which I was privileged to be a member; and finally for the brotherhood and friendship of The Association, Alpha Phi Alpha Fraternity, Inc., Sigma Pi Phi-Iota Boulé, the National Guardsmen, and the Detroit Guardsmen.

And to all of you, I simply say, thank you.

FOREWORD

DENNIS ARCHER has been blessed by God not only with brilliance, but with a commitment to help others.

I first met Dennis in 1967 when he was teaching school during the day and attending law school at night. When he worked in our law firm, I recognized the potential of this young man. He and I became very close friends.

I swore him in: when he passed the Michigan Bar Exam in 1970; as the President of the National Bar; as the President of the Wolverine Bar Association; as a Justice of the Michigan Supreme Court; as Mayor; and as the first black President of the American Bar Association, which represents all the lawyers in the country. I also administered the oath to his wife and to his son when they were admitted to the State Bar of Michigan. So, our families are very close.

Dennis Archer turned Detroit around. In my judgment — I really say this sincerely — I know of no other person, black or white, who laid the foundation for what Detroit is now, or who has done as much to keep this city where it is now.

This city would not be the same if it were not for Mayor Archer. He is the root of the Detroit Lions coming back to Detroit. Mr. William Clay Ford said that it was Dennis Archer who convinced him to come back to Detroit. And, of course, had it not been for Dennis Archer and his relationship with the CEO of Compuware, Mr. Peter Karmanos would not have brought Compuware to Detroit.

The corporate people had a strong liking for Mayor Archer and he's walked that thin line that few blacks can do. He hasn't lost his identity in the black community or his identity in the white community. The black community is still behind him 100 percent and so is the white community. He has respect in both communities, which is very important.

He is a man of integrity. That's important.

During his service as Mayor of the City of Detroit — this is critical — there wasn't one bit of anything about any criminality, any fraud or anything that brought dishonor to the mayor or his staff. That's wonderful. Mayor Archer has shown that one person who's dedicated and committed can make a difference. You don't need a bunch of people, just one person who has the ability and the commitment and the concern.

Coming from very little means, he's never forgotten his roots. And now he's helping young people, and has given more than $1 million in scholarships through the Dennis W. Archer Scholarship Fund for minority students at Western Michigan University and Wayne State University.

Mayor Archer is a person of color with character and integrity, who has walked with kings without any reservations and never lost the common touch; that describes this great man.

I have a saying: we're walking on floors we did not scrub, and going through doors we did not open. Dennis has scrubbed the floors so others can walk on them, and he has opened the doors for others to follow. What a compliment to pay a great man who's meant so much to the city, the state, and the country.

I salute him, and I hope this book will tell the true story of this great man and his family.

Judge Damon J. Keith
Senior Judge
United States Court of Appeals for the Sixth Circuit
November 24, 2015

INTRODUCTION

THE BLEAK CIRCUMSTANCES OF my birth offered no hint that my future would ever include a day like January 3, 1994, when I was publicly sworn in as mayor of America's eighth-largest city.

Nor did the days, when bigotry banned me from swimming in a lake 300 yards from where my father worked, indicate that one day I would serve on the Michigan Supreme Court as a justice charged with ensuring liberty, equality, and justice for all.

Likewise, my childhood days when I owned only one pair of shoes and lacked running water in our home could not have predicted a future when I would befriend presidents, travel the globe, host world leaders, and visit the White House, let alone sleep in the Lincoln Bedroom.

Growing up in the Village of Cassopolis, Michigan, with a population of about 1,200 people, where I met only two black professionals — a business owner and a schoolteacher — I had no vision of what I might become. And I had no idea that the path before me would ultimately allow me to lead the American Bar Association's 400,000 members as its first black president.

None of the above would have happened without the driving force of people close to me.

"Dennis, you are going to college and you will graduate," my loving but impoverished parents told me while growing up in rural Cassopolis, Michigan. Those who reiterated this edict had never set foot on a college campus. Yet they saw a future for me that I could not envision, and their encouragement made me work hard to bring their dream to reality.

At the same time, my childhood barber, a woman, declared, "Dennis, you're going to be somebody. You're going to do something in life."

I didn't know what that meant, but I believed it wholeheartedly and focused on education as my ticket to becoming that "somebody" and "doing something." Later, as the Civil Rights Movement persevered, Trudy, who became my wife, suggested that my work as a Detroit Public Schools teacher was admirable, but a career as a lawyer would bestow the power to advocate for equality and justice during an era of discrimination and deadly race riots across America. She discerned potential within me that may have otherwise remained dormant.

I've been very blessed with good people who cared enough to become mentors before I knew what a mentor was. They unabashedly critiqued, criticized, and guided me in ways that elevated my thinking, conduct, and qualifications to maximize my greatest potential to serve in positions that helped people.

One such person is Damon J. Keith, who hired me as a law student to work in his law firm. To my immense gratitude, Damon Keith's wise words have guided my life and career decisions for a half-century.

When I humbly heeded guidance from him and others, and worked hard to achieve ever-higher goals, the result always presented me with tremendous opportunities to help people on a broad scale.

Herein lies the motivation for sharing my life story on the pages of this book: to show young people that they can begin life with little or nothing, and they can climb up and out of any circumstances on faith, hard work, and help from others.

Just as importantly, I pray that my story will inspire men and women who are blessed with vision, achievement, and power to invest time, wisdom, and guidance in those who need it most.

Offering simple advice, shared in a few seconds, may engender a path toward success. Be that voice of wisdom and encouragement for a young person today; he or she may grow up to become a leader, a mayor, an inventor, a business owner, or even president.

Despite my conviction to convey this message, I must confess that embarking on the book-writing process began with a lot of reluctance and has been a long time in the making. It's far more appealing to focus attention on how I can help others, than to talk about myself.

Therefore, please allow me to thank my wife, retired State District Court Judge, Trudy DunCombe Archer, for inspiring the compilation of this record of my life. As we celebrate 50 years of marriage, I lack sufficient words to express my gratitude to Trudy for being the most exemplary wife, mother, grandmother, and life partner that a man could ever hope for.

Trudy reminded me that the local and national media have told my story their way. Now, LET THE FUTURE BEGIN is the chronicle of Dennis Wayne Archer's life and career, from my perspective.

This book also documents our family history for our sons, Dennis Wayne Archer Jr., and Vincent DunCombe Archer; our grandsons, Dennis Wayne Archer III and Chase Alexander Archer; as well as future members of the Archer family.

A final take-away: hard work does pay off. Integrity never goes out of style. And you can LET THE FUTURE BEGIN right now to create a life of meaning and impact on yourself and the world.

Dennis W. Archer
Former Justice, Michigan Supreme Court
Former Mayor, City of Detroit
Chairman and CEO, Dennis W. Archer PLLC
Chairman Emeritus, Dickinson Wright PLLC

PREFACE

OUR SON, DENNIS WAYNE ARCHER JR., spoke at my Inaugural swearing-in on January 3, 1994, at Detroit's historic Fox Theatre before 5,000 supporters and city, state, and national leaders.

Our son, Dennis Wayne Archer Jr. set the tone for an inspiring, emotional celebration during my Inaugural swearing-in ceremony.

When I woke up this morning, I had butterflies in my stomach because I realized that I had to come speak before you today. But having gone to the prayer breakfast and listening to the prolific Rev. Jesse Louis Jackson this morning, and then going to the ecumenical service and hearing again from Dr. Frederick G. Sampson of Tabernacle Missionary Baptist Church, I'm ready.

On October 27th, I drove from Ann Arbor to Detroit for the last time to work on my father's campaign. It was Wednesday and there was less than a week left to what had been the most stressful and trying period of my life. For the past four nights, I had not been able to fall asleep in my dorm. I later found out that my mother was also having problems sleeping. It was not surprising. But that night, I was back in my own room in my own bed and I was able to fall asleep. I had a dream that night. My father had been elected mayor and I was introducing him at his victory party. I told no one of this dream until now.

While others discussed victory celebrations, what we would do for the inauguration, and how our lives were going to be different, I chose to focus on the reality of the close race at hand. I thought of asking my aunt to allow me to speak at the victory party, but I decided against it for fear of jinxing my father. He never takes anything for granted, why should I?

November 3rd has come and gone. My dream is now reality. Dad won — we had a wonderful celebration. A couple of weeks later I called my aunt at home late one night and asked her if I could introduce Dad at the swearing in. She promised to get back with me. After a while, when I hadn't heard anything, and became caught up in my finals, I forgot about it. Then five days ago my father said they were taking away two of his 12 minutes so that I could make my comments. I was suddenly speechless. What would I say? What if I cried?

Well, I'm here today and I suppose my topic should be my father, his success, and our city's future. Booker T. Washington, in his book Up From Slavery *said, "To be successful, grow to the point where one completely forgets himself — that is, to lose himself in a great cause." I stand before you today, the son of a lost man — lost in the dreams and aspirations of our children, lost in the despair and plight of our homeless and disenfranchised, and lost in the possibilities and potential of the city he now leads.*

While he is lost, Detroit has made a great find. You have found a man who will dedicate his life to you. You have found a man who will relate to all of you, who will listen to all of you, and who will include all of you. I know this to be true because he has been a remarkable father.

Many of you ask, "How will he do this?" Deborah McGriff, in an August 25, 1991 Free Press *article said that "To be successful, you need to embrace change, learn to work with others, and make good choices." Well, Detroit, we have most definitely embraced change.*

As a matter of fact, we have demanded it and expect it. Rest assured it will come.

Will he work with others? I will let you be the judge of that. We had 6,000 campaign volunteers representing every race, religion, culture, and tax bracket. We will need assistance from both city and suburb — and since November 2nd, my father has been to the White House twice, to meet with the governor twice, and he has met with numerous religious and community groups here in the city.

Making good choices, that's an easy one. Akua Budu-Watkins, Emmett Baylor, Freman Hendrix, Ike McKinnon, Mike Sarafa, to name a few, all appointees. They are black, white, Hispanic, Lebanese, women, men, and all with impeccable resumes. All good choices. If Ms. McGriff's point to us was success is indeed an indicator, we are off to a good start.

And finally, to those who are asking whether the campaign had or will take my father away from our family, I answer a resounding NO! As a matter of fact, I thank Detroit for this campaign for our city. It brought my father and me even closer. Because I know what kind of father he is, I know what kind of mayor he will be. Congratulations, Detroit! You are very lucky!

❖ ❖ ❖

After his speech, tears filled the eyes of many of the 5,000 men, women, and children who had come to celebrate my Inaugural Swearing-In as the 67th Mayor of the City of Detroit. In the audience were Uncle Jimmy (Garner), Uncle Warren (Garner) and their wives; my wife's parents, Eleanor and James V. DunCombe; Trudy's sister and my campaign finance chair, C. Beth DunCombe and her husband, Joseph N. Brown; and many of our lifelong friends.

Though only 24 years old and a student at the University of Michigan School of Law, my son's eloquence inspired inexplicable pride within me — pride for both my family and for one of America's largest cities, one that I was now endowed with the honor of leading into a better, brighter future.

While the audience thundered with a standing ovation, I embraced Trudy, who for 26 years had been my loving partner in a rock-solid marriage that created Dennis Jr., and Vincent, who would, four years later, deliver an equally inspiring message at my second Inauguration as Mayor of Detroit.

Now, as I stood with Vincent, a 20-year-old political science major at the University of Michigan, Dennis Jr., and Trudy, time seemed to stand still. Cheers and applause fueled my spirit with immense joy, humility, and determination to power through the very long days and years ahead to accomplish all that I dreamed possible for Detroit. That moment in 1994 would remain the pinnacle of my life.

It encompassed everyone and everything that I love and value to this day. My family's love, guidance, and wisdom had helped mold me into the person who would now apply their values of respect, hard work, and altruism to transform Detroit into a globally celebrated boomtown where everyone thrived.

"If I'm optimistic today about our future, it's in part because of the road that I've traveled," I told the crowd. "And because of the lessons my parents taught me through their example, that hard work and determination can overcome great obstacles and break down barriers that seem insurmountable." At the time, Detroit's barriers indeed seemed insurmountable: crime, poverty, race relations, unemployment, population loss, poor schools, an eroding tax base, urban blight, and so much more. Detroit had become synonymous with all of the above, especially among late night comedians and media commentators. The Motor City's woes had also become fodder for sensationalist media reports, most notably in years past on Halloween eve when arsonists set hundreds of fires that attracted TV crews from around the world.

Naysayers had declared Detroit a dead city whose economic engine as an Arsenal of Democracy had thrived, then died, with a challenged automotive industry. However, I absolutely knew our beloved city could be revived with the help of thousands who had worked tirelessly on the mayoral campaign because they believed that together we could return Detroit to its status as a world-class city.

And it was my responsibility, my mission, and my vision to do just that. Thus, on that glorious day of January 3, 1994, I set out to fulfill my campaign goal to LET THE FUTURE BEGIN.

1

POOR, BUT RICH
WITH HOPE

SACRIFICING FOR A BETTER LIFE FOR BABY

MY STORY BEGINS ON A bitter winter night on the outskirts of a small village called Cassopolis, located near the southwest corner of Michigan. Its 1,200 residents lived a simple but wholesome life, with the men working in factories and on farms, and the women tending to homes and children. Venturing into town to shop or conduct business meant frequenting the flat-roofed, one block long, two-story brick storefronts adorned with awnings and signs.

Dominating the picturesque townscape, just one block from Main Street, stood the Romanesque-style Cass County Courthouse. Built in 1899, its three-and-a-half stories boasted a beige limestone façade. Rising above, its clock tower was visible, it seemed, for miles on the two-lane highways, M60 and M62, which intersected in the heart of Cassopolis as Main Street and Broadway, respectively.

A short drive south on M62 toward South Bend, Indiana, led to my parents' home, in the countryside where many of the town's black families lived. There, the winter wind whipped across snow-covered fields, howling against the two-story, wood-frame house. Though it was the Christmas season of 1941, and my parents were about to receive the blessing of a baby, their mood was hardly festive.

America had just declared war on Japan, which had bombed Pearl Harbor, Hawaii, on December 7th, killing 2,403 people. As a result, the United States' entry into World War II under President Franklin D. Roosevelt had cast an ominous and anxious pall over the country, as families braced themselves for the grim reality that their sons could be sent into battle and lose their lives.

My parents, however, were grappling with the reality of being too poor to provide for the son or daughter who had yet to be born.

I can almost envision the following: "Frances," said my father, Ernest James Archer, as he cast a worried look at my mother. She was sitting with him at the dining room table, grasping the sides of her pregnant belly that bulged beneath her floral-print housedress.

"You need to have this baby in the hospital," he said, "where it's clean and safe. Somehow we're going to get good medical care for the both of you." Wearing his usual bib overalls and a long-sleeved shirt, my father used his right hand to grasp hers.

"The problem is," he lamented, "without a car, I can't get you to the hospital. The one in Niles is 15 miles away, and we can forget about going 24 miles to the hospital in South Bend. Plus, we don't know how they feel about black folks in both those places —"

"We'll think of something," said my mother, Frances Marie Carroll Archer, squeezing his hand as anxiety pinched her face.

They sat silently in the red glow of the cast-iron, coal stove, the only source of heat for the old farmhouse.

"I want our baby to have so much more than I ever had," my father said, shaking his head. "Our child will go to college one day, and have a good life, not struggle like we do."

My father's struggle resulted from having only a third-grade education — and one arm. Being that cars had no air conditioning back then, my father had been driving on a hot summer day, shortly after returning to Cassopolis following his service in the U.S. Army. On that particular day, before I was born, he was catching a breeze through the open driver's side window — with his left arm leaning on the open window of the driver's car door. Another automobile sideswiped his vehicle, and he lost his arm above the elbow.

This handicap made it difficult for my father to find and sustain the kind of farming and factory work that dominated the economy of Cassopolis and the region. And while this challenge made him a resourceful entrepreneur with a knack for finding odd jobs, wintertime was especially harsh.

"How can we get you to a hospital?" he asked. He was well aware of the risks to both mother and baby when giving birth at home. "Frances, I promise you, we will come up with something."

The promises of equality and opportunity in the North had inspired my father's family to migrate from Northampton County, North Carolina, through Logan County, Ohio, before settling in Cassopolis. Likewise, my mother had come from Tazewell, Virginia, to Cassopolis with her mother and her sister. By the time of my birth, my mother's family had all since moved to Detroit.

But neither of their family histories seemed to matter as my parents contemplated the dilemma of how to bring me into the world inside the safety of a modern hospital.

"We didn't come this far to give up or give in," my father said, just before a train whistle blew. A locomotive rumbled behind the house on the railroad tracks, shaking the house as my father promised, "We will find a way."

Finding a way out of no way was a trait that both my parents had inherited from strong family lineages boasting men and women who had made extraordinary achievements during extremely oppressive times in the South.

And so, my parents drew upon the strength and resourcefulness endowed by prior generations to make a better way for their child.

"Frances," my father announced, "you need to go to Detroit, to a hospital there, and stay with your family for a while."

I suspect that one of my mother's brothers drove 187 miles to Cassopolis to pick her up and take her back to Detroit.

As my parents wished, I was born in Dorothy Rogers General Hospital on January 1, 1942. While many cultures around the world believe that New Year's Day babies are blessed with lifelong success, luck, and good fortune for themselves and their families, that proved true in the context of my mother's reality at the time.

Our good fortune came in the form of her supportive, financially stable relatives who welcomed us home from the hospital. First, we stayed with my grandmother's sister, Aunt Hattie, on McDougall Street in Detroit's famed Black Bottom neighborhood. Though named in the 1700's for its low elevation and fertile, dark soil by the French who founded Detroit as a fur-trading post, the name Black Bottom became associated with the fact that it had become home to most of the city's African Americans. There, black doctors, lawyers, teachers, and successful business owners lived among factory workers and others.

Many were among the 400,000 southerners who had flocked to Detroit since 1914 to earn the unprecedented five-dollars-a-day wages that Henry Ford was offering for jobs on the automobile assembly lines at Ford Motor Company. At the time of my birth, throngs of people were still crowding into the city to work at car factories, which had stopped producing commercial vehicles and were instead manufacturing B-24 bombers, Jeeps, and tanks for the Allies in World War II.

Though the United States was defending its ideals of democracy, liberty, and justice on a global scale, African Americans endured discrimination and segregation in Detroit. Because of discrimination, many African Americans could only live in what was known as Black Bottom.

Black Bottom is viewed through the nostalgic lens of history as an idyllic place when the constraints of the Jim Crow world created a black, minimetropolis that was self-sufficient, organized, united, and rich with culture and pride. The region bustled with thriving black businesses of every kind, including real estate agencies, pharmacies, ice cream shops, hospitals, funeral homes, bowling alleys, and so much more.

Just across Gratiot Avenue to the north was Paradise Valley, the black entertainment district whose electrifying glamour rivaled Harlem and Chicago's South Side. Nationally celebrated entertainers like Count Basie, Duke Ellington, Ella Fitzgerald, Billie Holliday, Sammy Davis Jr., and Cab Calloway performed in Paradise Valley clubs.

The world of the early 1940's barred them — along with Detroit visitors such as Rev. Adam Clayton Powell Jr., Harlem Renaissance

Author Langston Hughes, star athletes Jackie Robinson and Jessie Owens, and many others — from patronizing downtown hotels. Instead, they stayed at the black-owned Gotham Hotel, Detroit's most glamorous destination for dinners and social events for black people.

As Detroit's population continued to spike toward its peak of nearly two million by 1950, competition for jobs and housing strained race relations so much that a riot in 1943 — sparked by rumors based on racial stereotypes — exploded on the island park of Belle Isle when I was 18 months old. Twenty-five of the 34 people killed were black, many at the hands of police, and looting caused significant damage in Black Bottom.

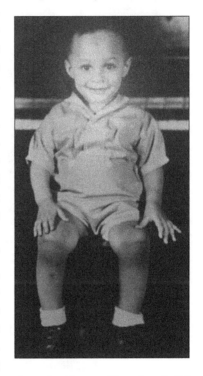

Such was the environment in which I lived as a toddler — between a gritty racial reality and the glamorous world of famous, high-powered black people who were making important economic and political marks on the world.

"See that house, Dennis?" my mother said one day, pointing to a home near Aunt Hattie's. "That's where Joe Louis' mother lives. He visits there all the time. He's the most famous black man in America, because he's the World Heavyweight Boxing Champion." I would later learn that the Brown Bomber held that title from 1937 until 1949, and his presence in the neighborhood set the historical perspective of my upbringing.

While I never met Joe Louis, I was impressed by the pride sparkling in my mother's eyes, and on the faces of children and my relatives who often referenced his presence in the neighborhood.

Before I was five years old, we moved a short distance to my maternal grandmother Letitia "Lettie" Carroll Garner's house on Rivard at Lafayette Boulevard, also in Black Bottom. One of the few photographs of me was taken at Grandma's around age two, smiling while sitting on a piano bench. In another photo, taken when I was four or five years old, I'm wearing a sailor suit and sitting on a metal-frame twin bed covered with an Indian-print blanket. With hands together in my lap and ankles crossed, I'm smiling slightly with a happy expression.

My grandmother, Letitia "Lettie" Carroll Garner

That was the feeling in the home of my grandmother, who was strong, elegant, and dignified. A retired schoolteacher, she had experienced the indignities of the Jim Crow South. My mother Frances, and her sister, Josephine, were born in Tazewell, Virginia, when Lettie was married to Gordon Cousins. She left Virginia and moved to Cassopolis with her two daughters, my mother, and her sister, Josephine. Later, Grandma married Chester Garner. They had three sons, Warren, James, and Ron. My grandmother, three uncles, and Aunt Jo moved to Detroit before I was born.

When my mother and I lived with Grandma, my uncles were serving in World War II, and Aunt Jo returned from living in Hawaii with her husband, Frank Lombardo.

Grandma was very practical. She filled me with the same words of wisdom that she had ingrained in her children, such as, "Pride comes from being a responsible, capable person." She frequently admonished, "Treat everyone you meet with respect. You never know who you might have to ask for a drink of water before you die."

Like my parents, Grandma insisted that I had to be twice as good as someone who was white to have a chance to be considered equal.

"Dennis, you can't do anything half way," she often said. "You have to do everything properly, by the books. Be ethical. And treat people with respect, no matter who they are. Because if you ever move up, the fall to the bottom can be swift and painful, but if you treat people with respect, someone may be there to help break the fall — to cushion it for you."

Grandma's values were passed down from a lineage that she traced back several hundred years along a family tree with two major branches: the Carrolls and the Warrens. Their histories are eloquently chronicled in three binders brimming with neatly typed histories, photographs, articles, wills, funeral programs and other documents. These narratives, composed by family members, feature story upon story of men and women who triumphed over immense challenges, defied unjust authority, and fought for freedom, justice, and racial equality.

Six generations later, our ancestors' spirit of patriotic military duty to our country inspired my three uncles to serve in the U.S. Armed Forces during World War II. Uncle Warren volunteered for the U.S. Army, and was awarded four bronze stars for fighting in Africa, Italy, Germany, and France.

Meanwhile, Cassopolis, where my father remained, could have been just as far away. I had yet to meet him as I celebrated my fifth birthday in Detroit.

Yet that did not seem unusual; I simply understood that Dad was back in Cassopolis, taking care of Mr. Wescott's summer home on nearby Diamond Lake. Aptly named for the sparkle of its pristine, blue-green water and luxurious cottages, the largest lake in southeast Michigan attracted wealthy, white, summer vacationers from across the state as well as Indiana and Illinois. Blacks could neither live nor swim there, but instead worked as domestics and caretakers.

My father had found employment with Floyd Wescott, owner of a tool and die shop in South Bend, Indiana. As the caretaker of his summer home, my father mowed the lawn, washed their car, tended to their garden that he planted, and made sure the house remained in good working order.

"Your father works real hard and cares a lot about you," my mother, grandmother, and uncles often reminded me. "He sent you here to make sure you were born in a good hospital in Detroit." All the while, I spent my days playing with kids in the neighborhood, and later attending kindergarten at Barstow Elementary School. At home, my mother, who had a high school diploma, taught me colors, numbers, the alphabet, and much more.

LIFE AS A BOY IN 1940's DETROIT

Some of my fondest memories involved outings with my mother and my grandmother, whom I adored. She was a walker, so we often

traveled by foot from home to the bustling downtown shopping district along Woodward Avenue.

Gripping Grandma's hand, I stared up at the ornate skyscrapers, including the Guardian Building, the Penobscot Building, with the big red ball on top that shone brightly at night, the Buhl Building, the David Broderick Tower, and the David Stott Building.

Everything seemed so big and busy on the streets crowded with men in suits wearing hats, and women in tailored blouses, full skirts, and heels. It was just awesome to walk amid the streams of people along the sidewalks past J.L. Hudson Department Store, the freestanding Kern Clock, and Grinnell's piano store as cars, buses, and streetcars whizzed past on the wide streets.

On the best days, Grandma would take me to Vernors. There she'd treat me to a float made from a scoop of vanilla ice cream atop golden, bubbling ginger ale that would become a world-famous, made-in-Detroit sensation. The store was a must-stop before the dock for the Boblo Boat, which I would ride during the summer with my mother and grandmother to Boblo Island Amusement Park down the Detroit River.

As for shopping downtown, another highlight was walking up Woodward Avenue toward State Street to S.S. Kresge Company. The vast store sold everything imaginable for a nickel or a dime. In the meat department, Grandma would buy chicken wings for 10 cents per pound. It filled me with delight and anticipation for the delicious dinner she would cook that night. Kresge had the most delicious smells wafting from the luncheonette that served hot meals, banana splits, and waffle cones filled with ice cream. My grandmother was the most outstanding cook that I've ever known. I especially loved Grandma's chicken, spaghetti, and apple cobbler.

While her food was perfectly seasoned, my grandmother peppered conversations with her trademark maxims. For example, if someone said they wanted something that they couldn't have, she would quip, "Yeah, people in hell want ice water." Stubbornness inspired her reminder that, "A hard head leads to a soft behind." And she thwarted gossip and criticism of others by cautioning, "If you don't have anything good to say about someone, then don't say anything."

Meanwhile, nothing was said to me about the racial climate of the mid-1940's — it was shown.

"Dennis, lay down on the seat," said Aunt Jo as her husband, Frank Lombardo, drove their car northward from Detroit toward their new home in the all-white suburb of Royal Oak.

They had recently moved from Hawaii and had given me a Christmas gift that became one of my most cherished toys. It was a Dick Tracy car, named for the popular comic strip detective, that I could wind up and race across the floor for hours. I adored Aunt Jo and Uncle Frank, because they lavished my mother and me with love.

Except I did not understand why they were telling me to lie down on the back seat. I was excited to visit their new home, so I did as I was told. The mystery continued when we pulled into their driveway, and I was guided to enter the house through the back door.

I later understood that Aunt Jo was "passing," which meant allowing people to conclude she was white because she had very fair skin, sharp features, and a fine hair texture. Back then, "passing for white" allowed blacks to enjoy better social and financial opportunities than those denied to people who were of color. Passing allowed Aunt Jo to obtain a very good position at the Michigan Employment Security Commission.

I later understood that she and Uncle Frank, who was white, had purchased a home in an all-white neighborhood in an all-white city, and my presence could expose their secret.

Likewise, my mother's very fair skin often led people to question why she — who in their eyes was a white woman — was shopping or walking with a black child.

"This is my son," she would respond proudly.

FROM A BUSTLING METROPOLIS TO RURAL CASSOPOLIS

"We all think it's time that you went home," Uncle Warren announced one day when he came to visit my grandmother's home. A short time later, he drove me and my mother to Cassopolis. As we left the buildings, paved streets, and densely populated neighborhood in Detroit, I stared out the car window, excited to meet my dad. Soon the city streets gave way to green fields and farms as we traversed the lowest part of Michigan along US 12.

"Dennis, this is Cassopolis," my mother said as Uncle Warren drove along a single block of Main Street. A drugstore stood on one side of the street, facing an A&P supermarket, with banks on either side, along with a clothing store, a taxi stand, and a bakery.

My mother, Frances Marie Carroll Archer. I have no photos of my father, Ernest James Archer.

Down one street stood a much bigger building with a tall clock tower, as well as houses, and a church with a tall steeple.

In a blink of an eye, we were passing houses on the left, and Stone Lake was on our right. We turned left and then right; houses lined both sides of the two-lane highway.

My heart pounded with anticipation to meet my father, but just as urgently, I needed to use the restroom as Uncle Warren pulled into a 30-yard, unpaved driveway leading toward a two-story, wooden house with a large front yard.

As we stepped out of the car, I was struck by the fresh air and silence, which was quite different than Detroit where cars, horns, sirens, streetcars, and neighbors created a constant cacophony of city noise. Across the two-lane road, back a bit, was a golf course.

Suddenly a deep, earth-shaking rumble and a train whistle drew my attention. A train chugged past along the railroad tracks just past the barn, the garden, and a fence.

"Hello, Dennis," my father said, gazing at me in a way that made me feel happy and loved. Wearing bibbed overalls and a shirt, with his left arm missing just above the elbow, he looked exactly as my family had described him. He was nice looking, my complexion, with gray eyes and a full head of hair. With a muscular build, Dad was a little shorter than my very tall Uncle Warren.

He hugged me, and I felt so happy. I couldn't wait to get to know my dad and spend time with him. But first I turned to my mother.

"Momma, I have to go to the bathroom," I announced. She took my hand and led me behind the house to a small wooden structure. As she creaked open the door, a foul odor hit my nose.

"This is where we use the toilet," she said. "It's not like Grandma's house with running water. We don't have a toilet or sinks or a bath tub inside the house."

I peered into the dark, closet-sized structure, which contained a wooden bench with a hole in the center. Flies buzzed around the hole, which seemed deep and appeared pitch black.

"What about at night and in the winter?" I asked nervously.

"We use the honey pot inside," my mother said, explaining that it was a chamber pot — a bowl-type container that substituted for a toilet. "Then you'll have to empty it here in the morning."

I was not a child who complained or whined. I respected authority, and accepted what I was told. But as I stepped into the outhouse, I sure didn't like it. I had a feeling that this indicated life here in Cassopolis, though now enriched by the presence of my father, would lack some of the comforts afforded by Grandma's house back in Detroit.

I would soon learn that having no modern plumbing required us to retrieve water for drinking and cooking from a well next to the house. When the well froze in the wintertime, we had to boil rainwater on the kerosene stove and pour it over the well to loosen the pump before water would come up. Then we'd store the bucket of water, covered with newspaper to keep dust out, on a table in the kitchen.

Another pump inside was connected to a container that collected rainwater from the eaves troughs. We used that water for washing dishes and bathing. Every Saturday night, I took a bath in a big metal tub before I went to bed.

When it came time to enroll in elementary school, personnel wanted me to repeat kindergarten.

"My son will begin first grade here," my mother insisted. "He has already completed kindergarten in Detroit, and he will not be held back."

Many of my classmates' fathers worked on farms and in factories, such as the Studebaker plant in South Bend, Indiana, or at the pickle, trailer, and furniture factories in and around Cassopolis. My classmates' mothers, like mine, were homemakers.

The town had no black section or white section; black families and white families lived, worked (except downtown), and attended school together. Many of the black families lived on farms outside the Cassopolis Village limits, where they, like us, relied on gardens for fresh vegetables. Some raised cows and pigs.

The people in Cassopolis were down to earth and genuine; we lived simple lives. Most were just like we were. My mother made certain that my clothes were clean, even if they did not match. A lot of my clothes came from my grandmother and uncles, who bought them in Detroit, or sent me nice hand-me-downs. Sometimes I wore my single pair of shoes whether I was going to church or school, or playing in a softball game.

At home, most of the time, food was usually abundant. My mother prepared most meals, and I enjoyed when my father shot and cooked rabbit or coon. At Thanksgiving, he always made sure we had a turkey.

When I was at school, the lunch program provided good, hot meals. As I got older, I worked in the lunchroom, which afforded me extra food. It also enabled me to indulge my fondness for ice-cold chocolate milk. Having access to the school's freezer, I placed the milk cartons inside before drinking them.

"You Have To Do Your Best!"

While I never went hungry or missed meals, a few occasions revealed our financial hardship, especially during the wintertime.

Dad earned $75 every other week during six months of the year. But just before Christmas, Mr. Wescott cut his biweekly pay in half, to $37.50 for the next six months.

"Dennis, come to the table," my mother called one winter night. I arrived to discover that our dinner, which she prepared on the burners and in the oven of the kerosene stove, consisted of biscuits — with no honey or jam — and sassafras tea. It was red and quite tasty, made from roots boiled in water.

At the time, I accepted this as the way things were. I would later learn that sometimes during the winter months, my father had to resort to applying for financial assistance from the Department of Social Services to help put food on the table.

With no television or exposure to wealthy people, I didn't know what we didn't have. We also had no camera, so I have no photographs of my father at all, and none of my mother during my childhood in Cassopolis.

However, while my parents were poor in terms of money, they were rich with hope for my future.

"Dennis, you're going to go to college and graduate," my father said over dinner. "Education is your ticket to having a good life."

My mother nodded in agreement as she sipped her tea. Nearby, the coal stove glowed red-hot as it heated the first floor.

"Now after you eat," Momma said, "I'll help you finish your homework. You need to earn the very best grades now, so you can go to college and graduate."

My mother was committed to helping me achieve that. She attended every parent-teacher conference, and inspected my desk as well as the classroom walls to make certain that I was being an exemplary student.

"Dennis," she warned on more than one occasion, "I saw your schoolwork on the bulletin board, but it had no stars from the teacher. I expect that the next time I see your work on display, your teacher will have marked it with gold stars. You have to do your best!"

At times, it seemed that the entire town felt this way.

"Dennis, let me see that report card," said the first of several neighbors who stopped me as I walked home from school. Cassopolis was a small village, and everyone — even adults who had no children — knew when the report cards came out, and they truly demonstrated the African proverb that "it takes a village" to raise a child.

"Come on over here," they called. "Let me see that report card." A good report card would be rewarded with a hug or a piece of candy. A low mark or critical comments from teachers would provoke a scolding: "Don't you come back this way with this next time. You can do better than that!"

I was not always the best student. In fact, sometimes I loved to cut up as the class clown. But I knew the difference between right and wrong, and restricted my mischief to harmless jokes and pranks.

"Dennis," my mother warned, "we expect you to act like a gentleman and earn better marks. Because you are going to go to college and graduate."

This was an oft-repeated declaration throughout my childhood from my parents, Aunt Jo, and my uncles when they visited us in Cassopolis, and from Grandma when I spent alternate Thanksgiving and Christmas holidays and two weeks in the summer with her in Detroit.

But neither they nor anyone at church or even my teachers provided any details for me to envision and dream about my future life on a college campus.

I contemplated this at night before going to sleep in my upstairs bedroom, which was heated only by what little warmth wafted upstairs from the coal stove on the first floor. On cold winter nights, my mother gave me a hot water bottle made of red rubber to keep my feet warm under the blankets.

If I needed to go to the bathroom, I would use the "honey pot." In the morning, it was my job to empty the chamber pot in the outhouse.

Meanwhile, as I tried to dream of college, I concluded that if going there would enable me to live in a house with a toilet, a bathtub, and sinks with running water, and if it would help me to make money to buy what I wanted, then I was ready.

MY FATHER: ONE OF MY GREATEST TEACHERS

My dad had a great mind; he was so skilled and industrious that I never thought of him as having a third-grade education, or being physically handicapped.

Though he was not worldly, he was wise, and endowed with the virtue of patience, which he exhibited with me while investing time to teach me everything he knew.

"Now, Dennis, watch this, because I'm going to show you how to grow a garden," Dad said as we stood on the soft, tilled rows of dirt in the back of our barn. "This is how you plant seeds that will grow into fruits and vegetables that we can eat, can them for the winter, and sell the surplus to neighbors. You're old enough to help me."

With only one hand, he demonstrated the mechanics of precise seed placement, offering instructions on watering, weeding, and finally, harvesting. Months later, we enjoyed eating the fruits and vegetables, especially rhubarb and collard greens. And I would join my father to sell them, or hustle on my own to sell along with red raspberries.

My father had an aptitude for working with electricity, and he bestowed this talent on me. To this day I can repair a broken lamp.

Sometimes I accompanied my father to the house on Diamond Lake where he worked. At the time, it was the biggest house I'd ever seen. I enjoyed those trips, because it provided me with the luxury of taking a shower.

"Mr. Wescott isn't here right now," my father said. "He's still down at their winter home in Sarasota, Florida."

One day, when Dad was driving his boss' car through the countryside, he parked on the side of the highway.

"See that over there?" he said. "That's where the Underground Railroad was."

I stared at the cornfields, seeing no train tracks or black-and-white striped gates indicating a railway crossing. I turned to my father with a baffled expression.

"Dad, how could they put a whole train and tracks underground?"

"Let me tell you," he said. "Cassopolis was a stop on the Underground Railroad. Here in Cass County, a lot of white people, called abolitionists, helped Negroes escape from slavery in the South."

I stared at the fields and trees. This was my first time hearing this; my teachers at school had never mentioned it.

"By railroad," my father continued, "that's what they called the secret route that blacks followed on foot or hidden in wagons. And the route wasn't really underground. It was under cover, because it was dangerous. The slave owners would hunt down the slaves who escaped. They could be taken back to the South and whipped or even killed."

I was horrified as my father explained what slavery was, and that it had been legal in the South. How could that be allowed? Why hadn't I learned about it in school?

"They were risking their lives to escape," Dad said, "and so were the people who hid them in houses, barns, and cellars along the way. It was illegal to help escaped slaves, even though they were doing the right thing."

My father then explained that some of the black people who made it to Cassopolis stayed, while others moved on to Detroit and into Canada.

I would later learn that by 1850, 74 households in Cass County were headed by a free black or mulatto, according to the U.S. Census, and half of those families had come from North Carolina. The Archers were among them.

One of my ancestors, Lemuel Archer, was mentioned several times in a 1902 article entitled "200 Years Under Freedom" and written by Booker T. Washington. In it, the educator and presidential advisor described visiting Cassopolis and expressed his amazement at the prosperity of the "colored" settlement. He said Archer is an English name, meaning "a person who shoots with a bow and arrow."

The earliest confirmed ancestor in my father's family was Lemuel Archer, born in 1777 in Northampton County, North Carolina. He married Dorothy Newsome in the early 1800's and had many children. Presumably born into slavery, they obtained freedom as evidenced by a document called a "free paper" in March 1831.

"This is an 1831 free paper used by Lemuel Archer and family for safe travels in the South and North," reads a caption under a copy of this half-page document preserved in an album containing articles, photographs, and documents about my father's lineage. At the top of the "free paper" is handwritten in large letters: "Lemuel Archer Colored Man."

The names of his wife and their six children were handwritten on the document, which they carried as one might carry a driver's license or passport to prove identity and citizenship. The Archer family's "free papers" were recorded on October 22, 1838, when they moved to Logan County, Ohio, after Dorothy's father willed them land there.

After a stay in Columbiana County, Ohio, near the Pennsylvania border, according to the 1860 Census, Lemuel Archer and his family moved to Cassopolis. My grandfather and grandmother were Joseph and Mary Archer. My dad had a brother, Floyd, and a sister, Malinda.

As my father introduced me to black history, I felt proud that our village and county had played an important role in leading people to freedom.

I also loved times like that with my father. Other endearing moments occurred when Dad took me hunting. Armed with his 10-gauge shotgun while I carried my BB gun, we hunted rabbits.

Another treat was heading into town to the bakery, where my dad would buy me a donut. While we were among the black customers in the businesses along Main Street, it was apparent and often discussed in private that no blacks worked in any visible positions along Main Street. Though I was unable to articulate it at the time, this realization played on my young conscience. It was society's way of showing me the "rules" of the game of life for blacks that I rejected in my mind and heart. Yet I had no idea how, when, or if the rules would ever change.

The absence of blacks working on Main Street was as close to racial injustice that I experienced in Cassopolis; blacks and whites lived in harmony together.

On Sundays, I attended church with my parents. During the summer, we enjoyed church picnics and church socials in Calvin Center.

These outings were special because my father would pick up his boss' car and drive us at a time when we were accustomed to walking as our main form of transportation.

Whether I was at church gatherings or at school, my parents insisted on exemplary behavior. Say please and thank you. Be polite, use correct English, and behave.

The wholesome, family-centered environment of Cassopolis provided me with a value system, the main tenet of which was to act like a gentleman who honored the Golden Rule at all times.

"Dennis," my parents often said, "always treat others the way you want them to treat you."

Momma and Dad also emphasized that teachers deserved my utmost respect at all times. Refuting a teacher's comments was taboo; it was the uncontestable truth that teachers were never wrong.

Though my teachers never discouraged me or told me that I was incapable of doing anything, I lacked a vision for who or what I could become.

Thankfully, one teacher in particular invested time and concern in me and other students by teaching us to take pride in ourselves.

"You know, Dennis, you can do good things," John Raihala, my government teacher for three years, told me. "You can be somebody."

Outhouse Causes Inferiority Complex

Undermining this encouragement was an inferiority complex triggered by embarrassment that our home had an outhouse. My classmates lived in houses with toilets, sinks, and bathtubs. Our lack thereof made me feel poorer than poor, and I vowed never to have a party that would expose my embarrassment to my classmates.

I was blessed with a close-knit group of friends that included Frankie Williams, whom I met in Mrs. Southworth's and Mrs. Hayden's classes. He lived in Cassopolis with his grandparents, about three-fourths of a mile from our home. We visited each other's homes to play and eat dinner; somehow I endured the embarrassment of our outhouse when my closest friends visited.

However, attending birthday parties and other gatherings at the homes of friends such as Winston Johnson, Dennis Ash, and Frankie Williams exacerbated my feelings of inferiority, because I was reminded of what we did not have.

As I grew older, my awareness of our poverty intensified during holiday visits and summertime stays in Detroit with relatives, as well as trips to Chicago to visit Aunt Maude and Uncle Jimmy, who worked for a railroad company.

During those trips, Grandma, my three uncles, and my Aunt Jo frequently reinforced my parents' mantra, "Dennis, you are going to college and you will graduate." Meanwhile, I enjoyed memorable conversations with my grandmother.

"Grandma, I just can't wait until I turn 18," I would say, or "I can't wait 'til I become 21, and then I can go to a bar and vote."

"Let me tell you something," she responded. "There's going to come a point in your life when time is going to fly. The older you get, you'll find that time goes faster than you can even imagine." Grandma also seemed to know everything that was on my mind. Every time I went out as a teenager, she warned, "Now don't you do so-and-so-and-so." I don't know how she knew what I was thinking about doing. But she was absolutely correct on everything.

While my relatives were enriching my mind and determination to excel in school, time in Detroit and Chicago exposed me to all that I was missing.

I don't ever remember thinking, "When I grow up, I'm gonna be rich." Instead, I remember thinking, "I'm going to be somebody because that's what the barber told me."

Quite simply, I wanted to graduate from high school, go to college, and return to Detroit, where I would enjoy running water.

2

SCHOOL, SPORTS,
AND MANY JOBS

A WORKING MAN AT AGE 8

WHEN I WAS EIGHT YEARS OLD, I walked into the small clubhouse at the Park Shore Golf Course across M62 from our home and asked, "Can I please become a caddy?"

I was approved! My father had not told me to do this; I had decided for myself that I needed a job to earn money so I could contribute to our family, as well as to buy tickets to the movies with my friends.

Park Shore Golf Course, a nine-hole golf course, served Cassopolis and the Diamond Lake area, where many young Notre Dame University students' families had summer homes.

This job instilled in me an appreciation for golf, as did Uncle Warren. He gave me a five iron, also called a mashie, and he taught me how to use it to drive, chip, get out of sand traps, and putt. Thus began my lifelong love for the game of golf — and working hard at whatever jobs I could get. These jobs included work at the local pickle factory. I continued to help my dad sell red raspberries and other produce grown in our garden.

When my friends and I began attending junior/senior high school, we worked weekends at the bowling alley in Cassopolis. It was hand-operated, so our job was to set the pins in the rack after each player bowled.

"We got nicked a few times," recalls Frankie Williams, "but it was nothing of a serious nature. For the most part, Dennis and I had fun and made a couple dollars on the weekends."

Around that time, a black businessman from Chicago named Charles Smith purchased the vacant land from my father that was next to our house. He built a factory called Smith Hoist & Manufacturing Company, named for the hoist that he had patented. A steady stream of trailer tractor rigs stopped at the factory to haul away hoists used by people and companies across America.

A very smart businessman, Mr. Smith hired me to sweep the factory and office floors. In the basement was a pool table; my friends and I would sneak through a window in the evening to play, and Mr. Smith, though he was aware, never said anything.

I really enjoyed caddying for Mr. Smith at the golf course across the street, and I raked leaves at his family's beautiful countryside home a few miles from our house.

Other than Charles Smith, for the longest time our town had no black professionals. Without first-person exposure to African-American doctors, dentists, lawyers, and accountants, it was possible to grow up unaware that such possibilities existed. We simply didn't know what we might become.

We had very little exposure to media. During the early-to-mid-1950's, I loved sitting around the radio with my parents, listening to *Amos 'n' Andy*, *The Shadow*, and other radio programs.

When I was 12 years old, I was captivated by conversations among my parents and the adults at church as they discussed how the U.S. Supreme Court had ruled in *Brown v. the Board of Education of Topeka Kansas* that segregation in public schools was unconstitutional. It seemed that everyone around me was talking about how a black lawyer named Thurgood Marshall had played a lead role in the case that said separating students by race in public schools was no longer legal. That decision could open the door for more civil rights advancements.

At the time, my understanding of that legal milestone was rudimentary at best, but I knew that it was good news for people of color. It also resonated because my family was always emphasizing education as the ticket to a better life, and this decision would help black kids, in far worse conditions than mine, to attend better schools.

Enjoying Sports Teams and Marching Band

A major highlight of junior high school was playing sports. Specifically, six-man football because our school was so small.

"We had to maintain a 2.0 Grade Point Average to play sports," Frankie remembers. "Dennis didn't have to worry. He probably had better than a 3.0 all the time. He was a pretty astute student in school."

Frankie, who recently retired after 41 years as Chief of the Cassopolis Police Department, adds, "Dennis was always a person who was accomplishing things. He wasn't a lazy person. You could tell that, down the road, he'd be blessed with his abilities."

Throughout high school, I played basketball, filling whatever position was needed. One year, we were undefeated until the Class C season playoffs, when we lost to Kalamazoo Christian High School.

Playing sports provided important lessons about teamwork; my every move could help or hurt the team, and the guys relied on each other to perform our best so that we could all win. This responsibility required giving my all during practice as well.

During the spring, I was on the golf team, playing with a set of used clubs provided by Uncle Warren. He and Uncle Jimmy were outstanding golfers. I could never beat them.

What I did beat was the bass drum, in the Cassopolis High School Marching Band. I enjoyed striking the two, felt-covered mallets against each side of the drum that was secured in front of me by a shoulder harness. My drumbeats joined with the rest of the band to create music that announced the Cassopolis Rangers' pride and victory. Our music electrified the players and fans who gathered to watch at our home football field and at other Class C schools.

My mother attended games. She had an especially proud sparkle in her eyes as we performed in band concerts and competitions, and when we marched in the Centreville Fair and the Blossomtime Parade in the nearby town of St. Joseph.

The marching band taught me about upholding my responsibility within a group whose performance depended on me. I had to attend band rehearsals, as well as practice at home. If I missed beats or failed to show up, the marching band — along with spectators — would suffer. This pressure inspired me to work hard to perform to the best of my ability. The pageantry of the marching band was fun; Momma made sure my blue-and-white uniform was clean and wrinkle-free, and I did my best to keep it that way.

FLIRTING WITH DEATH, ESCAPING UNSCATHED

The excitement was palpable as I got into Winston Johnson's car with Frankie Williams and a few other friends.

"Tonight's dance will be the best yet," Winston announced as he drove us 25 miles to the town of Paw Paw.

"It can't be better than last weekend in Detroit," Frankie said, reflecting on our road trip to stay with my uncle.

It was our junior year, and since Winston had his driver's license and a car, we took frequent outings to dances in a tavern on Eagle Lake. The ride there always inspired us to speculate about all the fun we would have with the black teenagers who convened there from nearby towns.

"I can't wait to get to the juke box," Winston said. "I want to play *A Star's Out Tonight* by The Flamingos."

After a fun night of dancing and socializing, we piled back into Winston's car to ride home.

"Ssshhh," Winston said, adjusting the radio dial as the static gave way to Ray Charles or Nat King Cole or Chuck Berry and R&B hit songs of the day. We listened while Winston cruised along the two-lane country road in the darkness.

"Here we are!" Frankie exclaimed as we reached a certain hilltop. At the bottom of its sharp slope was an intersection with a four-way stop.

"Let's do it!" we exclaimed.

Winston accelerated down the hill. Our hearts banged with excitement as we scanned for headlights on the road that we were about to intersect.

Winston turned off the headlights.

The car went flying down the hill, closer... closer...

We had done this countless times, always blowing through the four-way stop at a high rate of speed — in complete darkness. Mind you, this was a time before seatbelts and airbags.

"There's nothing coming!" someone shouted. "We can do it!"

We whooped with excitement.

Another time, we were in Cassopolis and not far from Winston's home, when he was driving down a hill. Suddenly the car went airborne.

It flipped over. After a few dizzying moments, we realized we were still alive — and unhurt. Amazingly, we all climbed out of the car and walked away from the crash.

While not flirting with death, the guys brazenly broke the rule that prohibited blacks from swimming in Diamond Lake. One sunny afternoon, we were having a great time when a white man shouted, "Yawl ain't supposed to be out there!"

As we scrambled away, I slipped and hit my knee on the rocks; it took two stitches to repair the gash.

Most of the time, my friends and I fished and swam in Stone Lake, just a few blocks from Old Main Street in the heart of Cassopolis.

During the summer, we rode about five miles to beautiful Paradise Lake in Calvin Center, about five miles from my home. This vibrant resort community was a mecca for black families from the surrounding areas in Chicago during a racial environment that precluded blacks from buying cottages, staying in hotels, or dining in restaurants in other areas. As a result, Paradise Lake was an oasis where blacks enjoyed all of the above, along with horseback riding, boating, tennis, swimming, and more.

My friends and I spent many a fun summer evening socializing with other young people on Paradise Lake. No matter what we were doing, we showed respect to adults, followed the rules, and honored our curfew.

"We didn't do anything that caused any problems for our parents," Frankie recalls. "We were taught that right is right and wrong is wrong. So, we always did what was right."

Back in Cassopolis, our outings took us to Dairy Queen and the A&W Root Beer stand. We also loved to frequent the Gem Theatre to watch Bob Hope movies like *Road to Bali*, as well as werewolf movies and *Frankenstein*.

After some movies, we were one scared group of kids walking home in the dark. With visions of werewolves and Frankenstein in our heads, we ran like our lives depended on it. My friends all lived within Cassopolis Village limits and had streetlights which lit their routes home. But I lived outside the village limits. And so, my solo sprint home was in pitch blackness save for the headlights of an occasional passing car or on the Smith Hoist building.

Other times, I joined my friends at someone's home to play bid whist. These gatherings were fun, but they often set off my inferiority complex because everyone had indoor plumbing except the Archers.

As for having visitors at our home, the guys would come over and we'd play football in our large front yard. But they left before using the bathroom became an issue.

Otherwise, I honored my secret pledge never to invite people to a party at our home where they would have to use the outhouse.

LIMITED LENS ON THE WORLD OPENS WIDER

The larger world began to reveal itself to me when I was 15. That's when my uncle brought our first TV, black-and-white, from Detroit. My dad went to Shank's TV store, where he purchased an antenna that was installed on the roof and dropped the wire down through a window. That enabled us to watch WKZO-TV in Kalamazoo, as well as stations from Chicago and South Bend.

At the time, shows like *Ozzie and Harriet* and *Leave It To Beaver* were popular. These and other programs featured few, if any, people of color that I could relate to. And so when I discovered a South Bend station showing state basketball tournaments in which many of the players were black, I was hooked. It was so unusual and exciting to see black people on TV, and playing a sport that I enjoyed. On the other hand, I once flipped to a station showing hockey, and because I did not know what it was, I changed channels.

Television opened my eyes to all that we did not have: nice homes, cars, clothing, and opportunities. In the late 1950's, TV also provided vivid and disturbing images of protests and marches in the South, where blacks were being beaten, attacked by dogs, sprayed with fire hoses, and arrested for demanding fair and equal treatment. While this was highly upsetting, the Civil Rights Movement felt far away. Cassopolis had no NAACP branch or protests, nor did any activists visit our town where blacks and whites lived, worked, and attended school without incident.

The occasional TV news reports that I saw showed Dr. Martin Luther King Jr. Prior to that, in the mid-1950's, I had often heard the adults at church talking about his efforts to provide voting rights, justice, and jobs for blacks in the South. They also talked about his quest to end bus discrimination in Montgomery, Alabama.

In Cassopolis, the arrival of a black teacher opened my eyes to other new possibilities. During my junior year, as Clarence Lusby began teaching math, his status as a black professional exemplified who and what a black man could become with a college degree.

"I Can't Afford to Send You to College"

During my junior year of high school, my father told me, "I can't afford to send you to college. I think you ought to join the Army and get the GI Bill to pay for your college."

When Uncle Warren heard this, he said, "You're going to work your way through college."

That inspired me to continue doing my best in school and at my latest job — mopping the floor at the bakery on Main Street. It required me to rise at 4 a.m., then walk a mile into town. While passing the houses and fields along two-lane M62, which had no sidewalk, I had to walk about two city blocks before reaching the first streetlight. On many occasions, strange sounds coming from the darkness prompted me to run — and run fast. Once I reached the bakery, I swept and mopped the floor. Then I'd walk home, sleep for an hour or so, get back up for school, eat breakfast, and walk to school.

This routine caught the attention of my friend's father, Mr. Edwin Johnson, who heard about me going to and from work at the bakery, and heard others talking about my grueling schedule. Impressed, Mr. Johnson hired me to work in the basement at his home, a job I held until graduation. In his basement workshop, Mr. Johnson demonstrated his excellent soldering and welding skills. He had me work on, and then clean, small metal items before he painted them and took them to Chicago to sell to an interior decorator.

"Dennis, with your work ethic, you can do great things in life," he said.

I had no vision of what those great things could be, but I was glad to know that he believed in me, and saw more in me than I saw in myself.

My senior photograph graduating from Cassopolis High School in 1959.

In May of 1959, I was among the largest class to ever graduate from Cassopolis High School. Of the 79 students, a fair number of us were black. A few attended college, and one, Gilbert Johnson, ultimately worked for the U.S. State Department. Most, however, married and raised families in Cassopolis.

My plan was to move to Detroit, live with my grandmother, and begin fall classes at Wayne State University. But first, I wanted to work all summer to save money to pay college tuition. So I applied at a local furniture company. I lied about my age, claiming I was older, but I got tripped up when I applied for health insurance. That's when they discovered I was really younger, and they fired me.

That forced me to move to Detroit earlier than planned. I was fortunate to land a job painting houses for the real estate company that employed Uncle Warren. The company also bought houses, renovated them, and sold them at a higher price. I soon discovered that painting was not for me. In the summer heat, as sweat poured down my face, the fumes from the oil-based paint seemed to burn my lungs, especially when I painted closets. I would frequently feel dizzy.

Then there was the terror of climbing an extension ladder to paint the eaves troughs or the outside windows, which required reaching up in a way that caused paint to drip down my arms.

Fortunately, I soon moved to another job down the street from the real estate office, at Alhambra Drugs at Woodward Avenue and Kenilworth. I stocked liquor and other supplies, then swept and mopped the floor. I enjoyed meeting all kinds of people and working for the owner and pharmacist, Mr. Bernstein, who wore a white jacket and filled prescriptions for customers.

DETROIT: THE RICHEST CITY IN AMERICA

At the time, Detroit was one of the richest cities in the United States, thanks to the booming auto industry. Known as "The Paris of the West," it was celebrated as one of the world's most important cities, where automobile company fortunes enabled families to build and inhabit mansions in neighborhoods such as the Boston-Edison District, Indian Village, and Palmer Woods. Detroit also boasted a thriving middle class and one of the best public school systems in the nation.

Louis Miriani was mayor, and Berry Gordy was in the process of founding Motown Records. Detroit was the place to be, and I was delighted to live with my grandmother to enjoy her wisdom, excellent cooking, and modern plumbing.

Leaving a rural town of about 1,200 people to live in America's fourth-largest city was exciting — and intimidating. Having little to my name besides the desire to attend college, I became acutely aware of all that I lacked.

While I rode the bus, sometimes two, to visit someone I was dating, I looked out on streets crowded with nice cars, many driven by guys my age. When I walked up Woodward Avenue, I lacked the money to patronize the country's second largest department store. I also became aware of the discrimination occurring inside, where blacks could work as elevator operators, but not on the sales floors to sell dresses or washing machines or perfume or anything else. Likewise, at the time, blacks and women were banned from joining the Detroit Athletic Club and blacks could not join the Detroit Golf Club, which were exclusive, white male enclaves where business deals were made over drinks, dinner, and golf.

I came to realize that while Detroit lacked the overt racism that designated "colored" drinking fountains or forced a black person to step off the sidewalk if a white person were coming in your direction, discrimination in the Motor City was institutionalized, resulting in the same void of brown and black faces in certain places and positions as I had experienced on the one block of Main Street back in Cassopolis. That was wrong, but I had no idea how, when, or if it could change.

For the time being, the top priority of Dennis Wayne Archer was to go to college and graduate.

"I'd Like to be a Pharmacist"

Stepping onto the vast campus of Wayne State University — located straight up Woodward Avenue from where we lived — I became the first in my immediate family to attend college. I can't recall any euphoric moment when I thought, "I have arrived."

Instead, it was somewhat intimidating to join the cosmopolitan, cultural mecca of a big-city campus bustling with thousands of people from around the world. Lurking beneath the surface of my friendly personality was that inferiority complex, often aggravated by jolting realizations that I was ill-prepared for the academic rigors of Wayne State University.

This was especially acute when I made a requisite appointment with a guidance counselor in 1959, prior to the start of classes.

"Dennis, what do you want to be?" he asked.

I stared back at him, hoping that my face did not expose my profound bewilderment. I had no idea what I wanted to be! I had never thought about what to study in college. I just wanted to get there. Now here I was, on the spot, in the glare of the counselor's probing eyes. Suddenly Mr. Bernstein came to mind. And I remembered chemistry class back in Cassopolis, but all I could recall was that we had made oxygen.

"What do you want to be?" the counselor demanded.

"I'd like to be a pharmacist," I said.

"Fine, you can go to Pharmacy School," he declared.

It took about 18 months for me and Pharmacy to not get along. Many of my classmates had attended much better high schools. I could not compete.

However, the campus atmosphere with so many new and interesting people was delightful. I enjoyed engaging in conversations that presented new ideas, opinions, and life experiences.

I purchased a four-door, 1949 Ford for $50 from Mr. Bernstein. The pharmacist had apparently backed up with his back door open on the driver's side and crunched it. I went to the junkyard and found a '49 Ford, bought a door, and put it on my car. The door was black; my car was blue. So, I called my car The Black Door. It eventually died, and I replaced it with a blue 1952 Studebaker.

Despite my academic challenges at Wayne State, it was important to project a good image. I may have felt poor and embarrassed about it, but I sure was not going to let anyone know it. Instead, I cultivated an engaging personality. Thankfully, my uncles helped me dress in proper styles.

On campus, I was especially impressed with members of Alpha Phi Alpha fraternity. Upperclassmen such as Steve Chennault and Elliott Hall were focused on education and always carried themselves with an air of sophistication and integrity that I admired. While they were fun to hang around at social gatherings, they lavished me with guidance and advice on how to navigate campus life.

"Hanging with the Alphas was important," recalls Elliott Hall, who was a junior when we met on campus. "We were academically centered and we had the highest honor point average than any fraternity on campus. We were absolutely focused on doing well with our educational careers and making sure we were hanging around with folks who had the same ideals. Dennis embraced that, and of course, wanted to do what these other Alpha brothers were doing. Most of them ended up being doctors, engineers, educators, and in some cases, lawyers."

I soon found myself pledging the fraternity — and questioning my judgment as I endured the kind of hazing that is no longer permitted. While "on line" during Hell Week, we had to shave our heads, wear a tuxedo and walk everywhere by taking two steps forward and one step back. On top of carrying our textbooks, we were required to carry a brick, and each day during Hell Week our elder brothers mandated that we add another brick. After seven days, we were lugging seven bricks across campus at all times.

I survived, and enjoyed the privilege of becoming an Alpha Man for life. Now, as I often tease my friends who are members of Kappa Alpha Psi and Omega Psi Phi fraternities, when it comes to being an Alpha, "Many are called, but few are chosen."

PLAYING FOR PRESIDENT KENNEDY'S INAUGURATION

A highlight was playing the bass drum in the Wayne State University Marching Band. All the excitement and responsibility of playing in the Cassopolis High School Marching Band was multiplied exponentially as we donned our black uniforms trimmed with the school colors of green and gold, and marched — 110 strong — into the football stadium.

Band Director Dr. Angelo Cucci required intensive practices and rehearsals. As a result, we performed flawlessly when the WSU Warriors competed with NCAA Division II teams in the Great Lakes Intercollegiate Athletic Conference.

We performed at home football games for the Detroit Lions as well as the Soap Box Derby in Akron, Ohio. Our showmanship attracted national attention, as did our status as America's only band that had performed in every elite musical convention in the United States.

Such honors earned the WSU Marching Band the privilege of representing the state of Michigan in President John F. Kennedy's Inaugural Parade in Washington, DC, on Friday, January 20, 1961.

During my first-ever trip to our nation's capital, I was over-whelmed with pride and excitement when we played "War March of the Tartars," our school song written by K.L. King, the former president of the American Band Directors Association.

Despite the bitter cold, it was a tremendous honor to play for President Kennedy, whom I had seen so many times on television throughout his election campaign. With him at the ceremony in the eastern portico of the U.S. Capitol was Vice President Lyndon B. Johnson.

"I Want to Teach"

Despite such incredible highlights of attending Wayne State, my dislike of the difficult classes required for a Pharmacy degree soon inspired me to attend the Detroit Institute of Technology. As an Arts and Sciences major, my grades became exceedingly better; I especially enjoyed my German class.

However, two years into the program, as I approached graduation, I asked myself, "What am I going to do with a degree in Arts and Sciences?"

I could not answer that question, until Steve Chennault and Donald Hobson came to mind. Both spoke often with me about their work as high school teachers. They inspired me to want to teach.

I also felt confident that if someone asked, "What do you do?" I could answer, "I'm a high school history teacher."

From the time I started at Wayne State, I was working part-time at Henry Ford Hospital in the Medical Records Department. I was among a group of college students whose job was to go through the hospital and annotate the location of every medical record. I was the first African American to hold this position.

This was significant, considering the times.

While I was attending college, whether it was at Wayne State University, Detroit Institute of Technology, and later Western Michigan University, students engaged in spirited conversations about the Civil Rights Movement and what was happening in the South. These conversations, which occurred when we gathered in the student union, at parties, picnics, and other events, changed significantly as news and historic events transpired.

Lawyers from the city of Detroit — including George Crockett Jr., Myron Wahls, and Claudia Morcom — traveled to Mississippi and other Southern states to help with voter registration, marches, and sit-ins. Back in Detroit, we heard about their experiences and shared opinions about how we hoped things would change.

Meanwhile, one of the most significant occurrences at the time in Detroit was the day Dr. King led 125,000 people in a march down Woodward Avenue on June 22, 1963, where he first delivered his "I Have a Dream" speech. Two months later, he would lead the historic March on Washington when his delivery of that speech became one of the most iconic moments in world history.

Around the same time, my friend, Creflo Mims, who would become a successful entrepreneur, invited me and a few other friends to take a weekend trip to Western Michigan University. After a two-hour drive west to Kalamazoo, Michigan, which is just 47 miles from Cassopolis, we attended a party. Meeting so many fun, interesting people motivated me to transfer to WMU to become a teacher. So, I drove there in my Studebaker. As soon as I pulled into the student lot, the car died.

Thankfully, it got me to my new destination in time to register and start classes.

"Dennis Had That Swag About Him"

"Dennis Wayne Archer came to campus like a storm," recalls William F. Pickard, who would become my second roommate and lifelong friend. "He had that Detroit flair, a charisma that made everyone in the room notice him. And he could drop names about people and places in Motown in ways that made him a celebrity. Everybody gravitated to Dennis Wayne Archer."

A native of the mid-Michigan automobile factory town of Flint, Bill says that guys like himself, from small cities such as Battle Creek, Dowagiac, and Paw Paw, saw Detroit as a cosmopolitan mecca of music, style, and glamour.

"Dennis had that swag about him," he says. "He was always neatly dressed. Polo shirts, belts, loafers, and khaki pants were in vogue. Dennis was always thin and neat, and his trademark pants were a little shorter. Plus, Dennis could dance!"

Bill, who would become extremely successful as Chairman and CEO of Global Automotive Alliance LLC, Detroit, and owner of multiple McDonald's restaurant franchises, adds that he dreamed of joining Alpha Phi Alpha fraternity.

"Dennis was already an Alpha when he got to Western," Bill recalls. "That added another part of the mystique because we were still trying to get an Alpha chapter at Western. That was something else that elevated him."

Despite Bill's glowing recollection of my presence on campus, living away from my family for the first time was a challenging adjustment. I had no idea how much I would miss my grandmother's extraordinary cooking — or access to food at all, for that matter.

But first, my most pressing order of business at Western Michigan University was to see a counselor to determine my course of study.

"What do you want to do?" the counselor asked.

"I want to teach high school history," I answered confidently.

"Where?"

"In Detroit."

"I want you to think about this," the counselor said. "Right now we've got so many high school history teachers in our state, you would be very lucky to teach junior high history. If you want to stay in Education, give some thought to a subject beyond teaching history. Or understand that you're likely to end up teaching junior high someplace."

This was heavy on my mind as I returned to Henry B. Vandercook Hall, a men's dormitory named for the State Representative who introduced the bill to establish WMU.

Inside my room, I discovered an 18-inch stack of mail addressed to George Waters, my first roommate who was a senior. The return addresses on the envelopes named school districts across Michigan.

"George, what are all these letters?" I asked when he arrived.

"Job offers." George, who was from the Detroit suburb of River Rouge and whose aunt was the actress Della Reese, explained that he would soon graduate with a degree in Special Education for the Educable Mentally Retarded, which meant kids with a below-average IQ.

"You could talk to them," he said, "and never know they were retarded unless you asked them to read or do math."

I glanced back at the towering stack of job offers, then met with my counselor to declare, "I want to study Special Education and find a job teaching 'Special A' in a Detroit elementary school."

Surviving "Hungry Hall"

Having a goal and a vision for my future boosted my confidence academically, and I began to thrive in Special Education courses.

Notwithstanding Bill Pickard's complimentary assessment of my social status, campus life provided constant and depressing reminders of my lowly financial status.

Vandercook Hall was known as "Hungry Hall," because it was the only dormitory on campus that had no cafeteria. Athletes and students who could not afford a meal plan lived in its stark rooms with bunk beds, desks, and communal bathrooms.

Thankfully, I met an older fraternity brother named William Moten who was responsible for one of the dormitories that served food. He got me a job making $1.35 per hour to wash pots and pans in the cafeteria. I chose to work the dinner hour so that I could eat a good meal every evening. Bill Pickard was hired for the breakfast shift. Each of us would bring enough food back to the dorm room to share later.

Another drawback of Vandercook? It was about a mile from campus. So, Bill and I had to walk or hitchhike to our jobs and classes.

I found it demoralizing that I was traveling by foot through snow and bitter winter winds to scrub greasy pots and pans, while many Western students had cars and meal plans.

Sundays were the worst, because the dormitory where I worked did not serve dinner. Instead, I worked the noon meal. Then Bill and I would wear baggy clothing to the buffet at Walgreens, where we'd eat seconds and thirds, while stuffing our pockets with food to eat later that evening. If we had extra money on Sundays, we would go to the popular White Castle-type hamburger place that sold burgers for 12-cents each.

"If we got real lucky," recalls Bill, "and somebody went home to Battle Creek, Flint, or Detroit for the weekend, their mother would send back a care package and they would come back on Sunday afternoons with enough chicken, potato salad, and dressing to share with all of us."

Most days, however, it was a struggle.

"Can you imagine being in Kalamazoo, Michigan, far away from home, and waking up in the morning with no credit card, no money, and no food to eat?" Bill asks. "Yet every day we ate, even though we didn't have a meal plan. We were on the LHM Plan. The Lord Have Mercy Plan."

With what little money we had, we stocked our room with "potted meat" which was ground pork in a can, along with Vienna sausage, soda crackers, and a powdered orange drink called Tang. Since we had no refrigerator, we stored the goods on the windowsill, which was cold during the winter months. We also had a hot plate.

"It was not unusual to heat a can of Chef Boyardee on that hot plate," Bill recalls. "Within 10 minutes, you were having a feast using paper plates and plastic forks."

Despite our hardships, we did not have "woe is me" conversations.

"You'll be a principal in no time," Bill would encourage me.

"And you'll be head of the Urban League before we know it," I would answer to Bill, who was studying sociology.

"We were both on a mission, and our only hope was education," Bill says. "Out of that grew a friendship and a sense of purpose that I might not have had with a different kind of roommate."

The education provided by Western Michigan University ultimately inspired a desire for success that also spurred three other friends and Western Michigan alumni — Ron Hall, S. Martin Taylor, and Roy S. Roberts — to extraordinary heights in later years.

"THE PRESIDENT'S BEEN SHOT!"

Just after lunch on November 22, 1963, I was washing pots and pans alongside others in the Student Union when somebody came running into the kitchen, shouting, "The president's been shot!"

We ran to the common area. Students had stopped studying, eating, and socializing. All eyes were turned toward the TV, where CBS News Anchor Walter Cronkite announced:

"From Dallas, Texas, the flash apparently official, President Kennedy died… at 2 p.m., Eastern Standard Time." A horrible, unforgettable feeling overwhelmed me. It was unthinkable that the most powerful person in the world, the President of the United States, had been assassinated.

Clearly struggling to maintain his composure, Walter Cronkite added that Vice President Lyndon Johnson had left the hospital in Dallas.

"Presumably he will be taking the oath of office shortly to become the 36th President of the United States," Cronkite said.

Success and Sorrow Conclude College Career

When I visited my parents in Cassopolis — a 45-minute drive from campus — they did not ask, "What's college like?" or "What are you learning?"

Instead, I sensed their immense pride that I was carrying out the dream that they had conceived before I was even born.

Unfortunately, my father never saw me graduate; he died during the fall of 1964. I was deeply saddened but more determined than ever to actualize his vision that I earn my degrees.

During my final semester, my field of study required that I get hands-on experience, so I left Western and became a student-teacher for Special Education at Bunche Elementary School in Detroit. It was located less than a mile east of where I first lived with Aunt Hattie and later my grandmother. I absolutely loved working with the students.

When I walked across the stage during the commencement ceremony to collect my degree, my mother was extremely proud, as were my grandmother, uncles, and Aunt Jo.

I was elated that — after six years on three different campuses — I had finally graduated.

Even better, I returned to Bunche Elementary School as a full-time teacher. My goal was to become the best teacher possible. I enjoyed it so much that I would return after school to play softball, meet with parents of students who needed help, and participate in special programs.

Thrilled to earn an annual salary of $5,500, I purchased some new clothes. I bought a car and moved into my first apartment, which Uncle Ron owned.

My family, fraternity brothers, and friends were all happy for me that I was teaching.

My scope was so limited that if someone had presented a contract on a desk in front of me and said, "Sign this contract and we promise to pay you $10,000 a year for the rest of your life," I would have signed on the dotted line, thinking I had, indeed, arrived.

3

A Career of Advocacy to Advance People of Color

IT WAS IRONIC THAT, DESPITE my initial preference to not teach junior high school, I found myself teaching six- to 14-year-olds at Bunche Elementary. The school was named after Ralph Bunche, the first American person of color to win the Nobel Peace Prize for mediating the Israeli conflict in the 1940's. In September of 1964, I began as a student-teacher for Learning Disabled children; in January of 1965, I became a teacher of Learning Disabled Students.

I fell in love with teaching. My students gave no outward signs of academic challenges, until they were asked to read or do math. Some were in my class simply because they acted out in their regular classrooms. Others had, after displaying difficulties in kindergarten or first grade, been tested to discover a below normal IQ.

Because they needed extra attention, the student-faculty ratio was 14-to-one, whereas regular classrooms could have 30 or more students with one teacher. Another difference was that the Special A students stayed in my class all day, as opposed to going to a different teacher for math, reading or science, as was the norm for their peers in regular grades. Special A students had the same type of curriculum as the rest of the school, but I tailored instruction for my students according to their needs, and focused on their progress. It was also thrilling to help a boy or a girl learn to read and do math at grade level, then transfer back into a regular classroom. Meanwhile, in my class, I often divided them into groups who were reading or writing on the same level.

Keeping the classroom interesting was a top priority, and it was fun to create dynamic bulletin boards celebrating Halloween, Thanksgiving, Christmas, and spring. I exposed the kids to worldly issues and current events by incorporating newspaper articles into my lesson plan. We talked about how Lyndon B. Johnson was the president, Detroit was known as the Motor City and provided cars for people around the world, and young soldiers from our neighborhoods were serving in the Vietnam War.

I am blessed with patience that enabled me to break down reading and math concepts by dissecting pronunciation of words as well as the basics of addition, subtraction, and division. My goal was to help my students achieve their absolute best. This required me to invest significant time and concentration. Planning what I would teach each day required me to strategize how to help the students achieve short-term and long-term goals for each academic subject, while fulfilling the requirements of the curriculum. Little did I know at the time how valuable this exercise would be; it trained me to think, plan, and structure my activities in terms of what I had to do each day to work toward achieving goals.

It was important to present a professional appearance for my students, so every day I wore a sport jacket or a suit and tie. After the school day ended, I returned to my apartment. I'd change into khaki pants or jeans, then return to school, where I'd join Bunche children for a pick-up softball game. I also made house calls to parents and caregivers to talk about how my students were performing.

I got along quite well with the other Bunche teachers. Among the many female teachers, I noticed one in particular, Trudy Ann DunCombe. A recent graduate of Eastern Michigan University, she was single and teaching first graders. Trudy impressed me because she was very intelligent, witty, cultured, attractive, and grounded in outstanding family values.

"I was living at home with my parents," Trudy remembers now, "and one evening in March of 1965 we were all having dinner when Dennis called. He asked if I was going to the Parent-Teacher Meeting and that maybe we could ride together. I said yes, and he picked me up and we went to the Parent-Teacher Meeting. I didn't consider that a date; I was dating someone else at the time."

Sam Simpson, who was a homeroom teacher at another elementary school, recalls, "I met Dennis when he was courting Trudy. Dennis was very humble. At the time, Trudy had a relationship with a dear friend of mine. Then Dennis came on the scene and shot him to the curb."

A week after the Parent-Teacher Meeting, Trudy and I went on a real date, and our relationship blossomed.

"When I first met him," Trudy says now, "I thought he was a different kind of guy. He had these sayings like, 'We'll see ya!' I was attracted to him because he was very smart and very ambitious. I knew that from the first time we talked. He was very interested in teaching, and becoming the best at it. And he wanted to become principal of a school someday."

WELCOMED INTO TRUDY'S FAMILY

I was delighted to get to know Trudy's parents, Eleanor and James DunCombe, as well as her younger sister, Beth, who was a junior at Detroit's Cass Technical High School, ranked among America's top 10 high schools. Trudy had attended Roosevelt Elementary, Durfee Junior High, and Central High School.

Mrs. DunCombe was a delightful cook, and honored me with invitations to family dinners where I learned about Trudy's family. Both parents had attended Wayne State University. Mr. DunCombe was a supervisor, then area superintendent at the U.S. Post Office, which was considered a very good job for African Americans at the time. Mrs. DunCombe was the first black teller hired at Bank of the Commonwealth.

While we were dating, Trudy did not reveal that her grandfather, James Vincent DunCombe, who emigrated from Kingston, Jamaica, was a lawyer. He graduated from the Detroit College of Law in 1929, and operated a general law practice from a home office while still working as an electrician at Ford Motor Company.

Dinnertime at the DunCombe's home was an absolute delight. A humorous moment that became family lore was when I bought my first new car, a burgundy 1965 Mustang.

"Dennis called and said, 'My new car has wall-to-wall carpeting!'" Beth remembers with a chuckle. "Back then, cars didn't have carpeting. But to call it wall-to-wall carpeting was just hilarious. That was the beginning of his success, and part of his fun-loving personality was that he said things a little differently. He later did a Richard Pryor imitation that always made us laugh."

Likewise, my humble upbringing in Cassopolis had not exposed me to many things, and I loved how Trudy had great taste and could help me with things that my parents could not teach me, such as following certain social protocols. Trudy had the polish, and I worked hard. I believed we would have a great life together.

We spent a lot of time together. I joined their family on Sunday mornings for Catholic church services.

"You Should Think About Going to Law School"

During my second year of teaching, Principal Violet Varty called me into her office for my performance review.

"You ought to think about becoming an assistant principal, and then become a principal," she said, adding that she was aware of how I committed afternoons and evenings to my students. "You get along very well with the other teachers, and you go above and beyond to help these kids. It's very impressive how you visit parents at home to talk about how they can help their children do their best in your class." To become a principal, she said, I would need a master's degree. I shared her vision for my future, and even aspired to become superintendent of Detroit Public Schools someday. So, I enrolled in two classes in the University of Michigan's Masters in Education Program; fortunately, classes were taught in the Rackham Building on Woodward Avenue across from the Detroit Institute of Arts, so I did not have to travel to Ann Arbor. When I purchased the two textbooks for the classes, I was surprised to discover that they were the same books that I had studied for education classes at Western Michigan University.

"I don't understand why these two classes are required," I complained to Trudy, who was studying for her Masters of Education in Guidance and Counseling. "I had these same books at Western, and I'm not learning anything new."

"Dennis," she said, "you should think about going to law school."

"I don't know anything about the law," I said. "I've never even been in a lawyer's office. I don't have a clue about what they do." Meanwhile, the more I complained about graduate school, the more she encouraged me to attend law school.

"Just take the Law School Admissions Test," she said, "to see how you might perform in law school."

I took Trudy's advice, and my LSAT score suggested that if I attended law school, I would have a good chance of graduating. So, after one semester at U of M, I dropped out and enrolled at the Detroit College of Law in their evening classes. I was fully aware that going to law school would not guarantee good grades, graduation, or passing the Bar Exam. It was a risk, but well worth it when I thought about the powerful impact that lawyers such as Thurgood Marshall were making in the United States.

I began law school in January of 1966, attending night classes while teaching school during the day. I fell in love with the law, but it was difficult. *Black's Law Dictionary* became my constant companion as I looked up legal terms that were completely foreign to me. But it was imperative to understand every facet of the cases which we were assigned to read before class. A few teachers scared the hell out of me and everybody else. That fear was a powerful motivator, because law professors randomly called on students and fired off a barrage of questions that you'd better know how to answer.

I was determined never to be called on and not know the answers. Success was all about preparation, and that was my middle name during law school. I would later learn that Edward Littlejohn and other classmates were part of a surge of black law students who helped the number of black lawyers in America spike from a paltry 2,400 in 1960 to more than 8,000 in 1970, according to the National Bar Association.

"Dennis treated law school like he treats everything else that he does, by applying himself 200 percent to make sure it's the best he can possibly do," Trudy says. "Since he was working full-time and taking classes on Monday, Tuesday, and Thursday nights, Wednesday was our date night. On the weekends, if we attended a party, we were always the first to leave because he would have to get up early to spend the entire next day studying. Always. Dennis is very driven. I did not know what Dennis was going to do ultimately, but I knew it was going to be something really extraordinary."

Our relationship grew and blossomed into something remarkable. At Christmastime, I asked Mr. DunCombe for permission to marry his daughter. He said yes, and I was a very happy man.

OUR WEDDING, HONEYMOON, AND FIRST HOME

When Trudy accepted my marriage proposal, I converted to Catholicism. This required taking classes and completing marriage

Trudy and I pose on our wedding day with (from left) her parents, James and Eleanor DunCombe, and my mother, Frances Marie Carroll Archer.

counseling, a mandate of marriage in the Catholic Church. It encouraged us to talk things through and never go to bed angry.

Thankfully, my parents had been good role models. In addition, Trudy's parents were exceptional role models for a successful marriage; they would celebrate their 70-year anniversary before Mr. DunCombe's passing.

On June 17, 1967, Trudy and I were overwhelmed with joy as we stood at the altar of the Cathedral of the Most Blessed Sacrament on Woodward Avenue in Detroit.

I could not take my eyes off Trudy, who was so beautiful in her gown. Beth was her maid-of-honor and she had six bridesmaids. I wore a black tuxedo with a gray, silk, striped ascot. My best man was Irving Victor Woods, and I had six groomsmen. I was so proud that my mother was there, as were my grandmother, my uncles, and Aunt Jo.

Though it rained earlier that day, Trudy and I were beaming like the sun, which came out as we exited the church. After the ceremony, we enjoyed a reception with family and friends at the new Howard Johnson's on West Grand Boulevard. After dinner at the DunCombes', we were driven to the airport for our flight to Miami, continuing to the Bahamas.

Nassau was an absolute dream. The weather was beautiful, and we loved sitting on the beach, enchanted by the turquoise water, hot sunshine, palm trees, and each other. We talked about our dreams, and having the ambition and desire to do whatever we wanted during our lifetime together. We met a tour guide who showed us the island and where he lived. Our honeymoon was so outstanding that we vowed to return to the Bahamas as often as possible.

Back in Detroit, we lived in Lafayette Park in a one-bedroom apartment at Central Park Plaza. It was built during the 1960's where Black Bottom had existed. We had a swimming pool and great neighbors.

I transferred to Duffield Elementary School, a five-minute drive from Bunche. Starting in the fall of 1967, I would teach Junior Special B to 14- to 18-year-old special-education students.

Working for Damon Keith During Trying Times for Detroit

Meanwhile, I had the privilege of meeting attorney Damon J. Keith. In the summer of 1967, he hired me to work in the law firm of Keith, Conyers, Anderson, Brown, and Wahls. He had established the law firm in 1964 with partners Nathan Conyers, Herman Anderson, Joseph N. Brown, and Myron Wahls.

Lawyers told me about the unfortunate plight of black lawyers, who were often belittled and disrespected by white judges, who treated white lawyers with respect and dignity. The courts assigned fewer cases to black lawyers. These factors inspired black clients to hire white lawyers, believing that they would have a better chance at winning their lawsuits.

The more I learned, the more I wanted to do to change the way things were. The mayor of Detroit, Jerome Cavanagh, was making progress, by integrating his administration with women and blacks such as Dr. Conrad Mallett Sr., the mayor's first African American Assistant and later Director of the Department of Housing and Urban Renewal. Mayor Cavanagh was admired by almost everybody that I knew.

Trudy and I loved being newlyweds. We had a thriving social life, and continued to enjoy family dinners with her parents. I cherished time with Mr. DunCombe, whom I called Dad. Some Sunday mornings I picked him up to play golf with several friends. On the morning of July 23, as I was driving him home, we saw smoke from a distance. As we approached the DunCombes' home, we smelled smoke. Sirens blared.

"I took your dad home and something is going on," I told Trudy when I arrived at home. She responded, "There was a disturbance over by 12th Street last night. The police raided a blind pig, and it set off looting."

Over the next few days, Mayor Jerome Cavanagh declared a state of emergency for the city of Detroit. Schools and businesses closed as people continued looting, shooting, and setting fires. We stayed home, convening with neighbors around the pool to talk about what was happening. All the while, gunfire echoed in the distance. The smell of smoke permeated the hot summer air. Things escalated to the point that Governor George W. Romney sent the Michigan Army National Guard into Detroit, and later, President Lyndon B. Johnson ordered U.S. Army troops into Detroit. They came in military tanks, and rifle-toting soldiers took to the streets to stop the violence and calm the unrest. In the end, 43 people died and 1,189 others were injured. Fires destroyed more than 2,000 buildings.

"It was terrible and frightening," Trudy recalls. "Everyone hung around the swimming pool, and we got to know our neighbors because we were trying to console each other. You could hear the shots and see the fires."

During the riot, snipers were also shooting randomly at people; one man was struck by a sniper's bullet and killed near the General Motors Building. Authorities set a 10:00 p.m. curfew for everyone to be off the streets. Meanwhile, 7,231 people were arrested, with more than half charged with looting. The jails and courts were so overwhelmed, the men and women were detained on Belle Isle in an open area. Courts were open 24 hours, and Recorder's Court judges put out a call for all lawyers to volunteer to help process the defendants, who needed to understand the charges they were facing. Keep in mind, most of those arrested by the white police force were black and poor. Most had little or no money for legal defense.

Among the many lawyers who felt an obligation and a calling to help were Damon Keith and his law partners. After observing how they did a masterful job of rendering legal services to people in need during a crisis, I couldn't get my law degree fast enough. The aftermath of the riots inspired a tremendous analysis of the problems that caused it. One of the most volatile triggers was that the predominantly white police force was harassing, beating, and even killing poor black people. At the same time, people who lived in black neighborhoods did not feel they were treated with respect by white merchants who operated grocery stores and other businesses there.

Later the same year, U.S. Senator Phil Hart nominated, and President Lyndon Johnson appointed, Damon Keith to serve as a judge on the United States District Court for the Eastern District of Michigan.

"You Can Distinguish Yourself"

One day during law school, one of the professors whom I most admired, Donald Campbell, called me to his office.

"Dennis, I know you helped start the Wolverine Bar Association's Law School Division here at the Detroit College of Law," he said. "We have very talented law students here, and after graduation they tend to gravitate toward the black bar association."

I listened intently.

"I urge you to consider joining both the black bar association and the Detroit Bar, which is an affiliate of the State Bar of Michigan. And you should also participate in the American Bar Association. They have a national conference where you can meet lawyers and judges from across the country, and you can attend seminars to learn about all the latest trends impacting the legal profession."

Professor Campbell continued, "Another way you can distinguish yourself among Michigan's 17,000 lawyers is to write articles from time to time for legal publications." I thanked him for his advice, and proceeded to join the American Bar Association's Law School Division and later the Detroit Bar Association's Young Lawyers Section, which is now the Barristers.

A Time of Unrest and Uncertainty

The day that Dr. Martin Luther King Jr. was assassinated, on April 4, 1968, was a scary time in Detroit and America. Deadly riots were exploding in cities across the country.

At the time, I was in law school and came home to Trudy. Less than a year after the Detroit rebellion, we were worried that violence could occur in our neighborhood.

Just five years after President John F. Kennedy was killed, we were baffled about why anyone would murder Dr. King, a minister who stood for nonviolence. It seemed surreal as we watched Dr. King's funeral on TV, as we had done for President Kennedy.

Then, on June 6, Trudy and I were awakened by her mother, who said, "Robert Kennedy has been assassinated in California after he won the California primary."

At the same time, the Vietnam War was raging and people were protesting America's involvement in this conflict that would kill or maim more than 211,000 Americans before it was all over. It always troubled me that our soldiers were treated so poorly upon return from a war that they had not started. All of this contributed to a deep sense of uncertainty about race, politics, and the world at large.

WORKING AT FORD MOTOR COMPANY

During the spring of 1968, Professor Donald Campbell asked me again to visit his office.

"Ford Motor Company's General Counsel office called," he said. "They're letting law schools know that they are an equal opportunity employer and they are looking for summer associates. I recommended you."

I was flattered and excited to spend the summer of 1968 working in the Legal Department of Ford Motor Company. It was an outstanding and fascinating learning experience because everything I observed coincided with the law classes that I had taken that spring. My work focused on commercial law and mostly entailed writing "claim and deliver" memos for the lawyers, and executing claims on property that Ford owned and wanted returned. It was a fabulous opportunity. I learned a lot. D. Allen Glenn, a student at the University of Michigan Law School, was another person of color who worked there for the summer. He helped me improve my writing skills.

"DENNIS KISSED THE DOCTOR"

Trudy and I were overjoyed when our first child, Dennis Wayne Archer Jr., was born weighing 6 pounds, 15 ounces at 7:15 p.m. on Saturday, March 1, 1969. Trudy stayed home for a year to take care of him.

"My mother and dad liked to tell the story," Trudy recalls, "that when Dennis found out the baby was a boy, he kissed the doctor!" Trudy's parents and Beth, like my mother, grandmother, aunt and uncles, were absolutely thrilled to welcome Denny into the world.

Soon thereafter, Trudy and I purchased a new townhouse on Thornhill Place in Elmwood Park. It had three bedrooms and a spacious patio in the back.

"Someday I'm Going to be Somebody!"

During the summer of 1968, I received special permission to leave Detroit Public Schools prior to the conclusion of the school year, so that I could run a program called Education for Life. Operated in a church, the program transported students to various locations around Highland Park and Detroit to hear guest speakers. In September, I returned to teach in the Detroit Public Schools at Duffield Elementary School.

"Dennis, you need to meet Robert Millender," my father-in-law repeatedly suggested as we teed off Sunday morning at Palmer Park Golf Course. He and Robert L. Millender, who was black, had served in the U.S. Army together in Italy, and were friends. "He's an outstanding lawyer, a brilliant strategist, and he can help you get your first job as an attorney. Bob runs one of the largest integrated law firms in the state."

In fact, Bob was a partner in Michigan's first integrated law firm — Goodman, Crockett, Eden, Millender, Goodman, and Bedrosian — formed in 1950 with offices in Detroit's Cadillac Tower which, at the time, refused to lease to blacks. I was familiar with Bob Millender because he was celebrated for serving as campaign manager for victorious black candidates, including U.S. Congressman John Conyers in 1964; attorney George Crockett in 1966, Recorder's Court Judge; and Robert Tindal and Erma Henderson, African Americans who served on the Detroit City Council. At the time in 1969, Bob was running the campaign of Richard Austin, a CPA, for Mayor of Detroit against Wayne County Sheriff Roman Gribbs in the general election.

I concluded that if I joined Richard Austin's campaign and impressed Bob Millender as a hard-working campaign volunteer who helped win the election, then his firm might hire me as a lawyer. So, I joined Austin's campaign with gusto, stuffing envelopes and doing odd jobs in the campaign office. We made mimeographed, letter-sized campaign flyers that said, "Please vote for Richard Austin." Then our car caravans would drive to supermarket parking lots where we placed our literature under windshield wipers on cars. We also handed out flyers in churches.

I encountered many other volunteers who were working to make Richard Austin the first black mayor of Detroit. Among them: my fellow Alpha and friend, Elliott Hall, whom I had not seen since he graduated from Wayne State. He had become a lawyer and, after working as an attorney for Chrysler for five years, had recently relocated downtown to represent criminal defendants, and had committed himself wholeheartedly to help those arrested during the 1967 riot. Elliott and I talked about our shared passion for becoming lawyers so that we could apply our legal abilities and ambition to help African Americans — including those in our own profession, because black lawyers were banned from leasing office space in most downtown buildings.

"Black folks were still really at the bottom of the rung in terms of socioeconomic status," Elliott recalls. "There was zero affirmative action. At the time, most blacks wanted Jewish lawyers, believing that they were smarter and more connected than black lawyers. As a result, most black lawyers worked in the Post Office and the auto factories while practicing law part-time."

Elliott and I were both very cognizant of the racial and political climate in America and Detroit. More than 1.5 million people lived in Detroit, with nearly half, 44.5 percent or 660,428, being African American, according to the 1970 U.S. Census. But blacks were prohibited from living in many neighborhoods, and the thriving residential and business district known as Black Bottom had been razed to create the "urban renewal" project of the upscale Lafayette Park neighborhood as well as the I-75 freeway.

Though the 1964 Civil Rights Act and the 1965 Voting Rights Act were slowly changing the racial landscape, many believed change was happening too slowly. As a result, radicalized groups were rising to prominence, including the Black Panther Party and the Nation of Islam, which appealed to people who believed more aggressive tactics were required to ensure equal rights and justice for people of color.

"The Civil Rights Movement was the reason we went to law school," Elliott recalls. "We didn't go into law school nor did we have a practice where we thought the only thing we'd do is make as much money as we could and take care of our families and to hell with everyone else. We had an obligation as talented black men to contribute to the community. We knew we had to give back. That's why politics was so important."

So, we campaigned hard in the black communities, learning from Bob Millender how canvassing entire neighborhoods to galvanize "voting blocs" of African Americans to the polls could ensure victory for black candidates. We also lobbied unions, the UAW and others, to support Austin, even though Roman Gribbs was favored by unions.

My hard work elevated me to head of the advance team — going to events first to assess the size and mood of the crowd. When Austin arrived, I would inform him of any hecklers, and where they were sitting. Then I would go to the next place.

While campaigning, I met Michigan State Senator Coleman A. Young, who was very respected and knowledgeable about the legislature. Accused of being a communist for his civil rights activism, he had been called to testify before the House Un-American Committee in Congress. Represented by attorney George Crockett, Coleman Young's defiant testimony created a larger-than-life reputation that epitomized how beneath his well-educated, gentlemanly exterior, he was strong as battery acid. When I first shook his hand, I knew I was in the presence of greatness.

When Election Day of 1969 finally arrived, it was rainy and cold. Inside the Book Cadillac Hotel, we watched election returns that indicated a close race, but Richard Austin lost. Roman Gribbs became mayor and took office in January of 1970.

By the way, I did not get the job in Bob Millender's firm, but we remained friends.

As my employment search continued, I was acutely aware that no large, majority law firm in Detroit, if not the state, employed a person of color as an associate or as a partner. I sent my resume — which showed I was on the Dean's List — along with a letter requesting an interview with a large law firm that, like most, employed no people of color.

"Thank you for coming in," said the attorney who interviewed me. "I want you to know that this law firm does not hire law students from the Detroit College of Law. We hire from Harvard, Yale, and the University of Michigan."

"Thank you very much," I said, finding this very interesting, because *he* had graduated from the Detroit College of Law. The message was clear: I was not welcome to work there because that firm did not hire black lawyers.

Fear of Failure Fuels Study Strategy

After the election, my most pressing task at hand was to pass both my law school final exams and the State Bar Exam. Taking the Bar scared me, but flunking it terrified me even more. So, I channeled that anxiety into a strategy that I hoped would ensure my success.

I would conclude law school with final exams in January of 1970, then take the Bar Exam exactly four weeks later in February. So, before studying for finals, I started reading the Bar Exam material during Thanksgiving break from school. While studying for my law school final exams, I also devoured the Nord Bar Review Course, which came in several big, thick books that I read cover to cover. Then we had Christmas break and I took the law school finals. When I started the bar review course, I'd already read everything. I also made time to study for the Bar by saving up a lot of sick days. Between studying during the day and taking the Bar Review Course at night, I devoted 12 to 14 hours to studying every day. My study partner was Ed Littlejohn, who was well-known among our peers for his brilliance. He also made it fun to study together.

We graduated from law school in January, and I was so proud as Trudy, her parents, my mother, my grandmother, Aunt Josephine, and my three uncles attended. They were exceedingly proud because I had not only graduated from college, but here I was earning my Juris Doctorate.

The Bar Exam spanned two-and-a-half grueling days. I took it alongside hundreds of other men and women in a large room at the University of Michigan in Ann Arbor. When the test was finally over, I felt relieved, and optimistic that I had passed because I had studied so hard.

MY FIRST JOB AS A LAWYER

While waiting for the Bar results, I encountered Elliott Hall as I was walking downtown Detroit. He had joined the law firm of two African American lawyers, Samuel C. Gardner and J. Robert Gragg. So, I joined the firm as a clerk. I continued to teach during the day, and worked as a law clerk at Gragg & Gardner, P.C. during the evenings.

I waited anxiously for the Bar Results, which would be published in the newspapers. The day before the results were released in early June, I received a phone call from Don Hobson, who had a list of the names of every black lawyer in Michigan, as well as every black person who took the Bar Exam.

"Dennis, you passed the Bar Exam," he said. "You'll get a letter in the mail on Saturday." When the mail carrier arrived that day, I ripped open that letter and sure enough, I had passed. "Thank you, God!" I exclaimed. I was so happy I didn't know what to do.

"Trudy, I passed!" I exclaimed when she phoned, as planned, from a phone booth at a luncheon.

"He was thrilled," she recalls. "That was very, very special."

The day only got better when I saw my name in one of the Detroit daily newspapers: "The State Board of Law Examiners Saturday announced that the following persons passed the March 1970 Michigan bar examinations." For Detroit, the article listed 29 names including "Dennis W. Archer" followed by my study partner, "Edward J. Littlejohn." Shortly thereafter, I concluded my public-school teaching career. Then on June 11, 1970, I joined a large group of lawyers who were sworn-in en masse in the auditorium in the City-County Building. After that, Trudy and I headed to the Federal Court Building for a private swearing-in by Judge Damon Keith. I was admitted to practice in all courts in Michigan and the Federal District Court of Eastern Michigan.

WORKING AS A FULL-TIME ATTORNEY

I was grateful that, unlike many black lawyers who had to work a full-time job while building up a law practice, I could begin full-time employment as a lawyer in an established law firm. Dressed in a suit and tie, and impassioned by my desire to help people, I found myself loving the experience of reporting to work at Gragg & Gardner, P.C. Attorneys at Law.

The law firm was in the Guardian Building, celebrated around the world for its Art Deco architecture and lobby whose soaring ceilings dazzled visitors with Native American tile patterns of turquoise, gold, and red. Stepping into this opulent building in the heart of downtown Detroit's Financial District was a daily and humbling reminder that I had truly come a long way from Cassopolis.

Yet the most thrilling aspect of my work in that building — which had opened office space to black lawyers because of Damon Keith's persistence — was that I immediately began to feel that I was making a positive difference in people's lives — because I won my first civil suit and my first criminal case, both by jury verdicts.

The two partners, Samuel C. Gardner and J. Robert Gragg, were thrilled, as were the three other associates: Elliott Hall, Alex J. Allen Jr., and Horace S. Stone.

The civil law suit involved an elderly African American woman who had been turned away from several law firms. She was suing the Detroit Police Department and a Detroit Department of Transportation bus driver who had waved to her, indicating that it was safe for her to cross in front of the bus, when she was suddenly struck by a Detroit Police car. I won that lawsuit in Wayne County Circuit Court Judge Blair Moody's courtroom.

My first criminal case involved an African American male, charged with a felony by the Wayne County Prosecuting Attorney's Office. I got him acquitted before Wayne County Circuit Court Judge James Ryan.

I was exhilarated!

My broad, general practice enabled me to learn about all aspects of practicing law, including traffic court and juvenile court. I even accompanied people to real estate closings, after reading all the documents and making sure my clients understood them clearly. At the same time, I often represented people who could not afford a lawyer.

I was making money. This filled me with a tremendous sense of accomplishment that began to dissolve the inferiority complex that I had felt growing up poor and without modern plumbing.

Thankfully, I was also being groomed by elder attorneys on how to cultivate great relationships with my clients.

"Keep a clean desk," Sam Gardner said, "so when someone comes in, they have a sense that they have your undivided attention. When they see you listening carefully to their needs and concerns, and writing notes, they'll get the feeling that the only thing you have to do is take care of their issue and their problem. When a client comes into the office, go get them yourself, greet them in the lobby, and escort them back to your office. This adds a personal touch that makes them feel valued, which engenders their trust in you." He also told me to return telephone calls the day they are received. "Even if it's a nagging client, you return that telephone call because they might refer the biggest case of your life."

Following the Calling into Politics

During my first year as a lawyer, Bob Millender called. He was helping Richard Austin campaign to become Michigan's Secretary of State, because incumbent James O'Hare was not going to run again.

"Dick needs the endorsement of the Michigan Democratic Party to run for office," Bob said. "The nominating convention is in Grand Rapids, but I'm having circulation problems in my legs. Dennis, I want you to go for me, and be my eyes and ears, walk around with Dick, report back to me every day." Bob wisely believed that if Richard Austin could get the nomination, he could win and become Secretary of State, the first African American to hold the position in the nation.

Attending my first Democratic State Convention was exciting. There I witnessed the proverbial smoke-filled rooms late at night as Richard Austin got the nod for the nomination, which I reported to Bob Millender. Back in Detroit, he asked me to help the campaign throughout Wayne, Oakland, and Macomb Counties. I was named Metro Campaign Manager. Later, my focus narrowed to Wayne County and Detroit. Working under Bob's direction enabled me to learn hands-on the wealth of information that made him such a brilliant political strategist.

We needed a good turnout, and Detroit was rich with African Americans, people whom we hoped would vote for Dick Austin.

We also needed a real energetic effort to get that vote out. At the same time, I was also trying to expose the law firm to a broader choice of potential clients so that I could try some high-powered cases. I accepted every opportunity to speak, and eagerly accepted my sister-in-law Beth DunCombe's invitation to address volunteers at the campaign headquarters of Congressman John Conyers, who was running for re-election to represent Michigan's 14th District in the U.S. House of Representatives.

"The night before the August primary, they had a rally at the campaign office for the workers," recalls Beth, who had graduated from the University of Michigan in May and was working on the Conyers campaign. "I told John, 'My brother-in-law would be a really good speaker at the rally; he could really get people going and encourage them.'"

He agreed.

"Dennis gave a get-out-the-vote speech at the campaign office, before at least 100 volunteers who were going to work the polls the next day. It was a hot summer night and people were fanning themselves. A woman who was standing behind me said, 'What church does he preach at?' I said, 'Oh, he's not a preacher, he's a lawyer.' That was the beginning of his barnstorming campaign speeches. He's so passionate when he speaks, he really gets people excited."

I found it exciting to get involved in the Congressional Districts alongside U.S. Representative Charles Diggs of the 13th District and U.S. Representative John Conyers of the 14th District. Each District had a Chair, an elected position that wielded tremendous influence on voters and decisions impacting residents and businesses in those districts. I met Prince Moon, chair of 13th Congressional District, who was very well respected and connected with the UAW. Meanwhile, on the campaign trail, I always met fascinating people, many of whom I had heard about and admired. One such person was prominent African American lawyer and high-powered Democrat, Kenneth Hylton.

"Dennis," he said, approaching with a young, white man. "I want you to meet Jim Blanchard. I think you two will have a lot in common." We shook hands, and I was impressed by his energy. Jim worked as a lawyer by day, and after work as a political advisor and organizer for Michigan Attorney General Frank Kelley, who was running for re-election.

"Dennis had a confident air about himself," recalls Jim Blanchard, from his law office in Washington, DC. "We were both from humble beginnings. We had drive, ambition, and prepared ourselves thoroughly for these challenges. We didn't have anybody in our family with a big name, we're Democrats, and we're in the state of Michigan, we like making things happen. Our birthdays are six months apart. We clicked. He's one of the more outstanding people that I've known in this world of politics and public service and government."

Meanwhile, I was awed by the close friendship of Frank Kelley and Richard Austin, which was a good thing because I sometimes found myself cramped with them and Jim in a four-person airplane, crisscrossing Michigan to campaign. I vividly remember one night, after a turbulent flight, how my eyes got as big as saucers when I first saw the control tower at Detroit City Airport up close and personal. Landing had never been more of a relief.

Election Day brought the same feeling. Both Richard Austin and Frank Kelley were victorious. This marked my first real victory in politics, and I was hooked! I decided that I would continue to help people that I liked run for office.

HALL, STONE, ALLEN & ARCHER, ATTORNEYS AT LAW

A number of issues precipitated a dramatic and fortuitous change at Gragg & Gardner. Elliott Hall, Horace Stone, Alex Allen, and I believed we were not being fairly compensated for the steady and lucrative work that we were bringing into the law firm. In a racially volatile climate where groups like the Black Panther Party and the NAACP were generating opportunities for black lawyers to represent both plaintiffs and defendants in court, we hungered to devote our passion and talent to the cause of racial justice. Those kinds of cases were not a priority at Gragg & Gardner.

"Dennis voiced objections to Sam Gardner and Bobby Gragg about how the office was operating and that we were not being treated fairly in a financial way," recalls Elliott. "What precipitated our leaving was they asked Dennis to leave because he spoke up. This is extremely important. That shows a side of Dennis that, even as a young lawyer, he had no fear about speaking up about anything pertaining to his moral code." This inspired the others to leave as well.

"I was close to Sam Gardner," Elliott recalls. "We went to law school together. So, it was then my task to tell him that we were going to leave with Dennis." Over the next month, we held organizational meetings to start Hall, Stone, Allen & Archer, P.C. Attorneys at Law on the 9th floor of the Guardian Building.

"Dennis became our managing partner, the treasurer of the firm," Elliot remembers, "because he had great organizational skills and was a strategic thinker."

We hit the ground running, paying ourselves each an annual salary of $12,000, which was a livable wage at the time. We had grand visions for our office, and applied at several banks for loans to purchase office furniture. All but black-owned First Independence Bank denied us a loan. The caveat? Our wives, who were all working, also had to sign the $20,000 loan. We ended up leasing office furniture, but we paid back the loan within one year.

"We never had a dull month in our first year of practice," Elliott says. "New business was coming through all the time. Dennis was an excellent office administrator. He gave inspiration to all of us… and we had monthly meetings so we knew where we were financially. Dennis was extremely efficient. When checks or money came into the firm, we gave it to Dennis. He was responsible for recording all the funds, the expenses, and the payment of expenses. Dennis, of course, had no problem getting in our ass if we didn't do what we were supposed to do. Everyone knew that when he did that, it was for the good of the office."

We were young, energetic lawyers running an extremely busy office as we handled probate, divorce, criminal, and real estate matters. I was a committed member of the Wolverine Bar Association, as well as the Young Lawyers Section of the Detroit Bar Association, for which I was elected as Secretary. The Young Lawyers were very active; we were photographed in the newspaper with Governor Milliken for Law Day USA on May 1 and another published picture showed us visiting the United States Supreme Court in Washington, DC.

Elliott, who was very popular in the community, started representing the Black Panther Party. Its members were often arrested and charged with misdemeanors for trying to sell newspapers in front of Hudson's downtown. He was also active with the NAACP, and joined the legal team of the NAACP to desegregate Detroit Public Schools.

"We were four, hard working, scrambling lawyers who were always out in the community passing out our business cards and building up the firm," Elliott recalls.

Horace Stone had an outsized personality and, being 15 years older than Elliott, was very helpful, as was Alex Allen, who went on to be Chief Judge of Detroit's 36th District Court. Both Horace and Alex have since died.

The four of us received excellent publicity from a photograph and article in *The Michigan Chronicle* for "June Brown Garner's Detroit." Married to my Uncle Warren, she showcased our law firm in a positive light while also exposing barriers that we faced every day. For example, some older blacks preferred to hire white lawyers who were perceived to have a greater chance of winning their lawsuit than black lawyers.

Detroit and America had a shortage of black lawyers, due to discriminatory practices in our profession and law schools.

The article explained that the four of us were on a quest to combat the negative stereotype that the *Amos 'n Andy* radio program portrayed, which was an unfavorable image of black lawyers. To combat that image, Detroit lawyer Myzell Sowell, who was Wolverine Bar President from 1963 to 1965, conceived the idea of an annual Wolverine Bar Association's Barrister's Ball, a black-tie soirée and fundraiser for scholarships, which Trudy and I attended every year after I became a lawyer, along with hundreds of lawyers, judges, celebrities, and dignitaries.

It was our desire and intent to be the absolute best lawyers possible. As a result, our firm was thriving. And we were so confident about our future that we all purchased brand new Lincoln Continentals. We also wanted to celebrate our success by throwing a Christmas party. Our soirée in the Thornhill Place clubhouse was a blowout! We invited judges, prosecuting attorneys, a lot of lawyers, and social friends. It was well-attended, and our wives were there.

"This party was outstanding for a young law firm," Elliott remembers. "Most of the African American guys who were practicing law thought we were moving too fast, buying these big Lincoln cars, having an office in the Guardian Building, and throwing a Christmas party."

Trudy knew better than anyone how hard I worked, and saw the party as a much-deserved celebration. "They were all thrilled and proud of themselves," Trudy recalls, "as well they should have been." Our success underscored her confidence in me.

"From the beginning," she says, "I knew that whatever Dennis was going to do, he would be successful. The dedication, the hours that he spent building his law practice, I was very supportive. He developed a passion for the legal profession, and he had a passion for politics. Both of those are demanding, requiring hours of being involved, especially when building a law practice. You have to be out there; you have to be seen. People have to know who you are in order to build a clientele. We sacrificed a lot, but I knew that we'd have some mighty extraordinary experiences. I could feel that."

GETTING ELLIOTT ELECTED AS NAACP PRESIDENT

Shortly after we opened our law firm, Elliott Hall ran for president of Detroit's NAACP chapter.

"Dennis was responsible for my being elected because he was my campaign manager," Elliott recalls. "People didn't think I had a chance. But we whipped a formidable opponent, Jimmy Watts, a leader in the UAW, which back in the 70's was like Goliath. Unions ruled the world." Suddenly, the political grapevine across town was buzzing about us, these young lawyers who were turning things around.

"Dennis did a number of great things to orchestrate my campaign," Elliott says.

So how did we do it? The keys to Elliott's successful campaign included a strong, well-researched platform, women, churches, and special events featuring high-profile supporters.

"Dennis helped me structure my platform," Elliott recalls, "that promised, among other things, to help black people find jobs; convince local theaters to stop showing *blacksploitation* movies that portrayed black people in a negative light; and integrate Detroit Public Schools by working hard to win the lawsuit against the state of Michigan." Next, we galvanized the power of women and black churches.

"We were up against a powerful political force," Elliott says, "so we did an alternative campaign. Dennis organized the NAACP's Sip-In Committee — made up of young women who did social things to raise money. They belonged to various black churches around the city and they became the captains for my campaign. Dennis convinced the pastors to endorse me, and help me attend the weekly meetings of 30 or 40 Baptist pastors, to introduce myself. Then I'd go to the churches and the preacher would say, 'Elliott Hall is here! Stand up! He's running for president of the NAACP and you should vote for him.'"

On Election Day, most of the folks who came out to vote were members of the churches as well as the UAW, because they were mostly factory workers. Elliott won the election!

By the way, when we met with theatre owners to ask them to stop showing movies that made black people look bad, they refused because those films were extremely popular at the time.

Meeting Black Legal Giants at the National Bar Association

In 1971, I attended my first National Bar Association convention in Atlanta, Georgia. Wayne County Circuit Court Judge Ed Bell was president. I met him through his good friend Sam Gardner. This personal association with the NBA president blessed me with extraordinary experiences with the 1,500 to 2,000 black lawyers who convened from across America for our annual meeting.

After the plenary sessions and seminars, Ed, along with Jimmy Cobb and O.T. Wells, invited me into hotel suites where lawyers and judges of legendary stature gathered to socialize and talk about their experiences of practicing law and opening doors for other people of color to enter the legal profession. They included George Crockett, Anna Diggs Taylor, Thurgood Marshall, Damon Keith, Constance Baker Motley, and lawyers of similar stature from all over the country.

I was both awed and acutely aware of this rare privilege to meet individuals of extraordinary caliber, and to sit at the feet of these giants. Second, I appreciated that this was a coveted experience that couldn't be bought; I was overwhelmed with a hunger to listen, observe, and learn as much as possible.

Thurgood Marshall, for example, described how he'd be invited to stay at someone's home in the South. When he was picked up, the person driving him insisted that he lie down in the back seat sometimes with a blanket over him because whites knew he was coming. When he spent the night at somebody's home, he never slept by the windows and sometimes didn't sleep in the bed because somebody might throw in a firebomb.

African American lawyers from Detroit, such as Myron Wahls, George Crockett, Claudia Morcom, and others shared stories about how they had traveled to the South to represent African Americans who were arrested while attempting to register to vote and participating in sit-ins, marches, and other civil rights demonstrations. Other lawyers spoke of how their homes had been firebombed because they were involved with racially charged cases in the South during the civil rights movement.

I wondered, *How can this be America? How could they treat black people like this? What about the laws that had been enacted to protect us?*

"If you look back on some of the legal decisions around race in America, such as the Dred Scott case and *Plessy v. Ferguson*," one of the legal giants commented, "You'll be reminded that we learned in law school, that the United States Supreme Court essentially said that blacks don't have any rights." I marveled at how these lawyers and judges had excelled and made history either as "firsts" or with landmark lawsuits despite the humiliation, discrimination, and barriers they had to overcome either in pursuit of their law degrees or in the practice of being the licensed ambassadors of justice in a country that sometimes robbed them of that right.

For example, Thurgood Marshall attended Howard University because he was black. He could not attend the law schools in his home state of Maryland; many others echoed this reality. Many were brilliant, graduating at the top of their law school class, but were not hired by white law firms. They also talked about how, in the courts in the South, black lawyers were banned from using the same libraries available to white lawyers.

Very importantly, these giants shared with me the history of the American Bar Association (ABA), whose official policy of excluding black lawyers had resulted in most black lawyers' passionate opposition to the ABA.

A lawyer and former dean of the Howard Law School, J. Clay Smith, wrote about three Negro lawyers who joined the American Bar Association in 1908. When the ABA discovered their race, the organization changed its membership application, requiring interested lawyers to list their ethnicity. If the ABA was unsure of an applicant's race, they would visit that person face-to-face in their office to confirm that he or she was not black.

As a result, the National Bar Association was founded in 1924 and incorporated in 1925 in Des Moines, Iowa, to provide black lawyers the opportunity to come together to stay on the "cutting edge" of their profession by attending continuing legal education seminars and networking. They were not welcomed to join the American Bar until 1943. Associate Justice of the United States Supreme Court Felix Frankfurter encouraged his law clerk, attorney William Thaddeus Coleman Jr. to join.

As I sat amid so many brilliant legal minds at the NBA, I thought about how much better our profession and America would be if the likes of William Hastie Jr., Charles Hamilton Houston, Constance Baker Motley, Damon Keith, Thurgood Marshall, and so many others had been invited to be young lawyers in the ABA and then be active in great debates and activities in the ABA and its House of Delegates.

The insights that I gained at the National Bar Association conventions inspired in me a deep commitment to leveling the playing field for black lawyers. I found it cruelly ironic that the men and women who had devoted their lives to serving as soldiers of justice for ordinary people were also victims of institutional discrimination.

Now, serendipitously during my first NBA convention, the ABA welcomed black lawyers to participate, and I was privy to hearing the pledge firsthand, thanks to my association with NBA President Ed Bell. He invited me to attend a private meeting with the NBA leadership and the incoming president of the ABA, Chesterfield Smith, whom I had never met. A lawyer from Florida, Mr. Smith told the group that the American Bar had made a horrible mistake in discriminating against black lawyers.

"We've been wrong," he said, "and we want you to come and get involved in the American Bar Association. And we've set up a seat in our House of Delegates, our final policy-making body, for a representative from the National Bar." He explained that the NBA could appoint that person to the position.

The NBA graciously accepted that opportunity. Little did I know, at the time, that I would later receive a personal invitation to participate in the American Bar Association.

"RUNNING THE MEETING LIKE HE'D BEEN AROUND 50 YEARS"

In 1972, Detroit lawyer John Krsul invited me to co-chair the Judicial Evaluation Committee of the Detroit Bar Association, which evaluated lawyers and judges who were running for judge in Detroit, County of Wayne, the Michigan Court of Appeals, and the Michigan Supreme Court.

"I didn't see how we could continue this committee without a person of color," recalls John, who is white. "We needed a diverse representation in the leadership because a lot of black lawyers and judges were running for office. Up pops this name, Dennis Archer, who was very recently out of law school. I had never met him, but he had made a name for himself, in a short time, with the things he had done."

I accepted the invitation, and relished the opportunity to get involved.

"I'm an A-type personality and I had been running the committee for four years," John says, "so I expected to play a prominent role. At our first organizational meeting, I called on Dennis to talk about his section. Lo and behold, this young lawyer starts running the meeting like he'd been around for 50 years! My eyes bugged out at how he exhibited his organizational and leadership abilities." The report was heavily covered by the *Detroit News* and the *Detroit Free Press*, so the public could see how we ranked judicial candidates. We rated a few "not qualified" which created a lot of headlines and an invitation for us to appear twice on Lou Gordon's popular TV show.

"Dennis acted as if he'd been around the courts and the law for a very long time," John says. "He exhibited a great TV personality ability. I was my usual subdued self and Dennis was the very energetic personality and quite remarkable in how he handled *The Lou Gordon Show*."

As our friendship deepened, John shared his experiences as chair of the Young Lawyers Section of the State Bar of Michigan, as well as how his five years of activity with the American Bar Association had earned him the position of Division Director, which helped execute the ABA's new commitment to involving young lawyers on national committees, an honor that had historically been given to veteran lawyers.

"I was in charge of finding appointments in the senior bar for young lawyers to get involved in committees," John said. "That involved working with the ABA Presidential Appointment Committee under Jimmy Fellers. Not surprisingly on my list was Dennis Archer, who… had a lot of talent and would bring diversity to the America Bar." One day, John visited my office. "Dennis," he said, "the incoming president of the Young Lawyers Section is Harry Hathaway. Harry wanted me to tell you that if you come out to the convention in San Francisco, he'll appoint you to a committee. Harry wants to make sure that everybody knows that the Young Lawyers Section is available and open to everyone."

As I reflected on the ABA's history of discrimination against lawyers of color, I responded to John's invitation by simply saying, "I'll be there."

Bar Associations: Black, White, or Both?

In 1972, I attended the NBA convention in Miami, Florida, along with 1,500 to 2,000 African American lawyers. That year began our tradition of making the convention a family affair: we took our three-year-old son, Dennis Jr.

"We're going to Miami," we told him, "and we're staying at the Fontainebleau Hotel, which has a beach on the ocean." As we began our travels, someone asked Denny, "Are you going to Miami?"

"Not YOUR-ami, it's MY-ami," he answered, much to the humor of the adults around him.

We had a wonderful trip, then returned to Detroit, where we left Denny with Trudy's parents before flying to San Francisco. There we attended our first American Bar Association Convention.

Former NBA President Ed Bell and others also attended, to follow up on his being appointed as the NBA member to its seat in the ABA House of Delegates.

Meanwhile, I honored my word to John Krsul and attended events for the Young Lawyers Section, which was comprised of more than 1,500 lawyers under age 35 and was the largest ABA Section. They came from every state, and countries such as Australia, France, and England were represented.

While I felt comfortable and was treated with courtesy by everyone we encountered, I was suddenly stunned by the stark contrast of leaving just as many black lawyers in Miami, to find myself in a ballroom with only three black lawyers. They were a Harvard law professor; a lawyer from the United States Army who was there to recruit for the JAG Corps; and myself. The crowd may have included a few Asian lawyers, but no identifiable Hispanics.

What I observed caused me to ask myself, "Do I want to get involved because of the ABA's history of not allowing lawyers of color to join, let alone be on a committee? Do I want to stay where there are so few of us? Or do I want to go back to the NBA where you see all these giants, people who look like me, and spend all of my time there?"

I decided to do both. I would try to simultaneously contribute to the strong history of the NBA, while working within the ABA's Young Lawyers Section where I hoped to open doors for lawyers of color to participate.

Once I made that decision, I stayed with it. I never second-guessed my commitment to making change, despite a frustrating lack of receptivity among some NBA members who demanded, "Why do you want to become active in the American Bar because of the history that so many of us had experienced before trying to become members?"

My response to them has always been to reiterate the importance of being able to make change from within. But that took patience, and being able to see the big picture.

INVIGORATED BY POLITICS AND PRACTICING LAW

In 1972, seven seats were opening on Detroit's Recorder's Court. Several people suggested that I run for a judgeship. Unsure, I visited the federal courthouse to consult with Judge Keith.

"Dennis," he said, "you keep practicing law, make some money, and take care of your family. There'll be a point that you will have to give that up. But now is not the time. Go practice law." So I did not run. But I did serve as Campaign Manager for Samuel C. Gardner, who won.

Also in 1972, I received the American Bar Association Young Lawyers Section Award and the Outstanding Young Man of America Award by the United States Jaycees. In addition, I was blessed with the privilege of becoming an Adjunct Professor at Detroit College of Law, a position I would hold for the next six years.

Meanwhile, the law firm was thriving.

"Dennis was very good at scoping out new talent, new lawyers that could benefit the firm," Elliott says. "He brought in Tom Chionos, who was Greek, and David Allen Glenn, and the firm became Hall, Stone, Allen, Archer, and Glenn. Tom and David contributed to the growth of the office and the diversity of the office."

Not only were we providing great employment opportunities for these lawyers, but by expanding the firm we were able to help more people. This exemplified something that Judge Keith had always instilled in me and many others:

"If you're in a position to do something and you don't, you might as well not have had the position in the first place. You hurt people if you don't help others along the way. Be the person who opens a door of opportunity for another, and who shares success secrets so the others may also succeed."

DIFFUSING A DEADLY DRAMA WITH THE BLACK PANTHER PARTY

After the 1967 rebellion, city officials implemented a police decoy unit called STRESS — Stop the Robberies and Enjoy Safe Streets. But rather than achieve that goal, the unit became notorious for rogue and racist police officers who were ultimately accused of killing 22 people, as well as beating, harassing, and falsely arresting hundreds more.

This reality convinced many in Detroit's growing majority African American community that law enforcement officers were there to hurt, not help, and that police brutality should be combatted with revolutionary tactics that included violence. Espousing this kind of philosophy was the Black Panther Party, led by Bobby Seale and Huey Newton. They believed that the United States had been extremely unfair to black folks, and the only way to achieve freedom was through armed rebellion.

As Elliott continued to represent the Black Panther Party, I became familiar with their beliefs and activities in Detroit and across America. One night, Sam Gardner and his wife were over having dinner with Trudy and me. After dinner, while we were sitting in our recreation room on Thornhill Place, I received a phone call from Mayor Ray Gribbs' Deputy Mayor, Walter Green.

"Dennis, this is Deputy Mayor Green. We got a problem. We need your help. A police officer was killed in front of a house where a group of 16 kids, Black Panthers, are inside," he said. "The neighborhood is in an uproar. Police cars have been turned over, and some fires have been set. We don't want the situation to explode." Officer Robert Bradford was dead, and I later learned that a former student of mine was among the 16 kids inside the house. Next, I received a call from Larry Horowitz, an aide to Congressman Conyers, "Dennis, I'm calling to ask you and Elliott to help diffuse the situation."

"How can we help?" I asked.

"We need you to talk these kids into exiting that house," Larry said.

I understood that failure to do so could result in a bloodbath that could potentially set off another rebellion as bad as or worse than that of 1967.

"We're on our way," I told him. Then I called Elliott.

Michigan Chronicle writer Nadine Brown, whom I knew, along with premiere Detroit radio deejay Martha Jean "The Queen" Steinberg, were at a location a distance from where the Black Panther Party members were holed up at 16th Street and Myrtle. Many of these men and women were barely in their 20's.

When we arrived, the house was surrounded by police vehicles and officers with rifles ready to shoot. The Detroit Police Department's urban tank stood ready to fire, and the air was thick with tension. Elliott and I complied with a request before we entered the house to remove our shirts to prove that we were not carrying guns. Then, as police led me, Elliott, and Nadine to the house, we observed that the police were heavily armed and ready to engage in a battle in what many militant blacks were calling a "revolution" against racism.

"If you don't surrender," Elliott told them, "the police are going to tear this place to shreds. They're surrounding the house, and they have an urban tank, ready for battle. You won't win."

"Let it be," said one of the female leaders.

"No, you can't do that," I said. "Not only would you be getting yourselves killed, but it would set off unrest, as we saw in 1967, that would get many more people in our community killed."

"That's what we've come to in America," one of them said. "We have to fight the oppressive powers."

"We can help you do that as lawyers in the court system," I said. "Right now, let's surrender without anybody getting hurt. We need to all walk calmly out of this house and allow justice to be served in a nonviolent manner." All the while, the young revolutionaries were on the phone with Huey Newton, who spoke with Elliott as well. They were also fueling their rebellion by reading magazines that espoused the Black Panther philosophy. Three of them decided to stay inside and have a gun battle with the police. We were able to convince 13 of the men and women to walk out with me, Elliott, and Nadine. To the great credit of the Detroit Police Department, they tear-gassed the house, and the three people inside surrendered and came out.

Meanwhile, Elliott, Nadine, and I were praised in the newspapers and on television reports for courageously diffusing a potentially explosive situation. The community took note that Elliott and I were two attorneys who truly were making a difference.

As more business poured into the firm, Trudy and I were blessed with news that we were expecting our second child.

Time for Detroit's First Black Mayor

Detroit was ready for its first black mayor, and political speculators agreed that the right candidate could win. Some pointed to Richard Austin, but it was unlikely that he would step down as Secretary of State, the third most powerful position in Michigan. Popular opinion pointed to State Senator Coleman A. Young as the most high-profile and promising contender.

My choice was Judge Ed Bell. In 1972, he left Wayne County Circuit Court to comply with a provision in our state statute that required members of the judiciary and the legislature to resign one year before a primary election if he or she wanted to run for a position outside of their respective arenas. Coleman Young did not resign.

I wholeheartedly endorsed Ed Bell's vision, and the newspapers announced when I was named his campaign manager. Our financial officer was a young Jewish lawyer named Lawrence Charfoos, and we became fast friends. I also clicked with another lawyer, David Christensen, who was Danish and who worked in the Charfoos & Charfoos law firm.

Meanwhile, I became deeply involved in plotting and planning Ed Bell's campaign, by conducting research across the city. My goal was to build a solid, fact-based platform to tell voters exactly what he would do to help the city, and how he would improve employment, housing, city services, the crime rate, and police-community relations.

At the same time, everyone was waiting to learn whether Senator Young would resign to announce his candidacy. When the deadline for compliance with the state statute passed, we breathed a sigh of relief that Ed Bell would be the only black candidate running for mayor. Without Coleman Young in the race, I believed we could get Ed Bell elected as Detroit's first black mayor.

As I worked hard campaigning for Ed Bell, representing my clients in court, and participating in the bar association committees, I was also sharing Trudy's excitement and anticipation for the birth of our second child, due in April. At the time, Denny was attending preschool at Grosse Pointe Academy, and Trudy was still teaching at Bellevue Elementary. On the evening of Friday, April 27, 1973, I received a call at the campaign office.

"I think we need to go to the hospital," Trudy said.

I immediately picked her up from our townhouse on Thornhill Place in Elmwood Park. We dropped off Denny at her parents' house nearby, and proceeded to the hospital. Just a few hours later, Vincent DunCombe Archer was born weighing 6 pounds, 13 ounces. We named him after his grandfather, James Vincent DunCombe. And we asked Beth to be his godmother.

"Dennis was happy again because he had another boy," recalls Trudy, who stopped teaching to stay home with Vincent and Denny. "It was a very happy time."

Meanwhile, on the campaign trail, we were gaining support for Ed Bell, and we were optimistic that he could win. Unbeknown to us, however, Senator Young had filed a lawsuit challenging the constitutionality of the state statute that prohibited legislators, unless they resigned one year before, from running for outside office. The Michigan Supreme Court declared the law unconstitutional, and State Senator Coleman Young became a mayoral candidate. Despite that, I was still determined to distinguish Ed Bell as the best mayoral candidate.

"Maybe we can work this out," I told Ed. "Let's talk with Bob Millender." We did, along with Coleman Young, while the four of us walked around a swimming pool behind someone's home in Palmer Woods.

"I think we should all support Ed Bell," I suggested.

Senator Young and Bob Millender laughed.

"We're going to run," they said.

Coleman Young and Police Commissioner John F. Nichols trounced Ed Bell in the primary election, becoming the two candidates in Detroit's 1973 general election for the mayoral race.

That night, Ed Bell and I committed our support to Coleman Young, and worked hard to help him become Detroit's first black mayor.

After Coleman A. Young won the general election in November, 1973, I was overwhelmed with the thrilling pride and honor of helping to make history. His victory made him one of the few black mayors of America's largest cities, taking office simultaneously with Maynard Jackson of Atlanta and Tom Bradley of Los Angeles.

In Detroit, African Americans celebrated Mayor Young's election as entrée into the top echelon of the city's power. That, they believed, would cultivate equality, safety, and progress for people of color. Unfortunately, Mayor Young's three days of inaugural festivities were overshadowed by the profoundly different ways that blacks and whites interpreted his proclamation that criminals had no place in Detroit:

"I issue an open warning to all dope pushers, to all rip-off artists, to all muggers," he said. "It is time to leave Detroit. Hit Eight Mile Road. And I don't give a damn if they are black or white, if they wear Superfly suits or blue uniforms with silver badges. Hit the road."

Those three sentences became a lightning rod of racial division. Many people of color understood Mayor Young to mean that criminals should leave town, because his administration would not tolerate crime. However, white suburbanites and Detroiters — most of whom had voted for Nichols — interpreted the comments as an invitation for criminals to fan out across Detroit's borders to wreak havoc in the mostly white suburbs. The fact that Eight Mile Road was and remains the border between predominantly black Detroit and mostly white suburbs, only exacerbated the inflammatory impact of this statement on the region's troubled race relations.

These words, sadly, cast a perception among many that Mayor Young was antagonistic toward whites in general and the suburbs in particular. And that accelerated middle-class whites' departure from the city alongside the business community's continued disinvestment by relocation to the suburbs. Compounding this was the city's high crime rate, and spiking unemployment due to the loss of auto industry jobs.

I was delighted that the Young campaign provided another opportunity to learn from Bob Millender about how to strategize a winning election. I demonstrated my commitment and ability to both him and Mayor Coleman Young that I was a hard-working ally. Meanwhile, I watched with fascination as Mayor Young eliminated the STRESS unit and began to integrate the police department.

At the same time, I was heeding my law professor's advice to contribute articles to various legal publications. One subject that I wrote about frequently was prepaid legal services, which I learned about through the American Bar Association. Just like car insurance, prepaid legal services were there when you needed them.

Many lawyers like myself wanted to convince everyday people to pay a nominal amount and for corporations to offer prepaid legal services as a benefit to their employees. The benefit would be that should someone need legal services, the costs would be covered. The UAW negotiated such a plan.

The First Black Associate at Charfoos & Charfoos P.C.

The fall of 1973 ushered in other major changes, as I left the law firm that I helped to start, and began practicing with Charfoos & Charfoos, P.C. in the First National Building. I became an associate. The other attorneys were Lawrence S. Charfoos, Samuel Charfoos, David F. Dickinson, Ronald R. Gilbert, and David Christensen. Larry Charfoos hired me as the firm's first black associate to reflect the city's growing African American population.

"The trend during the 1970's was for people in Detroit to realize that we had a growing African American community that had to be considered as our client base," recalls Larry. "As many of the white folks had left the city after the riots, we realized that we had better integrate our law firm to reflect the community. I had my eyes open to invite someone into a personal injury law firm, where there historically had been no black lawyers. Dennis Archer topped my list.

"When I worked with him on the campaign, he was outstanding in his personality and presentation, and after talking with others in the firm, I wanted to make him an offer — with a salary and a car. I said, 'Dennis, if you join us, we'll give you a Mercedes and a salary commensurate with the other lawyers in the office.'"

I was excited to work on big cases involving auto negligence, slip and fall, product liability, and malpractice. I also did criminal defense work, both assigned by the courts and retained.

"What impressed me with Dennis was whether he was retained or assigned, his client got the same, very high level of care," recalls

David Christensen. "When you take assigned work, it doesn't pay nearly as much as a retained client. You never knew it from Dennis. He zealously defended his criminal law defendants. Then, he increasingly did more personal injury work."

"I watched him in court during his first few trials, and was confident in his ability," Larry recalls. "That was affirmed when Wayne County Circuit Judge William J. Giovan told me that Dennis had tried cases in his courtroom on several occasions, and that, 'Dennis Archer is an absolutely first-class trial lawyer.'"

The firm name was later changed to Charfoos, Christensen and Archer, P.C.

The secret to my success? Old-fashioned hard work.

"Dennis works harder than anybody around him," says David, who led the practice of law at Charfoos & Christensen. "He gets it done. When you would walk into his office at the end of the day, his desk was clean. All the work was done and put away. The only thing on his desk was a yellow pad and a pen ready for the next morning's work. Everything else was spotless. He's always prepared. And he also returns phone calls right away. Dennis Archer simply outworks the next guy. And if you ever take a walk with him, you damn near need a scooter to keep up."

Cultivating Diversity and Inclusion in the Law Firm

Now that I was in a position to open the law firm's doors for other people of color, as Judge Keith had advised, I made it my business to do so whenever possible.

"Dennis insisted on bringing other black lawyers into the firm, including Sam Simpson and David Robinson, who went on to become a 36th District Court Judge," Larry says. At the time, Sam was Registrar and Chief Referee for the Wayne County Juvenile Court, and teaching law at DCL.

"I ran for Recorder's Court Judge," Sam says. "Subsequent to my loss, it was at Dennis' urging that I joined the Charfoos firm." David Robinson became a summer intern in 1972 and 1973 while attending the University of Michigan School of Law.

"In late April or May of 1975," David recalls, "I was literally walking down Woodward Avenue, coming back from lunch with colleagues, when I ran into Dennis."

"What are you doing?" I asked David.

"I'm working at the city," he said.

"Hey, come with me," I said.

"Next thing I know, I'm in the Charfoos office talking with Larry Charfoos," David says. "The firm had just had a significant victory with Larry and Dennis representing a young child injured on Belle Isle." David and Larry spoke. Next thing you know, David got hired by the Charfoos firm, working his way from associate to shareholder until he left in 1986.

"While at Charfoos," David says, "Dennis was always looking out to get young lawyers who look like us in the personal injury business. We had a summer internship program, and Dennis was responsible for that program and selecting several young black lawyers who worked with us." I got David involved in the local, state, and national bar associations. And I made a point to mentor him to teaching him how to be a good lawyer as he accompanied me to court.

"In court," I told him, "as a lawyer, you can only control two things: your degree of preparedness and being on time. Everything else, the person in the robe controls. You don't show up late. You don't show up unprepared. So, if the other lawyer is late or unprepared, you have an advantage. Everything you're doing, the lawyer on the other side is also trying to win. That lawyer has the same training, and is a member of the bar, too. Do the best job you can with what you can control." Other veteran lawyers joined me in schooling David on the ways of the legal world.

"As the youngest guy there," David recalls, "I'm learning by hearing these guys talk. They have knowledge and information that I don't have. They told me, 'If you can avoid one mistake because of what we're telling you, you'll be far ahead of the game.'"

I tried to instill in David that this is a business where you want to have good relationships with everyone. You represent your client zealously and fight as hard as you can. When the judge makes a call, you learn and move on.

"You don't hold a grudge," I told him as we ate lunch at the Fish Dock near Recorder's Court. "You're going to have wins and losses. You can't get too high or too low. If you win, you get 24 hours to enjoy. If you lose, you get 24 hours to sulk. In either event, that's it. You have to move on. You have other clients and obligations to handle. You can't get hung up on the highs and lows or you won't be able to function." David listened to everything that I and older lawyers told him.

"The courtroom is a stage," I said, "where lawyers play an adversarial role against each other. But once that courtroom door closes behind you and the other lawyer, it's time to say, 'Hey man, how you doin'? How are the kids?'"

David says that lesson impacted him profoundly. "When two doctors are in a room, one isn't trying to kill the patient while the other is trying to keep him alive. But that's the dynamic we operate in court. Dennis really taught me the importance of civility in the practice of law." David applied each lesson as he tried cases for the firm, and his success made me extremely proud.

And while I was encouraging the firm to hire more people of color, I did my best to acclimate my partners to black life and culture in Detroit.

"I'm a nice Jewish boy from northwest Detroit," Larry says, "and from the time Dennis joined the firm, he's dragging me to lots of black churches. He'd say, 'Larry, you've got to see this world and understand it, too.' I got immersed in the black community through him and learned about our community that I was not exposed to; that's commitment. I ended up marrying a black woman, so he really converted me." During that time, another family member joined us on the 40th floor of the First National Building: my father-in-law. Dave was especially fond of Mr. DunCombe, who had been friends with his father long before we met.

"As we worked together, Jim and I developed a special friendship," Dave says. "He did courier type work, delivering documents to court, and he'd pick up our expert witnesses at the airport. He loved to talk and tell stories to everyone he met. Invariably, whether they were a scientist or had some other fancy position, they were intrigued by Jim, and would ask, 'Who was that gentleman who picked me up?' He was much loved and worked with us for many years as a valued member of the firm."

In May of 1974, Trudy and I were so proud to take Denny and 13-month-old Vincent to Washington, DC, to attend Beth's graduation from Georgetown University Law Center. She then became an associate at Dickinson Wright law firm, where she later became the first black partner and spent 22 years. Dickinson Wright occupied the second half of the floor shared by Charfoos & Charfoos.

"Dennis was across the hall," Beth recalls, "and my father worked in the Charfoos firm after he retired from the United States Postal Service. It was a real family thing."

"I'm Ernie Archer's Son"

A year or two after joining the firm, Dave Christensen and I went to Chicago for a malpractice seminar. Driving my Mercedes, I was quite proud to stop in Cassopolis to show Dave around my hometown. We played golf, and then went into town and stopped at a bar for a beer.

"We drove to another bar whose front window made Dennis' Mercedes clearly visible from inside," Dave remembers. "When we walked in, nobody was in there except the bartender, one little old man, a skinny little fella, an African American man who talked like a farmer. We were wearing suits, and he studied us as we came in. After a few minutes of small talk, Dennis asked, 'Did you ever know a guy by the name of Ernie Archer?'"

"Oh, one-armed Ernie?" the bartender asked. "Oh yeah, I knew him."

"Well, that was my dad. My name is Dennis Archer."

Dave still gets goosebumps as he recalls what happened next: "That old man stuck his hand out and shook Dennis' hand and I thought that was kind of Dennis' way to go back to let Cassopolis know that Ernie Archer's kid did good in life."

Dave also recalls how his daughter's birth with profound brain damage in 1973 provided a heartwarming moment between us.

"Dennis came to me one day and he said something to the effect, 'Hey man, your daughter is in the hospital and you didn't tell me. You're supposed to let your friends know, it's important for me to follow up with that.' That meant a lot to me." Now, Dave says moments like that formed a solid foundation for our friendship.

"Dennis has that same, genuine human touch with everyone he meets," Dave adds. "If you walk down Woodward Avenue or on Griswold or Congress downtown Detroit, he greets every secretary, every courier, every person who ever worked in his office, every guy that ever parked his car, sold him a suit, shined his shoes, and he calls them all by name, stops and visits and finds out how they're doing. He's got a tremendous memory and a bigger heart."

LIVING THE AMERICAN DREAM

Our family needed more space; Trudy and I purchased a house in Palmer Woods. Home to many of Detroit's best-known executives, business leaders, doctors, lawyers, and politicians, the tree-lined neighborhood featured stately 1920's-era Tudor revival homes, as well as the city's only Frank Lloyd Wright-designed house, and the 35,000-square-foot mansion built by William Fisher of the Fisher Body automotive empire. Our two-story, gray limestone home had a circular driveway and a spacious yard for the boys to play. Both my family and Trudy's family were extremely proud of our home, where we hosted frequent gatherings for relatives and friends.

One day, David Robinson asked me to join him for a jog around Palmer Park. "I've been feeling sluggish," he said, "and I'm gaining weight. I need to run to get back in shape."

That began a daily ritual that soon included Dr. Charles Inniss, who lived nearby.

Trudy and I loved to entertain, and we have albums full of photos showcasing events such as a black-tie dinner for couples on New Year's Eve with a few of our closest friends, dinners prior to the formal Barrister's Ball, and birthday parties for our sons.

"Thanksgiving was great because we went to my grandparents' house," Denny remembers. "For Christmas, everyone would come to our house on Lincolnshire. For several years, the kids had a special tree in the basement, and our parents played Santa Claus."

A winter sleigh ride with the kids was one of many activities that Trudy enjoyed with them as part of Jack and Jill of America, Incorporated, which is, according to its website, "a membership organization of mothers with children ages 2–19, dedicated to nurturing future African American leaders by strengthening children through leadership development, volunteer service, philanthropic giving, and civic duty."

We traveled to Disney World and places such as Hawaii, Mexico City, and the Bahamas, to attend ABA meetings and conferences, while not missing an NBA annual meeting.

I fiercely guarded family time. I made a practice of getting up at 6:30 a.m. to make breakfast and eat with Denny and Vincent before they headed off to Detroit Country Day School.

"He made French toast, eggs, toast, and bacon before school," Denny recalls, "and he would verbally stress the importance of doing well in school. He had all kinds of sayings, including, 'A hard head makes for a soft behind,' and 'Loose lips sink ships.' Breakfast was his guaranteed time with us. Now I do the same thing with my sons, Trey and Chase."

In the evenings, Trudy would eat a small meal with the boys at six o'clock, then help them with homework and get them to bed.

"I always sat down and had absolutely marvelous gourmet dinners with Dennis when he got home at 9:30 or 10 o'clock at night," Trudy says. "That was our private time. On the weekends, he would always go to his office with the boys in the morning, then come home in the early afternoon. Saturday and Sundays were family time."

When our firm moved to the 40th floor of the Penobscot Building in 1976, our law firm began hosting an annual party on our balcony to watch Detroit's famed Fourth of July fireworks display.

"I remember going to his office as a kid and knowing everybody in the office," recalls Denny, who would intern at the firm during his high school summers. "His assistant gave me all kinds of stuff, like crayons to draw. And we used to watch the fireworks every year from that office. All of our parents' friends and their kids would come to watch the fireworks, which were literally right across the street."

Dave Christensen vividly remembers those days. "His family was awfully important to him. When the kids were little, you didn't find him at the downtown watering holes. He went home. He was very much a family guy."

My secretary, Marty Austin, who would remain with me through-out my entire career until she retired in 2014, handled my schedule and was awed by how I balanced my personal and professional lives.

"I don't know how he juggled everything," Marty says. "All the hours he was at work, he was in constant communication with his family. His family was very important to him; his kids were every-thing to him. He made it work. It was fun to watch those little guys grow up; they were just fun kids. He always seemed to have a great relationship with both sons."

At the time, I was handling a number of big cases and serv-ing as Chairman of the Young Lawyers Section of the Detroit Bar Association. I also served on the Board of Directors of the Detroit Bar Association and became Co-chairperson of the Public Advisory Committee. I was thrilled to get involved in Jim Blanchard's 1974 campaign for Congress, helping him get elected to the U.S. House of Representatives for Michigan's 18th District.

I was afforded the opportunity to discuss the political issues of the day by hosting a TV program. Mike Wahls, a Wayne County Circuit Court Judge, hosted a Sunday morning TV program called "Issues" on WXYZ, Detroit's ABC affiliate. He was appointed to the Michigan Court of Appeals, and resigned from the TV show, so I asked the producer, Ted Talbert, who was African American and extremely talented, if I could replace Mike. I did, and I loved it! The *Detroit Free Press* published a great photo of the three of us standing by a director's chair.

After that show, I became a legal consultant along with attorney Henry Baskin and another lawyer on "Good Afternoon Detroit with Marilyn Turner and John Kelly." We were presented with legal issues to answer.

"Walking one block with Dennis downtown Detroit would take 10 minutes," David Robinson recalls with a laugh, "because people would constantly stop him and say, 'Hey, I saw your show, it was great.'"

Trudy and I thought it was important for Denny and Vincent to learn about the city at an early age, and it made an impact. Denny recalls, "I can clearly remember that when Mayor Young was in office on Thanksgiving night, Damon Keith used to host black and white leaders in Detroit at his home on Outer Drive and have an off-the-record fireside chat about what's going on in Detroit. I went with my parents and Vincent, and I would sit and just listen, absorbing everything like a sponge. Those are amazing experiences."

CAMPAIGN MANAGER, COLEMAN A. YOUNG FOR MAYOR OF DETROIT

In 1977, Detroit was America's fifth largest city, and Mayor Young's leadership was ushering in a thrilling new era epitomized by the imminent unveiling of the Renaissance Center, a $500 million riverfront development backed by Henry Ford II and Ford Motor Company.

Its glass-covered skyscrapers included a 73-story hotel rising amid four, 39-story office towers, all set on a foundation of restaurants, shops, and financial companies. Begun in 1970 under Mayor Gribbs as a catalyst for Detroit's economy, the RenCen's completion during Mayor Young's impending re-election bid for a second term was fortuitous. It showcased him as the leader of a city that was literally on the rise, as the skyscraper development was now the tallest building in Michigan.

Very importantly, it would rev Detroit's economy by spawning more than $1 billion in financial growth within a year.

This crown jewel for our city, as its name suggests, was sparking a renaissance for Detroit a full decade after the ravages of the 1967 riots. It was a glimmering milestone for Mayor Young to showcase all that he was doing in the city — including integrating the police force in ways that improved police-community relations; creating jobs for Detroiters who worked on RenCen construction; and establishing the city as a mecca for shopping, dining, and hosting national conventions.

With this on Mayor Young's resume, the mayoral race was sure to be exciting, and I was eager to participate. So, I jumped at the opportunity when Bob Millender proposed this:

"Dennis, I'm the campaign director for Coleman Young's campaign for mayor. Would you like to be Coleman Young's campaign manager?"

Bob would call all the shots, and I would execute.

We had 15 campaign offices across the city, in addition to influential supporters at the City Resident's Committee on Livernois Avenue, as well as at the UAW and the AFL-CIO offices. Our campaign offices buzzed with activity, and I made my work — which consumed evenings and weekends — a family affair.

"I remember working in the campaign office, stuffing and licking envelopes, then people would push me around in these big mail bins on wheels," says Denny, who was eight years old. "I knew my dad was working on Mayor Young's campaign for re-election, but I didn't know he was the Campaign Manager. That was my first exposure to politics." Denny says all the activity and fast-moving people created an exciting atmosphere.

Among the many people I met while campaigning was Michael Cavanagh, whose brother, Jerome Cavanagh, had been mayor of Detroit from 1961 until 1968. The son of a teacher and a Ford Motor Company factory worker, he was a fellow Democrat who was passionate about Detroit and Mayor Young's leadership. Michael and I became fast friends.

Meanwhile, my passionate commitment to politics inspired my Aunt Jo to warn me: "Don't run for mayor. It's an enormous, thankless job. You can do a great job and it will take so much from you." I simply smiled and continued my work to help elect great leaders.

In this election, Mayor Young's principal opponent was Detroit City Councilmember Ernest Brown, who styled himself as a polished sophisticate determined to woo the city's growing black middle class comprised of doctors, lawyers, and business owners. His campaign attempted to paint Mayor Young as brash, unrefined, and therefore unable to represent the interests of black professionals.

That, of course, was untrue because Mayor Young's charm, wit, and brilliant understanding of the issues enabled him to appeal to people on society's lowest rungs while simultaneously cultivating excellent relationships with black and white professionals. He also enjoyed deep friendships and powerful business alliances with Ford Motor Company Chairman Henry Ford II, as well as billionaire developer Alfred Taubman and philanthropist Max M. Fisher, both of whom were Jewish.

As Mayor Young's campaign manager, I conceived an unprecedented strategy to ensure his victory on Election Day. I have never been one to underestimate the power of women in political campaigns. And with Mayor Young being a handsome, powerful, charming bachelor, I proposed a novel idea: "Let's host an outdoor event at the Manoogian Mansion for sororities and women's organizations to enjoy food, music, and the opportunity to get to know Mayor Young." The women came in large numbers, and it was an overwhelming success.

Likewise, I veered away from our typical format of small update meetings at our campaign offices, labor-union halls, and businesses hosted by our Livernois supporters.

"Let's have a series of huge meetings," I suggested. "We'll tell everybody that we're having a big campaign meeting on a certain day where they can shake Mayor Young's hand and take pictures

World Heavyweight Champion Muhammad Ali drew a huge crowd and positive media coverage when he attended a rally for Detroit Mayor Coleman Young in 1977. I was serving as campaign manager for his re-election.

with him. And we'll get them even more excited by announcing that celebrity supporters will be there." World Heavyweight Champion Muhammad Ali attended one meeting, drawing an enormous crowd and favorable media coverage.

Mayor Young was respected across the country as a leader within the U.S. Conference of Mayors. The national media spotlight also shined on Mayor Young because he was a friend and political ally of President Jimmy Carter, thanks to being an early supporter of his presidential bid in 1976. I studied their relationship and how, as a result, President Carter helped our city.

The mayor and president collaborated to create win-win programs and policies for Detroit and America. In fact, I still have a ticket number 115 that says "Admit One" for "A Meeting with President Jimmy Carter" on October 21, 1977, at Veterans Memorial Building, Detroit, Michigan. I also have a letter from The White House signed by President Jimmy Carter on June 12, 1979. I have a letter signed by Tim Kraft, assistant to President Jimmy Carter, thanking me for meeting with him and senior advisors on October 5, 1978.

"The meeting was extremely helpful to all of us, and the comments we heard were both enlightening and constructive," the letter said. "As you know, we are attempting to develop and expand our means of communication with the political leadership in the country. We need your advice and support. To facilitate and encourage this communication, I have assigned Mike Berman of the White House staff to provide you with direct access when you need it... We are looking forward to a closer working relationship with you."

That relationship evolved as I made my first trip to the White House for a briefing related to the Congressional Black Caucus.

All the while, I observed how Mayor Young finessed complicated business and political situations that sometimes involved an antagonistic press. He walked on water, swam, and didn't get wet. Mayor Young demonstrated that it's important to be principled, stand up for what you believe in, don't roll over or let somebody roll over you, fight when you need to fight, and make your case and bring people to your side of things. He was everywhere — in churches on Sunday, at union meetings, at the White House.

Very importantly, under his watch, crime had decreased after a severe budget crisis forced the layoffs of many police officers. He reassigned officers from desk jobs back onto the streets, resulting in more arrests, fewer shootings, and decreased complaints about police brutality and police harassment.

All the above accomplishments impressed voters on Election Day of 1977, when Coleman Young defeated Ernie Brown in a landslide, winning re-election to his second term as Detroit's mayor.

LOSING MY MOTHER TO CANCER

Sadly, my mother was diagnosed with stage four colon cancer in 1978. It was terminal.

"I do not want to have surgery," she told me. "I want some kind of quality of life while I'm here." We cherished many lengthy conversations as I expressed how important she was to me in my life and how motivating and supportive she had always been.

"Whatever I have done and will become," I told her, "will be in large measure thanks to you." I thanked her many times for instilling in me the values that were enabling me to achieve far beyond any of our imaginations while I was growing up in Cassopolis. We enjoyed Sunday dinners so that she could spend time with Denny and Vincent. In January of 1979, the hospital called to inform me that she had died. I felt relief for my mother.

I wish that Mom and Dad had lived to see all my accomplishments. Sadly, Aunt Jo died the following year. My grandmother had passed a few years before. I don't wear my religion on my sleeve, but I'm absolutely certain that my parents, my grandmother, my uncles, my aunt, and other relatives are looking down, pleased with what they see.

JOINING THE ASSOCIATION FOR
FUN WITH PROFESSIONAL FRIENDS

Through Trudy, I met many people who became lifelong friends. For example, Gil Fisher and Dr. Charles Inniss. Chuck recalls, "My wife, Marie Inniss, was friends with Trudy, and I remember going downtown to meet her and Dennis for the first time. We became good friends. We hung together and did things together socially."

Chuck and Gil invited me to join The Association, a social group comprised of 30 up-and-coming black male professionals who convened monthly in each other's homes. When I joined, the membership included a number of attorneys, including Myron Wahls, Joe Brown, and Sam Simpson. It was exciting to meet so many accomplished, ambitious black men who were eager to share advice and encouragement about becoming the best in our chosen fields. We always enjoyed our gatherings every third Friday evening of the month.

4

CHANGING THE GAME FOR PEOPLE OF COLOR IN THE LEGAL PROFESSION

INCREASING INVOLVEMENT IN THE WOLVERINE BAR ASSOCIATION

DURING THE LATE 1970's, Trudy began attending law school. At the same time, Beth urged me to take a leadership role in the Wolverine Bar Association.

"One day I said, 'Dennis, you really need to get involved in the Wolverine Bar,'" recalls Beth, who was moving up the chain toward the presidency. "'You really could make a difference.' I held off for a year, to insert him into the chain in my place."

I became Wolverine Bar Association President-Elect from 1978 until 1979, then President from 1979 until 1980. During that time, I was active as a Board Member of the State Board of Ethics for the State of Michigan. I also served as Secretary to the United States District Court Monitoring Commissioner for the Detroit School District. My political activities included serving as Director of the Michigan Democratic Party's Detroit Get-Out-The-Vote Campaign and Co-chairman of the Metropolitan Detroit Community Coalition for the Democratic Party.

"Dennis is a natural leader," Beth adds, "and the Wolverine Bar needed leadership because it was faltering." It had a reputation as a social organization whose sole objective was to host the annual Barrister's Ball. It had no bite in terms of advocating for the advancement of black lawyers or taking a stand on important issues impacting its members. At the time, a lot of black lawyers were coming out of law school. Affirmative action was controversial and hotly debated. And the Supreme Court was deciding cases that impacted the legal profession.

"When Dennis took the helm," Beth says, "the Wolverine Bar got on the map. People listened to him. He had a lot of contacts around the country with lawyers through the NBA and ABA, so he brought national respect to the organization."

We achieved that in many ways. We filed an amicus brief against discrimination. We started speaking up for black lawyers in the media. We also reached out to reporters who began calling on us for comments about news impacting black lawyers.

A big fight was brewing between the *Detroit News* and the *Detroit Free Press.* The *News* went after former Wayne County Circuit Judge Ed Bell and his relationship with Judge Sam Gardner, intimating that something inappropriate had occurred. The Wolverine Bar took out a big ad in the *Free Press,* challenging the *News* over how they were dealing with black judges.

Because I was active in the National Bar, I knew Elaine Jones, a brilliant lawyer and head of the NAACP's Legal Defense Fund. She called me and said President Carter was nominating Cornelia Kennedy, a federal trial court judge in the Eastern District of Michigan, to become a Judge on the United States Court of Appeals for the Sixth Circuit. She would become the first woman in that position. Elaine shared with me her opinion that Judge Kennedy dealt unfairly with federal inmates who filed in pro per (self-filed) cases.

"Dennis, will you come to Washington to testify in a Senate Committee against her elevation?" Elaine asked.

I agreed.

After that, I phoned Judge Kennedy to tell her that I could not support her, and that I had reached this decision after four lawyers and one law professor had reviewed 90 of her cases.

The Detroit Bar Association, the Women Lawyers Association, and the State Bar of Michigan supported her nomination. But the NAACP, and the 450 members of the Wolverine Bar and the National Conference of Black Lawyers, unanimously opposed the nomination. The mainstream bar groups were upset.

As President of the Wolverine Bar Association, I testified before the Senate Judiciary Committee that Judge Kennedy had an appalling record on civil rights in that she lacked qualities of reasonableness, and sensitivity, and was unfair to black prisoners who filed in pro per cases involving civil rights and constitutional issues. Joining me in the Senate hearing was former NBA President and Wayne County Circuit Court Judge Ed Bell.

As the controversy played out in the media, Beth told colleagues and interviewers alike that the Wolverine Bar's opposing stance was viewed as defiant by those who had not sought our organization's perspective prior to making their decisions.

I told interviewers that the negative response by the white power structure was triggered by the fact that Judge Kennedy was a nice person, but our viewpoint was that hurtful acts by a kind person were just as painful as those from a blatantly mean individual. Judge Kennedy and I, nevertheless, remained friendly throughout her service on the Sixth Circuit Court of Appeals.

This followed a big controversy sparked by a *Detroit News* columnist writing that Kennedy was being castigated by individuals who lacked class and intelligence.

Judge Kennedy's nomination was confirmed. But our high-profile stance against her showed that the Wolverine Bar meant business. As a result, membership grew. We hosted educational seminars and started a foundation to award scholarships to black law students.

"Dennis really made a difference and the organization pivoted to become more substantive," Beth says.

To substantiate my oft-repeated criticisms about the "opportunity gap" between black and white lawyers, The Wolverine Bar

Association conducted a study of our members. We publicized our findings in the media, at speaking events, and at meetings for bar associations and other organizations. Our survey revealed that only 47 percent of black attorneys worked in private practice, and that they worked in firms whose clients were also black. We also discovered that one-third of black lawyers who had been admitted to the bar would reconsider that career choice if made again.

"Unless white firms start hiring black lawyers, we are going to have a major problem," I warned, citing an ABA report that said the number of lawyers in America doubled from 1960 to 1980, and was projected to do the same between 1980 and 1995.

"I am a partner in a major law firm with 17 associates and partners, and we practice what I'm preaching," I often said, "because we are one of the most integrated law firms in the country, with four blacks, five Jewish people, an Italian, an Arab, a Dane, a Greek, three white women, and the rest white men."

Presenting solid statistics about the problem bolstered the impact of our message. For example, we discovered a 1 to 399 ratio of lawyers to citizens for whites, but only one black lawyer for every 1,215 blacks. At the same time, the numbers of black lawyers were declining.

"It is critical that we collectively strategize to serve the black community and to increase minority access to the profession," I told the National Bar Association members at their board of governors quarterly meeting in June in Cleveland.

At the time, about 2 percent of America's 500,000 lawyers were black and 4 percent of enrolled law students were black. Unfortunately, many factors were contributing to a decline in the number of black students who enrolled in and who graduated from law school. So, I participated in a campaign for the ABA to adopt Resolution/ Standard 212, which would require accredited law schools to prove that they offer "full opportunities for the study of law" to members of minority groups.

In February of 1980, I participated in a contentious debate with University of Michigan Law School Dean Terence Sandalow, who opposed it.

Thankfully, in August, after a two-hour debate, the House of Delegates, the policy-making body of the ABA, approved Standard 212 at our annual convention.

The national media reported that I gave a passionate testimony encouraging the House of Delegates to ratify the mandatory standard to help reverse the historic fact that the powerful and highly respected legal profession had excluded people of color.

"THE BROWNING OF THE
AMERICAN BAR ASSOCIATION"

In 1979, I still saw very few brown faces at ABA meetings and conventions. I was not happy, and was driven to action. So, I expressed my concerns at a Young Lawyers Division meeting. Now 37 years old, I had "aged out" of the group, and they needed to appoint a new crop of young lawyers to tackle this topic.

"When I first met Dennis Archer, he was talking about 'the browning of the ABA,'" recalls Rachel Patrick, who was hired by the ABA — at my urging — to work in its Chicago headquarters as a staff director for the Young Lawyers Division. After all, how could an organization with an all-white staff expect to attract members who were black, Hispanic, Asian, or Native American?

"I remember he said, 'You can count on one hand the minority lawyers who are active in the ABA, and I'm one of them,'" says Rachel, now Director of the Coalition on Racial & Ethnic Justice after 37 years of service with the ABA. "He said, 'This is ridiculous! This is basically a white organization. There are minority lawyers who want to get involved, but don't know how. We need to do something about this.'"

So, I considered four lawyers — Rachel, Jane H. Barrett, Robert Grey, and Cathy Vaughn — whom I believed could make a difference.

"When I met Dennis," recalls Virginia lawyer Robert Grey, "I could tell he was on a mission to create an environment and action agenda to improve diversity in the American Bar Association and in the profession."

Rachel agrees. "It was just amazing, the first time we met, and listened to him talk about his vision of what he wanted for the ABA with the help of this committee."

"I can make this happen, Dennis," said Jane H. Barrett, a California attorney who chaired the Young Lawyers Division. She created the Minorities in the Profession Committee to encourage and increase minority lawyers' participation in ABA activities.

"Dennis encouraged us to write a proposal to the senior bar so that he could present the proposal to them and ask them to support the initiative," Rachel says, "to create a permanent committee, a task force, so that everyone in the ABA could study the problem. Most white lawyers didn't think there was a discrimination problem."

Rachel recalls that because I had been building relationships and respect within the ABA, and had elevated past the young lawyer status, I was able to "transcend" difficult conversations about race. "When they heard him talking," Rachel says, "they didn't see black or white. They just saw Dennis Archer. He was everybody's role model. Even back in 1979, he was already being talked about as the first black president of the ABA."

The group called me "Anwar Sadat," who was the president of Egypt who won the Nobel Peace Prize for negotiating peace in the Middle East.

"We also called him the Right Reverend Dennis Archer," Rachel says. "Dennis was so smooth and articulate. Everyone was saying he should chair the committee."

Our endeavors would be more effectively represented, I explained, by someone who looked like those who had the power to make changes. Meanwhile, the committee worked hard to perfect exactly what to present to ABA leadership. We developed an action plan that included conducting informal surveys of minority lawyers' perceptions and attitudes, by sponsoring six conferences starting in 1980 through 1982.

"We'd be drafting the report late at night," Rachel recalls, "then Dennis would take it to the board, which said, 'You need to go back to those young lawyers and let them know A-B-C.' We went back and forth so much, many among us said, 'The ABA is not going to change. Anwar Sadat is not going to be successful.'"

My political activities in Detroit, however, were successful. In 1980, after U.S. Congressman Charles C. Diggs Jr. resigned, I ran George W. Crockett Jr.'s successful election campaign in a special election to fill his seat representing Detroit's 13th District. Trudy and I were invited to his swearing in, where I had the pleasure of seeing my all-time favorites — Peabo Bryson and Roberta Flack — perform at the Kennedy Center in Washington, DC.

The following year, I was campaign director for Shirley Robinson Hall for City Clerk of Detroit, as well as General Counsel for Mayor Young's re-election. My political involvement was exciting, and I was hosting a radio program — thanks to News Director Norman Miller — called "Inside Straight" on Detroit's WJLB-FM 98 Radio that provided a platform to discuss the issues that my candidates were emphasizing.

"Take Your Name Off of Dennis Archer's Application"

Around 1981, I applied to become the first black member of the exclusive Detroit Golf Club. I did not talk about it; I just quietly began the process. I had successfully convinced 12 members to write a letter on my behalf, as was the requirement for new applications. Likewise, I had identified two members on the board of directors to support my application.

When my name was posted on the bulletin board as a potential member, I was advised that one of the directors was told, "If you want to be president of the Detroit Golf Club, you need to take your name off of Dennis Archer's application."

I was also informed that two lawyers who were club members were asked to remove their names. As a result, I did not meet the qualifications and my application was never voted on. Though disappointed, I remained quiet — and fully committed to joining the Detroit Golf Club someday.

A Second Lawyer Joins the Family

In June of 1981, I was so proud of Trudy when she graduated from the Detroit College of Law. My friends gave me a "P.W.T." certificate, which stood for "Put Wife Through." That summer, as Trudy began studying for the Bar Exam, I took Denny and Vincent on a trip to

Jackson Hole, Wyoming. With the rugged backdrop of mountains and lakes, we went whitewater rafting and golfing, and had a ball.

Trudy passed the Bar Exam on the first try, but did not look for a job. "I decided to stay home," she says. "Vincent was eight and Denny was 12, so I took time off to devote to them."

That year I served on the Finance Committees for William Lucas for Wayne County Executive, James Blanchard for Governor, and U.S. Senator Donald W. Riegle's re-election. In 1982, I received the Distinguished Alumnus Award from Western Michigan University. In 1984, I helped the re-election campaign for U.S. Senator Carl Levin.

During this period, I was intrigued by a contentious dispute that exploded on the eve of Governor Blanchard's inauguration. Blair Moody Jr., was elected in November of 1982 to the Michigan Supreme Court. However, he died before taking office. Outgoing Governor William Milliken appointed Republican Dorothy Comstock Riley to the Court, much to the dismay of incoming Governor Blanchard, who believed that it was his right to appoint Moody's replacement. The Supreme Court agreed, voting 4–2 in February of 1983. In her place, Blanchard appointed Federal U.S. District Court Judge Patricia Boyle. This was a powerful lesson on how incoming and outgoing leaders could impact political appointments.

President Ronald Reagan was in office, and I often spoke out about how his administration was perpetuating an "old boy network" atmosphere in which blacks were not being hired and were first to be fired. It was affecting black lawyers, according to a *USA Today* report in 1985 that said the number of black attorneys in the country's top firms declined by almost half over the previous two years. The article said that women and Hispanics were making progress, but only 1.5 percent of lawyers in the top firms were African American, compared to 2.9 percent in 1982.

Reports like this fueled me to aggressively advocate to increase the numbers of black lawyers across America. I did this through my activity within the bar associations.

SEEKING THE PRESIDENCY OF THE NBA

In 1980, I was appointed Special Assistant to the President of the National Bar Association by President O.T. Wells.

"This was an opportunity to shadow the president and learn the operations of the bar," said John Crump, who served as the NBA's executive director for three decades. "Normally a president has four or five special assistants, and the position indicates that this is an individual who would be good for the bar association futuristically."

Well, I didn't want to wait that long. Though I had never held an elected NBA office, which was the typical route to the presidency, I felt that I could do a good job as president if given the chance. So, when Detroit hosted the national convention in 1981 at the Renaissance Center, I made a run for it. It seemed like everybody knew I was running.

My Wolverine Bar colleagues passed out my literature as I campaigned in a three-way race. When election results came in, I placed second. The next day, during a run-off, people kept saying, "Stay active in the NBA," as they entered the voting booths, as if they knew I would lose.

They were right; I got trounced by Warren Hope Dawson. Feeling terrible, I retreated to our suite in the Westin. Still, I attended the black tie annual dinner and congratulated Warren on becoming president.

The day after I lost, I started campaigning for the next year's election.

"If you knock Dennis down," Beth says, "he gets right back up. Some people would give up. But you can't keep him down long. If that's one of his goals, he's going to get there."

In 1982, the NBA convention was in Atlanta. I faced an election with two opponents.

"Vote for Dennis Archer for President-Elect, National Bar Association," my campaign literature said on trifold brochures that included my slogan, "Say Yes to Michigan!" which was inspired by our state's tourism campaign. Inside the brochure were photos of me with my family, Muhammad Ali holding Mayor Young's arm in victory, and Wolverine Bar Association leaders.

It also outlined my campaign platform to help black law students, lawyers, and judges, which included National and Community Involvement, Judiciary, Career Planning and Placement, Increased Membership, Fiscal Planning, and Long-Range Planning. The back of the brochure listed my professional and civic activities.

I was victorious, winning against two opponents on the first ballot to become president-elect for 1982–83. I still have a handmade card from Denny and Vincent congratulating me for the victory. I became president the following year.

Shirley and Elliott Hall threw a surprise party in Detroit to celebrate my NBA presidency just before I flew to Seattle to assume office.

Sharing a celebratory moment with Judge Damon Keith after he swore me in as President of the National Bar Association.

They had tricked me into believing that they would pick us up for dinner, but called to say, "We're running late. Can you come to our house instead?"

I became NBA President during the 58th annual meeting in Seattle in August 1983. When I took the helm, national travel consumed about half of my time. I maintained my pace at the firm by working until 10:00 p.m. or 11:00 p.m. and on weekends. Meanwhile, I met Johnny Cochran and other outstanding lawyers with whom I cultivated professional relationships.

"The NBA was facing big issues in 1983," John Crump says. "One was to make sure African American lawyers got hired in big law firms. Second was to get more federal and state judges on the bench. Third, we had to address major funding challenges."

I helped the NBA transition from dependency on grants and contracts to becoming self-sufficient through membership and sponsorship of the convention and other events.

"We made a trip to New York to the Ford Foundation," John says, "and through Dennis' leadership, they provided us with a bridge grant... to transition us over the whole process." We also added a midyear conference in a warm climate, in addition to one annual meeting for the bar and quarterly board meetings.

"When Dennis was president, the first meeting with judges was in Freeport, Bahamas," John says. "People brought their spouses, and it created a whole new atmosphere." As did adding classes and seminars for which people could earn six to eight hours of Continuing Legal Education (CLE) credits, which were required by most states.

"We became an accredited sponsor in all the states," John says. NBA membership spiked because people liked traveling to a sunny place during the winter while also fulfilling a state CLE requirement.

At the same time, the number of students of all races enrolled in American Bar Accredited Law Schools more than doubled from 50,000 to 60,000 in the early 1970's, to about 125,000 to 130,000 in the 1980's, Crump says. The numbers of black lawyers in the United States nearly doubled between 1970 and 1980, from just over 8,000 to 15,000.

Under my leadership, we purchased the building in Washington that we had been leasing for our NBA offices.

During NBA meetings, I was astounded by the fact that the 56-member board often brought just as many opinions to the table.

"Crump, man, how do you manage 56 lawyers in one room?" I asked.

"Just by sheer faith!" John responded. "Sheer faith!"

John said I handled it with diplomacy. "Dennis' biggest attribute is the ability to listen and ascertain the strong points before he makes a decision." Another milestone of my NBA leadership was to convince the ABA to allow two-year terms for our seat in the House of Delegates, which enabled the individual to gain traction and therefore have more impact. This helped Elaine Jones, who was General Counsel of the NAACP's Leadership Council, to ultimately get on the ABA Board of Governors.

I concluded my tenure at the NBA convention the following year in New Orleans, after traveling the country, convincing lawyers of the importance of their positions to help their communities. I had spoken before Congressional committees to convince them not to cut funds to black families that can lead to single-parent homes, as well as abuse of spouse and child. And I had urged black lawyers to do business with each other. I left office feeling that we had done so much, yet so much remained to be done.

ABA Private Club Controversy

Members of the Young Lawyers Section were having a ball, dancing at a private club during an American Bar Association midyear meeting in Philadelphia. Some of us were doing the hustle, when one of my colleagues said, "You know, if it wasn't for this meeting, you wouldn't be here."

"What are you talking about?" I asked.

"Well, the club does not admit black people as members," my colleague said.

Deeply troubled, I started talking to some of my white colleagues around the country and in Detroit. Then I put together a resolution that went before the House of Delegates, urging the ABA's policy-making body that the American Bar should not have paid functions at clubs that discriminate against people due to race or religion.

We had a huge debate, and we won. The House of Delegates voted to pass the proposal in January of 1982, that urged Congress to include private clubs that were used for business in the 1964 Civil Rights Act's ban on discrimination on the basis of race, color, religion, and national origin. The proposal said that the rules for public accommodations should apply to any club with 20 percent of its income derived from business-entertainment deductions.

That infuriated some country club members who feared that private courses would lose their exclusivity by becoming public. They cited the clubs' right to freedom of association as an argument against the House of Delegates' decision.

As a result, the House of Delegates voted 178–130 during the ABA's annual meeting in San Francisco to reverse its previous decision.

I was absolutely stunned! Their sudden repeal sent a message that discrimination was acceptable. As one of five black delegates at the meeting, I said, "What this means is that we can press our faces to the glass, but we're not allowed to go in to dinner."

During media interviews, I expressed outrage over the ABA's step backward.

I channeled my outrage into an article called "BLACKBALLED! The Case Against Private Clubs: An analysis of how the ABA condones discrimination" in the ABA's Spring 1983 edition of "Barrister."

We came back at the next ABA midyear meeting with a resolution and won it. The House of Delegates approved the proposal, and it stays as policy today.

FAMILY FUN AND FORUMS DURING VACATIONS ON MARTHA'S VINEYARD

Some of our family's fondest memories occurred during summer vacations on Martha's Vineyard, which we began taking in 1981 and continued for many years. We rented a condominium in Oak Bluffs, while many of our closest friends and their children occupied units in the same complex or nearby. We were first inspired to visit by Marie and Charles Inniss. Eventually, our group included the families of Wilson and Debbie Copeland, Elliott and Shirley Hall, Frank and Miriam Clark, Beth and Joe Brown, Anna Diggs Taylor and S. Martin Taylor, Nancy and Harold Varner, Mary Kay and Paul Piper, Nettie Seabrooks, Wendell Cox, and Nancy and Sam Simpson.

"Martha's Vineyard was always a blast," recalls Denny. "For several years in a row, we drove in a caravan with no less than four and up to seven cars. Dad had a white Cadillac Seville with a blue top. It was very Detroit. He loved George Benson, Roberta Flack, and Peabo Bryson, and we'd listen to cassettes during the 14-hour drive to catch the ferry at Woods Hole, Massachusetts. Those are some of my favorite songs to this day because of those trips."

Food was a highlight of the trip. "We'd pack the car with grapes and pop and get buckets of KFC. The Inniss family had a Trans Van which had a bathroom and mini kitchenette, and when we'd stop, the kids would all go in there."

We also loved to visit Bunch of Grapes bookstore in Vineyard Haven. We all liked to read. Denny enjoyed the Hardy Boys mysteries. Every morning, the guys staked out our spot on State Beach. There we made new friends from other states.

"Our entourage had about 20 people," Beth recalls. "We'd all go to the beach together, and we had a great time. It was a real family affair."

"We'd bring a hibachi out and cook hot dogs," Elliott says, "and we'd stay until three thirty or four at the beach, then we'd go to a bar downtown Oak Bluffs and have a beer. After that, everyone would go home, shower, and get ready for dinner."

Eating at our favorite restaurants or someone's vacation home was a pleasurable highlight of our Martha's Vineyard trips, as was the activity that followed. Some nights, after dinner we would gather and engage in spirited discussions about politics, current events, and, of course, all things Detroit.

In 1983, Trudy became Assistant Corporation Counsel for the City of Detroit, which afforded her fascinating insights into issues impacting the city.

"We'd sit around, have drinks in a very relaxed atmosphere, and assign a topic for the evening," Beth says. "Whatever was happening in the world became a topic of discussion. For example, we talked about Vanessa Williams when she lost her Miss America crown."

A few years later, the hot topic was President Ronald Reagan's re-election and continuously negative impact on affirmative action.

"I'm sure Dennis was recording all this in his head over the years," Beth says.

She's right. I don't learn a damn thing when I'm talking. But I learn a lot when I'm listening. Therefore, my preference, when sitting among the many CEOs, judges, lawyers, doctors, and business leaders who often joined our "think tanks," was to listen and learn.

During one of these events, I met Vernon Jordan, who sat on corporate boards of directors. I was fascinated as he described how he helped to make decisions that impacted how each corporation operated as well as how he worked to increase diversity.

"Dennis was always observing and asking questions, and ultimately saying, 'I can do that, too,'" Beth says. "He's always very patient. He might do it twenty years later, but he would start mapping his way and working toward that particular goal."

On one occasion, I had the opportunity to play golf with President Bill Clinton and Vernon Jordan at the Mink Meadows Golf Course.

SKI TRIPS WERE AS MUCH FUN AS MARTHA'S VINEYARD

Members of The Association enjoyed a family event every January at Shanty Creek Ski Resort in Northern Michigan. "It was amazing,"

Denny recalls. "Everybody packed their food on the bus, then we'd get to Shanty Creek, and take over the lodge. I loved it. These three-day weekends were equally as fun as Martha's Vineyard. All the kids would eat our meals at one table, while the adults were at others. Then we'd play hide and seek throughout the whole hotel."

Elliott, who took his daughters, Lannis and Tiffany, remembers it fondly. "The best time was at night sitting around the fire talking about everything under the sun. We knew the kids were safe because they had activities for them."

MORE FAMILY TIME

Bar Association conferences provided more opportunities for family trips, and we cherish photos of the kids together in Hawaii, Miami, and many other places.

"We'd see our NBA friends every year," Denny says. "I have friends right now that I'm still close with who live all over the country. Those relationships started at conventions. We'd go to the kiddie disco and when we were in New Orleans, we were old enough to

Denny and Vincent traveled with us to many major bar association events. For example, we attended the State Bar of Michigan meeting at the Grand Hotel on Mackinac Island.

go to the movies and see *Purple Rain*. We had a blast and have a lot of great memories."

Back at home, as the kids got older, we played tennis as a family every Saturday at Franklin Racket Club. It was always Denny and Trudy versus myself and Vincent. The winner got to pick where we'd have dinner: Carlos Murphys or Buddy's Pizza on Northwestern Highway.

"I remember playing basketball in the back yard with my dad; he had a little hook shot," Vincent says. "I love tennis and golf, and I know my love of golf came from hanging out with Dad. My brother had lessons at Palmer Park, then he and Dad would play, and they'd let me tag along. I had one club and kept hitting it. Dad used to play a lot and is a very good golfer. He definitely inspired me to love playing golf with him and my friends."

Trudy and I were also very active in activities at Country Day, including the Blue and Gold Club (the father's group), and fundraising activities.

"Between Mom and Dad, someone was always at a tennis match, or basketball game," Denny says. "They never missed anything."

MARKING MILESTONES FOR THE
ABA AND THE STATE BAR OF MICHIGAN

I continued to lobby the ABA to create a task force committed to the cause of studying barriers to — and solutions for — the advancement of minority lawyers in the legal profession.

I spoke as frequently as possible on this subject at meetings and during media interviews. I used words such as "abysmal" and "obnoxious" when noting that only about 18,000 of America's 650,000 lawyers were black. That was just under 3 percent, when blacks comprised 13 percent of the general population. I also referenced the *National Law Journal* findings, which for years had been pointing out the negligible numbers of women and lawyers of color at large law firms across the country.

In 1983, ABA President William Reece Smith and Young Lawyers Section Chair Jane Barrett hosted a meeting in Washington, DC, for African American, Asian, Hispanic, and Native American lawyers. They wanted to know why lawyers of color were not participating in the American Bar, as well as what obstacles were keeping people of color from the best opportunities in the legal profession. They would use the information to propose solutions for how to aggressively and urgently employ and promote those who were being excluded.

THE TASK FORCE ON MINORITIES IN THE LEGAL PROFESSION

They presented their findings that: America's largest law firms might have only one black associate or partner out of a staff of 400 lawyers; that lawyers of color as law school deans or as tenured track professors were few and far between unless they were at Historically Black Law Schools; and that judges typically hired clerks who looked like them.

Armed with this information, ABA leadership created the Task Force on Minorities in the Legal Profession.

ABA leadership appointed Calvin H. Udall, a member of the ABA Board of Governors, to chair the nine-member Task Force, which was charged with investigating the myths and realities impacting lawyers of color in America. It focused on Legal Education and Admissions to the Bar, Employment Opportunities, Judicial Administrative Division, and Bar Association Involvement. The Task Force gathered, received, and analyzed unprecedented data by conducting a survey of law firms nationwide, conducting meetings, and holding hearings across the country.

A concrete action plan that I hoped would result in a seismic shift for people of color to advance in the legal profession was beginning to take shape. The Task Force on Minorities in the Legal Profession embarked on an unprecedented investigation.

"We held closed-door meetings with the General Counsels of corporations, as well as with the partners of elite law firms across America," says Rachel, the task force director who secured the gatherings by assuring the attorneys that our discussions were top-secret and would not be leaked to the press. "We met with groups in Chicago, New York, New Jersey, Minneapolis-St. Paul, St. Louis, and Milwaukee."

"I'll never forget one of the meetings," Rachel recalls, "when they told us they couldn't give their work to black lawyers."

It happened in New York City, when Task Force member Norman Redlich, who was Dean of the New York University School of Law, arranged for us to meet with Manhattan's most exclusive silk stocking law firms. Though only one had a partner of color, they spoke very candidly with us.

When I said, "Tell me why you can't give your work to a black lawyer," their consistent response was this: "How would our client feel having somebody black handling top corporate issues? And why would we take a chance of losing a client who would be uncomfortable, not knowing if that lawyer of color was capable of handling a high-level corporate assignment?"

These elite lawyers also divulged that their clients from the world's top corporations had told them, "No, we don't want anybody black handling our work."

"We were stunned!" Rachel says. "We had some heated discussions, but Dennis was always very strategic."

Remembering that my grandmother used to say you can attract more with honey than with vinegar, I very diplomatically engaged these lawyers in dialogue to explore how we could create win-win solutions for everyone. I was convinced that we could wield significantly more influence for change from within the sacred space of these elite law firms, than to engage in rabble-rousing tactics from the outside, which would only inspire the law firms to slam the door on these groundbreaking conversations.

"Dennis knew everybody," Rachel says, "and he treated everybody with respect. I think he made people feel like, 'Listen, you can trust me, because I identify with what you're saying. We can fix this together.' It was almost like a spiritual leader; that's how compassionate and convincing and persuasive he was."

I did that by asking questions such as, "Can we talk about why you feel that you can't hire black lawyers? How and what would you do to hire a minority lawyer? What kind of test basis or pilot program could we establish to give it a try?"

After those meetings, Rachel remembers that Cal Udall would be amazed at how I finessed those conversations. "Cal would say, 'You have your finger on the pulse, Dennis. I'm so glad we're partners.'"

Those meetings inspired the Task Force to explore how to break this thought process, and identify what well-connected allies had the power to say, "This has to stop!"

TASK FORCE HEARINGS HIGHLIGHT THE PROBLEM

A classic Michigan snowstorm struck in February of 1985 as Detroit hosted the American Bar Association's Midyear Meeting. The highlight of this week-long event was one of four hearings that the Task Force on Minorities held across America.

Chairman Udall had sent invitation letters to 2,500 of the nation's largest law firms, asking them to testify about how to advance minorities in the legal profession. A paltry two firms sent representatives, both of whom were black. Yet more than 200 lawyers requested to testify! We were limited to accommodating 85 people in person, including law school deans, law students, lawyers, judges, and local and state bar leaders.

In attendance were Task Force members, including NYU Law School Dean Norman Redlich, as Task Force Chairman Calvin Udall led the two-day hearing — which stretched from 8:00 a.m. until midnight.

"We heard some real tear-jerkers from lawyers of color who testified about their experiences in the legal profession," recalls Rachel, adding that we accepted written testimony from 125 more people. "Their stories were received with such compassion in that room, it was indescribable." Trudy and I were delighted to host our ABA guests for dinner at our home.

I was also very proud to invite my colleagues to visit Charfoos, Christensen and Archer, because we exemplified the mission of the task force. In my office, I loved to point out my telescope, a gift from Trudy, which symbolized my long-term vision for advancing the legal profession. And I always told visitors about the print on my office wall, a Norman Rockwell lithograph. It shows a black girl escorted by U.S. marshals so she could attend school after *Brown v. the Board of Education* desegregated schools.

"I first saw this painting in a Chicago hotel, and had to get it," I told visitors. "I look at it every day because it expresses all my beliefs about life. The U.S. marshals symbolize the power of the American justice system to protect us in our pursuit of education and success in life.

Second, the young black girl is walking erect and proud, carrying her schoolbooks. She's proud and determined, not scared. She shows that we all have to take our bag of tools and our book of rules, with our values and life experiences, and apply all that to solve our problems."

I was doing that by filling days with my caseload, bar association work, travel, and sometimes four speaking engagements per week. This hard work earned my place on *Ebony* magazine's ranking of the 100 most influential black Americans.

During many interviews on the radio, on television, and in newspapers and magazines, reporters asked me to substantiate rumors that I may run for office. Instead, I expressed contentment with the independence of practicing law.

I did that with high energy and a youthful appearance, the media noted, thanks to my regimen of lifting weights and running three miles within 24 minutes around Palmer Park every morning.

I worked to execute the momentous vision of the task force. After the hearings, we combined our findings with our other research, which revealed that black women were least likely to find employment in private law firms, followed by black men, then Puerto Rican men.

Our findings also showed that attorneys of color:

- earned 56 percent of what their white peers earn;

- were more likely to have minority clientele; and

- usually worked in government offices or small firms, often consisting of one person;

We also learned that:

- Blacks, Indians, Hispanics, Chinese, and Japanese only comprised 8 percent of law school enrollment and 3 percent of lawyers in America's biggest 50 law firms;

- Blacks made up only 4 percent of law school student body enrollment;

- America's 170 accredited law schools had no minority faculty members to speak of and were few and far between on the country's federal benches; and

- Very few lawyers of color were tenured law professors at white law schools.

This data fueled my advocacy as I continued to write, speak, and do media interviews, never sugarcoating the issue. The term "good old boy network" peppered my comments about how lawyers of color were overlooked for jobs and promotions. I also emphasized that small firms followed bigger firms' bad example of not hiring blacks and other minorities. While keeping the problem front and center, I also highlighted the progress as more people realized the need for change.

Rachel adds that, "Calvin Udall, our task force chair, was a well-respected, conservative from Utah, and he became one of our most avid advocates. It was a revelation to him when he saw clearly Dennis' vision for the ABA's future as an association that embraced diversity and inclusion. He and Dennis became inseparable brothers around making the ABA a fair and equal place for lawyers of color. They'd stay at the ABA for a week at a time, politicking, meeting with the right people, and writing the Goal IX Report, which set a priority for how the ABA would spend its money to include opportunities for women and minorities. They defined the history of why the task force formed, and what action it recommended for the ABA to take." Once adopted by the ABA House of Delegates, it became policy.

"It was so exciting," Rachel says, "we were pinching ourselves."

In February of 1986, the Task Force presented to the Board of Governors our 76-page "Final Comprehensive Report of the Task Force on Minorities in the Legal Profession," which exposed that "residual discrimination still persists in some of the legal profession, and that some hiring and promotion processes and criteria continue to limit minorities' opportunities even though they are not intended to do so."

The group's subsequent recommendations included aggressively recruiting minority students for law schools, as well as helping white interviewers prepare to recruit law students of color. In August, the House of Delegates unanimously approved the Task Force's recommendation to grant a seat in the House of Delegates to the National Hispanic Bar Association.

More tangible change occurred after President-elect William Falsgraf wrote a letter in 1985 to section chairs, encouraging them to include women and minority lawyers as candidates to participate in and chair sections. As a result, 18 sections and divisions had special committees, programs, and activities that included conferences and seminars — all addressing the needs of minority law students and lawyers.

President Falsgraf put the Task Force's mission into practice by speaking at minority bar events across America. Nearly one-third of the people he appointed were women or people of color, or both. Despite progress within the ABA, its leadership concluded that the Task Force's findings demanded an action plan to conceive and implement solutions to generate and sustain opportunities for women and people of color to advance in the legal profession.

In 1986, the ABA created the 10-member Commission on Minorities in the Profession; I became its first chair, and we convened for the first time in December.

"The Commission was a very significant entity in the ABA," Rachel says.

Meanwhile, since 1984, we had been grappling with the question of how to advance white women — who were considered minorities at the time — while also advocating for men and women of color. As a result, the ABA created the Commission on Opportunities for Women in the Profession in 1987. Its first chair was the First Lady of Arkansas, Hillary Rodham Clinton. As she and I traveled the country together, Hillary was knocking out glass ceilings, and I was trying to open doors for ethnic minority lawyers. We held joint meetings once a year, to ensure that we were collaborating to advance our respective missions.

"When the Commission started," Rachel recalls, "Dennis handpicked a magnificent group of outstanding lawyers from different backgrounds — Asian, Hispanic, African American, Native Americans, and Caucasians. It was like creating a brain trust of the best legal minds in the profession who were all on the same wavelength."

Before we could propose solutions for people of color to get hired and promoted in law firms and in corporate America, we needed to better understand every aspect of how they recruited, retained, and advanced their employees. We began with a series of retreat-type meetings where we brought together diverse groups of lawyers who were willing to share their experiences and insights. Beth was instrumental in this process.

"I worked closely with Dennis on how you make partner because I was a partner in a major law firm at the time," Beth says. "We talked about how black lawyers struggled to retain clients if they were excluded from all-white country clubs where major business deals were made on the golf course."

Beth's perspective was bolstered by Commission member Phyllis James, who in 1985 became the third woman and the first African American partner at San Francisco-based Pillsbury, Madison, and Sutro (now Pillsbury Winthrop Shaw Pittman).

"Beth and I became the founding members of the Minority Partners in Majority Firms," Phyllis recalls, "which hosted annual events focusing attention on the dynamics impacting the hiring and retention of minority lawyers in majority firms."

At the same time, I sought understanding of how lawyers functioned in corporate America by consulting with white attorneys whom I knew, asking how minority law firms could get corporate business.

"Dennis represented a symbol of African American lawyers bridging that gap between what traditionally was the white mainstream and the parallel universe of minorities," Phyllis says. "He was a terrific role model for lawyers to navigate both worlds while demonstrating that you don't have to give up your identity as a minority in order to be a bona fide, respected member of mainstream organizations like the American Bar Association. That was really important."

At ABA receptions and dinners, I often spoke with Phyllis and other lawyers of color about the importance of using one's success to reach back and uplift others.

"You should never forget your roots," I advised. "Whatever you do, whatever degree of success you have, always remember to give something back to the black community."

Those words resonated with Phyllis. "That was a very important message. It wasn't 'Let's get rich and live in big houses, drive fancy cars, and go on fancy trips.' It was, 'Always do something to give back to your community in whatever way that you decide is meaningful for you.'"

A HISTORIC MOMENT:
FIRST BLACK PRESIDENT OF THE
STATE BAR OF MICHIGAN

Two other very qualified people were running for president of the State Bar of Michigan, which is always a hotly contested race. Each of us was vying for a majority of votes from our Board of Commissioners.

"There was a lot of politicking that day," recalls John Krsul, who had served as president from 1981 to 1982.

I set myself apart from the competition by positioning myself as an advocate for change, citing my role on the task force, and how I had reached out to the legal community in Metro Detroit and Grand Rapids, to talk about hiring and promoting lawyers of color.

"Dennis won by one vote," John says. "We walked out of that room, and I gave him a hug. 'My God,' I said, 'we did it!' Dennis and I were the young Turks leading other lawyers into leadership positions."

David Robinson was also there. "I was sitting at the table because of my affiliation with the Young Lawyers Section, which had 'voice and vote,'" he recalls. "I was one of the people who voted for him to become president. I thought it was a tremendous accomplishment. This was a guy that I felt real comfortable with on a professional level and as a human being, who was going to be the face of the legal profession for the state of Michigan."

On September 20, 1984, I was sworn in as the first black president of the State Bar of Michigan, just in time for our organization's 50th anniversary. As Trudy, Denny, and Vincent witnessed this historic moment, I was overwhelmed with pride and humility, as well as a burning drive to utilize the power and privilege of this position to make positive change.

While outgoing president Joel Boyden welcomed me to the helm in the ballroom of the Amway Grand Plaza Hotel in Grand Rapids, I looked out at hundreds of lawyers who were among The State Bar of Michigan's 23,000 members. Of those, only 3 to 4 percent were minorities.

I was determined to help change that during my leadership, which would make history for a second reason: Julia Donovan Darlow, a partner at Dickinson Wright, became the organization's first female vice president. She would ultimately become the first woman president of the State Bar of Michigan.

The October edition of the Michigan Bar Journal showed me on the cover with the headline "50th President." Inside, I wrote on The President's Page a two-page article entitled, "In the Coming Year," which began with news that the Bar was developing "a meaningful diversity program."[1]

I then pledged to champion the cause by meeting "with hiring partners, corporate counsel of businesses, chief judges in urban areas, and the chief judges of the federal district courts to discuss the presence of minority and women lawyers in the practice of law."

Further, I asked, "If we in the legal profession, who advocate equal justice under the law and equal opportunity, do not encourage and promote diversity within our own ranks, then how can we expect businesses, cities, and others to do the same?

"As lawyers, we race to the courthouse to file a claim for or to defend discrimination cases. As lawyers and judges, therefore, we must set the tone for the clients we represent, or for the rulings we make, regarding equal justice under law. I look forward to successfully developing a diversity program, supported by the Board of Commissioners and the officers of the State Bar of Michigan."

In the same edition, my sister-in-law, C. Beth DunCombe, wrote a lengthy article entitled, "An In-Law's Eye View of the President." After writing several personal anecdotes, she wrote about my contributions and concluded by saying that in 1985 Michigan lawyers will celebrate the 50th anniversary. "The positive irony," Beth wrote, "is that the State Bar's celebration of its 50th year will be led by its first black President, Dennis Archer."

David Robinson says that during my presidency, more young lawyers and lawyers of color began to participate in the State Bar.

"Michigan has 83 counties," David says. "Dennis sat down and broke bread with the county bar association in every county. This

---

[1]   *Text used with permission from the State Bar of Michigan. President's Page column in the Michigan Bar Journal.*

provided an opportunity to talk about bringing in people of color and being more inclusive."

In cities across the state, I also met with hiring partners of major law firms, with judges, law school deans, and officials of law departments of Fortune 500 and utility companies to understand the benefits of hiring and promoting women and minority lawyers as clerks, associates, partners, and general counsels. My oft-repeated admonition was this:

"If we as lawyers do not set the example for equal opportunity, then how can we as lawyers tell our clients to integrate and offer opportunities and upward mobility for women? If judges are not willing to hire minorities and women as their law clerks, how then can judges reasonably expect defendants to integrate willingly or stop practices that the court says are discriminatory?"

I used every possible opportunity to interject this message while appearing on behalf of the bench and Bar more than 100 times before local and out-of-state bar associations, in television and radio interviews, at administrative and legislative hearings, and at law schools, high schools, and grade schools. In doing so, I spent 60 to 70 percent of time serving the Bar, rolling up more than 25,000 miles on my odometer.

"We are getting to the point where it makes particularly good sense to have minorities involved, either by minority firms or having blacks in majority firms," said James Dyke, a partner in the Washington, DC, firm of Sidley & Austin who participated in the hearing. I quoted him on the President's Page of the June 1985 edition of the Michigan Bar Journal, under a headline, "Minorities in the Law: Not When; Now."[1]

Very importantly, James Dyke emphasized that it was good for business to bring minority lawyers in as partners, especially in cities that had people of color as elected officials. I concluded the article by quoting American Bar Association President John C. Shephard: "Everyone agrees that action must be taken to increase minority hiring. It is not when, but now. It is not who, but us."

That Michigan Bar Journal edition featured a 1920's-era black male lawyer with the headline, "Blacks In The Law." In it, I wrote,

---

[1] *Text used with permission from the State Bar of Michigan. President's Page column in the Michigan Bar Journal.*

"Since my President's Page in the November 1984 Bar Journal (entitled) 'Diversity in the Legal Profession,' many state bar journals had either devoted an entire issue on minorities in the profession, or have had major articles addressing the issue." I directed readers to the June 15, 1985 edition of The Pennsylvania Lawyer's article, "Black Lawyers Struggling for Acceptance."

My column continued by saying, "Many state and local bar associations have established committees to evaluate the status of minority students in law schools, hiring practices of corporations and large law firms, the low number of black and minority partners in law firms, and the scarcity of minority judicial clerks."

I pointed out that "state bar officers met in Detroit and Grand Rapids with hiring partners in law firms of 15 or more, judges from the Eastern and Western District Federal Courts, and representatives of corporations employing corporate counsel. Since then, some firms have begun (or have increased) their efforts to hire other minority attorneys, I am advised, and at least one is considering a lateral hire to partnership. Several federal judges in the Eastern and Western districts have personally confided their intent to make their next clerks minority lawyers. I thank all of you who make opportunity equal."

"It was a real whirlwind year," says Janet Welch, executive director of the State Bar of Michigan. "He went everywhere and talked to everyone. There wasn't any challenge that the Bar had that he ducked. He was completely involved and tried to get everybody on board. And his signature energy and congeniality brought together everything that was going on."

At the time, the Michigan Bar was grappling with weighty issues that were both coming to a head and beginning to brew.

"The Alan Faulk case was a First Amendment case dealing with the scope of the Bar's public policy advocacy and what it could or could not do as a mandatory Bar," Janet says. "It was a very big deal. It went to the heart of what the Bar was and what it could do."

On several occasions, Janet recalls that I applied my "powers of persuasion" to create positive outcomes for important issues such as state funding of the court, judicial salary and compensation, and judicial malpractice insurance. I met with both the governor and the chief justice more than once, while traveling the country, as well as to London for the ABA's annual meeting.

Throughout that year as president of the State Bar of Michigan, it was especially humbling and meaningful to visit Cassopolis. The newspaper hailed me as a hometown hero, publishing photos and articles when I talked with Cassopolis Middle School students about being their best, and when I spoke to the Cass County Bar Association at Dowagiac's Round Oak Restaurant.

"It was amazing that he was able to do everything that he did," Janet says.

All the while, I maintained a vigorous agenda of speaking out in the media when necessary and giving speeches. For example, in February of 1985, tensions were simmering after three people had been fatally shot in the Detroit area by people claiming self-defense.

"Firing through a door is not justified because it could be a Girl Scout selling cookies or a newsboy coming to collect, or a student selling magazines," I said at a news conference with WSU Professor Ed Littlejohn and Detroit Recorder's Court Chief Judge Sam Gardner. "Citizens should know they run the risk of becoming felons themselves. Self-defense could turn into self-destruction."

In March, I spoke at Lawyers Against Apartheid about how the State Bar of Michigan would consider endorsing its resolution condemning the use of South Africa's legal system to punish black protesters who were fighting to abolish apartheid. In the audience were Rosa Parks and U.S. Congressman John Conyers.

This occurred to a backdrop of Free South Africa protests in 23 cities across America, and a protest by lawyers and judges outside Detroit's City-County Building.

"Apartheid is a policy that has been imposed upon the black majority to maintain White supremacy," I told the group. "Apartheid has been found by the international court of justice to be a governmentally enforced policy of exclusion, distinctions, and limitations based on race, color, and national origin."

All the while, I remained very active in the ABA and NBA.

Despite my rigorous schedule, I still provided my clients at the law firm with impeccable legal representation. Janet Welch of the Michigan Bar says it was astonishing that, amid my travel and speaking schedule, that in my June report to the Board I said, "And in August, I'll be trying a capital murder case."

"It's jaw-dropping that he would be able to do that," she says.

Larry Charfoos remembers that well. "The State Bar dominated our life for a while. Dennis was totally involved and every once in a while, he'd drag me to Lansing. I was even on a couple committees because of him. With this and everything else he did, Dennis floored me on the level of his accomplishments because they went from verbal to realized, every time."

My hard work did not go unnoticed. In May of that year, *Ebony* magazine named me among the 100 Most Influential Black Americans. They selected these individuals for transcending their position "to command widespread influence among black people in ways that influence blacks nationwide in a positive way." The magazine called us "the most important people of our time." I was listed with Michigan Secretary of State Richard Austin, California State Assembly Speaker Willie Brown Jr., and Los Angeles Mayor Thomas Bradley.

Minority Counsel Demonstration Program Pioneers New Ground

Chairing the ABA's Commission On Opportunities for Minorities In The Profession inspired me to take its mission to another level by initiating the Minority Counsel Demonstration Program.

The NBA had a corporate program that was unselfishly started by Cora Walker from New York that aimed to inspire her clients in corporate America to do business with other law firms. I wanted to take that much further. So, as a project of the Commission, we consulted with Stephen B. Middlebrook, vice president and General Counsel of Aetna Life & Casualty Insurance Company, and his two direct reports, Sandy Cloud and Marida Gandara. Then we initiated the Minority Counsel Demonstration Program, whose mission was to demonstrate to corporate America that lawyers of color could do their work, do it exceedingly well, and receive the same quality legal service they had grown to expect.

"Dennis is one of the deep and global thinkers of his time," says Robert Grey. "He bought into an idea for a Minority Counsel Demonstration Program sparked by Steve Middlebrook, which was one of the projects created by the Commission. His idea was that we have got to change the trajectory of business being done by minority lawyers and minority law firms in the most sophisticated work available to lawyers. That to me and to everybody else at the time was almost like cracking the DaVinci code."

Rachel agreed. "That was one of the first programs that Dennis helped start, and it was a stellar program. We said, 'We need to get six corporations who will agree to be part of this pilot program.' Then we needed 21 of the best law firms of color in the country to work with these six corporations and six large majority law firms with lawyers of color to sit around the table and structure a program that breaks through barriers so that silk-stocking law firms would hire lawyers of color and general counsels would then hire minority lawyers in their firms and also hire minority-owned law firms."

I went straight to the top of corporate America to ask for participation, starting with Steve Middlebrook, then Leroy C. Richie who was General Counsel and Vice President of Automotive Legal Affairs for the Chrysler Corporation. Next, I visited America's largest corporation and met with Harry J. Pearce, Vice President and General Counsel at General Motors. Harry not only participated (or sent his second-in-command in his place) but he sent a six-page letter on February 29, 1988, to law firms that did work for GM. "The Harry Pearce Letter" became famous in the industry; here is an excerpt:

> A matter of great concern to me, and the entire bar, is the disappointingly slow pace at which minorities are being integrated into our legal profession, particularly at the practice level at which we must engage. Accordingly, I have asked the Legal Staff Recruiting Committee to more actively seek minority lawyers who may be interested in working for General Motors. Similarly, I am determined to increase our efforts to assure that more GM work is performed by minority attorneys in the outside firms we retain throughout the country. I also am seeking to establish ongoing business relationships with additional minority firms.

I am confident that these initiatives can be successfully achieved and that we can continue to have only attorneys of the highest caliber engaged to represent General Motors. I therefore ask you to be certain that minority lawyers in your firm, able to provide service at the requisite level, be included among those who represent GM. In addition, I am confident that you agree with me that we must make certain we are doing all we can to introduce additional able minority attorneys into our respective organizations.

In May 1988, the ABA made it official by unveiling The Minority Counsel Demonstration Program (MCDP) to "earmark work for minority law firms and individual minority lawyers," according to a booklet that it provided to corporate participants. It said the Minority Counsel had three objectives:

1. To retain minority law firms and lawyers to do more of the legal work of corporations and governmental entities than they have done in the past.

2. To encourage majority law firms to hire minority lawyers and to assign minority lawyers to significant projects.

3. To encourage and enhance joint ventures between majority and minority law firms.

"The Counsel began with a great deal of excitement and enthusiasm," Robert Grey says. "Dennis' strategy was a master stroke involving corporations and law firms. He created an inclusive group where everybody had something to gain. A lot of credit should go to the white lawyers that were leaders at the time with being open and receptive to Dennis. They saw him as an equal, not as somebody they were trying to make happy. They understood what he was doing and they bought into it. That made success very possible, very likely, and it was fascinating to watch Dennis do this."

General Motors, Chrysler, and Aetna Insurance were the first three corporations to join the program. When other companies and firms learned who was participating, the Counsel expanded quickly.

"We had more than 139 Fortune 500 corporations by 1989," Rachel says. They included American Airlines, Ford Motor Company, Pitney Bowes, Bank of New England, Bristol-Myers, Campbell's Soup, Clorox, Coca-Cola, FDIC, E. I. DuPont, Johnson Publishing, and Monsanto.

"People had to pinch themselves to believe this was happening," Rachel says. "The press couldn't get enough of Dennis. He was being bombarded with interview requests."

The MCDP meetings consisted of relaxed gatherings that aimed to build relationships between hiring executives from corporations and lawyers of color who were in minority-owned law firms or were in majority-owned law firms.

And I was not shy about delegating to those in attendance to recruit participation from others. To the general counsels, I would say, "Listen, I want you to talk to five general counsels that you know, and ask if they'll join this program. And I want you to get back to me in two weeks."

"No problem," they responded.

MCDP meetings usually began with a reception, followed by educational programs and open discussion programs for lawyers of color to showcase who and what their firms were about. Then we divided into small groups that included corporate general counsels, and we highlighted various firms of color. MCDP gatherings also enabled us to craft guidelines stating what we wanted those with hiring power to do. And because I wanted to equip lawyers of color with tools to succeed, I added an important lesson to the agenda.

"Dennis wanted people to play golf or tennis together," Rachel recalls. "That's where business is transacted. Everybody, men and women, got into it."

The Minority Counsel Demonstration Program was tremendously successful, resulting in hirings, promotions, partnerships, and very importantly, an acute awareness of the benefits of diversifying legal representation in corporate America.

Robert Grey cites one of many success stories as the creation of Wilder, Gregory and Martin law firm, with Douglas Wilder, who would become Virginia's first black governor; Roger Gregory, who would become Chief Judge of the United States Court of Appeals for the Fourth Circuit; and attorney George Martin.

"Their firm grew substantially from the opportunity to be in the program," Robert says.

The Minority Counsel Demonstration Program changed the legal environment of America. Corporations and law firms began to take an active approach to providing lawyers of color with opportunities to contribute their talent and achieve their greatest potential. For that, I am extremely proud.

DETROIT GOLF CLUB OPENS ITS DOORS

In 1985, when Mayor Young was running for re-election, we were sitting with him on the patio of a stately house overlooking the back nine holes of the North Course of the Detroit Golf Club. We were at the home of an oncologist who owned a pharmaceutical company. Dr. Arnold Curry was hosting a fundraiser for Mayor Young. The mayor, who was not a golfer, looked at the black faces around him, then glanced at the sprawling, green golf course.

"I know you all really enjoy playing golf over there," he said.

"Well, Mr. Mayor," we responded, "not one of us is able to join or belong to the Detroit Golf Club."

To that, the mayor spoke some choice Coleman Young-esque words. And the next thing we all knew, Cardinal Edmund Szoka advanced Mayor Young's name as a social member of the Detroit Golf Club. That meant he could eat, play tennis, and socialize there. Shortly thereafter, African Americans Walt Watkins from National Bank of Detroit, Avis Ford owner Walt Douglas, Detroit Edison executive S. Martin Taylor and others joined and became full members. I later became a member.

"MR. JUSTICE, HOW ARE YOU?"

In 1985 when I was finishing my tenure as president of the State Bar of Michigan, I was in Orange County, California, taking a deposition on a malpractice case. As was my habit, I called my secretary from the airport while awaiting my return flight to Detroit.

"Ed Farhat, [a lobbyist who represents the State Bar of Michigan], called and wants to talk to you," she said.

"Hook me up," I said.

"Dennis," Ed said, "you know that Justice James Ryan on the Michigan Supreme Court is going to resign because he has been appointed to go on the Sixth Circuit Court of Appeals. That will leave an opening on the Michigan Supreme Court."

I listened intently as he continued: "I'm going to play golf with Governor Blanchard, and I want to give him your name as someone to be considered. We have not had a black person on the court since Otis Smith."

An announcement boomed overhead: "Flight now boarding to Detroit." I was thinking that the chances of me being appointed were slim to none, and the best thing that could happen to me is that my name gets mentioned as a candidate. The benefit of that, I concluded, was that my clients would think that if he's good enough to be considered for the Michigan Supreme Court, I want him as my lawyer.

"Okay," I told him. "You can give him my name."

A few weeks later, my name was in the newspaper with Sam Gardner, Judge Keith, and former Judge and Solicitor General Wade McCree, then a law professor at the University of Michigan. There's no way, I thought, that between those giants, I would be appointed. So, I made two calls, one to Judge Keith and the other to Wade McCree.

Judge Keith said, "I'm not giving up a lifetime appointment in the federal court for the Michigan Supreme Court."

After I told Wade McCree that, "I'd be happy to be your campaign manager," he responded:

"Dennis, I've been on the Wayne Circuit Court, and the Eastern District Court of Michigan. I resigned from my position as a member of the Sixth Circuit Court of Appeals to become Solicitor General, and I'm very happy here at U of M. I have no interest. By the way, I have a couple people here for you to meet if you become Supreme Court Justice, some good law clerks."

I then believed that my name was being floated to see if anybody would come forward to say anything negative about my ability or that might embarrass the governor.

One week later, I was at a fundraiser for Jim Blanchard, who was running for re-election.

"Governor, how are you?" I asked as Trudy and I proceeded through the reception line.

"Mr. Justice," he said, "how are you doing?"

That confirmed without a doubt what was about to happen. I almost fell over. "Yeah, right," I responded playfully. "How are *you* doing?"

At the time, Trudy was Assistant Corporation Counsel for the City of Detroit. I was also an Adjunct Professor at Wayne State University Law School. Our salaries enabled us to maintain our home in Palmer Woods, pay for private school at Detroit Country Day for Denny and Vincent, and take trips every year.

In August of 1985, Trudy, Denny, Vincent, and I attended the American Bar Association Annual Meeting in London, in my capacity as President of the State Bar of Michigan. Denny was 16, and Vincent was 12. This was our first trip to Europe, and as I reflected on the reality of my own life at their age, I was grateful to provide such an experience for our sons.

"Dennis and I went to the Queen's Garden Party," Trudy recalls. "I wore my hat and my gloves, and it was just beautiful."

After the London meeting, we took the kids to Paris. We rode a train from London to Dover, then a hovercraft from Dover to Bologne, France, then a train to Paris. Trudy, Vincent, and our luggage were packed into a small car. It was pouring rain, and cabs were hard to find. Denny and I were running outside the train station to find a cab. We finally found one, and Denny used his French-speaking skills that he was learning in school to tell the driver where we were going.

Larry Charfoos and his wife, Trish — who owned a business and a condo in Paris — kindly provided our accommodations in their condo overlooking the Arc de Triomphe. Denny and I arrived at the apartment while Trudy, Vincent, and the driver whom Larry sent to pick us up, were unloading the car. Upstairs, a housekeeper was waiting for us, and she asked in French, "What would you like for breakfast?" I told her what we wanted to eat by speaking very slowly in English, enunciating in an exaggerated way.

"Dad," the kids said as they laughed, "just because you're speaking slowly doesn't mean she understands English!" Denny continued to be our translator.

Later, while we were in Paris, Judge Keith called.

"Dennis, you're going to get a telephone call from the governor," he said. "We've not had a person of color on the Michigan Supreme Court since Otis Smith 20 years ago. You've been president of the State Bar of Michigan, and you've spoken at different affiliated bar associations all across the state. You're the only one who can logically win the election to keep the seat on the court. You've been all over. People like you. People respect you."

I listened intently.

"Remember when you asked a long time ago if you should run for judge, and I said no? Well, all of us who served on the bench sacrificed so you can take advantage of this. Now is your time to say yes."

Overwhelmed, I simply said, "Let me talk to my wife."

Trudy was eagerly waiting to hear what Judge Keith had just said.

"Trudy," I said, "here's what's going on. If I get this appointment, my salary will be $81,400." Trudy was apprehensive. At the time, I was earning $200,000, the firm was having an excellent year, and I was on my way to surpassing an annual salary and bonus of $250,000. Trudy was working as an attorney in the Labor Section of the city of Detroit's corporate counsel's office. Unsure if we could handle our financial obligations on less than my current salary, Trudy sat down, did some calculations, and said, "It'll be tight, but we can make it."

After that, I spoke with the kids. "I don't know if it's going to take place. If it does, you will have to go to a college in Michigan. If it doesn't happen, I can send you to college wherever you want."

"Dad, if you get it, take it," they said almost instantaneously. "We'd be happy to go anywhere in Michigan."

During this period, I concluded my tenure as president of the State Bar of Michigan. It happened on September 11th at the 50th Annual Meeting at Hotel Pontchartrain and Cobo Hall in Detroit, where I, at the black-tie Annual Banquet, passed the baton to our next president, George T. Roumell. Our special guest at the conference was First Lady Rosalyn Carter, Reverend Jesse Jackson Jr. was the keynote speaker, and we were photographed in the media. That night, the Board gave me a plaque that says, "To Dennis Archer, to whom it's never been done before is a challenge to begin."

I thanked everybody under the sun, including Trudy, Denny, and Vincent for their understanding when I could not be home during the past year. I also expressed gratitude to everyone at Charfoos, Christensen and Archer.

A few months later, on Election Day of November 1985, I was sitting in my office when my secretary said, "Governor Blanchard is on the phone."

I picked up the phone, but no one was there. "You're messing with me," I said playfully.

But she was serious. On the third try, we connected.

"Dennis, this is Jim Blanchard. I'm here in DC and I'd like to know if you'd accept an appointment to the Michigan Supreme Court."

"Yes sir, I really would. Thank you very, very much."

Elated, I immediately called Trudy.

I would soon join the esteemed ranks of Chief Justice G. Mennen Williams, our former Michigan governor whom I had helped get elected to the Court. And I knew the five other justices through my work with the State Bar. My appointment would create a Democratic majority on the seven-member court, as Justices Michael Cavanagh, G. Mennen Williams, and Patricia Boyle were Democrats, while Justice Charles Levin was an independent.

Despite my excitement, I could make no public announcements until that was done by Governor Blanchard. His selection of me had roused anxiety for him, I am sure, because I had not followed the traditional trajectory to the Supreme Court of serving as a judge on a court first.

"I said, 'Gosh, it's not going to be easy picking someone who's never been judge,'" Governor Blanchard recalls from his office in Washington, DC. "We did a lot of political reconnaissance. Greg Morris said, 'We can do this. You know Dennis, we like Dennis, he's been good to you and everybody.' And having been president of the State Bar really helped. That confirmed our judgment because everyone had good things to say, so we decided we'd appoint Dennis even though he'd never been a judge. The appointment was very well received, and we were all really happy. I wanted to pick somebody who was widely respected."

Governor Blanchard consulted the head of the Judicial Qualifications Committee of the State Bar of Michigan, who was its former president and my friend, John Krsul.

"I got a call one day from Jim Blanchard to meet with him at the Capitol," John recalls. "When I arrived, he said, 'I want to talk to you about a candidate that I'd like to appoint to the Supreme Court. Dennis Archer. What do you think of him?' That was easy! The governor asked the committee to provide an evaluation, which we did."

Facing the Judicial Qualifications Committee in the State Bar of Michigan office was formidable. I sat on one side of a long table facing more than a dozen committee members, all of whom I had worked with while chairing State Bar committees and while serving as president. Now, however, nobody was cracking a smile. This was very serious, because they were reviewing every detail about me that I had provided on a questionnaire that was a required step in the process. They asked questions, and I answered every one of them. Then I stepped out of the room while they conferred.

"Dennis was highly recommended," John Krsul said.

Before Governor Blanchard made the announcement, the media buzzed with stories that my appointment was imminent. I neither confirmed nor denied this to reporters who cited long-standing rumors that Blanchard would appoint me.

At the announcement of my appointment to the Michigan Supreme Court. From left: Michigan Governor James Blanchard; Michigan Supreme Court Chief Justice G. Mennen "Soapy" Williams; me; former Michigan Supreme Court Justice Otis Smith, the first person of color appointed to the Michigan Supreme Court; and Damon Keith, Senior Judge on the U.S. Court of Appeals for the Sixth Circuit.

This sparked a speculation frenzy as journalists, political analysts, and other commentators shared two conclusions about why my appointment would be unusual and notable. First, it was uncommon for a lawyer who had never been a judge to ascend to the Michigan Supreme Court. Second, no person of color had sat on the Court for 20 years, since Justice Otis Smith was appointed by Governor John Swainson in 1961 and served until he lost the 1967 election to retain his seat. As such, pundits interjected race and politics into their analysis.

They said my appointment would boost Blanchard's standing amongst some black Democratic lawmakers who had criticized him for not aggressively helping the black voters whose support helped him win the gubernatorial election in 1982.

"ONE OF THE MOST EXCITING SUCCESS STORIES IN MICHIGAN"

Governor Blanchard made it official with a press conference in Lansing on November 11th. As I stood at his side facing the media, we were flanked by Judge Damon Keith, former Justice Otis Smith, Lieutenant Governor Martha Griffiths, State Attorney General Frank Kelley, and Chief Justice Williams.

"Dennis Wayne Archer has been named a member of the Michigan Supreme Court to replace Justice James Ryan who resigned to accept a federal judgeship," Governor Blanchard announced, referencing my "extensive involvement in the law and in the betterment of the legal profession at the national, state, and local levels." He called me "a leading figure in the legal profession in promoting opportunities for women and minorities."

Chief Justice Williams told the media, "I can't think of a judge in Michigan who isn't going to feel honored and pleased… because Dennis Archer has established a reputation, vis à vis the judiciary, that is really outstanding." He also referenced me as "one of the most distinguished trial lawyers in the state."

Governor Blanchard described me as "a man of extraordinary talent who came from ordinary circumstances. He's one of the most exciting success stories in Michigan."

During countless media interviews, I emphasized that, "Michigan is blessed with people having diverse backgrounds and social interactions. This appointment may eliminate any doubt blacks and minorities are essential to the success of Michigan's society." I added, "It's important for young women and minority students who have an idea of what they want, to be able to say, 'I can advance.' To say, 'Yes, I can,' is very important."

That was my mantra as I faced the next 10 months of campaigning across Michigan to keep my seat on the Michigan Supreme Court. First, I had to resign from the law firm, which celebrated my appointment with a cocktail reception on December 11th at the Millender Center in downtown Detroit.

"What law office in any state wouldn't be thrilled to have a member elevated to the state Supreme Court?" asked Larry Charfoos. Among 400 friends, judges, and law colleagues were filmmaker Sue Marx, Bell Broadcasting President Mrs. Haley Bell, former Mayor Roman Gribbs, former Michigan Supreme Court Justice Thomas Brennan, Wayne County Circuit Court Judge William Giovan, and Nettie Seabrooks, director of government relations for General Motors Corporation's North American Operations.

In late December, Chief Justice Williams swore me in during a private ceremony attended by Trudy, Denny, Vincent, and three of my law clerks, along with two of the Chief's law clerks.

Between the announcement and Justice Ryan's departure on January 1st, I embarked on a crash course to understand the responsibilities of my new position. I visited Otis Smith, the first person of color to serve as the general counsel for General Motors — as well as the first person of color to serve as general counsel of a Fortune 500 company. He graciously provided valuable insight and advice about how to excel as a Supreme Court Justice.

Then I observed the Justices in session in the Supreme Court Courtroom on the sixth floor of the Michigan Hall of Justice, near the State Capitol Building in Lansing. I studied the comments, behavior and observations of Patricia Boyle, Charles Levin, Michael Francis Cavanagh, James Brickley, James Ryan, and Dorothy Comstock Riley.

Left photo: Members of the Michigan Supreme Court following my swearing in.
Right photo: Judge Keith and I embracing in Detroit after he swore me in.

Photo credit: Michigan Supreme Court

(Despite being ousted in 1983, she was ultimately elected to the Court and would serve as chief justice from 1987 to 1991.)

I also asked Chief Justice Williams and my longtime friend Justice Michael Cavanagh, who was elected to the Court in 1982, about how they executed their duties, what they delegated to law clerks, and what I should know about daily operations.

SWEARING-IN WAS AN "OUT-OF-BODY EXPERIENCE"

The thoughts and emotions that ran through my mind on January 6, 1986, culminated in an out-of-body experience as I was sworn-in to execute my duties as an Associate Justice on the Michigan Supreme Court. I was simultaneously elated, honored, and solemn during two ceremonies, first at 10:00 a.m. in Lansing, followed by another at 2:00 p.m. in Detroit.

The day began in a wood-paneled courtroom of the Michigan Supreme Court in Lansing. I sat with Governor Blanchard while Trudy, Denny, and Vincent sat to my right. The courtroom was packed with family, friends, colleagues, and media. I was especially happy to see the pride beaming from the faces of Mr. and Mrs. DunCombe, Beth and my brother-in-law-to-be, Joe Brown, and my cousin, Eleanor Archer Lofton, who had flown in from Phoenix, Arizona.

The Supreme Court Justices, with Chief Justice Williams presiding, sat on the bench. Others in the courtroom included Senator

Jackie Vaughn; Senator Gary Corbin; Senator Mitch Irwin; Governor Blanchard's Chief of Staff Phil Jordan and Senior Staff members Greg Morris and Marilyn Hall; Michigan Department of Social Services Director Agnes Mansour; Michigan Court of Appeals Chief Judge Robert Danhoff; and the eight men and women who would speak during the program.

Chief Justice Williams served as Master of Ceremonies, first introducing George E. Bushnell, a member of the Board of Governors of the American Bar Association and past President of the State Bar of Michigan.

"My happy opportunity is to make record of Dennis' great contribution to the American Bar, and thus to the profession," George said. "A recounting of our new Justice's work with committees, sections, special commissions, and the House of Delegates of the American Bar would be significant in and of itself. But the unique contribution that Dennis has made, and I pray he will continue to make, has been to be the voice of the disenfranchised. The force to make the profession face its obligations and responsibilities to those unknown and uncared for. His dignified, but forceful demands, always fully documented, factual, and with just enough fire to emphasize his arguments have left his colleagues no option but to follow his leadership. And this we will continue to do.

"As a consequence, we, the American Bar Association, are extraordinarily proud of Dennis Archer."

Next, my former law professor George T. Roumell, who was now President of the State Bar of Michigan, referenced my attendance in his class in 1969, and predicted that I would provide an A-plus performance on the court. He suggested that my life story should be called "Grace Under Pressure II, the Story of Dennis Archer."

Especially touching were remarks from NBA President Fred Gray, who came from Alabama and who had been a lawyer for Rosa Parks and for Dr. Martin Luther King Jr., following Mrs. Parks' refusal to move to the back of the bus. Fred described me as "an eminent scholar of the law and as an eloquent advocate of diversity in the legal profession." He continued:

"He has never wavered in his effort to combat discrimination that has haunted minority lawyers for decades. Last year in my address before a number of groups, I have stressed the point that Dennis so eloquently expounded about diversity in the legal profession when he wrote in the November 1984 *Michigan Bar Journal* the following: 'We will seek solutions to the lack of equal employment opportunities of minorities and women lawyers, and the problem of upward mobility once hired. If we in the legal profession who advocate equal justice under the law, and equal opportunity, do not encourage and promote diversity within our ranks, then how can we expect other professions, businesses, or other economic groups to do the same?'"

Fred continued by saying, "The insightful manner in which he stated one of the more serious problems that faces the legal profession today is but an example to predict the forthright way in which he will seek solutions to matters that will come before him as a Justice to the Supreme Court."

Wolverine Bar Association President Sharon McPhail described me as "truly the American Dream realized," adding that, "America to this day has fulfilled its promise to Dennis Archer, and has moved itself one step closer to opening the doors for all of the black and white boys and girls of all of the Cassopolis' of this nation. We salute you, Dennis."

On behalf of the WBA, she gave me a gavel inscribed with my name and the court.

Deborah Miela, President of the Women Lawyers Association, and my former student in Evidence at DCL, lauded my commitment to advancing women in the legal profession.

Former Supreme Court Justice Thomas E. Brennan, who retired 12 years earlier, offered eloquent comments that included this: "Dennis Archer is an advocate. He brings to the chemistry of this Court an element of passionate persuasion which only a trial lawyer of his eminence can exude. I suspect the Court's deliberations will be livelier for his being in your midst. As anyone who loves the life of the intellect, I envy both the light and the heat that you will generate together in the conference room in the days to come."

Elliott Hall spoke as president of the Detroit Bar Association. "I've known Dennis Archer for over 25 years, and my first remembered view of him is on the corner of Cass and Putnam, on the Wayne State University campus, with several volumes of English 101 under his arm. There was no passage of the 1964 Civil Rights Act. There was no passage of the 1965 Voting Rights Act. Two black judges sat on the bench of this state at that time. The hope for many of us on campus was dim. But Dennis saw the opening as the 60's progressed. And he saw an undimmed view of opportunity, and ran to it, and has succeeded every goal that he has set for himself."

Next, Joel Boyden, past president of the State Bar of Michigan, told the Justices: "If you want a window to this man's soul, reflect on his lovely and gracious wife Trudy, and his two sons, Dennis and Vincent. And there, I think if you look closely, you will understand a large measure of Mr. Archer's strength and inspiration." He called me "an indefatigable worker" and a "lawyer's lawyer" who made integrity a way of life.

Then Chief Justice Williams read a letter from U.S. Senator Donald Riegle and his wife, Laurie: "Your keen knowledge of the law is a great strength. Yet an even greater strength may be your wisdom about injustice. We must understand injustice if we are to administer justice. I have every confidence that your careful judgment will see that justice is done. At this great milestone in your life journey, Trudy and your children share this achievement with you. That family love and strength will continue to be central in this new role."

At that point, Trudy teared up. "As we're sitting there and he's getting ready to be sworn in," she recalls, "I thought, this is for real; this is not a dream. He is standing there waiting to be sworn in. I felt extremely proud of Dennis because, after all, there were many out-standing lawyers and judges who could have been appointed to that position. And here he was. My husband was the one selected. I thought it was such an honor. I felt very proud for him. I teared up because I knew how he must have felt. When your hard work and what you have truly believed in allows you to rise to this level in your profession, it is a wonderful thing. It was a very emotional day, a very happy day."

Justice Williams then said, "And now I am honored to have been asked by our new Justice to swear him in personally."

Everyone stood, and I raised my right hand.

"Do you solemnly swear to support the Constitution of the United States and the Constitution of this State, and well and faithfully perform the duties of Justice of the Michigan Supreme Court to the best of your ability, so help you God?"

"I do," I answered.

I was suddenly and profoundly struck by the absolutely huge responsibility of being a member of the Michigan Supreme Court. It is the last stop in the judicial process for about 95 percent of all cases filed in Michigan. And though the Court reviewed 3,000 to 3,200 applications for leave to appeal, we would hear only 100 to 120 of those cases. In addition, we were responsible for the oversight and administration of all the courts in the state.

And so, in that moment as I accepted that responsibility, I also vowed to be my absolute best. I did not want to embarrass myself, nor did I want to create any shame for people of color. I knew full well that any failure on my part would hurt opportunities for minorities everywhere.

"I'd like to now call upon a former law partner of Dennis Archer's, David W. Christensen, to perform whatever he would prefer to do," Chief Justice Williams announced.

"That's an awful lot of leeway," Dave responded, rousing audience laughter. He began by saying that I had been a major influence on him for 12 years, and that I epitomized decency and goodness and kindness.

"The qualities that I admire and that you admire in Dennis," Dave began, "were instilled in him… by his mother and father, God rest their souls. Have been encouraged and enhanced by his wife Trudy. Have been nurtured by his distinguished and tremendous mother-in-law and father-in-law, James and Eleanor DunCombe, with an able assist from his sister-in-law Beth DunCombe. And probably to truly understand Dennis, we know that these qualities are then exemplified in his two children, Denny and Vincent."

Then he added that the court would be enriched "because Dennis will make it better.… I'm very, very proud that I get to present a robe. I'm going to ask Trudy, and Dennis, and Vincent to assist in the robing of Dennis."

After my family robed me, we embraced and I sobbed tears of joy and pride.

"I felt really proud of him," says Vincent, who was 12. "We saw every day how hard my dad was working at everything he was doing. So, to see all these people celebrating this accomplishment was amazing."

Both Vincent and Denny, who was 16, were old enough to understand the magnitude of my appointment. "I was a lot more cognizant of how hard he worked and I began to understand the respect he garnered as a member of the Bar," Denny says. "Governor Blanchard's confidence in him was illustrative of that."

As the ceremony continued, I stood at the podium on the judge's bench, between flags for Michigan and the United States.

"May it please the Court," I said, glancing at Governor Blanchard and Chief Justice Williams, then at Trudy, Denny and Vincent, and into the audience.

"As most of you know, I am not often at loss for words," I began. "But I do find it difficult to find the words, the right words, to express all of my feelings at this moment on this occasion here in this room, in the presence of so many people whose friendship and love I cherish. I want to thank each of you for being here to share in this ceremony today, and for what each of you has done to make it possible. That means, of course, Governor Blanchard, whose decision brings me here. It means my wife and children, and other members of my family. It means the members of my former law firm, and many, many other professional colleagues, and so many dear friends. Each of you had some part in shaping me into the person I am today, and share with me the joy and satisfaction of this occasion.

"I have been afforded a generous share of honors and satisfaction in my lifetime, professionally and personally. But this surely represents a high point in my life as a lawyer. To be a judge is a single honor for any lawyer. To be a justice of this Court at the heart of our system of justice is an honor so profound that I am truly hard put to describe my feelings about it. It is a humbling experience. It brings with it an obligation which cannot, even for a short while, be deferred while I get used to the idea of wearing this robe. There are but seven justices of this Court, and the load of work it must do is heavy in both qualitative and quantitative terms, and in terms both of the substance of law the Court is called upon to pronounce and the administrative responsibilities placed upon it by the constitution and statutes. I am ready to assume my share of that burden now."

My remarks, which filled four, single-spaced, typed pages of the official transcript, included my commitment to improving the judicial system's image.

"I do not fancy myself as a Moses come down to lead us out of the wilderness," I said. "It will take the efforts of many with greater talents than mine. And it will not all be done in a few short months. The Court has already initiated significant efforts to make itself and the entire judicial system more accessible, better understood by the public. I will have an opportunity to further that effort. Under our state's system of judicial selection, I face an election in ten short months for the seat I assume today. I face the election gladly, for it means that the people of our state will have the opportunity to ratify the Governor's judgment in appointing me to this Court. I will travel throughout our state in the next ten months, as far and as often as the duties of office permit. I want to meet the people. I want them to see me, to hear me, and to form some basis of judgment about me. In doing so I will represent the Supreme Court to the people I meet. I will articulate the nature of our system of justice and the role of the courts in making it work. In particular, the role of the Supreme Court, what it does, what it does not do, and the whys and the wherefores of both. I hope in some small way to dispel the myths and misconceptions and to help some people at least to understand what a marvel of freedom they have in a truly independent judiciary.

"Drawing upon my background as a public-school teacher and as an associate professor of law, I plan to make particular effort to bring this message directly to the young people in the schools of the communities that I visit. Many worthwhile curricular, and co-curricular programs touch upon such matters. The State Bar and judges of local courts throughout the state have devoted significant resources toward fostering a greater awareness of the judicial system among our young people. I believe that a real, live Supreme Court Justice, giving reality to the abstractions the students read and hear about, talking firsthand about the process and its meaning to them as citizens, can make a contribution. I plan, wherever possible, to visit a local school in every community where I make a campaign appearance. I realize that few in the audience will likely be able to vote for me in November." The audience laughed.

"But in all seriousness," I continued, "I believe the truism that our youth are our future. It is they we most need to persuade that the courts and the system of justice are the keys to their future liberties. That they have a very personal stake in preserving and improving the legal system. And I am certain that my time in that effort will be well spent."

In conclusion, I added, "Finally, the governor has my heartfelt thanks for the honor he has bestowed upon me by this appointment, and my personal gratitude for his expression of confidence in me as a lawyer, and as a person. But I cannot really be content until his judgment has been ratified by those whose office it really is to bestow, the people of our great state. This appointment will, under the law, be submitted to the people for their approval at the next general election in November, 1986. I will do my very best in the interim to earn their vote of confidence."

Then I acknowledged my family, adding that Trudy "now can lay claim to being the best lawyer in the family."

After that, we drove to Detroit for the second swearing-in ceremony at Cobo Hall.

"When we arrived," Trudy recalls, "we were surrounded by people we knew who were overjoyed and were congratulating us. Many had their children with them. It was a wonderful day." I was especially proud that Uncle Jimmy and Uncle Warren were there to witness this accomplishment that was rooted in their encouragement, along with that of my parents, grandmother, and Aunt Jo, to attend college. During the ceremony, Governor Blanchard spoke, as did Elliott Hall, Larry Charfoos, and Mayor Young, who humored the audience.

The event culminated with Judge Keith swearing me in. A photo of him hugging me, smiling with his eyes closed, his hands grasping my shoulders, was published in the local papers, as well as *Jet* magazine. I was also photographed with Detroit Mayor Coleman A. Young. I was walking on air, eager to begin executing my duties on the Court.

Supreme Court Justice Dennis W. Archer

When I first arrived at the Michigan Supreme Court, I immediately clicked with Justice Charles Levin. And I was happy to work with a long-time friend, Justice Michael Cavanagh, whom I had met while campaigning for Mayor Young during the 1970's.

"Dennis and I were quite close," recalls Justice Cavanagh, a former trial judge who sat on the Michigan Court of Appeals for eight years before joining the Supreme Court in 1983. "I think he knew I was always there for whatever advice I could give him. I really respect the man. I admire him and love him like a brother."

He said the task of being a Supreme Court Justice is daunting and requires a tremendous time commitment.

"Dennis was always a very, very hard worker and has always prided himself on being completely prepared. It was pretty amazing because even while he was on the Court, he had a 100 different things going at the same time. He was always going at 100 miles an hour. To his credit, he was always prepared for Court conferences and always prepared for oral arguments. He did this while having more extracurricular activities than anyone on the Court, and while maintaining a great family life. He accomplished this because he was a very bright individual whose work ethic enabled him to make a significant contribution to the Court."

That contribution, retired Justice Levin says now, favored the underdog.

"Archer and I tended to be for the weakest person in the lawsuit," said Justice Levin, who retired in 1996 after serving 23 years. "The Court was overwhelmingly pro-plaintiff in civil cases and inclined to be pro-defendant in criminal cases… but with criminal cases… their final appeal is usually the Michigan Court of Appeals. We were allies. I tended to be with the weakest person in the controversy, which is the defendant in the criminal case and the plaintiff in the civil case."

Justice Levin said that my experience as a plaintiff's lawyer made me inclined to decide in favor of people injured by medical malpractice, product liability, and automobile accidents. But he said I only made those decisions after a thorough analysis of the facts.

"One thing I admired a lot about him was his ability to analyze the issues, listen to arguments, and then make up his mind and make a decision," said Justice Cavanagh, who became Chief Justice in 1991 and retired in 2015. "He was pretty definite and firm once he came to rest on an issue. Another desirable quality he possessed was the willingness and ability to listen to different arguments. If you disagreed with a particular stance he had on an issue, and if you could muster the proof, you could convince him to change his mind. That is really important in any judge, but in particular when you're dealing with six other prima donnas on the Court, there are a lot of egos floating around. The willingness to listen and to change one's mind is an invaluable asset in that milieu."

Justice Levin added, "He was always on time, always moving ahead. He had so much on his mind all the time."

"Nobody Outcampaigned Me"

I shared the distinction with Justice Otis Smith as being an African American Justice on the Michigan Supreme Court. But I was determined to avoid his fate in 1966 when he lost the statewide election. So I set out to do everything in my power to convince voters across Michigan to vote for Justice Archer. Here was my chance to apply to my own campaign all that I had learned while helping to elect victorious candidates such as Mayor Young and Governor Blanchard.

Now, 24 people were running for two spots on the court: mine, and the one vacated when Chief Justice Williams would step down at the end of the year due to age limitations. Two candidates were nominated by the Republican Party; two were nominated by the Democratic Party; while others ran as independents.

While I was the only incumbent justice on the ballot, I wanted to ensure that I placed first or second when all the votes were counted. I was extraordinarily blessed with prior campaign experience and now, the fact that Chief Justice Williams took me under his wing to help me soar to victory.

"Here's what you need to do," he said. "Go to the Upper Peninsula to campaign." I was fine with that. As immediate past president of the State Bar of Michigan, I had recently spoken at most, if not all, of our 108 affiliates, including those in the UP. In fact, on May 16, 1985, the Sault Ste. Marie paper published a small article about how I would address the 50th Judicial Bar Association at Lake Superior State College.

Next, he advised me to visit county fairs, providing a list of fairs to attend in the Upper Peninsula.

Chief Justice Williams said, "When you walk back where the farm animals are kept to meet and greet people, watch where you step. Then go to the area where they have the pie-eating contests. Shake hands, say hi, and ask people to vote for you."

Chief Justice Williams told me to meet voters by visiting plant gates at the end of shifts. Though he was in his 70s, he got up early several mornings to join me — including on election day.

"Hi, I'm Dennis Archer, Michigan Supreme Court Justice," I told men and women who were getting off the night shift at 5:30 or 6:00 a.m. "When you get off work, please vote for me."

Justice Williams revealed another way to endear myself to voters. "When somebody has a function for you, whether it's a fundraiser or a meet and greet, and they serve food, you go back to the kitchen and thank everybody for the food they prepared and service they provided."

Grateful that such a brilliant, gracious person as Chief Justice Williams was coaching me toward campaign victory, I put his advice into action. At the same time, my campaign team reached out to people I'd met in cities statewide through Bar activities, asking them to connect me with their local Rotary Clubs, Kiwanis Clubs, economic clubs, radio programs, and TV shows.

Of course, a successful campaign requires financial backing to pay for travel, campaign literature, and radio and television advertising.

"Dennis did not believe in touching any money," recalls my sister-in-law and campaign finance director Beth DunCombe.

"Dennis never, ever reviewed or looked at how much money anybody gave him in the campaign," Beth says. "We set a limit saying we'd never accept more than a certain dollar amount, so no one could say, 'He got bought.' I actually had to send money back. That's Dennis' rule. He is a special breed of ethics in politics that I really applaud."

Beth accompanied me to events so that she could speak directly with contributors. When she wasn't with me, my mantra to those offering support was "Call Beth," or "Let me take your card and I'll have Beth call you."

My friends and supporters hosted many fundraising events, demonstrating the tremendous support I received from friends and the legal community. Detroit lawyer John O'Meara hosted an event at Cobo Hall that raised $100,000. For two hours, Trudy and I greeted guests who included Judge Keith, Chief Justice Williams, and attorney and civil rights activist Ken Cockrel. I also had the support of the United Auto Workers, then led by President Owen Bieber, which distributed campaign literature saying, "We encourage you to elect incumbent Supreme Court Justice Dennis Archer."

Longtime friends Dr. Lorna Thomas and Sam Thomas hosted a fundraiser at their home, which was attended by many friends and supporters. Unfortunately, the Michigan Chamber of Commerce challenged my candidacy, saying that because I was a plaintiff's lawyer, I would be too liberal. Coming to my defense was Richard Van Dusen, a partner at Dickinson Wright, who was also chair of the Greater Detroit Chamber of Commerce. He invited me to the Mackinac Policy Conference, which is Detroit's annual corporate retreat that occurs in late spring on Mackinac Island, which is located in Lake Huron in the Straits of Mackinac, between the Lower and Upper Peninsulas.

He invited me to speak before the plenary session, where I expressed my philosophies and commitment to equal justice. During that event, I met a lot of business leaders who ultimately confirmed that I was a safe candidate worthy of their support.

That summer, Trudy and I thought it would be a good idea to take the kids on a 10-day road trip through the Upper Peninsula. We would have to drive five hours north from Detroit, cross the five-mile-long Mackinac Bridge, and journey into the mostly rural and predominantly white UP. We still laugh about how this was not the boys' idea of a fun summer trip.

"At the time, I thought it was terrible," recalls Denny. "But now in retrospect, it was fun. I just remember my friend in the neighborhood was having a party on a Saturday and I was excited because the party was going to be amazing. Then, Thursday, my parents informed us that, 'You need to go with us.'"

Vincent also appreciates the trip — in hindsight.

"We had never been to the Upper Peninsula," he says. "With my Dad, there's no gray area. He was not going to use his government car for the Supreme Court while campaigning. So he rented a Pontiac 6000 and used campaign funds to pay for the gas, hotel, everything."

We visited the home of Joe Regnier, who was the executive director and general counsel of the Judicial Tenure Commission, the oversight body that monitored judges for inappropriate behavior. He and his wife hosted a fundraiser for me in Brighton.

We drove to Lansing. "My brother and I were in the back seat as usual," Vincent remembers, "and in Lansing, somebody gave our Dad a huge eagle, which had to sit in the middle of my brother and me for the rest of the trip. After that, we drove several hours north to Traverse City, and had to find a house with balloons where we were staying. The brand new home belonged to a supporter, but had no furniture, so we slept on the floor."

Denny remembers going to the Cherry Festival in Traverse City and "not seeing many black folks."

Then we crossed the Mackinac Bridge to the Upper Peninsula, heading to small towns such as Iron Mountain where my political consultant had set up meetings with civic organizations and media. My goal was to meet as many people as I possibly could, and give them campaign literature that was filling the trunk of my car.

"Then we went farther north to Escanaba," Denny says, "to a very uncomfortable hotel with hard beds, but they served phenomenal beef pasties."

Vincent added, "It was great to see, as we went across the state, how highly respected our dad was at that time."

Trudy was struck by the number of people who were surprised and delighted by our visits. "Many people said that Supreme Court Justices never campaigned in the Upper Peninsula. But Dennis was determined to do everything possible to ensure his success on election day."

At the conclusion of the trip, I resumed my solo travel with Tom Chionos, Joe Baltimore, and Mark Brewer, ultimately driving 25,000 miles as I crisscrossed the state, speaking to the 108 affiliates of the Michigan Bar Association.

At no time did my campaigning detract from my duties on the Supreme Court. That was my top priority, and my campaign activities were orchestrated around that.

In fact, it was not uncommon for me to sit in the back seat, illuminated by both back lights, so I could write, read commissioner reports, or dictate with a handheld Dictaphone, while a volunteer drove me three hours to Grand Rapids or four hours to Ludington or 90 minutes to Saginaw, then drove me back to Detroit afterward.

These travels also enabled me to honor my vow to speak to schools, civic groups, and others to educate them about the court system, to inspire young people to aim high, and to encourage people of color to succeed.

"Every minority has the responsibility to reach back," I told 100 people at the 10th annual Minority Leadership Conference at Western Michigan University on March 23, 1986, alongside TransAfrica Director Randall Robinson. "If you don't, then you spit on the graves of those who have given you the right to be here."

Likewise, at no time was I afraid to criticize where criticism was due, speaking out against President Ronald Reagan and U.S. Attorney General Edwin Meese for chipping away affirmative action and equal employment. I also spoke my mind about the state of black folks, and what needed to be done to reverse a negative cycle.

"I'm talking about aiming high," I often said when speaking to young people, such as a group of black students at Wayne State University on February 19, 1986. "Having a dream and having high standards in life to help and not to abandon your brothers and sisters out there who have no real role models other than those dudes in the streets riding in Cadillacs."

I encouraged them to get their education, participate in politics, exercise their right to vote, and break the cycle of crime and poverty. I urged them not to become a statistic that included black men in jail and prison, or black women raising babies out of wedlock.

When speaking before predominantly black audiences, my message focused on people of color helping each other, by remembering the civil rights struggles of the past.

"We've come a long way, but many young people who consider themselves yuppies and buppies don't seem to remember how we got where we are now," I told groups such as the Saginaw Frontiers Club. I encouraged them to make sure that their children studied history to appreciate how blacks were humiliated, beaten, and killed while fighting for the Emancipation Proclamation, the Bill of Rights, the 14th Amendment, *Brown v. the Board of Education,* affirmative action, and the NAACP.

"Take your children to church," I often emphasized. "Encourage them to read, and show respect to elders." I urged people of color to break free from "shackles of self-doubt" and become leaders.

One speech that I delivered often was entitled "How to Get Blacks to Support Blacks." I urged black professionals to stop behaving like crabs in a barrel pulling each other down, and instead reach back to uplift other people of color.

I urged them to enjoy the material fruits of their success without becoming self-centered or forgetful of their collective responsibility to help the entire race by uniting with African Americans.

I also encouraged black professionals to support black ministers who have the power to persuade thousands of people to vote for a particular candidate. I substantiated my speeches with statistics about black economic power that, during the mid-1980s, could make up the ninth largest nation in the world with an annual income of $175 billion to $190 billion.

"If you blow it because of ego-tripping, you will have hurt your respective families," I warned. "If you don't work with your own black people, what are you teaching your kids? If you operate singularly, you cannot be as effective as you can collectively." In closing, I quoted Dr. Benjamin Mays, former Morehouse College president: "Not failure but low aim is the sin." This was in an *Indianapolis Record* article entitled, "Networking, minority involvement in Games top agenda for local black professionals," by Colleen Heeter.

I was aiming high. Nobody outcampaigned me. I was all over the place. And Labor Day weekend exemplified my breakneck pace. It began with one of my clerks driving me up to Sault Ste. Marie, where I took a ferry to Mackinac Island and spent the night in the Governor's mansion, along with Governor Blanchard and Chief Justice Williams. The next morning, we rose before dawn, and we took the ferry to walk in the Labor Day Parade across the Mackinac Bridge. Afterward, Governor Blanchard and I took a plane to Detroit to walk in the Labor Day parade. Then we went to Hamtramck, to walk in their Labor Day parade.

"I was appointed to the Michigan Supreme Court by Governor Blanchard and sworn in by Chief Justice G. Mennen Williams," I said at every campaign stop. "I'm endorsed by education associations, law enforcement agencies, bar associations, and labor groups. And I'm the only candidate who is currently serving on the court."

Those four bullet points appeared under my photograph on my campaign literature that said, "Remember, you have not finished voting until you've voted for DENNIS W. ARCHER, JUSTICE OF THE SUPREME COURT." It also said, "Vote the Non-Partisan Ballot" on Tuesday, November 4.

A trifold brochure detailed my history and contributions to the legal profession, and featured photographs of me with Trudy, Denny and Vincent, as well as with Justice Williams swearing me in.

My supporters wore round, three-inch buttons pinned to their shirts and coats that said, "Retain Archer, Michigan Supreme Court" in kelly green letters on a white background.

Governor Blanchard's campaign literature also urged voters to cast a ballot for me. On one side, his kicker cards said, "Vote Governor Jim Blanchard and your Democratic team." And the other side featured his photo, along with Congressman John Conyers, Mayor Coleman Young, and Congressman George Crockett. Below that: "Vote for Justice Dennis W. Archer."

On election day, Trudy and I voted together. On the ballot, I appeared at the top of the list of 24 names; I was the only candidate on the non-partisan ballot with "Justice of the Supreme Court" under my name.

Former U.S. Senator Robert Griffin received more votes than me, but I came in second, so I won.

"Dennis was the first African American Supreme Court Justice in Michigan to get re-elected," recalls Jim Blanchard, who also won that year by the largest margin of any governor in state history.

"The following January 1," he says, "I had to have my second Inauguration, so Dennis swore me in."

SUPREME COURT JUSTICE MISTAKEN FOR THE VALET

Sadly, Chief Justice G. Mennen Williams died on February 2, 1988. Our family attended his funeral, then joined family and friends to visit his widow, Nancy, at the Williams home in Grosse Pointe, Michigan. At that time, Trudy was Assistant Dean at Detroit College of Law, a position she had taken the year before. Denny and Vincent were with us at the Williams' home.

"It was snowing," recalls Denny, then an undergraduate at the University of Michigan, "and a lot of people were coming to the house. Dad was just being Dad when he asked, 'Where's the shovel?' and he shoveled the driveway so people could pull up to the house. Some white cat gets out of the car, looks at Dad shoveling the walk, and throws him his keys, assuming he was the valet. Mind you, Dad's wearing a suit and cashmere coat.

"Most people would have a more volatile reaction. But Dad walked up to the man and said, 'I'm Dennis Archer, Michigan Supreme Court,' and handed the keys back."

WESTERN MICHIGAN UNIVERSITY NAMES A STREET "ARCHER DRIVE"

On December 12, 1989, Western Michigan University bestowed the tremendous honor of renaming a street "Dennis W. Archer Drive" on campus. This occurred after the Epsilon XI chapter of Alpha Phi Alpha suggested that the circular drive in front of the Bernard Center student union be renamed after me.

"Western Michigan University has provided me with an embarrassment of riches," I said during the naming ceremony attended by University President Diether Haenicke; president of the campus Alpha chapter, John Ambrose; WMU Board of Trustees chair Carol Waszkiewicz; and vice chair Geneva Jones Williams.

"First, an education, then a Distinguished Alumni Award in 1982, and Honorary Doctor of Laws in 1987, and now through a request by my fraternity and the acquiescence of the Board of Trustees, a street named after me. My debt is a heavy and joyful burden which I hope to repay by way of public service and my unflinching loyalty to Western Michigan University and Alpha Phi Alpha fraternity."

I concluded by saying, "Thank you for this tribute. You encourage me to reach for even greater heights."

WMU vice president for development and administrative affairs Chauncey Brinn said the University overwhelmingly supported my fraternity's suggestion for the street naming.

"His accomplishment and his exemplary work for our state are an inspiration for all of us, but especially for all students at WMU," he said. "The University would be pleased to honor its most successful and prominent alumni in this fashion."

Two years prior, I had delivered the commencement address in April of 1987, stressing the importance of graduates demanding equality and justice in their life's work. Five years later, I had the honor of delivering the keynote address for the 30th anniversary celebration of WMU's Alpha Phi Alpha fraternity during Homecoming weekend in October of 1992.

All the while, I have nurtured a strong relationship with current WMU President Dr. John Dunn.

"Dennis was always very good in advising me in my role as president to think about ways that we could be more inclusive," he says, "more responsive to the populations in ways that are positive. He always gives extremely good counsel."

It has been my honor and pleasure to participate as often as possible in programs that enhance students and the campus community.

"What I learned from him is what we know so well," Dr. Dunn says, "but it's great to see in individuals who validate the power of education, and who illustrate that talent and intellect come from all sectors, including the poorest of the poor. Some might say his upbringing in Cassopolis is a sad story, but it's got a richness, too, that includes affection for his father and his mother, and it shows the ability to overcome through the power of hard work and education, and to never give up."

PREPARE YOUR ARGUMENT BEFORE
APPROACHING THE BENCH — AT HOME

In 1989, Governor Blanchard appointed Trudy as a Judge on Detroit's 36th District Court. I swore her in. As a result, Denny and Vincent became well aware that having two parents who were judges presented a challenge when asking permission for something that could easily be denied.

"You couldn't just come up with something and ask for it," Vincent recalls. "You had to create your argument, and have all your talking points, your supporting evidence lined up, and you had to know how they would counter, and how you would counter them after that. But first you had to lead them down the path with easy questions that you can answer quickly."

Vincent says he had mastered this technique as a teenager when asking us to extend his curfew from 10:00 p.m. until midnight, so he could attend teen clubs that let out at 11:30 p.m. or midnight.

"That was a big deal," he said. "I went into the discussion strong because it's a two-hour jump, and I had to come up with the best reasoning so that they could not say no. I simply said, 'I have to talk about this curfew. I need it extended.'"

"My dad's immediate response was, 'No, you don't.' My mother asked, 'Why do you need it extended?' I said, 'All my friends are going out and everybody has a 12 o'clock curfew but me.' My parents said, 'They are not my child. You are.'"

Vincent said he formulated his argument around his group of friends.

"I said, 'Listen, I have a group of friends that you love and know their parents and you can pick up the phone and call them. So, you have to extend my curfew.'"

His strategy resulted in a curfew extension.

But his argument failed when he asked to attend a concert for a notorious rap music group at Joe Louis Arena in downtown Detroit.

"Even my friends at Country Day were going," Vincent remembered. "But my parents weren't buying that. They said no."

5

"THOUGHTS FOR A GREATER DETROIT"
THE CAMPAIGN, ELECTION, & TRANSITION

"DENNIS, YOU SHOULD CONSIDER RUNNING FOR MAYOR OF DETROIT"

A DEAD CITY.

The murder capital of America.

A place where the weak are killed and eaten.

Comparisons to bombed-out Beirut.

A real-life movie set of an apocalyptic cityscape.

Another "Rust Bucket" town left to crumble in the dust of automotive manufacturers seeking greener pastures in Kentucky, Mexico, Asia.

Such was the image of Detroit that many people held during the late 1980's and early 1990's when I was on the Michigan Supreme Court. The presumption was that I worked in Lansing, but my Court offices were in downtown Detroit.

Every day as I drove between our home in Palmer Woods, downtown and back, I passed increasing numbers of boarded-up and burned-out houses. Clusters of young black men loitered on street corners as opposed to being in school or at jobs. Piles of abandoned tires — hundreds of them at once — littered vacant lots overgrown with weeds. Men, women, and children huddled amid snow and frigid winds at bus stops, waiting for transportation that sometimes came hours late, if at all. If I were driving before dawn or after sunset, streets were dangerously dark under streetlights that were not working.

As I drove, I reflected on how Mayor Young was re-elected in 1989 to a fifth term, promising what most political observers viewed as four more years of Detroit's downward spiral. Many, including Richard Van Dusen — chairman of the prestigious law firm of Dickinson Wright and former chairman of the Greater Detroit Chamber of Commerce — had encouraged Mayor Young to abstain from another mayoral bid, hoping that new leadership could steer the city into better days.

All the while, I always gave high respect to Mayor Young for having achieved so much early on, as a powerful and impactful leader. His collaboration with Ford Motor Company Chairman Henry Ford II, business magnates Al Taubman and Max Fisher, and others, had created the gleaming towers of the Renaissance Center as a catalyst and symbol of Detroit's economic revival. In addition, Mayor Young had integrated the police and fire departments decades ahead of other major cities. Detroit became the first major city to have an African American police chief. (Sadly, a two-year federal investigation of Chief William Hart for embezzlement resulted in an indictment and prison sentence.)

But despite Mayor Young's many positive contributions to Detroit, one-third of our citizens lived in poverty. Disinvestment of the lifeblood of our city — the automobile industry —was facing challenges. When he took office, 16 automobile plants operated in Detroit. Now, only three remained. This long-term downsizing and disinvestment by the automobile industry robbed Detroit of one-third of its jobs, as well as one-third of its population since 1970. The remaining one million people — 75 percent of whom were African

American — were plagued by an unemployment rate double that of the suburbs, a 25 percent drop in per capita income, and a poverty rate that doubled. Ironically, 35 percent of adults in the Motor City could not afford to own a car.

Detroit had more children living in poverty than any other American city. Many children lived in crumbling neighborhoods pockmarked by 45,000 abandoned homes, and a decrepit, cash-strapped urban infrastructure that left streetlights dark, potholes rampant, parks overgrown and abandoned, and recreation centers shuttered.

This quintessential urban decay correlated with Mayor Young's increasing reclusiveness as he battled emphysema during his last two terms in office. Pushing him further out of public view were a combative media, budgetary woes, and a variety of critics who were quick to blame him for Detroit's continued demise. His rare public appearances inspired comparisons of the mayoral residence, the Manoogian Mansion, as a castle with a moat.

"Things have to change," I thought as I drove to work each day and tuned my car radio to Detroit's local AM radio news stations. The headlines crackled with Detroit's crack cocaine problem. Teenagers were killing each other over gym shoes, leather jackets, and designer eyeglasses. The latest standardized test scores for Detroit students were dismal, and the city's public school graduation rate was among the worst in the nation.

Too often, newscasters referenced the latest nighttime television comedians who made Detroit the butt of jokes... or someone of national prominence referenced my birthplace as the epitome of urban decay, crime, poverty, failing education, and abandonment by whites and big business.

Each news bulletin struck me to the core, setting off an urgency in me to fix them. This feeling only intensified as I drove into downtown.

Block after block of office towers, restaurants, and stores stood vacant or boarded up and dusty, like the ominous chorus of a Greek Tragedy, whispering that the city's economic engine was sputtering toward utter and irreversible failure.

"How can we turn this around?" I wondered.

I thought about Denny and Vincent, and the city they and hundreds of thousands of our city's children and young people would inherit. I thought about the countless families struggling to put food on the table, stay warm and safe, or find employment, or escape the cycle of poverty with better education and needing role models showing how to create a better life. I thought about the senior citizens whose homes were prisons of isolation and fear.

And I thought about all the thriving cities that I had visited across America and the world where people enjoyed an exemplary quality of life with good education, reliable city services, safe and stable neighborhoods, a vibrant downtown bustling with restaurants, exciting sports and entertainment, outdoor gathering places in city centers and along waterways, and the cosmopolitan flair of a destination city that could attract visitors, conventions, and major sporting events such as the Super Bowl.

"How can we make Detroit the world-class city that it was during the 1950's?" I asked myself. Back then, Detroit was so grand that it was called The Paris of the West. Now, if Paris epitomized class and culture, then Detroit was perceived as its polar opposite.

In contrast, I remembered Detroit as the vibrant, cosmopolitan downtown that I had experienced as a boy during the 1940's with my mother and grandmother and later as a college student during the 1960's. Now, even the J. L. Hudson tower — which once stood as the crown jewel of the Woodward Avenue shopping district — had closed in 1983. This stripped, shuttered, squatter-inhabited symbol of Detroit's economic rock bottom was surrounded by dusty-looking buildings, wig shops, and empty sidewalks. After 5:00 p.m., downtown became an eerie ghost town when office workers vacated via the freeways and went home.

As I continued to work downtown, the hopeless state of our city weighed heavily on my heart. I was a Supreme Court Justice, tasked with ensuring fairness and equality for the citizens of Michigan. But what justice was being served to Detroit's one million residents? And what could I do about it?

"Dennis, you should consider running for mayor," someone would inevitably say as I ventured outside for lunch. If it were a Wednesday, this oft-repeated encouragement would be given while standing in line at Silver's Café, a modern, cafeteria-style spot inside Silver's furniture store at Congress and Shelby. Their legendary Caesar salads with chicken and corn bread attracted a steady stream of downtown workers, including many from the legal and business communities.

"You should think about running for mayor," I often heard while attending evening and weekend events with Trudy around Metro Detroit. This encouragement came from a broad spectrum of the clergy, business leaders, community organizers, philanthropists, and people of every race, religion, and station in life. And it continued for years. At first, I blew it off, thinking, *They can't be talking about me.* Besides, it was a pleasure to serve on the Michigan Supreme Court with wonderful colleagues.

Then, in April of 1990, *Michigan Lawyers Weekly* magazine named me "Most Respected Judge in Michigan." This honor was bestowed by the lawyers and judges who subscribed to the magazine, and had voted to name the most respected 20 judges in the state. I was ranked number one. That gave me tremendous credibility, having served on the court for only four years. This high regard from my peers inspired comfort in those who were beginning to hear my name as a potential candidate for the office of mayor. This honor spoke to integrity, character, and wisdom. It spoke to my ability to listen and to work with others — so that was very helpful. This honor propelled me closer to thinking about the possibility of running for mayor of Detroit.

I concluded that I could not remain on the Supreme Court and attempt to help Detroit. The judicial canons of ethics preclude sitting judges from running for a political office outside of the judiciary. And I was obligated to abide by Michigan's constitution, which states that a Supreme Court Justice cannot campaign for another elected position outside of the judiciary before vacating that position for one year before the primary. Therefore, in order to campaign for mayor, I needed to leave the court. First, I engaged in a series of casual conversations with accomplished people whose opinions I valued.

"One day out of the blue," Nettie Seabrooks recalls, "Dennis called me and asked if I could meet him, and I agreed."

Over the years, I called upon Nettie, who was director of government affairs at General Motors. Her brilliant business mind enabled her to become deeply involved in the creation of the North American Free Trade Agreement with Canada and Mexico. Finally enacted in 1994, NAFTA aimed to eliminate trade and investment barriers between the U.S., Canada, and Mexico.

"I'm thinking of leaving the bench," I told her, "and running for mayor of Detroit."

"Are you crazy?" she asked, flabbergasted.

"Nettie, somebody's got to do it. Coleman Young has been mayor for 20 years, and his health is not good."

"Well, if there's anything I can do to help," said Nettie, who had never been interested in politics.

As I continued to consult with trusted voices about my growing interest in becoming mayor, something unexpected happened in November of 1990: Governor Blanchard lost his re-election bid to Republican Senate Majority Leader John Engler. My memory of the Blair Moody controversy, along with my unwavering commitment to reaching back and pulling a person of color into every position that I held, accelerated my decision to leave the court. It was imperative that a person of color replace me, and that could not be guaranteed should I step down after the departure of our Democratic governor who valued the importance of diverse perspectives on the Michigan Supreme Court.

"Jim, I'm seriously thinking about running for mayor," I told the governor, "and in order to make a run, I need to step down now. I need to know that you'd consider putting someone of color in my spot. Here are some names. Whomever you choose, it should be someone of color." He appointed Conrad Mallet Jr. to take my place.

"Dennis served with great distinction," recalls Jim Blanchard. "Then he came to me as I was leaving office unfortunately at that time and said he wanted to run for mayor and he would have to step down as a justice and give it a year before he could run for mayor."

On December 18, 1990, I announced that I would resign from the Michigan Supreme Court on December 28, 1990. On January 1, 1991, I returned to private practice, becoming an equity partner at Dickinson, Wright, Moon, Van Dusen & Freeman, Attorneys at Law.

Four months later, the *National Law Journal* selected me as one of the 100 Most Influential Lawyers in America for its March 1991 edition. This distinction further propelled my ambition to help Detroit. However, my political campaign experience had taught me to arm myself with facts and a strategy before facing voters and critics.

My Vision for Restoring Detroit to a "World-Class City"

As I contemplated how — if given the privilege — to help restore Detroit's status as a world-class city, my vivid recollection of watching Richard Austin and Roman Gribbs launch their mayoral campaigns during the 1970's inspired an idea.

Both candidates had followed the customary practice of holding a press conference and announcing, "My name is Richard Austin, and I've done all this in the city of Detroit, and now I'd like to bring my education and work experience to become the next mayor of the city of Detroit." At the announcement, the media would ask specific questions, such as, "What are you going to do about crime?" And the candidate would reply, "We're working on it." Candidates typically did not share a strategy at their announcement on how to combat crime or solve other problems.

My campaign, should I decide to launch one, would be different. First, I wanted to research Detroit's major problems; quantifying them would facilitate solving them. Second, I planned to consult with experts and citizens about the problems and possible solutions. Third, I wanted residents to tell me exactly what they wanted from their next mayor. Finally, I would compile this information into a report that would make the case for why I was running for mayor and what I would do if elected.

That report would be entitled, *Thoughts for a Greater DETROIT* which would serve as a blueprint for rebuilding Detroit into a world-class city and a bustling metropolis where it's desirable to live, work, play, and visit. That means a thriving economic environment where businesses feel welcome to operate downtown and throughout the city, and that they can draw upon a talented pool of employees, all the while strengthening the city's tax base.

My vision of a world-class city is one where people feel safe, with a low crime rate, and trustworthy police presence and response time. City services are outstanding, with streets, bridges, and roads in good condition. Streetlights work. Garbage is picked up in a timely manner. The word "neighbor" is reconnected with "hood" so that neighborhoods are nurturing, cohesive places where people come together to raise children who attend quality schools and play on clean, safe playgrounds and in exceptional recreation centers.

Municipal government operates efficiently and effectively as a one-stop shop where open communication, as well as policies and procedures, ensure the best, friendly service for citizens and businesses. Innovative partnerships between government, business, and organizations provide resources that improve the city on every level.

Sports stadiums, entertainment venues, and restaurants entertain people from across the region, and host high-profile gatherings such as the Democratic National Convention or the Republican National Convention, as well as national sporting events such as the World Series, the Stanley Cup, and the Super Bowl. The city's downtown offers an extraordinary gathering place that celebrates Detroit's unique history and affords unforgettable experiences with friends, concerts, and special events.

Transforming Detroit from its current reality into this vision was not something I could attempt to do alone. It would require unprecedented teamwork, collaboration, and cooperation on local, state, and federal levels, as well as between the city and the suburbs, the business community and municipal government, and people of every age, race, ethnicity, religion, and socioeconomic level.

To achieve this, I began assembling a team of people whom I thought possessed outstanding skills in every area necessary. I called Nettie Seabrooks and accepted her offer to help my campaign. "Nettie, I'd like you to start attending exploratory meetings on different subjects. And I want to produce a document called 'Thoughts for a Greater Detroit.'" Little did she know that she would help me write it. For the time being, I explained that the report would be a compilation of information that we would glean from national research, community meetings, and academic research to clearly define Detroit's devastating problems — and offer realistic, solid solutions to fix them. It was time to LET THE FUTURE BEGIN, and Nettie, along with many others, were going to help me discover how to do that.

Next, I asked University of Michigan President James Duderstadt if he could provide outstanding professors to work with me on several topics. Each one would take an assignment to identify people who share what they were doing about specific problems in their cities, and what solutions would work best in Detroit.

We hosted focus groups from February until May of 1991 at the home office of Philip Powers' *Observer and Eccentric* newspaper headquarters. The meetings addressed nine key areas:

1. Crime, Safety, and Drugs

2. Economic Development

3. Transportation

4. Job Training/Employment

5. Education

6. Health Care and Preventative Health Care

7. Housing (Rehabilitated, Public, and New)

8. Human Resources

9. Municipal Finance

We explored each issue in separate meetings with a core group of urban educators, a wide cross section of knowledgeable Detroiters, and individuals from other states. Every participant defined the problems and suggested solutions from the perspective of his or her own expertise and experience. A roundtable discussion followed. Despite our different backgrounds, we shared a common love for the city of Detroit and a sincere interest in its preservation, development, and revitalization. Our thoughtful analysis of the ideas convinced us that Detroit could become the most improved city in America by 2001 — if every person who had a stake in the city's future was willing to make the commitments and sacrifices to stabilize, revitalize, and prepare Detroit for success in the 21st century.

During this time, I supported Governor Bill Clinton's presidential campaign. His campaign promise of economic revival for America's cities through an Urban Agenda would bode well for Detroit. In addition, my longstanding friendship with his wife, Hillary Clinton, through the American Bar Association, had enabled me to meet him on several occasions. And when he made his bid for the White House, I let them know that I would do whatever possible in Detroit and Michigan to assist with building support for him.

"I'm here to volunteer," I told the Clinton campaign's regional director, Freman Hendrix, one evening when I entered his campaign office in Detroit. "I want to make some phone calls for Governor Clinton." At the time, Freman was Assistant Wayne County Executive for Wayne County Executive Ed McNamara, as well as president of the Northwest Detroit Democratic Club. We clicked immediately, thanks to a similar, shared vision about how to restore Detroit to a world-class city in terms of education, safety, business development, strong neighborhoods, and a vibrant city center. Freman and I enjoyed a spirited exchange about the positive impact that Governor Clinton could have on America as president — and that I might have on Detroit.

"I've been hearing speculation in the community since the late 1980's that you might run for mayor someday," Freman said. "I'd like to invite you to share your vision with community activists and precinct delegates in my home in northwest Detroit." I agreed.

"I sent a letter to my network," recalls Freman, "hoping for 20 people to attend, and we had nearly 50 people. After that, I was barraged by folks asking, 'Why didn't you invite me? I heard you had a meeting with Dennis Archer.' So I hosted three additional meetings. That's when I knew this was getting ready to happen."

During these casual conversations with small groups, I heard repeatedly that the current system was failing Detroit on every level, and it was time for change.

"Dennis stood in stark contrast in terms of his political style and his public persona to the image that had been cultivated with the Young administration," Freman says. "People saw Dennis as a beacon of hope and the embodiment of positive change for Detroit. He was a smart, good-looking guy, he had paid his dues, and he had incredible credentials. When I had a chance to listen to him in my living room up close and personal, I felt I got to know him, and learn where he stood on different issues. He was someone who was bold enough to shun the status quo and embark on his own path to do what's best for the city of Detroit." The meetings enabled participants to vent about crime, poverty, city services, education, and urban blight. And they wanted to know how I would fix these problems.

"I have some thoughts," I always responded, "but first tell me your ideas and concerns. Tell me, why are you angry?"

This approach, Freman says, made people believe in my sincere desire to help the city.

"I was so impressed by Dennis during those meetings because he was an extraordinary listener," Freman recalls. "He brought a judicial temperament that was his unique, stylized way of interacting with people. You could see him sitting there listening to somebody talk with undivided attention. Politicians are always so quick to tell you how smart they are, and why we should do this and that. But Dennis always started by saying, 'Tell me what you think.' I observed that and said, 'This guy is the real deal. I really, really like this.'"

As a result, Freman told me, "If you run for mayor, count me in. I'd be honored to work in whatever capacity you offer." Our natural affinity and shared vision made it natural to select Freman Hendrix as my co-campaign manager with Emmett Baylor Jr.

"Our very first meeting was a breakfast gathering on a Saturday morning in the basement of Dennis' home in Palmer Woods," Freman says. "Trudy served salmon, lox, bagels, cream cheese, fruit, and coffee. In attendance were Beth, Joe, Mr. and Mrs. DunCombe, and dozens of supporters. I walked into this meeting, and there must have been 30 people surrounding the perimeter of the basement. I didn't know anybody, which let me know that Dennis was reaching to places and people I'd never seen in the local political community. He was assembling a very eclectic group of people — city, suburb, black, white, Jewish, Arab, professional, blue collar, UAW people, carpenters, General Motors executives, everybody. At every meeting, Dennis was filtering ideas and feeling people out."

One day I was speaking with *Detroit Free Press* Publisher Neal Shine about my vision for our city's future.

"Dennis, if you're going to run for office," he advised, "you better talk to Ike McKinnon." Isaiah McKinnon had a long, illustrious history with the Detroit Police Department, having been one of few black officers when he joined the force in 1965, then working under Mayor Cavanagh, Mayor Gribbs, and Mayor Young. Now a University of Detroit Mercy professor and head of security for the Renaissance Center, Ike had lived through some of Detroit's most tumultuous times with the police department, including the 1967 rebellion, STRESS, layoffs, and ranking as one of America's worst crime rates.

I called Ike McKinnon; he said he was familiar with me as a former Supreme Court Justice and host of my Sunday TV program on Detroit's local ABC affiliate, WXYZ Channel 7.

"I'd like you to head my security team," I said, sparking a three-hour conversation about our shared vision for improving Detroit.

"Mr. Archer, I'll give you my undying loyalty," Ike said. "I'll support you 100 percent because so many wonderful things need to be done for the city." He proceeded to accompany me everywhere throughout the campaign. "I could see that the city really liked Dennis Archer," Ike recalls. "They saw this need for change. And they really wanted Dennis Archer to be their mayor."

My optimism surged as we conducted meetings with Detroit citizens during the winter and spring of 1992. At the same time, our team visited other cities to learn how they were converting problems into progress. Among them Cleveland, where Mayor Mike White was doing an outstanding job at rebuilding the city into a shining star of urban revitalization. After years of financial crisis, high unemployment, and derision as an undesirable destination, Mayor White helped attract new sports stadiums, downtown redevelopment, and cultural attractions that earned Cleveland media praise as a "comeback city."

I wanted to do the same for Detroit, so we studied Cleveland, as well as Baltimore and San Antonio, cities that had transformed their waterfronts into vibrant destinations bustling with restaurants, entertainment settings, and sports arenas.

Meanwhile, one day I had lunch with Oakland County Executive L. Brooks Patterson, and a newspaper reporter published a column about it. A Republican, Brooks was considered the archenemy of

Mayor Young and therefore was disliked among Mayor Young's supporters. Unfortunately, news of my meeting with him sparked rumors that I would "sell out" Detroit's jewels to the white suburbs. Rather than engage racial politics or criticisms that I knew were unmerited, I chose to "show" rather than "tell" my racial allegiance by working hard to find solutions to help our majority-black city.

After the research was compiled, and I was satisfied that we had collected a plethora of creative solutions for Detroit's grave problems, the writing process began. Between May and November of 1991, I was writing the document, even during vacation, with help from Nettie and my friend Al Lucarelli, the managing director of Ernst & Young, and Michael Franck, the Executive Director of the State Bar of Michigan, who were editing the overall document.

By mid-November, we completed *Thoughts for a Greater DETROIT*. This living, breathing document conveyed what I saw as a solution — and an invitation to everyone in our city and region to participate in the search of ideas, plans, and recommendations.

"Detroit is a city in serious trouble," I wrote at the start of *Thoughts for a Greater DETROIT*. "We know it. The entire nation knows it. We must repair the damage immediately. The future and economic viability of the entire State of Michigan is tied inextricably to Detroit. Our city must once more become an attractive, vibrant, and safe place for families and businesses." The report was a blueprint for building a better Detroit, so I included a description of how I envisioned our city one decade later.

"My View of Detroit 2001" spans the first five pages, as I describe our city a decade into the future, following the implementation of the ideas listed in *Thoughts for a Greater DETROIT*.

It starts in 2001, as my morning newspapers arrive, trumpeting Detroit's successes that are being praised in the major media outlets across America, and echoing a national news magazine's celebration of Detroit as its "Most Improved City of the Decade Award." Here is an excerpt:

> The city of Detroit is now "the" in place to live, raise a family, open a business and experience cultural diversity... We have

safe streets both in the neighborhoods and downtown. Our children enjoy an excellent public educational system. We have a great healthcare system. Detroit recognizes the dignity of its people.

We have a world-class waterfront development, a pristine and cherished Belle Isle and a transportation system that has become a model for other cities. Our unemployment rate has been drastically reduced.

Because our Cobo Hall Convention Center is always booked to capacity, the Detroit hotels enjoy a high occupancy rate and the restaurants in Detroit and its suburbs require reservations.

The major factors which led to this renaissance have been our strong neighborhoods, which continue to grow and prosper and a strong working relationship between the mayor and the business community. As a result, we have a reduced tax burden on our property and a reduction of our city income taxes is under consideration. Detroit is pro-business and has once again become competitive with other leading cities in the United States.

Some writers who engaged in in-depth analyses... credited the close working relationship between the public and private sector... the leadership skills of the administration... and the brightest people running each city department.

The vision also describes how local journalists credit Detroit's success to a strong and progressive working relationship between the mayor and all levels of local, state, and federal government, as well as community groups, suburban mayors, and organizations such as New Detroit, Inc., Detroit Renaissance, the Greater Detroit Chamber of Commerce, and other groups focused on Detroit's revitalization. After that, *Thoughts* examines how collaborations have vastly improved Detroit's safety, education, transportation, healthcare, housing, and business development.

I continued by writing, "I could go on, however, I have said enough to portray my view of the future. So, it is time to return to November 25, 1991. I suggest that what I have set forth is all quite possible and achievable. But it will take commitment, leadership, involvement, teamwork, vision, planning, sacrifice, and follow-through.

"And, how do we get there?"

The rest of the report explained exactly how, and those points became the major tenets of my campaign. The cover page of *Thoughts for a Greater DETROIT* said "Draft for Community Input" because it was *their* document. Turning the city around would require a team effort from the grassroots up to the offices of the mayor, the governor, and the U.S. president.

On November 25, 1991, we published the 64-page report and sent 1,000 copies to editorial boards, radio and TV stations, and leaders in business, religion, community, and government. I even sent a copy to Mayor Young. *Thoughts for a Greater DETROIT* sparked the local and national media to interview me and analyze the solutions we were proposing for our city.

Meanwhile, the major question was: would Mayor Young announce a bid for a sixth term? Many people maintained a very high regard for him; his political support base was formidable. As a result, potential mayoral candidates were waiting to see if he would announce by the June 1993 deadline. If he did, they believed that running against Mayor Young would be a losing game. If Mayor Young did not run, some contenders wanted his blessing so that his supporters would throw their voting power behind his anointed candidate.

I assumed that I would run against Mayor Young.

"It took tremendous courage and self-confidence to put an exploratory team together and issue a paper," Freman says. "It was unheard of for a candidate to do that, or to begin years in advance to so meticulously lay out a specific vision of how to bring the city back."

Confirming Family Commitment for a Mayoral Bid

Campaigning for and becoming the mayor of a major city would require a tremendous sacrifice of time and energy, both for myself and for our family. It was imperative that Trudy, Denny, and Vincent were agreeable to my commitment.

"We, as a family, were all supportive of him," says Denny, who at the time was attending law school at the University of Michigan, where Vincent was a sophomore. One weekend when Vincent was home, I called him into my upstairs study.

"I'm thinking about running for mayor," I told him. "What do you think?"

"Whatever you want to do, I'm going to support you," Vincent said. "What does Mom think? It's more about Mom than me."

Trudy encouraged my decision, even though her position as a judge precluded her from becoming actively involved in my political campaign.

"I was very supportive," she says, "but I could not go out speaking and encouraging people to vote for him. I could accompany him and sit there and be quiet."

We hosted many meetings in our home on Lincolnshire.

"Trudy was extremely gracious with all these folks in their home," says Judith McNeely, who worked diligently on my campaign and would later become my Executive Assistant. "The entire family — Dennis, Trudy, Beth, Joe, the DunCombes, Dennis Jr., and Vincent — everyone made a full and tireless commitment. It showed they were willing to work together to make a difference. That meant a lot to all of us. If the family could give a 500 percent commitment, then we all had to make the same commitment."

RECRUITING OUR CAMPAIGN COMMUNICATIONS TEAM

In August of 1992, I was facing an impressive team of communications professionals from Washington, DC. These sophisticated, corporate "K Street" individuals came highly recommended because they had masterminded many successful congressional and gubernatorial election campaigns.

Now, sitting in the conference room of the Dickinson Wright law firm, they were telling me, Nettie, Beth, Freman, the late Morri Gleicher, an experienced political consultant, and the late Joe Marshall why we should entrust them to design and disseminate advertisements and a communications strategy to inspire Detroiters to select me as the next mayor. They were quite convincing, as was the next team of equally impressive communications experts who had flown in from the nation's capital to interview with us.

At the conclusion of these interviews, a third individual entered the conference room wearing an Army fatigue jacket and casual summer clothing. David Axelrod was a talented, young, political consultant from Chicago who had helped Harold Washington, Chicago's first black mayor, win re-election. He had a reputation for helping black politicians triumph over the complicated racial and political dynamics of urban elections. Freman had introduced me to Axe, whom he had hired for the County to do public relations work for the airport.

"David Axelrod was invited because he wrote a letter to Dennis saying he wanted this job," Beth recalls. "The letter was long, like a term paper or dissertation, and it was very impressive because he captured the Dennis I had known for 25 years. He had researched Dennis by reading newspaper articles, which he included in the letter, and it was clear that he really understood Dennis. The letter also explained his really wonderful ideas for the campaign." During the interview, Axe elaborated on those ideas.

"I was immediately impressed with someone who didn't have the job and had yet gone through that effort and done a lot of the work up front," Beth says. "I must admit, he touched us two women first. Immediately after we had interviewed him, Nettie and I said, 'We gotta have him' and we quickly convinced Dennis and the other guys to hire him. This is one of my fondest memories. The interview process was really fun, and it was pretty exciting that Axelrod came on board."

He was tasked with creating and publicizing our campaign messages that included slogans, literature, commercials, and public relations. His ideas resonated with me; I trusted his expertise and experience, and as a result we had an excellent working relationship. Axe conceived the announcement strategy with his partner, Jon Kupper, and campaign volunteers. And David Axelrod created the campaign slogan, LET THE FUTURE BEGIN.

"We thought it was a very uplifting, forward-thinking slogan," Beth says. "It was positive, and the rest of the campaign messaging centered around that."

"An Ingenious Retail Campaign"
as an Institutional Outsider

"LET THE FUTURE BEGIN" announced a large banner behind me on the stage of Detroit's historic Gem Theatre on November 25, 1992, the day before Thanksgiving.

Hundreds of supporters packed the two levels of the 450-seat theater. Most wore "Dennis Archer for Mayor" buttons that were white with Kelly green print, which we had selected as the campaign theme colors. A huge surprise was U.S. Congressman George Crockett, who spoke and endorsed my candidacy.

"I am hereby announcing my candidacy to become the next mayor of the city of Detroit," I began my brief remarks as local TV news crews, reporters from newspapers and magazines, as well as media photographers captured the event.

I left the Gem Theatre and immediately started campaigning door-to-door on Detroit's East Side, telling citizen after citizen, "Hello, my name is Dennis Archer. I just announced that I'm running for Mayor of the City of Detroit."

I did that through the winter and for the duration of my campaign, in addition to attending meetings, participating in debates, and doing everything else required of a mayoral candidate.

"Are you sure you want to do this?" David Axelrod asked one day as we drove through a particularly devastated neighborhood. I responded with an emphatic yes.

"He was unwilling to accept this as Detroit's destiny," says David, now a Senior Political Commentator for CNN and director of the nonpartisan Institute of Politics in Chicago. His work as Chief Strategist for Barack Obama's presidential campaigns led to President Obama appointing him as Senior Advisor to the President. In 2011, he served as Senior Strategist for President Obama's successful 2012 re-election campaign.

"Dennis has a personal journey that was impressive to me," David recalls. "And it was striking that he was so committed to his family and his relationship with Trudy, who was a striking person in her own right, as was Beth. They gave you a sense that, here were these wholesome, good people with strong values, committed to public service. And Dennis was making a sacrifice to take on something like running for mayor of Detroit. The whole family had a palpable sense of commitment. And I sensed that when we were driving around in that car that day."

That commitment, Freman says, enabled me to sustain a campaign without the support of Detroit's powerful, political machine whose loyalty remained with Mayor Young.

"Dennis was campaigning as an institutional outsider," Freman says. "None of the influential pastors, the big labor unions like the UAW or AFL-CIO, or the civil rights groups such as the NAACP, supported him. They were very critical of Dennis because of their respect for Coleman Young and the legend he had become. Despite the desperate state of the city, the perception was that Dennis' campaign was disrespectful to Mayor Young, whom everyone assumed would run for a sixth term."

Some had, in fact, considered Coleman Young "mayor for life" because his support was so deeply entrenched among a good portion of Detroit's one million residents.

"Back then," Freman says, "the political status quo dictated waiting for Coleman Young to make the first move. Dennis didn't do that. So when he put together his exploratory committee, issued his *Thoughts for a Greater DETROIT*, and announced his bid, still looming over him was the specter of Mayor Young and the anger with Dennis for coming out while he was still in office, without giving his blessing to which candidate he wanted to support."

I did, however, have the backing of many people and organizations who shared my vision for transforming Detroit into a great place to live, work, play, and visit.

"A trail of folks beat a path to Dickinson Wright to meet with Dennis," Freman says. "I'm sure his door was swinging open six, seven days a week with people who wanted to meet with him and pledge their commitment of support."

The corporate business community also endorsed me, including the top leadership of General Motors, Chrysler, and Ford Motor Company. I had known GM Chairman Jack Smith, GM General Counsel Harry Pearce, Chrysler Chairman Bob Eaton, and Ford Motor Company Chairman William Clay Ford Jr. for many years.

When I shared my vision with them, I was extremely fortunate that they supported my bid for mayor.

Thanks to the timing of my announcement, Freman says, the public endorsed my bid, as evidenced by polls showing that I had 35 or 40 percent of the vote from people who wanted to see a change in Detroit's leadership.

"Dennis was outpolling the mayor," Freman says.

However, lacking the endorsement of Mayor Young and his supporters inspired our grassroots campaign strategy, in the spirit of old-fashioned "shaking hands and kissing babies" at local events where I could speak face-to-face with individual voters. This was essentially the same strategy that had proven successful during my campaign for the Michigan Supreme Court.

"Dennis was running this ingenious retail campaign," Freman says, "going to more places to address the same number of people that you would face at a big UAW convention with 1,000 people. He didn't have that kind of access in the early days of his campaign because of the status quo. Some people considered him a *persona non grata* and shut him out."

As a result, I spoke to voters at hundreds of community meetings, home meetings, small and midsized churches, senior citizen homes, community centers, and labor halls.

"During those early months, in late 1992 and early 1993," Freman says, "we didn't have that place with 5,000 people hanging off the rafters in support of Dennis Archer for Mayor. While the UAW and AFL-CIO controlled political endorsements, Dennis went to other labor unions, including carpenters and building trades."

All the while, Freman was coordinating my campaign around the following five pillars: satellite offices throughout the city; a religious coordinator who orchestrated my visits to churches, mosques, and other places of worship; a senior coordinator who scheduled talks with senior citizens; a volunteer coordinator; and home meetings, which became a campaign staple.

Our campaign showcased these events in our advertisements. They included a documentary-style series of ads that showed me speaking on various topics, as well as sound bites from a speech in a Detroit church.

"When he got in front of this crowd," recalls David Axelrod, who strategized the campaign's advertising for television, radio, newspapers, and magazines, "he spoke with a genuine passion that was not like a judge from the bench, but was like the leader of a community. He departed from the script and spoke very much from his heart… very passionately about the state of the city. He was particularly animated about the fact that it was intolerable to have kids shooting each other over jackets and gym shoes. It was moving. It was powerful. And these ads that we created from that speech gave Detroiters a different sense of who Dennis Archer was. They really showed that his passion for the city and for change was real."

Inevitably, these events inspired citizens to approach and ask, "How can I support the campaign? I don't have any money, but I want to help."

Our campaign always responded by saying, "Organize a meeting of your neighbors, friends, coworkers, and family members. Invite 25 or 30 people to your backyard or church basement."

At each meeting, Freman collected names to create our database to build support and attract volunteers.

Trudy often accompanied me. "Running for election was very exciting," she recalls. "I attended events with Dennis all over the city at places that I had never visited before and met people that, but for him running for election, I never would have interacted with. It was a very rewarding experience."

There was a lot to learn. One event in particular presented a valuable lesson about how to talk with people in a way that engenders their comfort and respect.

"I was disappointed in Dennis," a woman told Al Lucarelli in a conversation that he relayed back to me. The woman added, "I was talking to Dennis and I'm shorter than him, and he was looking at where he wanted to go and who he wanted to go talk to next." Al said the woman felt disregarded and devalued.

"It will not happen again," I promised. Her comment reminded me of why people adored then-presidential candidate Bill Clinton; he always made people feel like they were the only person in the world while he was speaking with them, and that left an unforgettably positive impression. Therefore, I vowed to improve how I connected with people. If I'm talking with you, I don't care who's in the room. I'm not going to leave our conversation until you and I have concluded it, and you know I'm talking to you. This facilitated my ability to garner support on a national scale as well, particularly through involvement with the American Bar Association.

"Dennis, why are you running for mayor of Detroit?" asked Phyllis James during a meeting of the House of Delegates, of which we were both members. "You're now part of the mainstream legal establishment, so why would you want to do that? You don't strike me as a politician."

I explained to her and many others who inquired that Detroit was languishing in dire circumstances as a predominantly black city; it was suffering tremendous economic depression resulting from many historical factors, and it required a dramatic new vision and a new influx of talent.

"It's important for me to take on this challenge," I said. "The city needs someone to step forward and try to put it on the right path."

Phyllis understood Detroit's legacy of segregation that largely resulted from both white discrimination patterns, and a degree of self-imposed isolation by the minority community. She also grasped that the key to the city's prosperity was to narrow the enormous gap between black and white while attracting corporate investment.

"Wow, I think you're probably the perfect guy to take on that challenge," Phyllis said. "The right person at the right place at the right time." She and other ABA lawyers expressed support for me embarking on this great public undertaking as a role model for others to take bold action to help in circumstances of desperate need.

"I felt like Dennis was truly practicing what he had been preaching to us minority lawyers for years," Phyllis says now, "about giving back to the black community in ways that are meaningful for you as an individual."

DENNIS ARCHER FOR MAYOR: BUILDING BRIDGES BOTH WAYS

In 1968, the Kerner Commission warned that, "Our nation is moving toward two societies, one black, one white — separate and unequal."

More than two decades later, as I campaigned for mayor, Detroit epitomized the grim conclusion of that federal commission appointed by President Lyndon B. Johnson during our city's 1967 insurrection. He wanted to identify why deadly uprisings were exploding in America's largely black, poor, urban centers — and how to solve the problems to prevent future unrest. Sadly, the Kerner Commission foretold even wider divisions in Detroit — between the city and surrounding communities, state and federal leadership, the business community, the rich and the poor, and the list went on.

Conciliation on every level was the key to our city's success. That's why I cast myself as a bridge-builder committed to healing these fractured relations. I wanted to reverse every problem that had been damaging our city, and *Thoughts for a Greater DETROIT* explained exactly how I would do that. I reiterated these solutions in each media interview, community meeting, face-to-face introduction with citizens as I stood on their front porches asking for their support, business forums such as the Economic Club of Detroit, and discussions with corporate leaders such as GM Chairman Jack Smith and Vice Chairman Harry Pearce.

I did the same with community builders such as Focus: HOPE Founder Father Bill Cunningham and his partner Eleanor Josaitis, as well as leaders with Detroit Renaissance, New Detroit, Inc., and the Greater Detroit Chamber of Commerce. The list went on, and my message remained the same. By establishing myself as an agent of change for citizens and businesses alike, my core campaign pledges always included:

Crime: Transferring at least 300 police officers from desk jobs back on the streets. I reached this conclusion after consulting with Police Department officials who said 276 to 380 police officers could be reassigned to street patrols.

City Services: Implementing a "total quality management" refurbishment of city departments, with the goal of improving customer service at city hall, improving garbage pickup, fixing potholes, repairing broken streetlights, improving bus service, cleaning up playgrounds, and transforming recreation centers into thriving oases for children, families, and seniors.

This included changing the employee culture within city government, and hiring people who provided services in a spirit of excellence and dedication. Likewise, success in other cities hinged on harmonious cooperation between the mayor's office and the city council; healing those rifts would enable Detroit to advance exponentially.

Finance: Tackling the budget deficit that resulted from years of financing the cash flow by spending more than what the city was taking in, and going to the bond market. Now we needed to boost Detroit's low bond rating, which was below investment grade, to a respectable level. We needed to pay the city's bills on time to build good credit with contractors and improve Detroit's economic standing.

Economic Development: Cultivating a pro-business city to create jobs and strengthen the tax base. Establishing a "one-stop shop" that would encourage businesses to open in Detroit with minimal bureaucratic red tape; this would obliterate delays and obstacles in what had become an unwieldly, regulatory maze that deterred business. This economic development office would expedite applications, licensing, and permits, as well as answer questions within 72 hours. This would repair the city's reputation for being hostile toward new business, a sentiment often reinforced by a belief that Mayor Young bashed business for disinvesting in Detroit and causing its financial collapse.

Encouraging churches and other faith-based organizations to start nonprofit businesses, such as grocery stores, which had abandoned Detroit's neighborhoods due to crime, would be another way to enhance Detroit's economy.

We also needed to ensure that black businesses had access to loans that enabled them to open offices and stores downtown. This commitment inspired me to visit Detroit Renaissance — a private organization promoting economic development — and discuss how businesses of color could not get financing. I requested the creation of a $50 million fund of corporate dollars to loan or provide in exchange for equity to level the downtown development playing field for businesses owned by African Americans, Latinos, Arab Americans, and other minority groups.

Downtown Development: Luring business back downtown and into the city. Our goal was to find the best resolution for the Hudson's building, and reestablish downtown as a retail shopping destination.

Waterfront: Transforming the world's most underdeveloped waterfront into an attraction for residents and visitors alike, as cities like Cleveland, Pittsburgh, and Baltimore had revitalized their waterfronts with restaurants, parks, hotels, businesses, and entertainment. Our international waterway that we shared with Windsor, Canada, was a blank slate with infinite possibilities.

A Master Plan: Creating a Master Plan by assembling a task force of city and suburban experts that included architects, engineers, planners, preservationists, neighborhood and community group leaders, and others to propose a Master Plan within 120 days.

Housing: Appointing a housing expert for the city to improve Detroit's delinquent status with the U.S. Department of Housing and Urban Development (HUD) as well as assess existing housing and future development. At the time, the city had delinquent status with HUD, which had vowed to take over Detroit's ill-managed and poorly maintained housing projects.

Casinos: Maintaining my opposition to casino gaming in Detroit, where four previous attempts to create casinos in Detroit had failed under Mayor Young.

Sports & Entertainment: Making Detroit a sports and entertainment mecca. I wanted to lure our sports teams back to the city from suburban stadiums, and build new, state-of-the-art structures that made sporting events exciting for fans, families, and out-of-town visitors.

At the time, the Lions played football 30 miles north in the Pontiac Silverdome. Pistons basketball games were held 35 miles away at The Palace of Auburn Hills. An antiquated, run-down stadium in the city housed Tigers baseball games. And Red Wings hockey matches took place downtown at Joe Louis Arena. In terms of entertainment, revitalizing the Fox Theatre district and other performance venues would make Detroit attractive for concerts and other events.

This outline for restoring Detroit to a world-class city made national news as media outlets announced my candidacy and campaign promises.

Let the Fundraising Begin

From the beginning, I established a campaign that would exemplify immaculate integrity in terms of donations, supporters, and endorsements. I intended for the notorious "pay to play" culture that had dominated Detroit politics for decades to become a vestige of the past under my campaign and, should I be so fortunate to win the election, my mayoralty.

To ensure this, I appointed my sister-in-law, C. Beth DunCombe, as my campaign finance director. Her impeccable reputation as an attorney and partner for two decades at Dickinson Wright, one of Detroit's most respected law firms, endowed her with the authority to demand that contributions were always given directly to her or another high-ranking campaign official.

"Dennis never touched the money," Beth says. "We always had a witness, so no one could say, 'I paid Dennis.' So, for example, when we held fundraising meetings, a campaign representative always attended with Dennis. Knowing there would be an 'ask' for money, we never wanted Dennis to ask, and we never wanted him to get the money himself."

The first campaign fundraiser at the end of 1992 was a citywide mailing. The goal was to capture all the voters in the city, so the mailing included campaign literature detailing my platform, along with an envelope requesting contributions ranging from one dollar to $25. The idea was to inspire voters to buy into the campaign with a small contribution.

With the bulk mail rate, the mailing to every address in the city cost about $7,000. We raised $15,000 — with an average contribution of two dollars. Raising sufficient funds to pay for the campaign materials and small expenses made our first fundraiser a success, which boosted our campaign's confidence.

"The results of that mailing were wonderful and energizing," Beth says. "We had the sweetest feeling when people mailed in a single dollar. That was very motivating to Dennis and the campaign."

CELEBRATING PRESIDENT CLINTON'S INAUGURATION

In January of 1993, Trudy and I, along with Beth and Joe, had the honor of attending President Clinton's Inauguration in Washington, DC. His election victory promised to usher America into a new era after President George H. W. Bush. Now, cultivating good relations in Washington had the potential to garner tremendous benefits for Detroit.

By February of 1993, we had a full-blown campaign going, with an average of two small fundraisers every day. Then we began having fundraising parties in the neighborhoods.

"Someone would volunteer," Beth says, "by telling us, 'I live in such-and-such neighborhood, and my neighbors want to have a fundraiser.'"

Beth's assistant, Tory Inniss — who is Chuck Inniss' and Marie Inniss' daughter — worked full time for the campaign, and attended many of these neighborhood fundraisers, which aimed to grow community support for my mayoral bid. Tory made them festive with balloons imprinted with "Let the Future Begin." She sat at the front door with a cash box for donations. Even the smallest contributions signified support, which encouraged us.

At larger fundraisers, we requested donations of $200. We even had meetings where some people would give $25,000. Back then, no limits existed on how much one person could donate to a mayoral campaign.

"Dennis' money seemed unlimited," Freman says. "It was coming from so many places. He originated what Barack Obama took on a mass scale with contributions from individuals, corporations, and groups."

Donors who gave at least $1,000 were called a "Friend of Archer" and received a gold pin designed by a professional ad agency.

"That became a fundraising hit," Beth says. "All these people gave $1,000 just to get a pin to wear around Detroit. It was really wild. The pins looked expensive. People were wearing them everywhere, and they were so popular, we had to get a second shipment. We also developed stationery for Friends of Archer with all the donors' names on it, and that made people really want to get their names listed on the stationery."

We also had a few Friends of Archer events, including a weekday breakfast featuring a talk with David Axelrod. Another gathering enabled supporters to hear from Paul Maslin, our pollster from San Francisco. People loved to hear about our strategy and the latest poll results.

"When opponents attempted to portray Dennis as an elitist attorney who was out of touch with everyday Detroiters," Beth says, "we purchased ads in newsletters and newspapers published by 300 block clubs across the city. These groups invited Dennis to speak at their picnics, and we invited them to our many Archer Picnics on Belle Isle. Those were always well-attended, as volunteers came and donated food."

One significant nonmonetary donation came from a large ad agency used by one of the Big Three automakers.

"The big ad agencies volunteered to put together a logo for the campaign," Beth says, "and that logo was an image of the Spirit of Detroit sculpture looking up, and it had an archer bow and arrow. They were so clever."

As the fundraising continued in early 1993, I selected Beth's husband, attorney Joe Brown, to locate our campaign offices and initiate the leases. We needed six to eight offices in different neighborhoods around the city. We wanted our main campaign office on the Jefferson corridor near downtown, Beth says, but one of our first choices would not rent to us because they were loyal to Coleman Young. That led us to establish our main campaign office in the Harbortown strip mall, which is a five-minute drive east of downtown. It was spacious, with rooms for volunteers, and unlimited parking. From there, we expanded our campaign staff to include outstanding individuals such as Judith McNeely, who helped with communications, along with Cathy Nedd.

"Harbortown became a beehive of campaign staff and volunteers," Freman says. "Revenue for that whole strip mall went up 200 percent because of all the people coming to our campaign office."

SECOND CANDIDATE JOINS THE MAYORAL RACE

In January of 1993, an African American female lawyer whom I had known for many years, announced that she was running for mayor. Sharon McPhail was a supervisor in the Wayne County Prosecutor's Office and treasurer of the Detroit Branch of the NAACP. In 1985, Mayor Young had appointed her to the Board of Police Commissioners, where she served five years.

During her announcement, two of Mayor Young's longtime supporters joined her: former Detroit Pistons star-turned-businessman Dave Bing; and U.S. Representative Barbara-Rose Collins. Sharon was also backed by many grassroots individuals and groups. From the start, Sharon and her supporters attempted to portray me as a bourgeoisie lawyer who was out of touch with the average Detroiter, and not black enough to lead a city that was 75 percent African American. She also tried to cast me as a tool of the business elite and white establishment who would sell out the city to the suburbs and the business community.

This rhetoric became more inflammatory as the campaign heated up in June of 1993, after Coleman Young declined to join the race just before the filing deadline. With that, the mayoral race became flooded with a total of 23 candidates, most of whom had been waiting in the wings to see if Mayor Young would file. These candidates included U.S. Congressman John Conyers.

Another candidate, Wayne County Commission Chairman Arthur Blackwell II, echoed Sharon's us-against-them mentality by referencing me with vile, slave-era terminology that described blacks who toiled in the fields versus those relegated to the less brutal environment of the plantation house. Mayor Young endorsed Art Blackwell for mayor.

My response was always diplomatic in what the media frequently described as my trademark lawyerly and low-key manner.

"Detroit is not an island to itself," I often said, "nor are the suburbs an island. We need to work together to create and enjoy a world-class city." It helped to have *Thoughts for a Greater DETROIT* to show people our solid strategy for achieving that. No other candidate had conducted research or prepared a document detailing their vision for how to fix Detroit's gargantuan problems.

"By the time Coleman Young finally decided," Freman said, "Dennis had already put down roots, built a formidable base of voter support, raised money, and put organizations together. And by the time the other people came into the race, he was already well down the road to victory."

My preparation and tireless campaigning paid off. During the September 14 primary election, 95,962 Detroiters cast their votes for Dennis Archer for Mayor. Sharon McPhail earned less than half that — 47,733 votes. I won 53 percent of the vote, while she had 26 percent. Art Blackwell placed a distant third.

"I will say to you that I am an underdog, and I will fight as hard I can to earn the right to lead," I declared to my supporters. "I take no frontrunner status."

Freman saw otherwise. "Right after the primary, I said, 'We got this! This is done!' We had so many volunteers, and I managed them along with Emmett Baylor and Akua Budu-Watkins. We'd meet every Saturday at Harbortown around this big table. It was phenomenal!"

Thanks to the outpouring of support, my campaign raised about $3 million. This included contributions from out-of-state lawyers, as well as businesses, suburban communities, and Detroiters representing every ethnic and socioeconomic group. In contrast, my opponent generated about $500,000 in donations.

Sadly, a highly-respected Detroit pastor fanned Sharon's flames of racial rhetoric. Reverend Charles Adams of Detroit's prestigious Hartford Memorial Baptist Church, who was former president of the local NAACP chapter, made national headlines by declaring: "They (the suburbs) want a mayor to shuffle when he's not going anywhere, scratch when he's not itching, and grin when he's not tickled."

My diplomatic responses emphasized how I would improve our city. I also said that the election was not about "talking trash." It was about "picking up trash." But Reverend Adams' criticism and harsh words from others were especially hard on my family.

"I remember," Trudy says, "on many occasions being upset with some of the reports regarding the opposition, but being a wife and a judge, I could never express how I felt."

Reverend Adams later apologized for what was widely viewed as a lightning-rod moment in the mayoral contest. His comments illuminated the irony of race dominating the showdown between two African American candidates in a mostly black city. Unfortunately, this distraction from the real issues continued as I participated in election debates with my opponent.

Coleman Young endorsed Sharon McPhail for mayor, which emboldened her attempts to question my racial allegiance during our live, televised political debates. At one point, she demanded to know whether I — if elected — would keep Mayor Young's career appointees in their high-ranking positions.

"I can't promise you that," I responded.

She proceeded to harp on the idea that I would wipe out Mayor Young's appointees and replace them with people whose allegiances were to white suburbanites and big business. All while she stressed her devotion to Mayor Young's people.

"She tried to paint a picture of a man who is the antithesis of Dad," recalls Denny, who was watching the debate with Trudy in a local TV studio as it aired live throughout Southeast Michigan. He took a light course load in law school to spend as much time on the campaign trail as possible, which included visiting multiple churches on a Sunday, or advising our team from his perspective as a 24-year-old African American Detroiter with a diverse set of friends in the city and suburbs. This perspective, and his understanding of my humble beginnings in Cassopolis, made it extremely difficult for Denny to watch my opponent attempt to question my lifelong commitment to advance people of color.

"She was portraying him as a rich, out-of-touch black 'working for the man' in the corporate law firm," Denny says. "The sell-out, Uncle Tom insult only got worse as she compared him to Clarence Thomas during the first debate. She was spewing boldface lies on camera, making accusations, and attempting to goad Dad. She then asked, 'What have you ever done for black people?' He was livid! He probably wanted to explode on her, but he paused to stifle his anger. My dad knew better than to stoop to that level and say something negative that would get replayed over and over in the media. The alternative, however, was that he froze on live TV for what seemed like eternity. Mom started crying. I was like, 'Is he going to come out of this?'"

Following the debacle of that first debate, I underwent intense debate preparation prior to subsequent debates, and took charge.

"The debates were difficult and stressful," Denny says. "To hear people say mean-spirited, untrue stuff about your dad is an uncomfortable thing. Later, I was in my room crying. 'It's just politics,' Dad said. 'You need a thicker skin going forward.' I toughened up about it, but it still upset Mom. Big city politics is a dirty game; it took time for me to get used to that."

An Attempt at Skewing Public Opinion with Suspicious Polling

Another difficult moment that occurred between the primary and general election related to a poll. We hired San Francisco pollster Paul Maslin, who had worked on many campaigns across America. Immediately after the primary, he conducted a private, scientific poll that accurately measured support within plus-or-minus 3 percent.

"The poll showed that Dennis was clearly in the lead," Beth recalls. "But we did not share the results with the media. At the same time, a local TV station broadcast poll results showing Sharon beating Dennis. That poll was conducted during the same timespan that Paul Maslin's scientific poll showed Dennis leading the race. Dennis was stunned, and Paul was absolutely furious, because he knew that poll was not scientific. The discrepancy was so great between his results and their results. Paul wrote a letter demanding how someone in the news organization could hire someone on the cheap with this cheap result. Maslin felt someone was undermining his credibility. Meanwhile, it helped Sharon a lot. She was excited to think she was winning. It was really ugly, not a good feeling in late September of 1993."

A few weeks later, polls by the local newspapers reflected our results, confirming that the TV station's poll was a fluke.

THE FINAL STRETCH TO ELECTION DAY: CAMPAIGN FUNDRAISER IS STANDING ROOM ONLY

As election day approached, it became increasingly apparent that I would be victorious, and support expanded exponentially. In fact, UAW President Owen Bieber and other high-ranking union officials endorsed me. This overwhelming support was evident at our final fundraiser, held about a week before Election Day in the Renaissance Center's main ballroom, which holds 2,000 people.

"It was standing room only," Beth says, adding that it became our largest fundraiser. "You could not get in the ballroom. We almost didn't have enough people to take the money at the door. People knew Dennis was going to win, and when people perceive you're a winner, the money flows in. Most people paid $200 to enter, but a few donated $25,000. We raised almost $500,000 in one day!"

On the eve of Election Day, I called a meeting with Nettie and S. Martin Taylor, executive vice president of DTE Energy Company and my co-campaign director.

"We're going to win tomorrow," I said. "I want both of you to ask your organizations for a two-month, paid leave of absence, so you can run my transition team. I need the answer by this time tomorrow in the afternoon."

"Dennis, GM can't make a decision that fast," Nettie said.

Chairman Jack Smith was a major supporter; he said yes and granted Nettie's leave of absence.

On Election Day morning, our campaign team and our supporters expressed guarded euphoria. Finally, it was time to vote, and casting a ballot for my own name in that voting booth was invigorating beyond measure. We have a photo showing me voting at the 12th Detroit Police Precinct with Trudy, Denny, and Vincent. All the while, a multitude of reporters and photographers recorded the moment, and continued as we proceeded to greet voters outside.

"When we got to Election Night, it was a wrap," Freman says. "David Axelrod wrote one speech. A victory speech."

That evening we watched the election results in the Westin Hotel in the Renaissance Center. The suite was packed with our core campaign team, along with Denny, Vincent, Beth, Joe, Mr. and Mrs. DunCombe, and close friends like Martha Barnett, who traveled from Tallahassee, Florida, to campaign for the day.

"My parents were so proud of Dennis," Trudy says. "To them, he was their son."

Just before 11:00 p.m., the announcement was made: I won the election with 56 percent of the vote. As thousands of supporters waited in the ballroom downstairs to hear my victory speech and celebrate, our suite buzzed with excitement. Several poignant photographs included one taken behind me as I watched Sharon McPhail on television while she delivered her concession speech.

"The room was packed," Trudy says. "I didn't hear a telephone ring, but I saw Dennis speaking on the phone. He was talking to President Bill Clinton, who had called to congratulate him."

Trudy and my Executive Assistant Judith McNeely watch as I take a telephone call from President Clinton as he congratulates me on being elected Mayor of Detroit. Leroy Richie, vice president and general counsel at Chrysler Corporation, stands behind my right shoulder.

Photo Credit: Bill Sanders

My election was an asset to the president, as our relationship would serve as a foundation for him advancing his Urban Agenda through relationships with the new breed of mayors celebrating victories in other cities as we prepared to take the helms.

"After Dennis had his conversation with President Clinton," Trudy says, "I spoke with him on the phone. That's what I remember most about Election Night, along with all the well-wishers. It was a wonderful evening."

When it was time to go down to give my victory speech in the ballroom, I turned to Ike McKinnon, who had assembled a team of off-duty Detroit police officers. As they escorted us down to the ballroom, I asked, "Okay, how are we going to do this?"

"Let's go into a side door," he said. "We can get you to the podium in about five minutes."

Ike led our family onto the stage as our campaign theme song — *Aint No Stoppin' Us Now*, the 1979 hit by McFadden & Whitehead — blasted through the ballroom. The crowd went wild.

"An absolutely euphoric feeling was electrifying the ballroom as thousands of people cheered," Ike recalls. "It was unlike anything I had experienced. As I was leading Judge Archer, I said, 'Stay with me' while Officers David Simmons and Garrett Ochalek were leading the mayor-elect."

As I stepped to the podium, the crowd pressed toward the stage. I delivered an impassioned victory speech that was televised live on the local 11 o'clock TV news programs. After that, we celebrated with a victory party, finally retreating to the suite around 2:00 a.m.

"We're going to Lansing tomorrow," I told my campaign team.

"I hope you guys enjoy it," Ike said.

"You're going with me."

Exhausted, Ike shook his head. "I have a job here at the Ren-Cen."

"No, you're going with me," I said.

BIPARTISAN BRIDGE BUILDING BEGINS TO UNIFY CITY-STATE RELATIONS

The next morning, we rose early and had breakfast at a restaurant east of downtown. Then we drove to Lansing, where the media photographed a moment that conveyed my urgency to improve relations between Detroit, Republican Governor John Engler, the legislature, and the people across Michigan. The photo showed me, Denny, Freman, Ike, and several other key campaign members descending the steps of the Executive Office Building. This meeting set a tone and sent a message that my administration was committed to working across partisan lines to make decisions that benefited both Detroit and the rest of the state.

"This wasn't a Kumbaya meeting with the governor, the mayor, and their respective staff members exchanging pleasantries," recalls one of my top advisors, David Smydra. "This was a roll-up-your-sleeves collaboration where they acknowledged, 'You're a powerful Republican, I'm a powerful Democrat, and we've got a legislature and a city council that are difficult to deal with. We have an outstate view of Detroit that is negative in the extreme. We have a view in the city that's negative in the extreme of outstate Michigan. How do we solve some of the problems that face us in terms of everyday governance?'"

The answer was that Governor Engler and I created a positive, productive relationship because we shared a common vision for collaborating to resolve the tough challenges facing Detroit and Michigan.

"Because he's a good lawyer, Dennis Archer is a very collegial person to work with," says Governor Engler, now president of the Washington, DC-based lobbying group, the Business Roundtable, an association of CEOs of top U.S. corporations that together generate $7.4 trillion in annual revenues and provide jobs for more than 16 million people. "His communication style is not a fist pounding on the table. You could discuss all topics. We found him to be a perfectly reasonable and informed advocate for the city of Detroit. He appointed good people to run agencies and departments. He worked hard on improving the administration and performance of government. There were a number of things we were able to get done."

I was motivated to work with Governor Engler because I needed his assistance to get things through the legislature to benefit the city.

"When Dennis set up these regularly scheduled meetings with the governor," Freman says, "John Engler was hated by many in Detroit because he was forcing people off welfare; closing Lafayette Clinic, which forced a lot of mentally ill people onto the streets; and threatening to shut down local courts. It was unprecedented for the Archer administration and the Engler administration to share and talk and do things together, and it ushered in a new era of cooperation."

Ike, who was aware of icy relations between the Republican-dominated state capital and Detroit's city hall, was awed by the warm reception.

"We were met with people who were just as euphoric about the mayor being elected as the crowd the night before," he says. "The reception was tremendous."

It was also important to make a positive impression on the constituents of our state lawmakers in Lansing. I was receiving favorable ratings in statewide polls, and wanted to harness that positive perception to benefit Detroit.

"A lot of people don't know," Freman says, "that Dennis got into his car in the early weeks and months of his first and second years, and he was driving to these little hamlets in Pontiac, Grand Rapids, Saginaw, and meeting with groups like the Little Sisters of the Poor and the Knights of Columbus. I was with him on many drives, thinking, 'What are we doing out here talking to these people so far away from Detroit?' Then it hit me: 'This guy gets it.'"

People across Michigan held such a negative image of Detroit for so many years, that in the legislature, a whole generation of lawmakers had come to Lansing from cities and towns and got elected by criticizing Detroit. When they got to Lansing, anything they could do to withhold from Detroit, they were doing it and getting away with it. Every day was a fight, a controversy.

"What does Dennis do?" Freman asks. "He takes this really good feeling that people are having, not just here in Southeast Michigan, but polls across Michigan were giving him very favorable ratings. So Dennis doubled down on that by going directly to those people and meeting them up close and personal. Then he solidified their support of him. As a result, when Dennis went to Lansing, these same lawmakers who didn't want to do anything for Detroit, are now saying, 'We should help Detroit.' The cold war thawed. Dennis turned things around on the strength of his personality, his style, his transparency, his let's-work-together, and on his bridge-building mission."

CLINTON FRIENDSHIP BENEFITS DETROIT

As I embarked on a quest to build bridges across Michigan, the Clinton Administration was cultivating a win-win relationship with Detroit.

"The message went out really early that Dennis was going to have a strong relationship with the president," Freman says. "Since a friendship between Hillary and Dennis predated the Clintons' time in the White House, it was a natural bridge for Dennis to build a great rapport with the president and first lady. And it fit very nicely with Bill Clinton's campaign strategy and philosophy of cultivating big city mayors because so many governors were Republican. Bill Clinton went after the Democratic mayors as his base to build his coalition. And Dennis sat at the top of Bill Clinton's list of favorite mayors. As a result, he had a direct pipeline into the White House, which enabled him to develop relationships with the department heads, and people such as Transportation Secretary Rodney Slater, Chief of Staff Rahm Emanuel, Secretary of Commerce Ron Brown, and Housing and Urban Development Secretary Henry Cisneros."

These relationships helped desperately needed resources flow into Detroit. Shortly after I became mayor-elect, Secretary Cisneros visited our city to announce grants to upgrade our public housing. These included $38.9 million for the Parkside complex and a $500,000 grant for the Jeffries Homes. This was a clear reversal of the contentious relationship that had festered between the city and HUD prior to my election, tarnishing our city with delinquent status with HUD. I found these new developments exceedingly encouraging as a foretelling of good things to come for Detroit's future.

BUILDING THE DENNIS ARCHER BRIDGE
TO A BETTER DETROIT

On November 7, 1993, *Detroit Free Press* political cartoonist Bill Day autographed a large, framed copy of what had run in the newspaper: a black-and-white sketch of the Ambassador Bridge, spanning a huge, black rock promontory on the left, and an equally big, white rock formation on the right. The caption says, "Coming Soon: The Dennis Archer Bridge." Scrolled across the top is the handwritten note from Bill to me offering best wishes for the future.

This hangs in my home office today as a symbol of my role as a conciliator to unite a racially, economically, and geographically fractured region. To do that, I needed to assemble the most outstanding transition team possible.

"Instead of going back to my office at GM," Nettie recalls, "I reported to a whole floor at PVS Chemicals that Jim Nicholson had given to the mayor for the transition team. I tried to put together an administration, thinking, 'In two months, this assignment will be complete and I'll return to GM.' At the same time, I called him 'Mayor' because I wanted to respect his office and be an example for all these other young people."

I appointed Freman as my Chief of Staff, and assigned him to the office adjacent to mine. This happened as we shared a surreal moment on a sunny November afternoon after the election, when we were granted an opportunity to visit the mayor's office to look around. We were standing in the mayor's office, just the two of us, gazing out at the Detroit River toward the Renaissance Center.

"Fre," I said, turning to him. "We're here now. We are here now!"

"Mr. Mayor, it's going to be awesome!"

Freman chuckles at the memory of how I declared those words like, *It's on!*

He adds, "I thought to myself, 'Boy, this is a pretty powerful moment!'"

Meanwhile, we continued to build our transition team. David Axelrod remained as an advisor. Judith McNeely became my executive assistant, handling communications with local, state, and federal governments. Shortly after the Lansing trip, I invited Ike McKinnon to our home.

"Ike," I said, "I want you to be the police chief."

"Thank you," said Ike, who had no intention of becoming police chief despite encouragement by many to do so. "Did you clear your request with my wife, Pat?" My response was, "I have to. This is going to be a journey and an adventure for all of us. We have a lot of things to do." Meanwhile, reporters were camped outside the house, and calling me and others for a scoop about who would become Detroit's next Chief of Police.

"I had to sneak out of the mayor's house to my car, which I'd parked down the street," Ike says. "When I got home that night, Channel 4 reported on the 11 o'clock news that it would be me."

Ike needed a strong Deputy Chief, so I interviewed Commander Benny Napoleon, whose father was a long-time, respected minister in the city. My former law clerk, attorney Reggie Turner, who was instrumental in my campaign and transition, had set up a meeting at his home for me to meet Benny for the first time during the campaign.

I asked him, "What are your thoughts on fighting crime, improving delivery of services to the citizens, improving the police department overall, and what would be the best way to approach it?"

Benny, who had been Ike McKinnon's driver when Ike was an Inspector, gave innovative and impressive answers. I told him to talk with Ike, who then asked Benny to write a proposal on how to re-organize the department to make it more effective. After consulting with several others, Benny presented what became our blueprint for restructuring the department.

TRANSITION TEAM CREATES COALITION: COMMUNITY, LABOR, & BUSINESS

In mid-November, I announced that our transition team would begin an intensive, four-week assessment of municipal government by meeting with department heads and key employees.

I tasked them with gathering departmental information and data, such as current organizational structure and responsibilities, budget, staffing patterns, attrition, and on-going projects. I also asked them to identify critical departmental issues that I would encounter during the first 90 days, the second 90 days, and the first six months in office.

The team was required to compile their findings in transition books, delivered to me in December. I planned to use them as background data in both appointing executive and administrative staff, and in formulating action plans to maximize each department's efficiency and effectiveness.

"The team we've put together represents a strong coalition of leadership necessary to move Detroit forward into the 21st century," I said during a press conference to announce the transition team.

"We've called upon a cross section of business, civic, community, education, religious, and union leaders to help us in this effort."

My transition committee consisted of the following, plus many others:

    Chairman: S. Martin Taylor
    Chief of Staff: Nettie Seabrooks
    Search: George F. Francis III
    Vice Chairs:
        Economic Development: James B. Nicholson
        Finance: Jay Alix
        Human Resources: Roderick D. Gillum
        Law and Public Safety: Leroy C. Richie
        Neighborhood & Community Services: Maggie Desantis
        General Counsel: Victoria Roberts
        Special Counsel: Curtis Blessing

After the teams presented the 44 transition books to me, I chose not to share the findings with the public because I did not want to scare off the business community. However, the information proved enormously helpful in identifying the critical areas where appointees, department heads, and employees should focus their energy to improve every aspect of city government.

Meanwhile, throughout the holiday season, we had much to celebrate. During the annual Thanksgiving Day parade, we were invited to walk with the Blue Cross Blue Shield float. It was thrilling to walk down Woodward Avenue with Trudy, Denny, and Vincent amid throngs of cheering Metro Detroiters.

Mayoral Appointments

On December 21, I had a private swearing-in at the city clerk's office. I felt an urgent need to assemble my leadership team with the best and the brightest urban innovators from Detroit and across America. First, Nettie Seabrooks did such an outstanding job with *Thoughts for a Greater DETROIT*, the campaign, and transition, I invited her to our home and asked her to become my deputy mayor.

"Now, why would I do that?" she asked. "I love my job at General Motors."

Thankfully, she agreed, and reported to her office at the City-County Building immediately following my swearing-in. A week into the job, WXYZ-TV news anchor Bill Bonds interviewed her on the local ABC station and asked, "What do deputy mayors do?"

"I don't know," Nettie responded playfully. "I'll let you know as soon as I find out."

Meanwhile, George Francis, my vice-chair of transition teams, helped find dynamic people to help with the selection process and work in my administration. One especially impressive person was Gary Dent, a human resources expert from General Motors, who helped identify appointees through a vetting process that George and Nettie created.

"It was exciting," Gary recalls, "to find people like Phyllis James and Gloria Robinson and many other wonderful people who were going to help Mayor Archer to do great things."

Phyllis came to us through a strange but fortuitous twist of fate, when she called to ask me to serve as a reference for her application to become a White House Fellow.

"Why do you want to do this White House Fellowship program?" I asked.

"This would be a good opportunity," she said, "and you always encouraged us to do some kind of public service."

"If you're really interested in true public service," I said, "then I have a better suggestion for you."

"What is that?"

"How would you like to come and be my general counsel here in Detroit?"

"Why would I want to do that?" Phyllis asked.

"The White House Fellowship is a wonderful program," I told her. "But it really would not be a challenge for someone with your level of professional accomplishment. Although it would be prestigious, if you were here in Detroit, you would have the opportunity to be part of an administration that could make a contribution to the turnaround of a very economically depressed and severely challenged, predominantly black community." I explained that she could run the Law Department, which desperately needed reform as well as leadership by a dynamic attorney who could administer a large-scale city law department.

"How do you know I know how to do that?" she asked.

"Trust me, I'm sure you can do that," I responded. "If you can achieve partnership at the Pillsbury firm, you can do this. It will not be a walk in the park. It's not going to be glamorous like being a White House Fellow. It's going to be hard, grueling work, but I think it will stretch you as a professional, and it's a great opportunity for doing that and giving back to an African American community in a way that suits your professional calling."

"I'll think about it," she said.

A short time later, Phyllis received a call from my law partner, Joe Marshall, followed by another call from Roy Richie, General Counsel for Chrysler, who told her, "You should say yes to this. It's not every day that a big-city mayor asks you twice for an important appointment. This will be a thousand times better as a career enhancer than being a White House Fellow. A hard professional experience, but more rewarding."

Phyllis took a three-year leave of absence from the Pillsbury law firm and became corporation counsel for the city of Detroit (where she remained during my eight years as mayor). As her deputy director, I retained Thomas Walters.

A surprise also facilitated our hiring of Gloria Robinson as Director of the Planning Department and the Community and Economic Development Department. It happened after Gary Dent called the American Planning Association to initiate a national search to fill that position.

"You have one of the best planners in the country in Detroit," an Association spokesperson told Gary. "Her name is Gloria Robinson. She has a master's degree in urban planning from Michigan State University and has been working in private practice for many years. Her work includes serving as planning director of Wayne County's Department of Jobs and Economic Development." Her experience also included empowering community groups by connecting them with professional firms.

I knew Gloria. She happened to be married to my longtime friend and former law partner, Judge David Robinson, and she and Beth were sorority sisters and had lived together at the University of Michigan for two years.

Gloria recalls that she was impressed by my vision for Detroit. "He wanted to combine the two departments that I was running in separate buildings," she recalls. "It was a challenge, but I shared the commitment to make a difference in the city."

For some appointments, we were unable to find the best candidates, so we hired executives loaned from corporations. For example, I appointed David DenBaas, Comerica Bank's vice president of purchasing services, to a six-month interim position as director of the Purchasing Department.

Meanwhile, Gary thought he had finished his work with the transition team, and that he could return to his job at General Motors. He still chuckles at the memory of when I entered the office where the team was working and said, "Gary, there's one more job to fill, and I'd like to talk to you about it."

Gary shook his head. "No, I have the list here, and we've done everything. There isn't another job."

"Oh, yes there is," I said. "The HR job."

"I'll get on that right away."

"Actually," I said, "I want you to consider that job."

"Oh, heck no," Gary said. "I'm not doing that. I know too much about this."

He returned to work, where GM's top-ranking Human Resources leaders — Roy Roberts, Helen Moy, and George Francis — encouraged him to take the job.

"No, I like my career," Gary said.

Then GM Chairman Jack Smith visited his office and said, "I understand you talked with George and Roy, and we'd like you to go."

Gary became the HR Director for the city of Detroit.

"I was so impressed with Dennis Archer as a human being," Gary says. "I was also intrigued that a person who had no real management and leadership experience wanted to take on that job."

Thanks to the help of Gary and our team, I appointed 59 people, 23 of whom remained from the Young administration. National searches enabled us to fill other key positions with outstanding individuals such as Betty Turner, who became our Housing Department Director. As the former Housing and Redevelopment Agency Director in California's capital city, Sacramento, she had cultivated both a positive relationship with the U.S. Department of Housing and Urban Development as well as national prominence as a public-housing expert. Her appointment assured HUD officials that Detroit was committed to repairing past problems and moving forward in a spirit of cooperation to improve housing in Detroit.

Recruiting a strong team was the first step toward ensuring that we could achieve the vision for our city's future that I had described in *Thoughts for a Greater DETROIT.*

6

THE INAUGURAL
CELEBRATION

"DETROIT FOR ALL, ALL FOR DETROIT"

OUR ELECTION VICTORY WAS rooted in support from people from every walk of life who shared our vision for working together to make Detroit a world-class city.

"This was the first time in 20 years that Detroit was celebrating a new mayor," Trudy says, "so we wanted to make the celebrations very special and inclusive of everyone."

I named Beth as our Inaugural Chairperson, tasked with planning a three-day extravaganza of festivities that would involve and celebrate everyone. She led a team that included Oscar-winning filmmaker Sue Marx and David Axelrod to brainstorm events that would convey a spirit of cooperation as well as generate momentum for the hard work ahead.

"The thought was to involve people from every station in life," Beth says. "So our team came up with the slogan, 'Detroit for All, All for Detroit.' I had gone to the Clinton Inaugural in 1993, and made mental notes. The pressure was on; we had to orchestrate his inaugural in 45 days. Right after the election, everyone went on vacation for a week. I sat on a beach on St. Barts and strategized his inaugural. We had something for everyone."

The cover of the inaugural program booklet announced, "Detroit for All, All for Detroit" in a jazzy script font. The words angled upward on a cream-colored background, framed by a gold border adorned with a subtle, ethnic pattern of starbursts and stick-people holding hands. The inside page showed a family photo that included our family dog, Bogie, along with a message signed by me, Trudy, Dennis Jr., and Vincent. It said:

"We wish to express our sincere thanks to all of the volunteers and voters who gave us the privilege of becoming Detroit's first family. We pledge our individual and collective best efforts to live up to your expectations. As Detroiters, we all must dedicate ourselves to improve Detroit's quality of life and Detroit's image. Our children must feel safe, secure, and motivated to take our places and become the leaders of tomorrow. We believe that if you will match our commitment — then together, the City of Detroit will return to its rightful place as a world-class city as we enter the 21st century."

The booklet also included a page for the 1994 Detroit Inaugural Committee, first listing Chairperson C. Beth DunCombe, followed by Honorary Co-chairpersons:

- Owen Bieber, President, International Union, UAW

- Robert Eaton, Chairman and Chief Executive Officer, Chrysler Corporation

- Iona Echols, President, Lexington Village Tenants Council

- Jack Smith Jr., Chief Executive Officer, General Motors Corporation

- Myzell Sowell, Attorney

- Alex Trotman, Chairman and Chief Executive Officer, Ford Motor Company

- Flora Walker, President, Michigan Council 25, American Federation of State, County, and Municipal Employees

- Geneva Williams, President, United Community Services of Metropolitan Detroit

The facing page listed dozens of volunteers from each committee, starting with Coordinator Victoria (Tory) Inniss and Assistant Coordinators Paul J. Piper, Leona Stallworth, Renée T. Walker, and Anisa Ward. No city dollars paid for Inaugural events. Instead, costs were financed by ticket sales, corporate and business sponsorships, and volunteer work.

In addition, we published an official program, made of a heavy cardstock, that was decorated with a gold cover with black script on the front: *1994 Detroit Inaugural Swearing-In Ceremony.*

BECOMING MAYOR ON MY 52ND BIRTHDAY

The booklet read "Happy Birthday, Dennis" on Saturday, January 1, 1994, to mark a pre-Inaugural event hosted by Inaugural co-chairs Emmett R. Baylor Jr., Liz Jackson, and many volunteers.

"Detroit kicks off with a traditional New Year's feast" read the headline. A celebratory mood filled the Riverfront ballroom of Cobo Hall. The food was outstanding: baked ham, turkey, macaroni and cheese, collard greens, and black-eyed peas — which are good luck in the Southern tradition when eaten on New Year's Day — candied yams, mashed potatoes and gravy, stuffing, corn muffins, apple pie, and sweet potato pie. Ten sheet cakes were decorated with my photo and "Happy Birthday" as well as "Detroit for All, All for Detroit." Those attending, while too many to list, included Ike McKinnon, Reggie Turner, Cathy Nedd, U.S. Senator Carl Levin, Councilwomen Sheila Cockrel, Kay Everett, and Maryann Mahaffey.

DAY TWO OF THE INAUGURAL EVENTS

Nearly 1,200 people convened at the Detroit Institute of Arts on January 2 for the First Lady's Luncheon called "A Salute to Detroit's First Lady, The Honorable Trudy DunCombe Archer."

The event — co-chaired by Akua Budu-Watkins and Aretha Marshall, with help from Eleanor DunCombe and Lanie Pincus — began in the auditorium. It was a wonderful display of Detroit's finest: Bates Academy String Orchestra played four songs; Soloist Damon Dandridge gave a stunning performance of *Lift Every Voice and Sing;* the Renaissance Men's Ensemble sang; and the Detroit-Windsor Dance Academy also performed. Facing an audience that included Democratic State Senator Debbie Stabenow from Lansing and Democratic gubernatorial candidate Howard Wolpe, Trudy pledged to champion the cause of children.

"There are far too many of our children who are living in a dysfunctional environment through no fault of their own, and they are lacking in love," she said. "I ask you to help me put our children first, and to extend yourself." After her remarks, she received a giant bouquet of flowers, as I stood up from the front row and blew her a kiss. Lunch followed in the Prentis Court, where the tables were adorned with pink rose centerpieces.

That evening, the Inaugural Sponsors' Dinner at Joe Muer's Restaurant celebrated our sponsors, while some of Detroit's finest restaurants — including Opus One, Roma Café, The Rattlesnake Club, Van Dyke Place, and The Whitney — presented culinary creations. This lovely event was organized by co-chairs Julia D. Darlow and Elliott S. Hall.

The night did not end there by any means. Chair Marie Scruggs Inniss arranged for an Inaugural Concert at the New Masonic Temple Theatre starring Ray Charles, The Contours, and Mary Wilson of the Supremes. Amyre Makupson, a news anchor at WKBD-TV Fox 50, served as the Mistress of Ceremonies. More than 5,000 people attended what Councilwoman Kay Everett called "a Hollywood premiere for the Archer administration," as the music celebrated Detroit's golden era of Motown. The who's who crowd included Reverend Jesse Jackson; Harry Pearce and his wife, Kathy; and cable TV businessman Don Barden and his wife, Bella Marshall, who had been Mayor Young's finance director.

DAY THREE OF INAUGURAL CELEBRATION: THE SWEARING-IN & FORMAL BALLS

Expressing our gratitude for this new spirit of cooperation sweeping our city was the focus of an interdenominational prayer breakfast at Cobo Hall. Reverend Jesse Jackson gave the keynote, followed by a prayer for Detroit by Reverend William Holly of Detroit's New Rising Star Baptist Church. Representatives from several religions led prayers, including: a prayer for families and children by Imam Abdullah El-Amin of The Muslim Center of Detroit; a prayer for unity by Rabbi Noah Gamze of the Downtown Jewish Synagogue; and a prayer for me, the new mayor, by our priest, Father James F. Lotze, S.J., from Gesu Church, a Catholic, Jesuit Parish.

Chaired by Virginia W. Wadsworth and Timothy O. Winn, the event featured performances by The Clark Sisters and a welcome from Michigan Governor John Engler. After my remarks, the breakfast closed with a benediction by Carol Dixon of Going Forth Ministries.

From there, we headed to the Ecumenical/Interfaith Service at Blessed Sacrament Cathedral, which was packed with leaders and everyday people representing many religious denominations.

Following a welcome by Monsignor James P. Robinson of Blessed Sacrament, Imam Mitchell Shamsud-Din led a call to prayer, followed by words of faith by Archbishop Adam J. Maida of the Archdiocese of Detroit. Reverend Ruth Mosley, Pastor of West Side Unity Church, led a Litany for Peace.

One of the most poignant photographs of the day, which is framed and displayed in our home, shows me kneeling at the altar with my hands extended while the Renaissance High School Choir performed. The local newspapers published this photo which Trudy describes as "a very powerful image that is still embedded in my memory."

Rabbi Efry Spectre of the Michigan Board of Rabbis gave an Inaugural Blessing, followed by an Inaugural Prayer by Archbishop Maida and all religious leaders. The words of faith and prayer continued as Dr. Frederick G. Sampson, Pastor of Tabernacle Missionary Baptist Church, spoke next.

THE BIG EVENT:
THE INAUGURAL SWEARING-IN AT THE FOX THEATRE

The euphoria of my election victory culminated in an indescribably electrifying feeling in the Fox Theatre on the morning of Monday, January 3, 1994. About 5,000 people from every walk of life filled the ornate theatre, including local and national dignitaries, urban and suburban residents, and people of every age, race, and ethnicity.

Mr. and Mrs. DunCombe, Beth and Joe, and Elsie Fondren, who had been with us since shortly after Denny was born, were in the audience, along with my campaign staff, as well as countless friends and colleagues. Local and national media, including C-SPAN, gathered to broadcast the event live, and to file news reports for publication and broadcast around the world.

The program began with the Detroit City Council members taking their oath of office: President Maryann Mahaffey, President Pro Tempore Gil Hill, Clyde Cleveland, Sheila M. Cockrel, Kay Everett, Nicholas Hood III, Mel Ravitz, Brenda M. Scott, and Alberta Tinsley-Williams.

One of my favorite moments during the three-day Inauguration celebration in 1994: kneeling at the altar of Blessed Sacrament Cathedral during a multi-faith service attended by thousands of people and led by a cornucopia of faith leaders. This photograph is framed and displayed in our home.

Photo Credit: The Detroit News

The Honorable Margie Braxton, a Judge in Recorder's Court, swore in City Clerk Jackie L. Currie. The City Clerk designated the President and Pro Tem of the City Council, after which City Council President Mahaffey spoke, giving an excellent farewell message to Mayor Young.

The Detroit Symphony Orchestra performed and Detroit's own Queen of Soul Aretha Franklin gave a soul-shuddering rendition of *Lift Every Voice And Sing*.

As we walked on stage as a family, Trudy carried a red Bible. I stood with her, Denny, and Vincent at the podium, where City Council President Mahaffey shook my hand. Then I raised my right hand, facing The Honorable Anna Diggs Taylor of the United States District

Court, Eastern District of Michigan, and The Honorable Michael F. Cavanagh, Justice, Michigan Supreme Court.

They swore me in, speaking my oath of office in unison, and I repeated after them: "I, Dennis Wayne Archer, do solemnly swear that I will support the constitution of the United States and the constitution of the state of Michigan and that I will faithfully discharge the duties and responsibilities of the office of mayor of Detroit to the best of my ability, so help me God."

"Congratulations," they said, shaking my hand. As the audience thundered with applause and cheers, I kissed Trudy, then hugged Vincent and Denny. Denny went to the podium and spoke:

When I woke up this morning, I had butterflies in my stomach because I realized that I had to come speak before you today. But having gone to the prayer breakfast and listening to the prolific Rev. Jesse Louis Jackson this morning, and then going to the ecumenical service and hearing again from Dr. Frederick G. Sampson of Tabernacle Missionary Baptist Church, I'm ready.

On October 27th, I drove from Ann Arbor to Detroit for the last time to work on my father's campaign. It was Wednesday and there was less than a week left to what had been the most stressful and trying period of my life. For the past four nights, I had not been able to fall asleep in my dorm. I later found out that my mother was also having problems sleeping. It was not surprising. But that night, I was back in my own room in my own bed and I was able to fall asleep. I had a dream that night. My father had been elected mayor and I was introducing him at his victory party. I told no one of this dream until now.

While others discussed victory celebrations, what we would do for the inauguration, and how our lives were going to be different, I chose to focus on the reality of the close race at hand. I thought of asking my aunt to allow me to speak at the victory party, but I decided against it for fear of jinxing my father. He never takes anything for granted, why should I?

November 3rd has come and gone. My dream is now reality. Dad won — we had a wonderful celebration. A couple of weeks later I called my aunt at home late one night and asked her if I could introduce Dad

United States District Judge Anna Diggs Taylor and Michigan Supreme Court Justice
Michael F. Cavanagh administer my oath of office.   Photo Credit: Bill Sanders

at the swearing in. She promised to get back with me. After a while,
when I hadn't heard anything, and became caught up in my finals,
I forgot about it. Then five days ago my father said they were taking
away two of his 12 minutes so that I could make my comments. I was
suddenly speechless. What would I say? What if I cried?

Well, I'm here today and I suppose my topic should be my father,
his success, and our city's future. Booker T. Washington, in his book
Up From Slavery said, 'To be successful, grow to the point where
one completely forgets himself — that is, to lose himself in a great
cause.' I stand before you today, the son of a lost man —

The audience exploded with applause. Trudy and I and Vincent
were fighting tears, and my heart swelled with pride.

— lost in the dreams and aspirations of our children, lost in the
despair and plight of our homeless and disenfranchised, and lost in
the possibilities and potential of the city he now leads.

While he is lost, Detroit has made a great find. You have found a
man who will dedicate his life to you. You have found a man who will
relate to all of you, who will listen to all of you, and who will include all
of you. I know this to be true because he has been a remarkable father.

The whole time he spoke, I was rubbing Denny's back. Everyone was fighting back tears.

Many of you ask, "How will he do this?" Deborah McGriff, in an Aug. 25, 1991, Free Press article said that "To be successful, you need to embrace change, learn to work with others, and make good choices." Well, Detroit, we have most definitely embraced change. As a matter of fact, we have demanded it and expect it. Rest assured it will come.

Will he work with others? I will let you be the judge of that. We had 6,000 campaign volunteers representing every race, religion, culture, and tax bracket. We will need assistance from both city and suburb — and since November 2nd, my father has been to the White House twice, to meet with the governor twice, and he has met with numerous religious and community groups here in the city.

Making good choices, that's an easy one. Akua Budu-Watkins, Emmett Baylor, Freman Hendrix, Ike McKinnon, Mike Sarafa, to name a few, all appointees. They are black, white, Hispanic, Lebanese, women, men, and all with impeccable resumes. All good choices. If Ms. McGriff's point to us was success is indeed an indicator, we are off to a good start.

And finally, to those who are asking whether the campaign had or will take my father away from our family, I answer a resounding no! As a matter of fact, I thank Detroit for this campaign for our city. It brought my father and me even closer. Because I know what kind of father he is, I know what kind of mayor he will be. Congratulations, Detroit! You are very lucky!

There wasn't a dry eye in the place as the audience stood up for a long, loud, standing ovation. I was overwhelmed with pride and emotion. Vincent reached over and rubbed Denny's head, and they hugged. This affectionate gesture broke the tension, rousing laughter. We had a huge family embrace.

"It was crazy," recalls Vincent, who was 20. "It was hard to see my brother get choked up."

Then, as I took the podium alone, I wiped my eyes and told the audience, "We have somewhat of a sensitive family."

I began with Psalms 127-1: *Except the Lord build the house, they labour in vain that build it: Except the Lord keep the city the watchman waketh but in vain.*

Welcome friends to a new day in Detroit. We are here today — men, women, and children — black and white — Jew, Gentile, Christian, Muslim, Chaldean, and Asian — through the grace of a freedom born in the dreams and won through the efforts of those who came before. They have left us a full and colorful history. Full — but not complete.

Now the task is ours to decide what we will do with this legacy and the new challenges that lay before us. We have the vision — we have the will — we have the determination to make this community what we want it to be.

Fifty-two years ago, I was born on the East Side of Detroit, to parents who were proud but poor. And I can only imagine how daunting the road to this moment would have looked to them. My mom and dad are no longer alive, but my two uncles, James and Warren Garner, my parents by marriage, James and Eleanor DunCombe, my closest friend and Trudy's sister, C. Beth DunCombe and her husband, Joe Brown, represent my close family unit outside of my wife, Trudy, and our sons, Dennis Jr. and Vincent.

So, if I'm optimistic about our future today, it's in part because of the road I've traveled, and because of the lesson my parents taught me through their example: That hard work and determination can overcome great obstacles and break down barriers that seem insurmountable. Barriers to the election of an African American mayor at one time seemed to be insurmountable.

But one tough and inspired leader broke those barriers down, and has spent the last 20 years in service to this city and its people. Today, as we launch a new chapter, we cannot forget the contribution of a truly monumental figure in Detroit's history, Coleman A. Young.

The audience responded with rousing applause.

Thank you, Mr. Mayor. You're a tough act to follow. And I have no illusions about the difficulties that lie ahead. For Detroit to do better, we first must be willing to believe that we can do better, we must believe again in ourselves — and in our city.

I'm here today because I believe so strongly that, with great effort and a new spirit of openness and cooperation, we can meet the challenges we face as a city. We are all here today because we love Detroit.

When these next four years are history, let it be said that, together, we helped make Detroit safer and stronger. But most of all, let it be said that we helped restore hope that Detroit's future will indeed be bright. City government must play a central role in that process. And it begins with one, simple commitment: We will provide to the citizens of this city the basic services which they demand and to which they are entitled.

In what some have described as the excitement of a preacher at a revival, my voice crescendoed as I proceeded, gesturing with my hands and arms to emphasize each point.

We will pick up the garbage —

The crowd cheered loudly.

— light the street lamps and, yes, put more police on the streets, in order to restore public confidence and a decent quality of life for our people.

The audience applauded.

I look forward to working with our great city employees, those represented by unions and those not represented by unions, and each and every member of City Council to provide quality services to every neighborhood. That is something people have a right to demand of their government, and something a responsive government must deliver.

While we are faced with a budget shortfall of extraordinary proportions, a deficit we must confront openly and honestly, we cannot, however, deprive the people of Detroit — our valued customers — the services they need.

In the areas of finance and budgeting, we indeed face numerous significant and difficult challenges. In the short term, we must "fix" the current financial situation. On the revenue side, the tax burden is already too high in addition to being at the legal limit in most areas. On the expenditure side, the city has been spending more than it takes in, and it must stop.

We must manage more with less. We'll need to cut spending and become more productive in all areas. We'll be calling on all parties to contribute their fair share to the solution of expenditure reductions. Everything must be and will be reevaluated. Specifically, it is my plan to hold taxes, cut spending, seek efficiencies, perhaps sell certain assets, and refinance certain debt. The plan must be in place by the deadline for budget submission in April. We must develop a comprehensive, workable, economic revival and development plan. We must set priorities and utilize all of our great physical and geographic resources along with our political and economic influence.

If we do not take the hard steps now, then we must accept the choice of not having a future.

That is a choice I will not accept!

But let us not expect nor promise too much, and fuel the cynicism so many of our people already feel. The truth is that city government alone cannot solve all of Detroit's problems. We can and we will work, day and night, to improve the economic climate and attract more investment to our city. But we, in turn, must ask the business community to match its encouraging words of support with tangible commitments that create real jobs.

For this great crusade to redeem our city to succeed, everyone must pitch in. I am going to make the revitalization of our neighborhoods one of my highest priorities. However, every citizen must take responsibility. Everyone who has an interest in Detroit must do their part. Sweep the sidewalk in front of your house.

Cheers and clapping exploded throughout the Fox Theatre.

Clean the rubbish from the storm sewer on your street.

The applause got louder.

Pick up the broken glass in your alley. Go with your neighbors to cut the weeds in the lot down the way on your street. Demand! Demand that I get the trash picked up — on time. Insist that I make the buses run — on time. Let yourself see that our police and our firefighters and our emergency medical workers are working hard on our behalf. Recognize their contribution. Praise it. Help them do their jobs. Demand that I see to it that they do it right.

Get a grip on your life, and the lives of your children!

The audience thundered with applause and whistles during a standing ovation.

With them rests the destiny or the destruction of our community. In their hands is the future of our society.

My voice became increasingly loud and impassioned, as I raised my hands for emphasis.

Stand with me when I tell the dope man: Get off our streets! Leave our children alone! Get out of our way! We're taking back our children! We're taking back our streets!

People were cheering, clapping, crying. And I was exhilarated with faith and spiritual energy that would enable me to make these promises a reality.

With all of us standing together — believe me when I say this — hear me — and believe it. We will prevail. Through greater cooperation between the police and the community, we can begin to roll back this tidal wave of crime.

We can and we must provide better alternatives for our children. Through a greater cooperation between our schools and churches and, most importantly, parents throughout our city, can we truly save our most precious resource — our children.

To our friends in neighboring communities, I say that you, too, have a great stake in Detroit's future, as we are the hub of this region. You benefit from our assets as a city, and you cannot wall off our problems. You have much to offer us, and we have much to offer you. In recognition of these mutual interests, I extend a warm hand of cooperation and look forward to productive ways in which we might work closely together, in a spirit of mutual respect.

In that same spirit, I say to the governor and legislative leaders that we are ready to make the case for Detroit because Michigan has a huge stake in the future of its greatest city. We ask only for what is fair and just. Help Detroit help itself, and you will have made a great investment in Michigan's future.

For Detroiters, I ask you to reach out. Talk to your neighbor. Reach out. See who needs some help — and give it. Reach out when you need some help. Believe that someone cares. Believe that help is coming. See it when it's offered. Accept it when it comes. Give it back to the next one who can use a hand. Reach out your hand. See? That takes you halfway to the person next to you.

Reach out from Jefferson/Chalmers — to Brightmoor from Clark Park to Palmer Park — from the river to the Fairgrounds. Reach out across Woodward Avenue that, for too long, has divided Eastsiders from Westsiders. Reach out across Eight Mile Road — across Telegraph —across our beautiful river — an asset too long wasted. Tell our friends in Birmingham — in Dearborn — in Mount Clemens — in Windsor — we're in this thing together — and we're in it for the long haul — each tied to the other in ways we can't deny, even if we wanted to.

Very few people have felt the thrill I experienced today, taking office as mayor of this great city. And with that thrill comes a profound sense of gratitude — to the thousands of volunteers and supporters who helped make this day possible; to my wonderful wife, Judge Trudy DunCombe Archer, and our spectacular sons, Dennis and Vincent.

I have been truly blessed to be the instrument of a great movement. But I know that with honor comes responsibility — the responsibility to work as hard as I know how to achieve our shared vision of a Detroit on the mend and on the move. A Detroit where our streets are once again safe and our children and senior citizens are secure. A Detroit where good jobs abound, and our people have the education and training to fill them. A Detroit where all of us live together

in an atmosphere of trust and cooperation. A Detroit that is known
and appreciated the world over.

As I close — I ask you today to put your hand in my hand.

Take the hand of the person next to you. Stand up. Stand hand
in hand — side by side. Lift your spirit. Raise your hopes. Come with
me. Ain't nothin' going to stop us now!

Detroit for all and all for Detroit! *I shouted.*

A standing ovation thundered through the Fox Theatre, and I
could not have felt more excited or determined to make Detroit the
comeback city of the millennium.

REFLECTIONS ON THE INAUGURAL SPEECHES

"It was very emotional," Trudy says. "Aretha sang, and it was
just absolutely wonderful — I got chills. Then when Denny took the
podium to speak, I didn't know what he was going to say. It was
all new. It was very emotional. Very sincere. And the audience just
erupted. That's what brought tears of joy and tears of pride."

Denny says his passion for quotes inspired his speechwrit-
ing method. "I collect books of quotations, so I read quotes, then
thought of words: 'leader, family, loyalty, commitment.' Then I went
to quote books and looked up the words, and I wrote the speech
around the quotes."

Prior to the event, Denny practiced his speech at our home in front
of me, David Axelrod, and a teleprompter. He believed the emotional
rehearsal would enable him to stay calm on Inauguration Day.

"I gave the speech," he recalls, "and I started bawling. Everybody
was bawling. I was thinking, 'This is not cool. I'm on live TV crying.
This is embarrassing.' It was a surreal moment. I was proud to do it.
Originally, there was no plan to have one of the kids speak. I wasn't
nervous or excited. I didn't understand the magnitude. I'm not shy
talking to people; my concern was keeping it together. I knew the
campaign supporters would be in the room. When I spoke, my family was behind me, and I couldn't see the audience."

The real impact struck immediately afterward, when Denny
walked up the aisle of the Fox to leave. "All these people came up

to me," he says. "At that point, I still don't think it's a big deal. I was thinking, 'Oh they must've dug it,' because these strangers were so emotional and hugging me. When I started seeing the news, *Jet*, *Ebony*, then I started realizing that the impact that the speech had on people was a lot bigger than I knew."

David Axelrod recalls that the ceremony highlighted Dennis Jr. and Vincent as "a great reflection on their parents. We all hope to raise children with good values, strong character, and who are successful. They were, and they had inculcated that value system from their folks."

Trudy remembers: "Dennis received e-mails, letters, and calls from people who had lived in Detroit — he didn't know them — from Italy and other parts of the world who had seen it. They were so proud of Denny and said how proud he should be about such a wonderful tribute to his dad."

She believes the audience's standing ovation occurred because I had the courage to say what so many were thinking. "When Dennis said pick up the paper in front of your house, the people applauded loudly because they too believed that sentiment, and some of them would be reluctant to say that. He said it, and people were in support of him. They were there for Dennis, and because he had a vision for what they wanted the city they loved to be, he represented their hope."

Inaugural Luncheon Celebrates Elected Officials

President Clinton welcomed elected officials via videotape to this luncheon at the Detroit Institute of Arts, where Governor John Engler welcomed government leaders, including U.S. Senator Don Riegle, U.S. Senator Carl Levin, and Congressman John Dingell. At this private event, Congressman George Crockett emceed and Reverend Jim Holley gave the invocation before lunch. Co-chaired by Freman Hendrix, Thomas Lewand, and Carol Walters, the luncheon enabled me to thank my supporters and emphasize the importance of working together across partisan lines, geographical boundaries, and historic divisions.

Children's Inaugural Party
Offers Food and Fun

Wearing festive dresses and suits, hundreds of children and their families converged on the Detroit Historical Museum for an event featuring food, art, and music.

Co-chaired by Detroit Superintendent David L. Snead and Detroit School Board Member April Howard Coleman, the event included fun activities organized by teachers Carolyn Baltimore, Carmen N'Namdi, and Mary Turner. The children enjoyed face painting, caricature artists, and a puppet show, as well as performances by a mariachi band, a Greek musician, an accordion player, and a Suzuki violin. A magician and storytellers entertained, and the kids watched a video of Mayor Archer called, *The Boy Who Would Be Mayor.*

Honoring a Campaign Promise to
Dance with a Senior Supporter

When I entered the Ambassador Ballroom in Cobo Hall at 4:00 p.m. for the Big Band Memories: A Senior Gala, I was looking forward to the first dance. Trudy was not with me; she was getting ready for the formal Inaugural Balls that evening.

However, she was overjoyed that I was about to honor a campaign promise to save the first dance for Iona Echols, whom I had met while campaigning among Detroit's seniors. The newspapers photographed us dancing to the Bob Hopkins Band, as people surrounded us, clapping. Ms. Echols wore a beautiful, sparkling turquoise dress and I wore my tux.

I loved the Senior Gala, chaired by Deierdre L. Weir, because I felt a special bond with the many senior citizens I met on the campaign trail. As mayor, I was eager to make changes so they would feel safe and celebrated in a city that too many had grown to fear.

Enjoying the Inaugural Dinner Dance
and Inaugural Ball

The Inaugural Dinner Dance began with cocktails and music by Alexander Zonjic. The 1,800 people attending enjoyed a delicious dinner of smoked shrimp and scallops with crispy onions, baby greens with tomato chutney, filet mignon with salmon rosette on a bed of roasted pepper and tarragon, and white chocolate terrine with wild cranberry sauce.

Governor Jim Blanchard gave a champagne toast, after which Trudy and I led off the dancing with music provided by the Duke Ellington Band and the Johnny Trudell's Band. Trudy had selected a beautiful, emerald green satin and black lace gown for this very special night. Her childhood friend, Miriam Martin-Clark, chaired this event. "The dinner, and the dance, were elegant," Trudy says. "Every detail was perfect."

Next, Trudy and I headed to the Riverfront Ballroom at Cobo Center for the Inaugural Ball: "A Taste of Detroit." Jimmy McKee and the Upsetters, and a special performance by the Spinners, kept 3,000 people jamming into the night. One special moment occurred when Trudy and I, along with hundreds, danced to our victory theme song, *Aint No Stoppin' Us Now*. Wilson Copeland and Mary Kay Piper chaired this outstanding event. They know how to throw a party.

"It was a whirlwind," Trudy says. "We had been up since 6:00 a.m. and were still going strong. I was very, very proud of Dennis. The entire three days inspired a feeling of pride, and excitement, and joy."

YOUNG PEOPLE CELEBRATE AT THE INAUGURAL JAM

Trudy and I left the Inaugural Ball and headed up Woodward Avenue to the State Theatre, where Denny, Vincent, and their friends, John David Simpson and Tory Inniss, hosted a party for young adults. Dennis Jr., who was 24, and Vincent, who was 20, invited their longtime friends from the city and suburbs. The evening included a video salute to the mayor, as well as performances by Detroit R&B group UNV or Universal Nubian Voices. Music was also provided by Kim James and Stacey "Hot Wax" Hale. Vincent and his friends celebrated with a drive. "We all got in the big limousine," he says, "and rode around Belle Isle because we wanted to do something in the spirit of celebrating Detroit."

Trudy and I dance to our campaign's theme song, Ain't No Stopping Us Now by McFadden & Whitehead, at the Inaugural Ball.
Photo Credit: Bill Sanders

EXTRA INAUGURAL FUNDS REFLECT SUPPORT FOR CHANGE

At the end of the three-day Inaugural celebration, nearly $200,000 in donated funds remained. I thanked Beth for doing an outstanding job as Chairperson of the Inaugural Committee. And I expressed gratitude to the Inaugural Committee and co-chairpersons: Owen

Bieber, Robert Eaton, Iona Echols, John Smith Jr., Myzell Sowell, Alex Trotman, Flora Walker, and Geneva Williams.

Thanks to their diligence in fundraising from corporations, businesses, and individuals to cover the costs of the inauguration itself, we distributed the remaining $185,000 to 29 organizations for homeless people, cultural arts, and scholarships. We also gave $62,000 to the Detroit Compact Scholarship Fund, which provides a tuition-free option to a four-year college degree based on academic standards.

Meanwhile, thousands of people left the inaugural festivities feeling filled with hope and excitement that true change was possible for Detroit. As they hung the official inaugural poster in their homes, businesses, and classrooms, they cultivated the new spirit of cooperation conveyed on the poster. Sold during the festivities for $5, it shows 10 rows of people representing Detroiters, including people dancing, musicians playing instruments, and waiters holding flaming cheese in Greektown.

"The inaugural festivities," Trudy says, "brought together so many people who love Detroit, people from different walks of life. The comments and the warmth gave me the sense you get when you know you're in the midst of something special. There was a feeling like we're all in this together. They were there in support of Dennis and for his visions for the city that they love."

7

AN URBAN OVERHAUL:
CITY HALL, CITY SERVICES, HUMAN RESOURCES, MUNICIPAL FINANCE, PHILANTHROPY

"THE PACE WAS FRENETIC; CRISIS MANAGEMENT WAS CONSTANT"

MY TEAM HIT THE GROUND RUNNING on Tuesday, January 4, 1994, for a marathon budget meeting. It was imperative that we resuscitate the city's finances, which had been deprived of a healthy cash flow for decades. A fresh influx of cash would pump new life into our crippled city services and fractured infrastructure.

As we worked through the day in a conference room on the eleventh floor of the City-County Building, hundreds of the world's automotive leaders, car enthusiasts, and international journalists were assembling two long blocks down Jefferson Avenue at Cobo Hall. They were in town for the Motor City's most important business and social event: the North American International Auto Show.

This two-week extravaganza is our sparkling crown jewel. It begins with Press Week, which is highlighted by press conferences, receptions, and unveilings of new car models as well as sleek concept cars, for the world's TV, radio, and print journalists to showcase across America and around the globe. Press Week always concluded on Friday evening with the black-tie Charity Preview, where the world's leading automotive executives, as well as leaders from business, government, the clergy, community groups, and others gathered to toast the industry that was synonymous with Detroit.

The following day, the Auto Show officially opens to the public, with tens of thousands of people entering Cobo Center's exhibition hall to check out concept cars and the automakers' latest models. The world is watching Detroit during the Auto Show, and I was thrilled to set the tone that we were on the road to becoming the world-class city promised by my administration.

Also during my inaugural week, the global spotlight focused on Detroit because we were hosting the U.S. Figure Skating Championships at Cobo Arena. Many of the competitors were preparing for the upcoming Winter Olympics in Lillehammer, Norway. On Thursday, January 6, figure skater Nancy Kerrigan, who had won an Olympic medal in 1992, was practicing at Cobo Arena. After leaving the ice, she entered a corridor flanked by spectator seats. Out of nowhere, someone whacked her right knee with a police baton.

"Why, why, why?" she cried, grabbing her knee as attendants helped her. That image and her cries were caught on video that would dominate media reports around the world, doing nothing to improve Detroit's image.

"We both got the call," says Benny Napoleon. "When the attack happened, we were out in the city. We headed over to Cobo Arena and started the investigation. I was Ike McKinnon's number one guy as chief of detectives, in charge of all criminal investigations throughout the city. I became the lead person investigating this international incident. Ike looked at me, and said, 'Okay, you better not mess this up.'"

Ike and Benny called me in the mayor's office.

"We have to go there," I told Judith McNeely. "We have to address this crime in the city and what it means." At Cobo, I met with Ike and Benny, then talked with the skaters.

"He wasn't sitting in his office getting reports back," Judith says. "He was immediately there, front and center, dealing with the problem."

I told Ike and Benny, who interviewed Nancy in the hospital, that we had to solve this crime — quickly. It was a golden opportunity to show that Detroit was serious about fighting crime. Ike and I said exactly that during interviews with the local and national media.

The day after the incident, which was Friday and the final day of Press Week for the Auto Show, I was preparing to approach the podium at the prestigious Economic Club of Detroit's most well-attended luncheon. I was excited to address hundreds of automotive executives, members of the media, and the business elite in Cobo's Riverfront Ballroom. But before I made it to the podium to speak about my strategy for transforming Detroit into the comeback city of the millennium, Judith informed me of another crisis at Cobo.

"We have a major problem with broken pipes," Judith whispered, "and the complex is losing heat."

That would be bad news any day, but this was the worst possible time. That evening, many of the people at this luncheon would gather for the black-tie Charity Preview at Cobo, joining thousands of women in sequined gowns and men in tuxedos to sip champagne amid gleaming vehicles to raise money for children's charities. And the following day, the Auto Show would open to the public.

I made a joke at the podium about another crisis, then immediately left the luncheon to meet with department directors about how to get the heat turned on full force in the building.

"He was unflinching in pulling people together to get this addressed," Judith says. "He got it resolved, and we hosted a successful charity preview. It was an example of strong leadership getting people tasked to resolve challenges. He was incredibly resilient."

Meanwhile, the Kerrigan investigation continued to shine a global media spotlight on Detroit. Benny recalls that, "Every time there was a news report about the Winter Olympics, somebody from the press called me. I got calls from all over the world." Ike and Benny briefed me constantly, and I asked them a lot of questions.

"I think he came to trust us," Benny says, "and we were very capable of doing the things we were asked to do, and we kept him informed."

Ike had a hunch that the perpetrator was not local: "I wondered, 'Why would someone from Detroit hit this woman across the leg?' The national media was all over it. I went on *The Today Show* with Katie Couric and *Good Morning America* with Charles Gibson. The mayor did interviews, too. It let people know we were serious about solving this crime. Our determination showed that Detroit was not a second-class city. I was very clear in my belief that this crime was not specific to Detroit."

Benny received the tip that ultimately solved the case. "I was home in bed, and at 5:00 a.m., I got a phone call from the command center. The caller had said, 'I won't talk to anybody but Benny Napoleon.' My first thought was that this was a false alert, but I talked to the caller, and asked probing questions. I was convinced that she was not just some person rambling. It was true. The next day, Ike and I reported to police headquarters and shared the information with the FBI. They verified the caller's information that the attacker was Shane Stant of Clackamas County, Oregon, and was linked to Kerrigan's skating competitor, Tonya Harding."

Ike continues: "We solved that case within the first week. That unfortunate incident threw the spotlight on the police department, and the results were that the people trusted us. They saw that we were serious about combatting crimes."

That inspired trust in the police department, and affirmed my belief that one of the best appointments I made was naming Isaiah McKinnon as my Chief of Police. By empowering him to choose his executive management team, and go about the business of making Detroit a safe city, I trusted that we would soon see results, and we did. In fact, violent crimes in Detroit decreased 6 percent between 1993 and 1994, and the overall crime rate declined every year that I was in office. My simultaneous ability to increase the recreation department created positive options for our young people.

I was especially proud of Chief McKinnon's commitment to community policing, and utilizing the Gang Squad to reduce gang violence. Ike and Benny demonstrated their success a few months later, when 12 inmates escaped from the medium-security Ryan Correctional Facility on Detroit's west side. The national media covered the story.

"Within a week," Benny says, "we had eight or nine people back in custody. One of the escapees was found dead in an alley on the west side. The mayor was really impressed with the speed at which we closed prominent cases."

That incident inspired the creation of the violent crime task force, which had a significant impact on making our city safer. Meanwhile, breaking news and ongoing investigations only intensified the frenetic pace of the mayor's office.

"Crisis management was constant," Freman recalls. "It was pretty harrowing and relentless, but we adapted to the pace. When you walk into the city of Detroit, there's always a crisis somewhere. A water main break, a shooting, you name it. Everything was laid out in the newspapers in the morning when you walked in."

Back then, the 24/7 live news cycle and the nonstop onslaught of social media had yet to become reality. But e-mails and phone messages did stack up, awaiting responses after 7:00 p.m. when the pace subsided somewhat.

"The office was a beehive," Freman says. "Dennis had a policy of doors open, especially on the heels of the previous administration when everything was bunkered and you couldn't get in unless you knew someone. Dennis came in with a fresh start, no favorites. Anybody who wants a meeting will have a meeting. With all this transparency and openness, we had a constant stream of people in and out of the office, in the lobby area, in the waiting area. It was just always going, going, going."

On many days, I walked visitors from my office suite about 10 steps over to Freman's office and said, "Freman, this is Mr. Jones. He's got this issue. I want him to sit down with you and see if you can help him."

The executive staff was on call 24 hours a day, seven days a week, recalls Greg Bowens, a business journalist who later became my press secretary. "This was not a nine-to-five corporate job. This was a commitment to the people of Detroit. You had to be available to deal with any emergency whenever it happened. No one was allowed to go on a vacation that they could not get back from in 24 to 48 hours." Another rule? "Mayor Archer insisted that we all drive American cars," Greg adds, "because this is, after all, the Motor City."

RUNNING REVS ENERGY FOR
DAILY MARATHON OF MAYORAL DUTIES

When I took office, I was 52 years old, and invigorated to expend every possible ounce of energy on transforming the city of Detroit to achieve its highest potential. My daily regimen included running, stretching, lifting weights, and eating healthy foods.

"Security marveled at how he could come home at 10 or 11 at night, sleep four hours, get up at five in the morning, and run seven-minute miles," Judith says. "He never skipped the run. Dennis had this insatiable desire to exercise every morning. He *ran* Belle Isle. He didn't jog."

I logged three miles every morning, year-round.

"One requirement for executive protection detail was that the men and women had to run with him in the morning," Judith recalls. "It was the bane of their existence. Those who weren't runners had to become runners. Some tried to keep up on bikes. It was funny because the police officers would say, 'Oh my God, Chief, the mayor can run! And he's older than us!'"

Likewise, my Press Secretary Anthony Neely joined me a few times, hoping that we could talk outside of the bustling office.

"Ironically, I am a runner and can easily do three miles," Anthony recalls. "But I was so worn out every day, usually working from eight in the morning until 11 at night, I could barely keep up. Plus, this was his quiet time, and I didn't want to intrude on that."

Quite honestly, my morning jog on the beautiful island park, alongside the river amid trees and geese, was a calming confidence booster. In fact, during the most challenging stretches of my mayoral tenure, my morning run felt like that day's most successful accomplishment. My morning routine continued at home with a light breakfast of orange juice and a bowl of bran cereal, a habit which I continue today. Then I would get to the office by 7:00 or 8:00 a.m.

"No matter how early I got to the office in the morning," Greg recalls, "the mayor was already there."

I worked 16 to 18 hours every day of the week. At times I was exhausted, but never discouraged or overwhelmed. I went into this job with my eyes wide open, and was energized beyond measure by the excitement of so many individuals, community groups, businesses, and government leaders stepping up to become a united catalyst for change.

If somebody invited me to speak or wanted to talk about starting a new business, I was there. If someone opened a little mom-and-pop store, or if they opened a business in a telephone booth for that matter, I would have gone to the ribbon-cutting. I wanted people to know that all businesses were important and that we needed to support them.

"He would go anywhere and talk to anybody," Greg recalls. "If three people wanted to do something good for Detroit, he was game, even though he had serious pressures on his time. Often we'd go places and be the only black people there. For example, it was me, him, Judith, and his driver, Detroit Police Officer Ralph Godbee, when he spoke at the Grosse Pointe Optimist Club in a ballroom at the Grosse Pointe War Memorial, overlooking Lake St. Clair. He talked about investing in Detroit and a couple hundred people gave him a standing ovation. That would happen time and time again, from Detroit to the Upper Peninsula."

Judith was always at my side, taking notes, scheduling meetings and events, and putting me in touch with experts as the need arose.

"He said yes to everything, and after a full day, he could have two or three evening events and stops," she says. "Managing his schedule was daunting. We were all committed. It was more than any of us could have imagined. None of us had any idea what it would be like. We were working on adrenaline, excitement, and commitment. Dennis leads by example. He'll always work you under the table, but he won't ask you to work any harder than he'll work himself."

Every day was different. While my calendar listed that day's scheduled meetings and events, an unexpected incident or development could require my immediate attention for the city, the governor, or the president. When the president called and asked, "Can you come to the White House? We're going to make an announcement, and we'd like you to join us," I rearranged my schedule to go. At the office, unless I was attending a luncheon, my preference was to have a brown bag lunch at my desk so I could keep working. Favorite staples included a corned beef and chopped liver sandwich from Star Deli and the chicken Caesar salad from Silver's Café.

Entering a restaurant as mayor could be quite time-consuming because I wanted to greet everyone and talk about their concerns for the city. At the same time, conducting a business meeting in public was difficult due to the potential of other diners overhearing confidential information. Working through lunch in my office enabled me to maximize my productivity throughout the day.

"Dennis is the hardest worker I've ever known," says Marty Austin, who was my secretary and executive assistant. "I saw other people with a good work ethic, but he had them topped by leaps and bounds. He would never ask anyone to do anything he wouldn't do himself. When we were in the throes of government work, he worked an awful lot of hours, evenings, and weekends. He was right in there working with everyone else, and everyone who worked with him put in tons of hours."

DETROIT'S MASTER PLAN TASK FORCE

Manifesting the goals of *Thoughts for a Greater DETROIT* required building coalitions of accomplished, visionary individuals who had the experience and expertise to rebuild our city. That inspired my selection of members of my Detroit Master Plan Task Force, which was charged with providing a final report to me in May. I assigned Executive Assistant Marge Byington and Planning Department and the Community and Economic Development Department Director Gloria Robinson to work with the Master Plan Task Force, which was composed of a diverse cross section of men, women, and a student.

The members were: David Schervish, architect/developer; Charlene Johnson, community development; Ned Fawaz, community development; Byung Park, community development; Yolanda Gomez-Stupka, community development; Alan Young, community development; Eugene Miller, finance; David Snead, education; Tamara Craig, student; Stephen D'Arcy, business/accounting; Gail Warden, health care/hospitals; Dennis Tuffelo, retailers; Bronce Henderson, industry; James Kokas, restaurants; Joseph Thompson, restaurants; Lawrence Alexander, hotels; Charles Brown, developer; Fred Goldberg, mall developer; John David Simpson, arts; Leon Cohan, arts; Flora Walker, union; C. Beth DunCombe, attorney; Marian Ilitch, business; John Lobbia, utilities; Diane Edgecomb, Central Business District

Association; Harold Varner, architect; Joseph Hudson, foundation; Lawrence Marantette, developer; Robert Larson, developer; Larry Ledebur, higher education; Katherine Beebe, planner; Nellie Varner, business; Liz Jackson, senior; and Charles Allen, finance.

"Dennis demonstrated tireless compassion and commitment to get the job done by surrounding himself with brilliant people to get the job done with innovation and excellence," says Phyllis James. "Dennis always aimed for the sky. He was an aspirational leader who always did it in a way to motivate you to do more."

PHILANTHROPY: PIONEERING A NEW WAY TO FINANCE DETROIT'S FUTURE

Our city's desperate financial state required innovation, which resulted from brilliant ideas from people such as Gilbert Hudson from the Dayton Hudson Foundation. He called me and indicated that he knew of my high regard for foundations through my work on the Community Foundation of Southeastern Michigan. Gilbert said his organization would underwrite the cost of a person to work for the city if that person would report directly to me. I immediately accepted; David Smydra from my transition team was appointed to seek philanthropic support for Detroit's economic resuscitation.

David was no new kid on the block to this sort of endeavor. He understood philanthropy. He was familiar with the local nonprofits. He knew the board presidents of local foundations. He was the best man for the job. Because he was so knowledgeable on a local level, he quickly learned how to find the significant players in the realm of national grants and fundraising. I attribute much of the success of this new partnership to David's ability to hit the ground running, as well as his past work experience, and his connections. This concept was different, as cities needing money historically raised taxes and relied heavily on federal grants. I knew additional dollars were out there, and David was the person to get them for the city.

"I was the first person in the country," David says, "to be used by a mayor for purposes of linking philanthropy and their funding missions to a mayoral agenda for addressing municipal issues."

Over the course of my eight-year administration, David brought in roughly $500 million in new dollars to the city of Detroit. To put it mildly, David was a liaison extraordinaire. He explains, in italics below, how this evolved.

A key issue for the mayor, was bringing in new private dollars from philanthropy and from private interests that would begin to formulate a new downtown and support for neighborhoods in Detroit. That was a very conscious, well-thought-out, strategic approach in which we were able to go ahead and bring philanthropy to the table with large dollars, and corporate interest to the city led by Bob Larsen, who was vice chairman of the Taubman Realty Group. He was a very large supporter of Dennis. Bob's role basically to Dennis was that of being the go-to between Dennis and the broader corporate leadership, so Dennis didn't have to go out one-to-one with everyone. Dennis could go to Bob and say, "This is what we're interested in; what do you think? Can you sway others to do such-and-such?" The decision was made that what we would go aggressively toward was placemaking and structural redevelopment downtown: hence the creation of Campus Martius; the creation of the riverfront development (now Riverfront Conservancy); the demolition of the Hudson's building; the relocation of some of the initial corporations downtown; Blue Cross coming downtown; and the courting of Peter Karmanos of Compuware. These were strategic actions coming out of a steering committee that Dennis put together between himself and top corporate and philanthropic leadership.

When Dennis and Bob Larson were putting together the Detroit Downtown Partnership, it was an important decision. There was no magic. Dennis had a grasp on what philanthropy could do as a partner in municipal rejuvenation. Mayors still don't have a grasp on that. Dennis had the experience of being on the community foundation board prior to being mayor. That exposure helped him when the Hudson Webber Foundation approached him about using me. They gave him a briefing in terms of what the collective philanthropic interest of this region was and how that might come together with corporate funding. That along with his ability

*to attract government funding — and the fact that he was a quick
learner — got it done.*

*It enabled me to be an ambassador with power. I was empowered.
When philanthropists spoke with me, they knew they were speaking
with the mayor. Dennis gave me a free hand. I can't appreciate suf-
ficiently or state strongly enough what an extraordinarily valuable
tool that was. The president of the Robert Wood Johnson Foundation
based in Princeton decided to do a major youth health initiative across
eight cities in the US. They were searching for cities, and their vice
president called me to feel out the interest. He knew that my responses
were the mayor's response.*

*Having that kind of a capacity was the real trick to doing it. It
was common for me to receive three or four calls a day from presidents
of foundations from across the country about ideas that they had for
investing millions of dollars in Detroit. They wanted to know how
to go about it, and how to fit in with other things that were going on.
A major article on me came out in the Chronicle of Philanthropy, the
bible of philanthropy, in 1995 or 1996. That was like sending up a
rocket nationally that Detroit was engaging in a municipal-mayoral
philanthropic partnership that was truly unique. And that was why
we were able to get $500 million.*

*Philanthropy and corporations — based on what they had done
in other locales, such as riverfront development in San Antonio —
were examples that could be readily transformable in concept to
Detroit. The people who wrote the checks were comfortable writing the checks because they'd seen the work; they were willing to
transfer that to Detroit. This was a cornerstone of Dennis' mayoralty. I became one of his speechwriters to articulate and formulate
his agenda going forward to take the initial campaign agenda and
turning campaign promises, if you will, into a reality. I was the
guy down the hall when people were discussing issues, and Dennis
would say, "Let's get David."*

Meanwhile, David attended meetings when I could not, and
from there, we formulated a strategy on how to proceed. His salary
was paid by a conglomerate of Detroit-area grant makers. During

my second term, his salary was incorporated into the city budget: he became a member of the administration.

"Group Executive became my title with responsibilities over all the staff agencies of city government," David says. "I kept this 'Let David do it' role. As one of his speechwriters, I had the responsibility of helping a big-city mayor articulate a vision and substance to rebuild a city."

No More "Pay to Play"

My first Executive Order was that no person in my administration would have to buy or sell any fundraising ticket in exchange for favor, promotions, contracts, or anything else. This abolished the "pay to play" culture. The new policy also confused city employees because they were accustomed to selling tickets to functions. In fact, people had quotas; their stature was determined by their ticket sales.

"You don't need to sell a ticket or buy a ticket to be considered for promotion in this city," I repeated. Likewise, I never met with people who wanted something. If they needed something done, I would bring in a department head who would make it happen if the request was reasonable and fair.

"Whenever Dennis had a fundraiser," Freman says, "people would call and say, 'How many tickets do you want me to buy? I want to buy my tickets from you.' I would answer, 'We're not selling tickets.'"

To combat this practice, Beth oversaw all ticket sales.

"Dennis kept politics very, very separate," Freman says. "He didn't allow that kind of stuff to creep into the day-to-day goings-on of running city government. We had a private fax machine and a private phone in my office that no city budget money paid for. In case I got a political fax, it did not come over the city of Detroit's fax machine. If I took a political phone call, I had the person call me back on a different phone number. We routinely supported other candidates and their fundraising."

Beth organized my fundraisers, and when people called offering support, my response was: "Call Beth. I'm running the city right now."

We made it very clear to the city's employees that we had a zero tolerance for anything lacking integrity and honesty.

"Folks who were used to not following the rules didn't even know what the rules were," Gary says. "We implemented training programs to teach them the rules. Dennis always said, 'If there's a rule, we follow it. If it's broken badly, we have to update it.' Phyllis, Val Johnson, the city Finance Director, and I were constantly echoing Dennis by telling people, 'We have to follow the law and we have to follow the rules, and if the rules are bad, change them.' We also had to educate our vendors, who were used to walking into offices and saying, 'Here's a gift. I'd like this contract.' Dennis said, 'No, that's not how we do business.' I was happy to work for a guy who was full of integrity."

Benny Napoleon emphasized that point, when it came to celebrities and crime.

"After I became Police Chief, one of the things I respected a whole lot about the mayor," he says, "was how he handled famous people, and prominent local folks, who got arrested or in trouble with the police department. Mayor Archer never once would call. If it was someone newsworthy, he'd call and ask me what happened, so he'd be able to say what happened, but he never once asked me to do something untoward in my official capacity as the chief. He never hinted, suggested, asked, inquired, or anything, that would cause me to not go to sleep at night. Instead, he simply said, 'Do what you would normally do,' and that would be the end of it. That was to me a huge measure of the man's character and integrity."

ANOTHER VESTIGE OF DAYS GONE BY:
A "CLOSED DOOR" POLICY

As a bridge-builder, conciliator, and instrument of change for our city, I felt an urgent need to broadcast a loud, clear message that my doors were always open to everyone, and that I was available, visible, and receptive to new ideas to help our city. This included an open relationship with the media, with whom I had built a rapport and relationships during my long campaign.

"Dennis Archer is making quite a show of lifting the veil," wrote Ric Bohy in a February 14, 1994, article in *Crain's Detroit Business* entitled "Blinded by the Light of Archer's Open Door."

The article continued: "He walks the halls of the City-County Building and uses the common restroom. When gripes begin to build about the three-week backlog of uncollected garbage — accompanied by not-so-gentle reminders about a very clear campaign promise — he not only calls a news conference to take the heat, but trots out department heads to do the same. He even has returned reporters' phone calls, personally."

This shocked reporters because Mayor Young's relationship with the media had become so contentious during his final years that he refused to respond to the simplest questions, instead ordering media outlets to file FOIAs, a lengthy and time-consuming legal process involving the Freedom of Information Act, even for the most innocuous information.

Likewise, the Young administration had cultivated a "closed door" policy at city hall — for employees, department heads, and the citizens of Detroit. He had even divulged that he had never visited some floors of the City-County Building.

I was determined to change all of the above. So I implemented several recurring events to show that I was the people's mayor whose doors were always open.

Mayor's Night In

During a visit to Cleveland, Mayor Mike White shared with me one of his secrets to successfully transforming his city from crumbling to successful: "Mayor's Night In." He invited people to visit his office and talk for 10 minutes about the topics of their choice. Department heads attended as well, so if a resident complained about a pothole, or garbage not picked up, or nonworking streetlights, the head of the appropriate department could address the problem right away.

I was excited to host my first Mayor's Night In in the mayor's conference room. One problem: I forgot to consult the *TV Guide*. I had scheduled our event for the night of the NCAA basketball finals! However, Detroiters were undaunted; so many people attended the 6:00 p.m. event that we did not finish until I had spoken with the final person at 12:30 a.m.

The crowds at the next Mayor's Night In became so large, we held the ongoing events in the 13th floor auditorium of the City-County Building. I also hosted Town Hall meetings throughout the city for many years.

"Those of us on staff knew Mayor Archer's commitment to the poorest, most disenfranchised residents of the city," recalls Anthony Neely, my Press Secretary and one of my speech writers. "It was clear to me as I watched him at evening town hall meetings around the city. He would make a detailed presentation about improvements underway, then field an hour of questions from the audience, and afterward, he would patiently listen to a dozen people who stood in line to speak to him, one by one. He would call over a department director — or me — and ask us to take notes about what the person's problem was, then promise the person that the mayor's office would follow up. I can guarantee that by 8:00 or 9:00 p.m., I was exhausted. But he seemed to be able to stand there and deal with repetition, uninformed questions and comments, and tedious details until the cows came home."

Meetings with Employees

We replicated this free flow of ideas and communication that we enjoyed with citizens during Mayor's Night In — by doing the same with employees in each city department.

This evolved after Nettie Seabrooks suggested that I visit every city department during my first year and conduct a "diagonal slice" meeting with employees without the presence of the director or deputy director whom I had appointed. Instead, employees met with me and Judith, who took notes.

"What are we not doing that would make the city better able to serve the people?" I asked. "What tools do you need to provide the best services for the public? How can we improve our services?"

My questions provoked blank stares and elusive chatter among many employees, who at first were nervous and fearful. The concept of open, honest communication and problem-solving — while sitting face-to-face with the mayor — was such a foreign concept, many employees sat for a good 15 minutes without saying much of anything. So I assured them: "We're here because this is our city and we care about our city."

"And we're not writing your names down," Judy said. "We're writing your thoughts and ideas down."

"If you'd rather not talk," I said, "just send me a letter with your ideas."

Then something clicked, and *whoomph!* they relaxed and unleashed their ideas.

Arbitration

Many employees were reluctant to speak openly and honestly with me because they were furious about long-delayed arbitrations. Their complaints and labor disputes had festered for months, even years, intensifying their anger and hindering their ability to cultivate a productive work environment.

So I called upon Flo Walker, president of the American Federation of State, County & Municipal Employees (AFSCME) Union, and my HR Director, Gary Dent, to resolve this problem.

I held a meeting at Cobo Hall on a Saturday and vowed to stay as long as necessary to hear every employee's complaint.

Nearly 2,000 people showed up! They came, and we listened to an earful of complaints and problems. We hosted three more events, each drawing increasingly smaller crowds.

"Hundreds of people would come and stand in line," Gary recalls. "They'd never sat one-on-one with a mayor of Detroit. And they were just amazed to have the mayor turn to the human resources or facilities or police person and say, 'Fix this problem.' On top of that, Mayor Archer would write the person back. It was astounding! People really loved that about Dennis."

At the conclusion of our meetings, when we believed we had heard everything, we got to work resolving the problems. Gary and Flo addressed the unresolved arbitrations by making a joint application to the U.S. Department of Labor to fund a project that would reduce management-labor strife. This endeavor later proved so successful, starting at the end of my first year in office, that Gary and Flo were invited to the Harvard Business School to share how they conceived and mastered the program to successfully resolve the city's horrific backlog of arbitrations.

All the while, Gary unearthed a plethora of problems that we worked aggressively to resolve.

"I could not fathom how employees were treated so poorly and still came to work every day," says Gary, who now lives in Cincinnati and runs his own consulting company. "I always give the employees of Detroit huge credit for turning the city around once we started listening to them and hearing from them through the suggestion program and getting things done."

OVERHAULING A HUMAN RESOURCES MESS

Culture shock is a polite way of describing Gary Dent's reaction to the bureaucratic debacle that greeted him as our Human Resources Director. His experience and expertise were honed at General Motors, one of the world's largest corporations, where efficiency and military-precise business policies and procedures had enabled GM to dominate the global economy for many years.

Detroit presented perhaps the polar opposite of that, Gary says, yet a glorious sense of accomplishment when our innovative teamwork resolved seemingly impossible problems in ways that attracted national praise — all within a matter of years.

Human Resources Problem #1:
More Than 50 Unions!

The first startling thing was that Detroit had more than 50 unions. Gary was shocked. General Motors had the UAW. In Dayton, there were the United Rebel Workers, Electrical Workers, et cetera. The city of Detroit had the American Federation of State, County & Municipal Employees (AFSCME). It had 50 unions with 110 bargaining agreements. These people were working for the city and not being taken care of.

"Coleman Young had brought on people who were not city employees," Gary recalls. "They were on the payroll, but not all of them had gone through the civil service process. They were brought in to sell tickets for Coleman Young and to do his bidding. I was told, 'Gary, you have to fix that problem.'"

Gary remembers that he had to respect the fact that some of these folks had been on the payroll for a decade or more. "But they had to come off," he says. "I went back to Dennis and said, 'Here's the answer: with 10 and 20 years on the payroll, we're going to have to understand and respect it.' I convinced Dennis to allow these people to take the civil service test and whatever job they qualified for, they should apply and receive that job, assuming a vacancy."

I agreed with his strategy, and believed we owed these city employees the respect they deserved for their long-term service to the city of Detroit. They were able to take the civil service exams and fill vacant jobs for which they were qualified. Fortunately, we were able to keep them at their current salaries.

Gary recalls, "That was the most notable bad experience for me. What Dennis had to do — he cared for people — it wasn't their fault, but he needed to correct it. It took me about eight months to resolve that. I had to go to each of the 50 unions, and say, 'This happened under your watch. You're as much at fault because you let people be in the unions.' They did work with us and gave us the opportunity to put people into jobs by the rule."

Human Resources Problem #2:
DO-WOP, and it wasn't the Motown Sound

Gary says the second thing that startled him working with the city was, "Do-Wop. Not the Motown sound. This was Days Off Without Pay. Lots of city employees were working and being paid below what their contract required. They were told that they were to work, but would not be paid for day-to-day work, particularly those in management. If they were scheduled to work five days, they'd work four days and not be paid for the fifth day."

Gary came to me, and filled me in on this problem. "We have to understand," he said. "We have federal laws. We can't force people to work overtime and not pay them if they're not exempt."

"Tell me what we need to do," I said.

"In order to get that done," Gary says now, "Phyllis James became my best buddy. I would always go to her and say, 'Explain the law on this to Dennis.' She would talk to her labor lawyers, and tell Dennis he was right. We couldn't go to these people and not pay them appropriately."

During staff meetings, I expressed my amazement at what was going on.

"We gotta fix this problem," I said. So I talked to directors and told them we had to find savings and use the savings to pay people for the work they've done. Then I told Phyllis and Gary to get this done.

"Dennis, through this hard work, was able to restore the pay to bring people back to where they should've been and to have them work the five days that their labor agreements called for. Dennis trusted me," Gary says. "Trust and verify. Phyllis would verify that the law and labor agreements were being followed. That took us about two years to finally get all of that resolved and to get people paid and assure the governance that we were back within following the law and labor agreements. I admire Phyllis," Gary says now. "She was right there as a person of integrity who worked for the mayor."

Human Resources Problem #3:
Carbon Paper and Typewriters!

Gary was astounded by the city's archaic practices and crippling culture. The first item he was asked to sign was a requisition for carbon paper.

"Why are you bringing me this?" he asked. "And why are you using carbon paper?"

The employee showed him a used stack of carbon paper.

"When we hire a clerk," the employee said, "we put carbon paper between the sheets and press down really hard to make copies so 15 people can sign the hiring document."

Gary thought it was foolish to expend all that effort to hire a clerk. So he made a big speech to his staff about doing things correctly in a technically competent way, and that we had to get into the 20th century.

Then he came to me and physically walked me through a hiring contract. He showed me the individual people who had to sign the contract before we could hire a clerk, and that all those people had to press through this carbon matrix to get it signed.

"You're kidding, right?" I asked.

Gary was not kidding. He assembled a group of employees, and he reduced the number of required signatures for hiring from 15 to five.

This is one example of how he implemented new policies that saved money so that we could train people to purchase trucks.

"I can't run this office with carbon paper and typewriters," he told a friend at EDS. "I need to ask you for the computers that you just threw out."

Then he came to me, Nettie, and Freman and said, "I can get us 100 computers, but I need to know how to legally get these computers donated to the city of Detroit."

Human Resources Problem #4:
Crumbling Trucks & Broken Equipment

One day, Gary invited me and several directors to take a walk through various city departments to see that our employees could not work effectively or efficiently because they lacked space, tools, and equipment.

First, we looked at the city's fleet of trucks. Snow plow trucks, for example, had not been replaced in decades. Cardboard and plywood covered the floor boards. Drivers risked falling through the floor if they took a wrong step.

"We can't have employees being unsafe," I said.

As we toured other city vehicles, Gary said, "Our employees are sitting on bare springs in police cars."

That walking tour resulted in numerous innovations that included restoring pay to certain employees who would work on acquiring safety equipment for employees who were ambulance drivers, EMS technicians, power and light pole workers, and sewer system workers.

We also met with our unions. Gary told them, "We know we owe you this money. We're going to take care of that. We need you to do a fair day's work. We need you to get here on time, drive that bus, pick up people on time, and do this huge change to show citizens that you're about them. It's not your fault. We have to really step our game up."

In addition, we started a quality control program in which we took our employees across America to witness municipal employees who were doing a great job in Baltimore, Philadelphia, Washington, DC, and Seattle. We took Detroit labor leaders with us, convincing them that working together would provide solutions for improving our service to the citizens of Detroit.

The quality program began with a training budget of $100,000 that grew — thanks to cost-saving in other areas — to nearly $5 million annually as we expanded it to train supervisors, employees, and skilled trade workers.

Human Resources Problem #5:
Reorganizing Departments and Strategic Purchasing

Teamwork was the key to our success, but even good teams need reorganizing to ensure victory. When viewing our management structure through his perspective honed by General Motors, Gary was instrumental in transforming our management structure.

One day during a staff meeting, as 50 department heads and other key employees competed for my attention, it became apparent that our management structure could be more efficient.

"The mayor can't manage 50 people at once," Gary said. "I'd like to propose a structure that the mayor would have four people reporting directly to him — Nettie, Freman, and a few others. Everybody else would report to Nettie and Freman. We'll call them general managers or general directors."

I loved Gary's idea, and gave him the green light to restructure our management hierarchy to maximize efficiency and effectiveness.

He also noted that different departments competed for the same resources.

"For example, the fire, police, and parking departments all do similar things, but never talk to each other," Gary said. "In fact, they competed for budget and other resources. That's why we can't get things done. So, rather than have the fire department buy fire trucks and not talk to the public service department, what if Freman brought all the people who needed trucks together, and we make a larger buy. Then we can go to GM, and rather than buying 10 trucks, we're going to get 100 trucks, where we can ask, 'What savings can we get?'"

I gave Finance Director Valerie Johnson the authority to negotiate with GM to do this, and it saved the city a small fortune. We then repeated this across every city department.

All the while, Gary applied his cost-saving skills to the Human Resources department, ultimately reducing his staff of 600 people to 300. Likewise, over the course of eight years, he helped reduce the number of city employees from about 21,000 to about 18,000.

Gary's tremendous impact on improving city government exemplified the importance of hiring excellent, talented people to help transform Detroit. I always gave credit where credit was due.

Gary recalls, "The mayor said, 'Great job! I knew there was a reason I hired you.'"

"The City's Infrastructure Was Light Years Behind Other Cities"

When Gloria Robinson began work as Director of Planning, she was astounded by the antiquated environment in our municipal offices.

"The city's infrastructure was light years behind other cities," she says. "When we came into office, there was literally nothing. A couple of computers, no network. Everything was done by paper."

The lack of supplies, structures, and organization also shocked Nettie Seabrooks. "When we went into the mayor's office, there was not one sheet of paper there. We had nothing. No files, no nothing. We tried to put it on a more solid footing, like a director's meeting at seven thirty every other Tuesday morning to help everybody organize. It's very hard to articulate what I did. I tried to apply what I had learned at General Motors all those years on how to organize."

Gloria was stunned that the telephone system was decades behind modern technology. "I remember the planning department had a switchboard, but not individual phones. You couldn't leave voicemail messages. The city — from a functioning, infrastructure point of view — was in dire straits. It needed everything. Knowing Dennis and his focus and his abilities and dedication, I just felt like he was the person who was going to be able to do this. He brought resources to bear that no one else could. He got the private sector to dedicate staff and resources to address the issues and problems."

But it took work. "When I got to the city," Gloria said, "there were no processes, no equipment, and the staff was demoralized. When Coleman Young was sick at the end of his last term, he wasn't coming into work regularly. Things just weren't getting done. There had been cutbacks in staff because of budget issues. Everything had to be built from the ground up in terms of having a functioning government."

Morale was a major problem, Gloria noted. "Also was the issue of trust and building bridges through relationships and partnership that the mayor was so good at. The history of relationships between the former mayor and the city council was awful. Dennis had to rebuild those relationships. Nor were there relationships with the business community or suburban community. He was masterful at rebuilding those relationships and bringing a lot of goodwill and resources to bear on the problems. There was a lot of anxiety from not having relationships."

Gloria jumped to action.

"The first thing we tried to do was put processes in place. Businesses complained to the mayor, saying 'You can't get anything done in this city, and the processes are too cumbersome.' I remember a company telling me when I first came in, when the Planning Department and Community Economic Department were a partnership, they kept getting bounced between the two departments. One said, yes, and one said no. I wanted to create a central intake process for development projects that consisted of planning and development and all the departments that played a role, including the Department of Public Works, roads, public lighting, buildings and safety, the council site, and the planning commission, which also does site planning review for city council."

Gloria wanted one central entry, one application. The developer of a significant project could call and schedule a meeting with the intake group and complete an application with everyone together in the same room. Questions could be asked and answered rather than having a waiting period. This process helped significantly in streamlining things.

"The mayor directed buildings and safety to come up with a one-stop licensing and permit process," Gloria says. "We had the joint application and site plan review process. That started to speed up development approval through the city. The other thing that I faced: we didn't have quality staff in the planning department. The city's human resource process was set up so you had a generic title throughout the city. If you were Manager-1 or Administrator-1, you could go to any department in the city with that title."

Gloria spent hours writing job descriptions for professional planners to be hired in the department, then having to go through human resources, which was sympathetic to her needs. But it all took time.

"I felt like I needed another layer of appointed management below myself," she continues. "I asked the mayor if I could have appointed people to run those groups. It took me forever to get that through city council. They were suspicious that I was trying to avoid the unions and civil service. I said, 'That's not the point of this,' and finally got approval."

Gloria oversaw major areas: planning, housing, economic development, grants management (which included some rather large grants for the city's planning), development, zoning, and homeless issues. She demonstrated her leadership when she suggested doing team building and social activities for the demoralized employees.

"I said to my two deputies, 'Let's do some team building, some social activities to form a cohesive department,'" Gloria recalls. "The culture was very different. The mayor has his staff, along with two appointments in each department, including a director and a deputy director. You can't change an organization with two people. That's always a challenge and remains a challenge. How to motivate the career people, who have essentially 'retired on the job,' particularly when at the end of the Young administration, a lack of accountability for staff was the culture."

Nettie says during that time she would meet with anyone. "It was not hierarchal. I was trying to flatten it out."

Judith had the same focus. She refers to it as getting the city right-sided.

"I respect Mayor Young," Judy says. "I struggle with the notion that we had to fix the city, but we had to get it back on track where it needed to go as times were changing. We were figuratively rebuilding bridges that were weathered or worn over the years."

TRANSPORTATION: CANNIBALIZING BUSES TO PROVIDE 24/7 SERVICE

Detroit is known as the Motor City, but a good portion of its residents cannot afford to own a car — or pay the highest car insurance rates in the nation. As a result, they rely on city buses to go to work and otherwise get from one part of town to another. Sadly, Detroit's Department of Transportation had a terrible reputation for buses that, when they did show up often several hours late, they did not run properly. Nor were they clean or safe.

This dismal state of affairs for the city's only public transportation except for the Detroit People Mover, whose service was limited to a specific, mile loop around downtown, resulted from the crippling budget deficit that Mayor Young had faced during the 1990 recession under President George H. W. Bush.

While struggling to balance the city's budget, Mayor Young had to lay off bus drivers and could not buy new buses or repair existing ones. Meanwhile, the city's financial woes had bred distrust from companies that refused to provide service, parts, or new buses on credit.

Given this reality, I made it an urgent and top priority to get our city's buses running again.

Two years into my administration, in April of 1996, I announced that for the first time in five years, the Detroit Department of Transportation (DDOT) was offering bus service for 24 hours, seven days per week. It began on 14 major bus routes that included the main corridors of Jefferson, Mack, Gratiot, Michigan, Woodward, and Crosstown.

This triumphant follow-through on my inaugural promise to provide reliable bus service exemplified getting the job done despite the city's financially crippled resources. The sad fact of the matter was that we ordered brand new buses, only to be told that the bus manufacturer did not have time to deliver new buses because other cities wanted more buses than us.

"We need to get these buses up and running," I told the mechanics.

They went through the entire bus yard and cannibalized the good parts from the bus fleet, then assembled 50 buses that, by the time they hit the streets, were like brand new.

During the media announcement, I praised the teamwork of our DDOT mechanics for reconditioning 50 buses that had been out of operation. I also emphasized that the city saved money by doing the work in-house rather than sending the buses to Chicago for major overhauls.

More good news: we were creating jobs. Since the prior year, we had certified and hired 129 new bus drivers. They were equipped with radios for better communication and emergency calls, and thanks to collaboration with the police department, officers were giving increased priority for DDOT calls.

This was a case of "making do" with the limited resources that we had.

Diplomacy Resolves Conflict Over Regional Transportation

A $9 million federal transportation grant for our region was awaiting my endorsement, but I refused. The Detroit Department of Transportation's relationship with the SMART suburban bus system was so fractured and contentious, I would agree to nothing until we reached a truce, then promised to work in a spirit of harmony for the sake of advancing our region.

The problem came to a boiling point when SMART leaders announced they would charge double fares for DDOT monthly pass holders as transportation leaders attempted to implement a regional pass. SMART had announced it would stop honoring the $42 monthly DDOT passes, which would force Detroit residents to purchase a regional pass for $49.50.

SMART had also said it would no longer honor DDOT transfers, tickets, or passes in response to DDOT's demand that SMART pay $500,000 for what amounted to free rides for SMART passengers on DDOT buses in 1994 and 1995.

DDOT Director Albert Martin and I demonstrated coolness under fire as we negotiated an agreement that would benefit both DDOT and SMART bus riders. We agreed that those who wanted to use both systems would purchase a regional pass for $49.50. The plan was for the two systems to split the revenue from the passes.

The most important development from this agreement was that the two systems agreed to work together in a spirit of cooperation to provide the best service for people in Detroit and the surrounding communities.

8

MAKING OUR CITY CLEAN, SAFE, AND FIRE-FREE:
CRIME, CLEAN SWEEP & ANGELS' NIGHT

REDUCING CRIME AND MAKING Detroit safe was a top campaign pledge, and number one in *Thoughts for a Greater DETROIT*. My relationship with the Clinton White House helped secure resources to make our city safer. We were in and out of Washington on a regular basis, and our lobbyist advocated on behalf of our city.

"Dennis was able to parlay his relationship with the president and first lady to bring tons of resources back to Detroit," Freman says. "The Clinton administration was very pro-city, trying to give cities a hand *up* rather than a hand *out*."

This proved especially helpful in our fight against crime, which we reduced every year that I was in office. Very importantly, President Clinton awarded significant funding through his COPS program, which enabled us to put an additional 100-plus police officers on the streets of Detroit.

Attorney General Janet Reno announced the establishment of the Office of Community Oriented Policing Services (COPS) in October 1994 to administer these grants. They resulted from President Clinton's $30 billion Violent Crime Control and Law Enforcement Act of 1994, also known as the federal crime bill, a nationwide effort to increase the number of officers in 30 cities and counties. The program was designed to have a 75–25 percent split in costs, with the federal government picking up the bulk of expenses for the new officers. For Detroit, this financial boost represented nearly an entire precinct.

Chief McKinnon and I visited the White House with a number of mayors and police chiefs. The president, attorney general, and vice president hosted these events to strategize solutions for the drug problems and drug organizations that were ravaging cities across the country.

"Each city had its own problems," Chief McKinnon recalls. "We talked about people working deep under cover. President Clinton, Vice President Gore, and Attorney General Janet Reno had a great relationship with our mayor, and they came here, too. They gave us so much assistance to help turn the city around in terms of this fight in drug trafficking."

We were also active with the National Association of Police Chiefs and NOBLE, the National Organization of Black Law Enforcement Executives.

Here at home, Chief McKinnon transferred 300 officers from desk jobs onto the streets. At the same time, he discovered that about 700 of our 4,000 officers were out on long-term disability. Some were on excessive, bogus leave. Many had moved out of Detroit, but were still receiving pay from the city. Ike talked to doctors and unions and, in the end, 60 of the 700 on long-term disability returned to work.

"We locked people up," Ike says, "while people in the neighborhoods were simultaneously thanking us for closing down the drug houses. People knew if they had a problem, they could call me. If they knew of a drug house, they could call and report it. We raided countless drug houses by repairing fractured relations with the DEA and other agencies."

I agreed with Ike that we had to change citizens' perception of the police department and our officers. Most importantly, we needed to inspire their trust in the police department again. We had to show them that our officers were honest, that they had great response time, and that they were responsive to what the citizens needed and wanted. So we worked hard to build their trust, one person at a time. For example, one day I received a phone call from a woman in the 10th precinct.

"Someone has a boom box outside in the street and the noise is disturbing me," she said. "I live on the west side, at Oakman and Linwood. I called the precinct last night and again at 10 this morning, but nobody came out to make them turn down that noise."

I called Ike, relayed the story and gave her number.

"Mr. Mayor, I'll take care of it."

Ike called the woman, and he could hear the noise in the background.

"Hello, ma'am, this is the police chief calling."

"The police chief is calling me?" she asked, shocked.

"Ma'am, of course I'm calling you. The mayor is concerned about you. What's the problem?"

"Can you hear the music outside? I'm 70 years old! I can't sleep with that noise."

"I will make sure it's taken care of. If things haven't changed in 15 minutes, you give me a call back."

Ike gave her his private number, then called the Lieutenant on the desk at the 10th precinct.

"No one has done anything about the noise," Ike said. "Now listen, that's going to stop right now. Not tomorrow, not later today. Right now. Lieutenant, I want you to go over there, talk to this lady after you stop the noise, the music, then you call me."

The woman called Chief McKinnon within 10 minutes, crying with gratitude. Then she called me to say thank you, and I called Ike to do the same.

"Ike, this is the way we have to do it," I said.

"Mr. Mayor, I'm here to serve."

On another occasion, a 10-year-old called me and said, "Mr. Mayor, there's a drug house down the street from my house. I'm afraid that they're going to have a shootout and kill us."

I took his address and phone number, and told the boy, "I'll have Chief McKinnon take care of that."

Detroit police raided the drug house that day and shut it down. The boy called me to say thank you. Similar daily occurrences restored trust between the citizens of Detroit and our police department.

"It was meaningful," Ike says, "to have an administration within the mayor's office and police department that truly cared about the people in the city."

I regularly visited the police department because it was an important element to a cohesive community.

"We had a mayor of the city of Detroit pulling up in front of the building, walking in, and shaking hands with people, and asking what we could do to improve our city," Ike recalls. "That says a lot about how much they trusted him with the city's difficulties. This was so important to what he did."

We attended countless community meetings where people said, "Thank you, Mayor Archer and Chief McKinnon. You're making a difference. You guys are everywhere. You're doing great things in the city and making us feel loved and needed."

Collaborating with other law enforcement agencies, who had experienced strained relations in the past with Detroit Police, became a priority that helped reduce crime.

"We started working religiously with other agencies, the FBI, and police departments in other communities," Ike says. "Crime does not stop at borders — not Eight Mile Road — it goes right through to the suburbs. It was important to stem the tide of crime. Working with these other agencies was a great functioning togetherness of all of us pursuing one common goal. As things started to work together, an understanding of the importance of all law enforcement officers working together was tremendous. We were seeing a decrease in crime in the city."

At the same time, thanks to brainstorming sessions with Ike early on about how to upgrade the quality of DPD leadership, I mandated that all command staff have college degrees. A graduate degree was required to excel beyond the junior executive level to the upper echelon. That was unique among any police agency in the country at the time. I also required all command staff to undergo command leadership training at Northwestern University or the FBI National

Academy. State funds enabled us to send about eight people a year for this training.

Chief McKinnon was working 12 to 14 hours a day, visiting churches, community groups, businesses, and doing media interviews to reassure the public that we were making things safe.

"This made a significant impact on the people," Ike recalls. "Senior citizens told me, 'You know, Chief, if something happens, we wait to hear something from you.' They would wait for me to come on TV because they said, 'We know you'll tell the truth, Chief. We still trust you.' This made me feel wonderful."

Our major crime problems were deeply tied to the booming drug sales in crack houses, which devastated whole blocks with shootings, noise, constant traffic, and terrified parents who forced children to stay indoors.

"We had some guys who were robbing drug houses with military-like precision," Ike recalls. "There would be 10 of them in a van, dressed in dark clothing, carrying automatic weapons. Sometimes they would shoot people in the houses. Other times they'd rape women."

An informant told us who they were; some were ex-military. DPD, the FBI, and State Police orchestrated a plan to take them down on the freeway.

"It's going down this evening," they said.

"Ike, I don't want you out there," I said.

"Mr. Mayor, these are my officers."

"Listen, I don't want you out there."

We compromised, by listening to the events — gunfire during the shootout — from Ike's office at police headquarters. Two officers were wounded, not seriously, and one bandit was killed.

Another situation involved a barricaded gunman.

"Ike, be careful," I said. "Remember your family."

"I do remember my family and the families of the officers out there doing this, too."

Ike went on the raid, where he got into a tank with the officers as they approached the house.

"Chief," they said, "We want you to know, this tank is not armor-plated. We have this vest."

They gave him a vest that would stop an AK-47 round.

"What happens if a bullet strikes me in the head?" Ike asked.

"Your head won't stop it," they said.

"Well, then I'll step back and let you guys handle it." Ike never went on another raid.

Supporting Police Officers Injured or Killed in the Line of Duty

It was customary for mayors to attend funerals of police officers killed in the line of duty, but I chose to go to the hospital any time an officer was seriously hurt.

"The mayor was there, every time," Ike says. "This was way beyond anyone's imagination. It had never been done, and I had been on the force since 1965."

My presence showed officers that I supported them as they served our city. "No matter what time it was," Benny adds, "if he was in town, he would show up. He was a legitimately compassionate person when it came to the people in the police department."

On May 25, 1995, I was with Trudy at Henry Ford Museum for a gala celebration of the Motown exhibit.

"Mr. Mayor, I just received a text that an officer was gravely wounded," said Ike, who was also attending the event with his family. "Let me get to the hospital and find out what was happening."

By the time he arrived at Detroit Receiving Hospital, 28-year-old Officer Jerry Philpot had expired. Ike called me; Trudy and I went to the hospital, where the corridors were lined with countless officers.

"When the mayor arrived," Ike recalls, "he was embracing these officers. He's in tears. They're in tears. They had never seen this before. They'd never seen a leader respond that way before. It had a profound impact on them."

We learned that Officer Philpot had been shot with an AK-47 assault rifle during a dispute with the Latin Counts gang in Southwest Detroit. The gunman was sentenced to life in prison.

At the hospital, Trudy was consoling Officer Philpot's family, including his widow, who was very active in the police department.

"Judge Archer," Mrs. Philpot said, "I want you to know how much my husband admired you. He appeared before you in court."

That was a touching moment. "I will always remember that," Trudy says, "for her to say that to me in time of her sorrow."

Introducing Police Chief Benny Napoleon

After four-and-a-half years of working every day, the stress of Chief McKinnon's job triggered excruciating migraine headaches. He retired, and returned to his position as a University of Detroit Mercy professor. In his place, I appointed Benny Napoleon as Chief of Police. The following are his recollections, italicized to indicate that the passages are from his perspective:

> *"Chief, are you going to be at home in the morning?" asked John Clark, the deputy chief, as he came into my office at Detroit Police Headquarters.*
>
> *"Yeah, why?"*
>
> *"We have to install a phone for you." He explained that the police department in Detroit at that time was on an enclosed phone system where you could tell that you were talking to someone from the police department. An outsider couldn't just call. You could verify it was an official police department number.*
>
> *"So if I called someone or if they were calling me," he said, laughing, "it was official."*
>
> *This is a true story. They put this red phone in my bedroom. It was really red, like a hotline. So whenever things would happen, the control center, the hub of the police department, would call my house and that's the phone they would call me on. I never went through one night without getting a phone call. Obviously if a police officer had been seriously hurt, I would call the mayor right away. If it was a major incident, arrest of prominent person, barricaded gunman, multiple murders, children under a certain age being shot, they called me, and I'd brief the mayor.*

Chief of Police Gets to Work

Once I became Chief of Police, the mayor asked, "How are you going to reduce violent crime in the city?"

We came up with a crime reduction plan that focused on four essential strategies: community policing; crime prevention; problem-oriented policing; and directed enforcement. These were all well-known terms in law enforcement.

We reorganized the department, with heavy force on the narcotics environment, and focusing on career criminals who were victimizing people in Detroit. It was a unique focus to fighting crime in the city of Detroit. When I presented the plan to the mayor, he looked at it, sat back, and thought about it.

"Okay, Benny," he said, and asked how different things would be impacted by having my focus on the most aggressive narcotics force the city has ever seen.

After he talked about where he wanted to go, he asked why I wanted to do it, and what would be the impact of my proposed reorganization.

"Mr. Mayor, you're going to have people complaining about speeding cars. Response by police might be a little late. Would you prefer that I get there in a hurry after you become a victim? I'd rather stop you from being a victim."

It took almost a year for my crime-fighting plan to get approved by the board of police commissioners because they had never seen anything like it. They were having hearings. I was like, "You guys don't understand; this is going to reduce crime in our town."

And it did. We started getting large catches of narcotics. After we reorganized the focus onto narcotics enforcement, I used to call the mayor whenever we had a seizure of a kilo — with street value $50,000, a pretty significant hit — just so he'd be aware of it. A kilo of heroin or cocaine for a local police department is a pretty nice seizure.

"Good job, Benny," he'd say.

Then we started getting three, four, five kilos.

"You don't have to call me with a kilo anymore," he said. "Just call with multiple kilos."

My plan was working. We started getting all these major narcotics seizures. That's why the crime numbers were going down because we were doing serious interruption of business for the drug dealers. A lot of it would never go public because we were working up a chain.

We were reducing the number of kids who were shot. I remember as a young inspector, we had eight kids shot in Detroit Public Schools in one day. One day — eight! The entire time I was Chief of Police, not one kid was shot in DPS. It used to be a common occurrence.

We were notorious for having young people under the age of 16 shot. We were averaging about 200 kids a year and about 22 who were 16-and-under killed during a year. Something I should not have to talk about, but I was very proud of a very focused and determined effort to make our schools safe. We really focused on some problems that were plaguing the city that we hadn't quite gotten a handle on.

During the first five years of the mayor's administration, crime went down 2.5 percent total. Then when I was chief, crime went down 28 percent.

It's important for folks to really understand the commitment that Dennis Archer had to this community. He had a protective detail. I had access to his schedule. This man worked almost every day of the week from about 5:00–5:30 in the morning till midnight. I would look at his schedule, and just shake my head. Every day for the eight years, if he was in town, that was his schedule. People need to understand the measure of this man's commitment to his community. It's unlike anything I've ever seen. He was amazing.

Chief Napoleon: Solving A Range of Major Crimes

We had a serial killer raping and killing prostitutes in Southwest Detroit. That was an incredible case. I believe from the moment we discovered that we had a serial killer, we wound up catching him within a week. Our investigation revealed this person had been in the military, and had killed people all over the world. He came here thinking he could get away with something. This guy is put away forever. He had cases all over the world.

I remember a group of guys committing home invasions. These guys had committed more than 100 home invasions in the Detroit area, Michigan, and Ohio. These were some very bad people. I remember they would pose as police officers. They'd go in like a raid van for narcotics, dressed in raid suits, and go to known drug houses. They'd go in and rob them. The problem was that some of these houses were former drug houses, and now had innocent people in them. So in the course of these "raids," they had raped several women and shot several people. We were working the violent crime task force. It was a secret, and they were very active with secret protection.

We had to go brief the mayor. The local head of State Police, the captain, the local head of the state FBI office, and myself went to the mayor's office to let him know we had these guys under surveillance. We told him what they had done and how frequently they had done it. We told him, "Mr. Mayor, these are some very dangerous people, and there's no way — when we try to arrest these people — that someone won't get hurt."

He looked at us, and asked questions, and said basically, "Be careful. Do whatever you can to make sure nobody gets hurt, but you have to take these people off the street."

We had wire taps. We followed them, not by cars, but by airplanes during our surveillance. We had this whole scheme. We knew they were going to go out a certain night, but we had to wait until they hit a house to make our case. After they hit the house, when they came back out in the van, we started to chase them.

We had people behind them, and my SWAT team in an EMS truck that cut them off at the end of the street. They rammed the EMS truck and disabled my SWAT team and took off down the street. And then we were chasing them, weaving through the 10th precinct near Dexter and Oakman. They're shooting at police officers, and one guy gets out of the car in the Dexter/Davison area. He starts running on foot. My surveillance officers chased him. He ran between houses, and my surveillance officer lost sight of him. Then he ran into the back yard, and my officer shot him three or four times in the chest and killed him. There's the casualty we knew would happen.

Another night, I'm sitting at Oakman and Portland in my unmarked police car, and I get the call that something is about to happen. I'm listening to my radio, following the chase which comes down Oakman to Cortland. A police car is chasing a van, and I get *in behind the van by myself. The van crashes with the car, and there's a shootout there. I'm the chief right in the middle of this stuff. That's probably the most intense street encounter that I had in my 26 years in the Detroit Police Department. It was unbelievable.*

I was not scared. Fear is something when you're in that moment, you revert to your training automatically. When it's over, that's when I start getting nervous. While all that stuff is going on I'm just trying to stay alive. Panic and fear will get you killed. I was very cautious following my training. Fortunately for us no police officers were hurt badly. After we briefed the mayor, he was very happy we took these guys down. That was a big one.

COMPASSION FOR ALL

The city has suites in Joe Louis Arena and Comerica Park, and the mayor would routinely give those tickets to the police department for the officers. That was common — he'd call and say, "Give this to the folks who are out on the streets working."

He didn't have to do that. He really looked out for the troops.

He would come up with a baseball cap on, and sometimes it would say "Mayor" or have a police logo. I don't recall ever seeing him pull up to a location where there were police officers present and not stop and talk to them on the way to talk to me. He would never pull out of an engagement, then get in his car and leave. He would always talk to the officers and inquire how they're doing.

He was compassionate and concerned about the people who worked with us. He was a tough boss, though. Obviously he's a very smart man. He would ask you some very probing questions. He was a no-nonsense kind of guy, trust me.

We were at a meeting one day in his office — he probably doesn't remember this stuff — it makes an impression on people like me. This was one of the first meetings I had in his office when I was first appointed chief. Ike always went to those meetings. I was at a conference table with a few other people around the table and the mayor at the head of the table. I leaned over and said something to someone next to me. The mayor said, "Benny, we're having one meeting." That's the last time I talked to anybody in a meeting.

He'd have "*diagonal slice meetings*" in which he'd come into the agency and talk to people of all different ranks. When we couldn't be in the meeting, he was very accessible. He was always talking to the officers. He's the mayor, people should have access to him. They all vote. He was always hands-on with citizens.

One of the biggest complaints was that we had so many drug houses, which is why I was so intent on stepping up our enforcement and going from three raids a day to 30. I got criticized for it by the local papers saying, "Napoleon is hitting these minor drug dealers." That was and is common practice for me.

One afternoon, I was at a play with my daughter, and a woman there with her grandkid came up to me and said, "Chief, can I talk to you?"

"Sure."

"I don't want to do it here," she said, so I gave her my private number.

Later when we spoke, she told me about a drug house on her street. I told her I would take care of it.

I went over to her neighborhood and talked to the guys at the house.

I said, "You guys know I'm the police chief, right?"

"Yeah, we know who you are," they said.

"Let me tell you this: You can't sell dope here. If you open up, we'll be right back. You understand what I'm saying?"

They said, "We do." They left, but got arrested three months later. They got out; again, I went to the house.

"Guys, what don't you understand? You can't sell drugs here."

Five months later they opened back up, and I was right back.

"What don't you understand? The day you start back up, we're going to raid you. You can't do it here."

They stopped. Ultimately, our investigation led to one of the biggest seizures we ever had at a house in Southfield, and it started from the information I got from that lady.

About two months after the last raid, she called me and said, "Chief, everybody is mad at you over here."

"Why are they mad at me?"

She said, "They said you're picking on these people."

"I'm picking on the dope man! Really?"

I think I told the mayor, and his response was, "They can just be mad. That's the kind of thing that happens to people who sympathize with that nonsense in their neighborhood."

NOT IN DETROIT: PREVENTING CHAOS AT ECONOMIC SUMMIT

I remember the Economic Summit. They had gone to Seattle and tore Seattle up. Went to Toronto, tore Toronto up. Went to DC, tore it up. Went to Montreal and tore it up.

They were coming to Detroit. They were protesters for the Economic Summit. They were going everywhere and causing problems. I had to go meet with the mayor. I had footage from all these cities where they had just rioted. He didn't want to cancel the event — it was a huge event. The president was coming to town.

In his typical Dennis Archer way, when you tried to really make a point, he would sit and tilt his head and sort of raise his eyebrows and look at you. After he looked at all this stuff that's going on, he can't cancel its coming to Detroit.

In his office I said, "Mr. Mayor, I got this, don't worry about it, it won't happen."

He looked at me with that look and said, "Are you sure?"

"Mr. Mayor, I promise you, there won't be any problems."

We had the event, and I think we arrested one guy on a bicycle. What we did, we did because over the course of my career I've been involved in tons of civil disobedience. I understand mob mentality.

What we did was come up with an enforcement strategy that incorporated plainclothes police officers into the crowd to quietly extract the rabble-rousers. The overwhelming majority of people were coming to protest peacefully. When people tried to agitate and got disorderly, they immediately got arrested. We were very fortunate that folks saw we had that kind of presence and we weren't going to let anything escalate, so it just didn't happen. It was an amazing thing.

Of course he was happy.

And I said to him, "I told you, I got this."

Crimes Against Children

After one particularly grueling crime, I almost called the mayor to quit my job. I've never told him this, about that day I walked into a house where five small children had been killed.

In the house the kids were all in this room, and they were so small, they looked like little baby dolls. This guy had cut their throats because he was mad at someone in the house for taking his car.

I have seen people murdered in all kinds of ways as the chief of detectives. Working for the former chief of detectives, we had been to so many murder scenes, but that one stuck with me for a long time. I couldn't get that out of my mind, and couldn't sleep for three months. I was saying to myself, "This is a sign for me to go," because nothing stuck with me in my career.

Ultimately I worked my way through it and got back to the business of chiefing. That was one of the most difficult things in my career. I did not talk with the mayor about it. I probably should have in retrospect — or somebody — but I didn't. We did catch the guy responsible very quickly, I might add.

"Student Safe Streets Program" Inspires Community Collaboration to Stop Attacks on Children

During the fall of 1999, girls were being attacked while walking to school. While Detroit Police investigated each incident and worked hard to find the attacker, I called upon ministers and residents to help patrol the neighborhoods, keep porch lights on, and be on the lookout for suspicious people.

"This is personal for all of us," I said during a press conference to announce the Student Safe Streets Program.

This exemplified the multilevel collaborations that my administration orchestrated to use creative ways to solve major problems that put our citizens at risk.

As a father, former teacher and as mayor, protecting our school-children was unquestionably a top priority. So we initiated the Student Safe Streets Program as a cooperative, long-term effort between

Detroit Public Schools, the Detroit Police Department, the religious community, and residents.

During church services, ministers across the city echoed my plea: "Get personally involved today. Everybody can be a volunteer. And this is how you can help." The media also published articles and ran stories on the radio and television, explaining how citizens could protect children and teens walking to and from school:

- First turn on your porch lights in the predawn mornings.

- Between the hours of 7:00 a.m. to 9:00 a.m. and 2:00 p.m. to 4:00 p.m. look out your house window.

- Get off the freeway and drive the surface streets to work.

- Patrol on your way to work by putting on your hazard lights and headlights so that students can feel your presence.

- If you see suspicious activity, blow your horn, yell out the window, or call the police.

- We're not asking any volunteers to have direct contact with the children (i.e., giving rides, etc.).

- Parents form walking groups to and from school.

- Parents, guardians, teachers, and principals should be the principal individuals to have contact with the children.

- Public Lighting, Detroit Water and Sewerage, Detroit Recreation, Department of Transportation, and Department of Public Works vehicles will be on alert beginning immediately.

- The mayor is asking citizens to especially patrol along school routes in their neighborhood.

- Everybody has a role to play. Get involved now.

At the same time, we outlined several ways for DPS, DPD, and others to work together. Detroit Police assigned a police officer to every one of the city's 263 public schools.

We reached out for help from the parent community, as well as the city's database of 30,000 volunteers for Angels' Night and Clean Sweep. We had a team of school principals identify any open and dangerous structures that became vacant since the city began demolition of nearly 5,000 structures previously identified. We also directed all city departments to identify morning and afternoon fleet vehicles to press into patrol service along school routes. We also asked all businesses that had fleets — cab companies, newspaper delivery, store delivery trucks, etc. — to patrol the streets. Lastly, we explored new ways to get senior citizens involved. We stopped the assaults against our female students by making timely arrests and by maintaining our community involvement.

DETROIT CLEAN SWEEP PUTS CAMPAIGN PROMISE INTO ACTION

During my Inaugural Address, I asked everyone who had an interest in Detroit to sweep the sidewalk in front of their homes, to clean their alleys, and to clear rubbish from storm drains on their blocks.

We got the whole city involved with the first annual Detroit Clean Sweep in April of 1994. This day united thousands of men, women, and children from Detroit and surrounding communities to pick up trash, rake leaves, and clear litter from neighborhoods and parks. Folks showed up, ready for work, in hard-sole shoes, long pants, long sleeves, and gloves. They represented a variety of local organizations, including New Detroit, Inc., the United Citizens of Southwest Detroit community organization, and Boynton Middle School.

All in all, nearly 10,000 volunteers comprised of city residents and several hundred of our suburban neighbors did the dirty work of cleaning our parks. A few weeks later, the Wayne County Commission led the Fourth Annual Tire Sweep, during which volunteers collected thousands of abandoned tires for proper disposal.

The Clean Sweep became an annual event, and grew in size every year. In 1995, several hundred community groups, neighborhood clubs, churches, organizations, schools, and businesses preregistered to sweep, clear garbage, and bag debris into 30-gallon plastic bags from eight in the morning until three in the afternoon. Folks brought their own rakes, shovels, gloves, brooms, and trash bags.

That same day in May, the Detroit Police Department had an Abandoned Vehicle Blitz. About 150 volunteer tow truck drivers, with the assistance of the Detroit Police Department, towed away previously tagged, abandoned vehicles. Shortly thereafter, the Wayne County Commission had a Tire Sweep that collected thousands of discarded tires and tire scraps.

By 1996, Detroit Clean Sweep involved more than 22,000 volunteers representing 896 community groups and organizations. That year, we filled more than 320,000 bags of litter, and removed 4,800 tires from vacant lots. Meanwhile, the Detroit Police Department's third Abandoned Vehicle Blitz tagged 6,154 abandoned vehicles, towed 1,483 more, and recovered 121 stolen vehicles.

Corporate support for Detroit Clean Sweep included GM, Ford and Chrysler, BCBSM, Frito-Lay, Henry Ford Health System, the Salvation Army, and the Booker T. Washington Business Association. Many businesses donated food and supplies.

Every year, I wore a baseball cap that said MAYOR and white coveralls embroidered with my name on the breast pocket. This inspired endless amusement for my staff.

"Everybody would get a laugh out of Mayor Archer's uniform," says Anthony Neely. "One year somebody said, 'Mayor Archer, you don't have to wear that this year,' and he looked at them like, 'This is the uniform!'"

By the end of the day, the white sanitation suit was dirty, because I was out there cleaning up our neighborhoods.

"We tried for years to get him out of that ridiculous jumpsuit," says Greg Bowens, "but he liked it."

Even more importantly, Greg adds, "He was a former Supreme Court justice and mayor of one of the 10 largest cities in the country, but he was not afraid to do the work he asked others to do. If the mayor is picking up trash, then you need to pick up trash, too. He was like, 'Judy, put on your blue jeans — put your schedule book down. Pick up some trash. Freman, you better be somewhere picking up trash.' Corporation Counsel was expected to pick up trash. It was that kind of party."

One powerful snapshot during the Detroit Clean Sweep was when Oakland County Executive L. Brooks Patterson joined me in picking up trash in Detroit's low-income Brightmoor neighborhood.

"That sent a strong message that we're all going to work together," Freman says.

Operation Clean Sweep had created so much momentum, the clean-up began a week before in preparation for the main event on Saturday. Trees were planted, mass ticketing of abandoned vehicles occurred, and business violation ticketing increased.

Nothing is greater than the act of people coming together to achieve a common good for their neighbors. We made a special appeal to our neighborhood businesses, asking them to participate by cleaning the grounds of their businesses. For example, Thyssen Inc., headquartered in Detroit, sent more than 50 volunteers. The company had invested nearly $80 million in its Detroit facilities and aimed to be a good neighbor to the residents of the community neighboring its material management and service company.

UAW members were participating with supporting partners including the Sharing and Caring Block Club, the West Warren Avenue Merchants Association, the Children's Crusade, and the Parkdale/N. Campbell/Wesson Club. St. John Hospital and Medical Center, Holy Cross/Saratoga Hospitals, and St. John Hospital-Macomb Center served as Ambassadors for the Clean Sweep.

Countless local businesses, including Detroit-based American Axle & Manufacturing, Inc. (AAM) — which had spent millions on training programs and created 1,600 new jobs — sent volunteers. As a result, more than 26,000 citizens of Detroit and surrounding communities cleaned up the city's streets, sidewalks, parks, and playfields.

Each year, people continued to work together to make positive things happen in our Detroit. Their enduring dedication and enthusiasm made Detroit stand out as a role model for volunteerism throughout the country.

As my final Clean Sweep as mayor neared, I strongly encouraged all candidates for Mayor, City Council, and City Clerk, to join Detroiters in our six-day Clean Sweep. City Council Members Gil Hill, Maryann Mahaffey, Sheila Cockrel, Nicholas Hood, Alberta Tinsley-Talabi, and Kay Everett (in conjunction with her Keep

Detroit Beautiful Task Force), as well as City Clerk Jackie Currie, all participated.

I was excited and encouraged by this overwhelming community support. Our citizens were setting an example for all urban communities to follow. The idea of working together on such a critical, yet often overlooked issue — one piece of trash at a time — convinced me that we could make Detroit a clean, safe environment for everyone, whether they worked, lived, or simply visited on occasion. At the end of the day, I gave thanks to everyone who participated. I told them they were the reason Detroit was second-to-none in volunteer action. Their efforts greatly enhanced our sense of community, our city's image, and our quality of life.

In the end, Clean Sweep became the largest volunteer clean-up event in America. It put Detroit on display for a good reason, and I could not have been more proud.

Angels Take the Devil Out of Devil's Night

In the past, on the night before Halloween, the city of Detroit became a global spectacle year after year as hundreds of fires consumed vacant houses, piles of debris, and abandoned cars. This annual Devil's Night travesty attracted TV news crews from around the world, reinforcing Detroit's notorious reputation as a dangerous, apocalyptic place. Mayor Young had dramatically reduced Devil's Night fires by imposing a curfew on young people, increasing police patrols, and recruiting thousands of citizen volunteers who took to the streets.

In the wake of the euphoria and positive momentum of my election, we let our guard down on Halloween Eve in 1994. We got burned, literally, with a significant spike in fires. On an average night, 40 to 60 fires occur in Detroit. That Devil's Night, 186 fires were set to houses, both abandoned and occupied, as well as parked cars, and debris piles. We went out that night with a schedule of fire houses to visit. I wanted to thank the fire fighters, and I wanted to be present to witness for myself what was happening in the city.

"I remember driving past the Chene and Mack area, where there were gutted homes," Judy says. "We watched the fires spike as we drove by, and the mayor wanted to get out of the car. We're running down the alley, and the fire fighters are saying, 'You gotta stay back, Mr. Mayor.' You could see people starting fires. He wanted to see it, and he wanted to talk to residents, the media, neighborhood city halls."

After that, we vowed to never get burned again.

"The first year, Devil's Night was really awful," says Nettie, who was in her office working the Sunday after Halloween when we discussed how to resolve this problem.

"You've got to look at it as a campaign," she said. "You can't just think about it in September. We need to put together an organization, and have meetings and assignments for everybody, including community volunteers. And the Police Department needs to assign one person to do this. We need to have a press conference announcing our strategy for next year and every year after that."

We did exactly that, and volunteers signed up in droves to say, "Enough is enough." I would not tolerate a repeat of that night, nor would the citizens, the police, or the fire department.

First, at the suggestion of John George, who founded Motor City Blight Busters in 1988, we shifted the perception of the three-day period from October 29 through 31 by renaming it "Angels' Night."

It was especially important that Halloween 1995 be void of the nightmarish images of raging fires because on Friday, October 25, the city announced that private and public backing for the $235-million, 42,000-seat open-air, natural turf baseball stadium had been obtained. Ten days prior to that, Standard Federal Bank announced its interest in building 400 houses along the west side of the Detroit River. We did not need any bad news!

Having a successful first Angels' Night was critical to the momentum we were building. We needed to demonstrate to ourselves, to the state, to the country, that Detroit was on its way to greatness. At this early juncture, we did not need to taint our progress with a repeat of the previous year's Halloween Eve with excessive arson and humiliating headlines.

With nearly a year to prepare, we began recruiting thousands of volunteers, and coordinated community patrols with the police and fire departments.

Organizers went into schools to spread the word about the curfew for minors. They were to stay off the streets from 6:00 p.m. until

6:00 a.m. Violators would be fined $100 and be required to perform 40 hours of community clean-up on Belle Isle and other Detroit nature areas. Thousands of students vowed to respect the curfew and stay out of trouble.

We had a ban on containers of gas. We had an Adopt-A-House program where citizens agreed to keep a watchful eye on abandoned properties.

We received support from all sorts of businesses: Ameritech donated phones to volunteers with a special code for reporting suspicious activity directly to the Arson Task Force. AAA of Michigan had 50 of their trucks patrolling the streets in addition to performing their regular roadside assistance. AAA also donated funds for refreshments for volunteers.

The volunteers were truly the backbone — all 30,000 of them, including many who had recently participated in the Million Man March in Washington, DC, just two weeks earlier. Volunteers received bright orange lapel ribbons to wear, flashlights, and two-way radios.

On October 30, only 41 fires were reported. Again, on an average night between 40 and 60 fires were reported. The citizens who volunteered made it happen in cooperation with the countless city departments carrying out their dedicated roles.

We made a statement that year: we can do it. We can control our city. News media around the country reported our success, constantly comparing it to the prior year and the worst years in the 1980's.

The impact out of Angels' Night rang across the United States and around the world. Shortly after that night, I went to the National League of Cities Annual Meeting in Phoenix and received congratulations on a job well done. I also went to Japan, and while there, I paid a respectful visit to our Ambassador, Walter Mondale. He said conversations in Japan's business sector had been, "What's going to happen in Detroit over Halloween, over Devil's Night?"

Nothing, we showed them, *because we took the devil out of Devil's Night*. Those are little steps, baby steps. I love hitting home runs, but I'm satisfied if we can keep moving base runners with singles every time we go to bat. I wanted successes like Angels' Night to inspire people to say, "You know, the city of Detroit is changing. It's getting better."

The following year, 1996, again, more than 30,000 volunteers patrolled the streets, more private tow truck companies and drivers watched the streets, more phones were donated, and again fires were in the normal range over the three-day period. We were creating momentum. We were changing the perception. We were bound and determined to keep it going.

The three-day period of what we now affirmed as Angels' Night was no exception to the incredible dedication people had to their city.

With each passing year, creativity abounded: libraries were open late with children's programs; McDonald's was providing coffee and cookies to volunteers throughout the night. And the total number of volunteers rose to nearly 35,000, including many of our suburban neighbors, who came into the city to demonstrate their commitment to their neighbor's well-being.

By 1998, we referred to our volunteers as Angels — all 35,000 of them. This was the first year fires reported over the three-day period were below normal levels. But we didn't rest on our laurels: we had created something wonderful, and we had to keep it up. In 1999, unseasonably warm temperatures for the Halloween season sparked concern that this would increase fires, but fires didn't increase. It just made for a more pleasant night for our patrolling Angels.

When all was said and done, the arsons were below the daily average. I truly felt we had come a long way. I also credit my staff for getting out every year to patrol our city. All evening, I traveled from neighborhood to neighborhood, trying to get to as many community stations as I could, shaking hands, talking to people, and thanking volunteers.

"The mayor wanted to patrol and visit all six neighborhood city halls where volunteers were gathering," says Greg Bowens. "That sent a message to all of us that if the mayor is out there on patrol, you better be out there doing your thing. I don't care if you're the youth director. Everybody got a flashlight and a car. What could you say? He worked all day and got to work before you did! He'd have all these meetings and deal with a crisis, but when six or seven o'clock came, it was time to kick off Angels' Night. He took off his suit and tie and put on a baseball cap and an orange shirt and got out there. He'd have three or four media hits in line with the news cycle at six, eight, and 11, as the media was keeping track of what was going on."

In the final two years of my second term, the trend continued, with arsons on Angels' Night remaining average or slightly below average.

No single person could ever take responsibility for this. This expansive, community-wide effort proved that when we work together, the collective good is the only outcome we can achieve.

9

THE CLINTON CONNECTION:
BUILDING BRIDGES TO SPUR
ECONOMIC DEVELOPMENT

SPENDING THE NIGHT IN THE
LINCOLN BEDROOM AT THE WHITE HOUSE

DURING MY FIRST MONTH IN OFFICE, I received a phone call from the White House prior to a trip to Washington, DC, for my first midyear meeting of the U.S. Conference of Mayors.

"Mayor Archer," the White House staff person said, "Would you like to spend the night at the White House during the conference?"

"Yes," I responded. But I kept it quiet, even from Trudy, because if plans changed, I did not want to explain why it did not happen. Once I arrived in Washington, I watched the president deliver his State of Union Address. Then I went to the White House, where a butler escorted me to the Lincoln Bedroom.

"Mayor Archer," he said, "you probably won't be seeing the president until the morning, because he has a sore throat."

"Please give him my regards and I hope he feels better," I said, before getting comfortable and calling home. "Trudy, I'm in the Lincoln Bedroom for the night." She was elated.

A short time later, someone knocked on the door, and I assumed the butler was delivering food. I opened the door.

"Hi, Dennis," the president said, holding a steaming cup of tea. He came in, sat down, and joined me in watching a University of Arkansas basketball game. The relaxed atmosphere and our casual conversation provided the perfect segue for me to ask his advice on how to juggle my schedule and my desire to be the best mayor possible.

"I'm going nuts," I said. "I've been in office a whole month and I'm making two or three speeches a day. I'm all over the city. If there's someone opening a business and they want me to cut the ribbon, I go, to show people and the press how enthusiastic I am."

President Clinton listened with focus in his eyes and an attentive expression that made me feel like I was the only person in the world.

"I'm just a mayor," I said. "You've got the whole world to worry about. What do you do?"

"I learned when I was governor," he answered, "try to not ever make an important decision when tired. Think about it, then move with as much information as you can gather, but try not to make a decision when you're tired. Invariably, you'll make a mistake. Take your time and make your decision."

That was some of the most valuable advice I received, because I applied it to my work back in Detroit to make the best decisions for the citizens of our city. As we talked, someone knocked on the door. And in walked 13-year-old Chelsea. She sat on her father's lap.

"I hope it snows so we have a day off school tomorrow," she said.

I marveled at the moment. There I was, a caretaker's son with meager beginnings in rural Cassopolis, Michigan, now sitting in the Lincoln Bedroom of the White House with the President of the United States and his daughter.

Detroit Hosts World Leaders for Annual G7 Conference

Not long after my stay in the Lincoln Bedroom at the White House, I was attending the American Bar Association's annual mid-year meeting in early February when I received a message to call the White House.

"Congratulations, Mr. Mayor," said a member of President Clinton's staff. "The president decided to bring the G7 Jobs Conference to Detroit. We're sending a team tomorrow to meet with your Deputy Mayor."

"Thank you very much," I said, amazed that President Clinton had not dropped a single hint about this when we were together in Washington. "I'm excited."

I immediately called Nettie to discuss her meeting with the White House team the next day. We talked about how the annual "Group of 7" event enabled global leadership to explore ways to stimulate employment and develop the world's economy. The group included Canada, France, Germany, Italy, Japan, Great Britain, and the United States. G7 members represent nearly two-thirds of the world's net wealth, and have the highest global rankings in terms of life expectancy, per capita income, and education.

"Host cities usually have a year to prepare for this," Nettie said. "We have six weeks."

How many times had I pledged to make Detroit a world-class city? This was truly a be-careful-what-you-wish-for-because-you-just-might-get-it moment, because here we were, just weeks into the term, and the world was coming to us — fast!

Given such a momentous opportunity to make our city shine, it was my desire to showcase Detroit in the best possible light. But given its financial woes, how would we pay for first-class hospitality? I called Beth, who immediately began fundraising for the two-day event set for March 14th and 15th.

"He made me chair of the G7 because I had to raise money so we could entertain these dignitaries and give them gifts," Beth says. "We set up a 501(c)(3) and asked the corporate community to cover the costs of food, decorations, accommodations, and transportation. We ultimately raised $1.3 million."

Detroit's corporate community provided unprecedented financial support. Chrysler, Ford, and GM contributed $100,000 each toward G7 expenses. Comerica, Little Caesars, NBD Bank, Omnicare Health Plan, and United America Healthcare Corporation contributed $50,000 each.

Meanwhile, Nettie worked with White House representatives and handled the momentous task of orchestrating every detail, such as establishing Cobo Center as the headquarters. She also convinced Ford, GM, and Chrysler to donate vehicles to transport the international dignitaries from the airport to downtown hotels.

As we were planning the conference, Freman got an idea for what would create an iconic moment for my administration. "I thought, 'Dennis likes to jog, the president likes to jog, the vice president likes to jog.' So before I consulted with Dennis, I set it in motion. I called Rahm Emanuel, and said, 'Rahm, the G7 Jobs Conference is coming. The mayor would like to jog with the president. We've got the perfect place, Belle Isle, early in the morning, we can lock the island down with security.' Rahm said, 'Let me check.' When he came back with a yes, I said, 'Mr. Mayor, the president wants to jog,' and it was on."

Meanwhile, Trudy and her bridge club, called "The Finished Product," teamed up to showcase Detroit's consummate hospitality.

"One Friday before the G7 Conference," Trudy recalls, "I was with my bridge club, and we got word that more than 100 gifts that would be presented to all the G7 participants needed to be wrapped."

Beth, who was in the bridge club, said a spirit of "instant volunteerism" inspired the dozen ladies to purchase beautiful gift wrapping paper and ribbons, then convene in a mayoral conference room on Saturday morning to wrap the gifts. They included a brown leather passport cover, a crystal box, and a fountain pen in a wooden box that said G7 on it.

"That was a really memorable day," Beth says, "because everyone was excited to help present our city in the best possible light."

Then, just two-and-a-half months after I was sworn in as mayor, I stood with Trudy and Denny on the tarmac, greeting Air Force One.

Trudy was so proud that President Clinton had chosen Detroit for this international honor. "I was thinking, 'Oh my goodness, Dennis has been mayor for two-and-a-half months. If this is any indication of what's to come, then it's going to be a whirlwind for all of us.' It was exciting that something wonderful happened so quickly. Dennis wanted things to change. He wanted positive events to be happening in the city, getting people excited. Here we were just into his mayoralty, and here we are meeting the president."

When the two-day conference began, Cobo Center was decorated beautifully for the formal international meetings and security was ensured by black drapes on all the windows in the huge ballroom overlooking the river.

As the world's seven industrial powers convened for the first time to discuss unemployment on a global scale, they discussed how to create jobs for about 30 million people. Many cited "technophobia" as a culprit, as people feared that technological advancements were obliterating jobs. Interestingly, some of the proposed solutions — such as encouraging the growth of small businesses, and providing job training, were solutions that we were discussing as ways to improve Detroit's unemployment rate.

Following the finance ministers was a small army of media, representing 186 news agencies from around the world. Nettie set up an outstanding, 24-hour media center for them to file stories in different time zones in Europe and Asia. The media station was stocked with newspapers from around the world, as well as interpreters, enabling the journalists to participate in the meetings and other events, which were closed to the public.

As for food, The Roostertail owner and caterer extraordinaire Tom Schoenith created food stations at Cobo Center offering cuisine from around the world to appeal to everyone's taste.

On the first night, the Secret Service called to arrange our run on Belle Isle.

"Go to the Millender Center where the president is staying," they told Freman. The Secret Service had chosen that downtown hotel for its covered carport, which enhanced security. The next morning, five black GMC Yukons with bulletproof windows pulled up, and they called us to come down. I wore a sweatshirt with the G7 logo, Denny wore a windbreaker and jogging pants, and Freman wore an Eastern Michigan University sweatshirt.

We met the president, who came out drinking coffee. The whole experience was fascinating. I felt like an observer rather than a participant because we were with the president, the vice president, and their counterparts. We hopped into the back of the SUV with the president in front. I was in awe of all the security; the Secret Service men had assault rifles.

The motorcade headed down Larned to Mt. Elliott to Jefferson
Avenue and made a right turn onto Belle Isle. The Secret Service had
locked down the one-and-a-half-square-mile island, and the U.S.
Coast Guard was patrolling the Detroit River.

"I remember thinking, '*This is a moment!*'" Freman says now.

Fortunately, the media caught that moment in a photograph
that was published around the world and became one of the most
celebrated images of the Archer administration. The photo captured

*Running on Belle Isle with Denny, President Bill Clinton, Vice President Al Gore, and
my Chief of Staff, Freman Hendrix.*   Photo Credit: Diane Weiss / The Detroit News

President Clinton and Vice President Al Gore running with myself,
Dennis Jr., and Chief of Staff Freman Hendrix, flanked by Secret
Service personnel and two members of my security team. The photo
ran on page one of the daily newspapers, and it hangs framed in my
office today.

"Knowing my father's background," Denny says, "and where he
came from and experiencing him jogging around Belle Isle with the
President and Vice President of the United States, chatting as if old

friends, it will always be one of my most prideful moments, seeing the respect they had and knowing the respect they still have for him."

After we jogged nearly three miles, the president looked over and said, "I think Al has had enough."

So we hopped in the car and came back downtown.

That was one of many positive moments during the conference. A photograph of Mr. and Mrs. DunCombe shaking President Clinton's hand became a family keepsake. Police Chief McKinnon did an excellent job coordinating security. The gifts that Trudy's bridge club wrapped were presented at a dinner at the Detroit Institute of Arts. As we showed off the city, it was gratifying to make a positive impression on world leaders and the media that followed them.

Many international journalists commented that the Archer administration's optimistic and electrifying momentum was the key ingredient for revitalizing our city and our economy.

The conference concluded at the Fox Theatre, where President Clinton's keynote address emphasized the importance of discussing global finance in terms of how it impacts "the economic well-being of ordinary people."

That was exactly the impact of the G7 conference for Detroit. "It was foretelling of things to come in terms of the relationship between Dennis Archer and Bill Clinton, and how strong we were with that administration," Freman says. "The resources and benefits that we got for the people of the city of Detroit and the region as a result of that were immense. Dennis' star just took off. Party politics held no more, since he was the new fresh face of cooperation and bridge-building, bringing Detroit together with the suburbs."

Surrounding myself with talented, exceptional people was key, and I especially valued David Axelrod's experience and expertise. Because he understood urban issues and political strategizing, he was always at my side, in Detroit, in Lansing, in Washington, helping me manage the most impactful ways to help Detroit.

I would routinely ask him, "Look, I'm going to be talking to the president. What do you think about this...?"

Freman credits David's subsequent success with helping to get President Barack Obama elected with the experience he gained and the relationships he nurtured while working with me.

"To me, if you think about Dennis Archer," Freman says, "he was the first Barack Obama, only in Michigan. There were no politicians of Dennis' ilk. There were no politicians like Dennis Archer running for election in cities at that time. In a victim-politician blaming atmosphere with a lot of divisiveness, all that changed when Dennis came along: he was the original model of Barack Obama."

Freman adds, "It's no coincidence that the manner in which David Axelrod cut his teeth under Dennis Archer was perfected when he became head of Barack Obama's campaign team. David Axelrod brought those same ideas and nurturing qualities to Obama."

David's help bolstered my ability to get things done on a national level, which enhanced my win-win relationship with President Clinton. That became fodder for my mayoral colleagues during my involvement with organizations that advanced the needs of mayors across America.

"Dammit, Dennis, every time I turn around, you're getting this and that," teased Philadelphia Mayor Ed Rendell.

And Republican mayors would say, "Man, you're always at the White House."

TRUDY'S RECOLLECTION OF OUR MANY WHITE HOUSE VISITS

Trudy and I enjoyed many visits to the White House, and cherished the honor of each invitation. Here, Trudy reflections on those trips. The passage is italicized to denote her point of view.

Those were good times. We attended our first Clinton Inaugural ball in January of 1993, prior to Dennis' election. After Dennis was elected, we received a series of invitations from the White House. We attended two state dinners, and Christmas parties every year that Dennis was in office. One of my favorite photos from those visits shows Hillary Clinton on December 18, 1999, wearing a beautiful, red dress. That's one of countless photos from the Clinton years that we have prominently displayed in our home.

In January of 2000, we were invited to the White House for President Bill Clinton's final State of Union address on January 27, 2000. We did not go to the Capitol to sit and listen to the speech live,

Trudy and I attended many events at the White House during the Clinton years. Here we pose with First Lady Hillary Clinton and President Bill Clinton during their annual Christmas Party on December 18, 1999. This is one of our favorite photos, which we have prominently displayed in our home.   Photo Credit: The White House

but we were in the White House, which had TVs in different rooms broadcasting it. We had flown to Washington that morning, and I had packed knowing we were going to spend the night in the White House. When we arrived, a butler led us up to The Queen's Room. We unpacked and then participated in the White House activities.

After the President's address, there was a cocktail reception. We mixed and mingled and everyone congratulated him. A select few were invited to go up to the private living quarters. That was the first time I'd been there. He was sitting at a desk, and someone had brought a book, one of his books, and he was sitting there signing the book. Dorothy Rodham, the first lady's mother, was there, along with Hillary's brother, Chelsea, and some other people.

The following morning, we went back to the Clintons' private dining room, where we had breakfast. Again, Hillary's mom was there. It was a very warm, intimate experience.

When you go through something like that, it's happening so fast, and you're looking around trying to take it in, it's just so much. Not only are you in the White House, you are in the president's private dining room having your breakfast. I enjoyed it, but it was sometime afterward that I realized exactly what we had experienced. How many people get to do that?! So much has occurred during our lifetime, but there are certain experiences you just have to stop and think: What is this? What have I just done?

The state dinners were phenomenal; the Christmas parties were fun. We never sat together. I sat with Lenny Kravitz one year. I remember dancing afterward, and I enjoyed watching Secretary of State Madeleine Albright dance. After seeing her in her professional capacity on the news, it was fun to see her enjoying herself on the dance floor.

Those were fun times going to the White House. That sleepover was the best.

My secretary, Marty Austin, recalls that I kept everything in stride, always staying focused on the work required to transform Detroit.

"He never stopped to carry on about how excited he was about the thrills in life that the rest of us would think were really exciting," Marty says. "You stayed in the Lincoln bedroom? No big deal. He put his whole heart into everything that he did, and had a great outcome, but he always went on to the next project without much fanfare. Especially during the mayoral years when he worked around the clock, he would have a meeting overseas or in another state, and he'd come back, get off the plane, and go to a meeting in Detroit. I would ask him, 'Why don't you fall off the radar for a day or two? The meeting ends on this day, so why don't you stay over a couple days and rest?' Nope. He would just look at me and smile. It was kind of like, 'That's a nice thought, Marty.' And he would say, 'No I have this, this, and this to do,' and he went on with it. Never one time did he ever stay over. Never one time."

MAKING THE MANOOGIAN MANSION OUR NEW HOME

The Manoogian Mansion has been the residence for the mayor of Detroit for decades. Trudy and I felt strongly that the home on the Detroit River should be renovated and updated from top to bottom before we moved in. No major reconditioning had occurred since Mayor Young began calling it home in 1973. So we asked Beth to oversee the renovations with Grosse Pointe Farms designer D.J. Kennedy and Grosse Pointe contractor Chris Blake.

The original owner of the Manoogian, built in 1928, lost it during the Great Depression. In 1939, Taylor, Michigan-based Masco

We lived in the Manoogian Mansion, the official residence for the mayor of Detroit. This photo, taken by family friend and attorney Curtis Blessing, shows the back of our home, which faced the swimming pool and Detroit River. The irises were a gift from the Blessing family.   Photo Credit: Curtis Blessing

Corporation founder Alex Manoogian, a prominent Armenian American businessman, bought the home. In an act of generosity and philanthropy that exemplified Manoogian's love for Detroit, he and his wife, Marie, donated the house to the city of Detroit in 1965 as the official residence of the mayor.

With Beth overseeing renovations and the renovation budget, we felt confident that the city of Detroit and its taxpayers would not have to pay for the makeover.

"We set up the Manoogian Mansion Restoration Society, a 501(c)(3) entity, for the restoration of the Manoogian Mansion," Beth says. "Its Board of Directors consisted of Richard Manoogian as chairman, Cynthia Ford, Beth Sachs, Wilson Copeland, and me as president. We also had leftover funds from the G7 visit sitting in the host committee's 501(c)(3). Our lawyers determined that the G7 nonprofit could donate its surplus to the Manoogian Mansion Restoration Society nonprofit fund. We were granted permission by the G7 donors to use the leftover funds in this manner, and everyone agreed. The board collaborated on the extent of the renovations and decorations, but left the final design decisions to Trudy and D.J. Kennedy.

"We had a lot of work to do — there was a lot to restore," Beth says. "So we made a list of various local companies that might be helpful. Donations made to the Manoogian Mansion Restoration Society were tax deductible."

The house had no air conditioning; adding it to a 1920's house was difficult and expensive. A local heating and cooling company donated that part of the project. The bowling alley in the basement was restored thanks to a donation from First Independence Bank. The bulk of the donations came from Masco Corporation and its affiliates.

After the house was complete, Richard Manoogian, Chairman of MASCO and son of Alex Manoogian, came into the house. He looked around at the work with an approving expression, and noticed the first-floor bathroom sink. He said, "Oh, boy, this is really a neat bathroom sink."

I said, "Richard, one of your companies made this sink."

"Really, which one?" he asked.

Masco Corporation Founder Alex Manoogian had invented the Delta faucet, among other things. In fact, when D.J. Kennedy went shopping to make purchases, he was like a kid in a candy shop. He went to several MASCO showrooms; it turned out that at the time the Masco Corporation owned just about everything necessary to decorate a house: cabinets, plumbing products, and fine furniture by companies such as Henderon, Sherle Wagner, and Marge Carson.

Trudy decided to have the gardens completely renovated, too. Beth Sachs, a member of the Manoogian Mansion Restoration Board and the founder of the Greening of Detroit, was involved with the gardens. Her husband, Sam, was then-director of the Detroit Institute of Arts. The DIA loaned several works of fine art to the Manoogian Mansion, as did a renowed art collector, Dr. Walter Evans, and two local art galleries, Sherry Washington Art Gallery and George R. N'Namdi Gallery. All of the furnishings and artwork were either owned by or loaned to the Manoogian Mansion Restoration Society.

We moved into the Manoogian in November of 1994. Denny and Vincent lived on the third floor for a short while, until Denny bought a condo in Indian Village Manor and Vincent moved to New York.

Our dog, Bogie, had the run of the house. He was a real fixture, greeting everybody. Bogie was at all the parties, hoping someone would drop some food for him. He was four years old, and he grew attached to the security folks. In fact, we were all very close to the security team. They were so much like family that we often had parties just for them.

In the spring of 1995, beautiful yellow tulips came up. The City of Detroit Recreation Department was in charge of the city's parks, as well as the Manoogian Mansion grounds. They did a beautiful job of planting.

Our Christmas photo with Bogie taken at the Manoogian Mansion.

One day Trudy received a call from security while she was at court.

"There's a gentleman here named Alex Manoogian," security told her. "He saw these yellow tulips and he wanted to come see the gardens. Should we let him in?"

"Of course!" Trudy said. "It's his house!"

By then Mr. Manoogian was about 90 years old, and was there with his driver.

As soon as we moved in, we began entertaining often.

We were especially proud to host Denny's wedding to Roberta "Robbie" Orr, an attorney, and a daughter of Mrs. Alvera Orr and Dr. Robert C. Orr of Detroit, on the grounds of the Manoogian Mansion on September 15, 2001. Just days after the September 11 attack on the World Trade Center, many of our guests from other states arrived in town via car because all airplanes were grounded. Despite this challenge, the wedding and reception made Denny and Roberta's wedding day one of our family's most cherished memories.

All the while, we created an especially enjoyable annual tradition at the Manoogian Mansion when we hosted our first Christmas party. Our personal Christmas parties in the evening included friends, family, and people from a vast cross section of our local, regional, and national communities.

Rather than pulling names and exchanging gifts with each other, my appointees and staff adopted public elementary schools. Teachers and principals selected students who were invited to the Mansion, and they were welcome to bring their brothers and sisters. Each of our staff members randomly pulled the names of the students and their siblings, and we each purchased gifts for all the children.

The party featured food, performers who entertained the children with magic tricks, and my reading of The Night Before Christmas. After that, the children saw Santa Claus, played by Derrick "Rico" Dixon from our Executive Protection Unit. He was simply outstanding, and the children loved him. The event culminated with the youngsters receiving gifts. Watching them laugh and have fun was absolutely delightful.

One of the most memorable Christmas parties was when one of the guests began playing and singing at the large grand piano in the living room. The guest was Aretha Franklin. Standing nearby, listening to Aretha was Duke Fakir, one of the members of the Four Tops singing group. Similarly, an unplanned event occurred at the Manoogian Mansion when Bobby Short, the famed New York café society entertainer, stopped by after his performance at a fundraiser for me at Cobo Hall. He, too, sat at the piano, and played a few songs.

Another guest whom we welcomed into the Manoogian Mansion for our annual holiday soirée was Harry the Barber, a gentleman who inspired a special fondness in me. Throughout my tenure as mayor, I visited Harry's barbershop on Detroit's east side, where he

The many esteemed guests who attended our annual Christmas party at the Manoogian Mansion included Ford Motor Company Director Edsel B. Ford (top); and "Queen of Soul" Aretha Franklin (bottom left). The singer/pianist Bobby Short entertained at the Manoogian Mansion following a fundraiser in my honor (bottom right).

Photo Credit: Bill Sanders

cut my beard and doled out wisdom to me and other patrons as if he were a minister and psychologist all in one. Harry could easily have been an investment banker, lawyer, or captain of industry in another profession. Yet he chose a career that enabled him to make people look nice.

I also invited him to attend baseball games with me, and later, I had the honor of speaking at his funeral in 2016. I talked about how we shared good times, and how he represented the countless unsung heroes who lived and worked every day in the city of Detroit, making it a special place to live. I paid final tribute to Harry by eulogizing him with a quote that he personified by Dr. Martin Luther King Jr.:

> "If a man is called to be a street sweeper, he should sweep streets even as a Michelangelo painted, or Beethoven composed music or Shakespeare wrote poetry. He should sweep streets so well that all the hosts of heaven and earth will pause to say, 'Here lived a great street sweeper who did his job well.'"

Harry did his job well, and those of us whose lives he touched, are all better for it.

Empowerment Zone Victory:
Crowning Achievement of First Year in Office

Shortly after I took office, Henry Cisneros, the U.S. Secretary of Housing and Urban Development (HUD), came to town and explained how our city could compete to win $100 million for an Empowerment Zone to spur economic development.

I was familiar with the concept because President Clinton had campaigned on the promise to help revitalize cities with Empowerment Zones that provide tax incentives and federal grants to economically distressed communities. These zones aim to attract business investment which strengthens the city's tax base while creating jobs and new opportunities that empower people to prosper and improve their lives.

In early 1994, Secretary Cisneros hosted a huge event for cities in Michigan and other states at Cobo Hall. Six cities and three rural areas across America, he said, would compete in the $3.8 billion Empowerment Zone program, by completing a rigorous application within a deadline. Winning would require us to create a strategic plan outlining exactly where and how the federal investment, along with local dollars, would be used to revitalize an economically devastated portion of our city.

Detroit desperately needed the Empowerment Zone. But to many, investing in Detroit — given its past crime rate, epic budgetary woes, racial conflicts, dismal educational system, declining population, and abandonment by business — might have seemed as logical as rearranging deck chairs on the Titanic. Yet, buoyed by the momentum of the election, the hope of the people who electrified the Fox Theatre and the entire city during our three-day Inaugural festivities, and my unwavering commitment to fulfill my campaign promises, I set my sights on Detroit winning an Empowerment Zone. That would be a bright flashpoint for Detroiters, the state of Michigan, as well as people across America. It would leave no doubt — Detroit would be the quintessential comeback city of the millennium.

That said, we got to work!

I selected Planning and Development Director Gloria Robinson to lead the endeavor with the help of David Smydra, Nettie, Freman, and other city leaders. Together they reviewed the stringent requirements and strategized how we could position Detroit for victory.

Meanwhile, I also called in Bob Larson, a vice chairman of the Taubman Company, who had a brilliant expertise for business and real estate. I told him, "Bob, I want you to take on the responsibility to look at the entire city of Detroit and tell us how the city should be divided up into zones." I gave him 120 days to deliver this Land Use Task Force report. They divided the city into 10 zones. Then we invited the public to a big meeting at Cobo Hall so that we could hear their ideas on how to develop each of these zones. A huge crowd gathered, insisting that the zones not exacerbate existing problems such as an abundance of adult entertainment clubs along Eight Mile Road, or add fast-food restaurants to the glut of drive-through eateries in certain parts of our city that consistently ranked too high on annual reports of America's obesity rate. Instead, people wanted more recreation centers, grocery stores, family restaurants, and programs.

The synergy of the community coming together with our experts, for this and a follow-up meeting, was exciting. While Bob Larson's task force was doing its work, unfortunately, national media reports about the Empowerment Zone process never named Detroit as a serious contender. Additionally, our local fundraising was not viewed as competitive to win the Empowerment Zone. I expressed this concern to Brenda L. Schneider, first vice-president of development for Comerica Bank and head of a group of lenders in the zone. Comerica Bank, whose world headquarters were downtown Detroit, was spearheading corporate fundraising to match funds for the Empowerment Zone application. Brenda told me, "We've met with banks and came up with half a billion dollars to invest."I told her, "Brenda, nobody gives Detroit a prayer. Detroit is not mentioned as a serious contender in any of the national media reports I've seen about the Empowerment Zone. They mention New York, Los Angeles, Philadelphia, Camden, New Jersey, Kansas City, Missouri and Kansas City, Kansas. What can we do to launch Detroit to the front of the line?"

We sat in silent contemplation for a moment.

"Go back and get me a billion dollars," I said.

Brenda explained that the bank's computerized system could project how her bank could provide loans over a decade. Ever optimistic, she got to work.

"We have $1.92 billion committed," she told me at our subsequent meeting. What a star and a blessing Brenda Schneider turned out to be! The banks committed $1 billion to loan over 10 years. Ford, Chrysler, and GM vowed to invest $600 million over 10 years, along with law firms, CPA firms, professional service companies, and others who said they would provide reduced rates in the Empowerment Zone. This pledge of $1.92 billion was remarkable, but not a guarantee.

"I don't think we have the right package to put us over," I told Brenda. So I consulted with Peter Schweizer of Campbell Ewald, who assembled a team to create a *pro bono* video about Detroit, lacing the engaging narrative with convincing financial lingo to guarantee support.

Meanwhile, I flew to Washington, DC, to ask Michigan's Congressional leaders — including U.S. Senator Don Riegle,

U.S. Senator Carl Levin, U.S. Representative John Dingell, U.S. Representative John Conyers and the entire Michigan delegation — to campaign across party lines to garner support for Detroit to win the Empowerment Zone.

I told them, "I need your help to press for the city of Detroit and let lawmakers and Secretary Cisneros know that Detroit will deliver."

While other cities were hiring consultants, our local firms donated staff, and we emphasized the importance of allowing our local community to lead this endeavor.

Gloria Robinson led a cross section of thousands of people from banks, corporations, neighborhoods, community groups, and businesses across the city in a series of meetings to review the contest criteria and select the best swath of the city to nominate for the Empowerment Zone.

"The concept of the Empowerment Zone was a grassroots up process," Gloria says. "We had a small group of community organizations that we brought to the planning department conference room, to help us select the area that would go into the Empowerment Zone. My staff took every census track and put little stickies on them, with the area size, population, income levels, and other selection criteria. When the meeting started, I said to the organizations, 'You get to pick which of these tracts will become the Empowerment Zone.' They looked at me like I was crazy. They were not used to being given any kind of decision-making power by city officials."

Gloria epitomized grace under pressure.

"She did a wonderful job, given the fact that she had advocacy groups coming at her from 20 directions in terms of what they wanted addressed," Smydra says.

"We held endless meetings throughout the empowerment zone process where everybody got a chance to participate and have their say. We gave regular reports out to the community with updates."

Ultimately, by studying maps, census tracts, socioeconomic data and more, we delineated our Empowerment Zone as an 18.35-square-mile swath of economically challenged neighborhoods and business districts zigzagging eastward from Southwest Detroit, through Corktown, and extending well into the east side, then extending northward from the Detroit River up to the I-94 Freeway. More specifically, this area extended from Fort and the Rouge River to the southwest, Balfour to the east, Oakland Avenue to the north, and Jefferson and the Fisher Freeway to the southeast. That area was home to 101,279 residents and 9,000 businesses.

Our strategic plan comprised a huge document focusing on three major themes: creating economic opportunities, creating healthy and safe families, and restoring neighborhoods. We listed the problems and solutions, then identified specific programs that we would implement, which was far more detailed than other plans submitted. Our plan also included a lot of graphics, which editorial cartoonists at the local newspapers kindly created for us.

"They are supposed to be impartial," Gloria says, "but they said yes because this was the first major initiative for the mayor. Everybody was so excited about him being elected mayor. A breath of fresh air had gone through the city. Everybody wanted to participate, and everybody could participate."

Preparing the application — which we titled "Jump Starting the Motor City" — required round-the-clock work to meet the submission deadline.

"We would spend the night in the office sometimes," Gloria recalls. "People would joke, 'Don't come to the Planning Department. You'll never be seen again!'"

Unfortunately, two weeks before the deadline, the writing was still not strong enough.

"You need to rewrite this," Gloria told the team. "They are not going to give us $100 million based on this section of the plan. This has got to be the best plan we can do."

She echoed our belief that it would be phenomenal to win something that was expected by most to go to New York, Chicago, Los Angeles, and other big cities.

The application also required specific financial commitments from a wide net of supporters, including social service agencies, business groups, banks, and corporate organizations.

"We obtained letters of commitment that were not required," Gloria says, "but we wanted the federal government to see how serious we were. Every dollar committed in terms of private investment we backed up with a letter in the application. Every company stated what the money was for."

It is important to note that the commitments were not contingent upon winning the Empowerment Zone designation, as Secretary Henry Cisneros admonished, the commitments were irreversible. We had almost $2 billion in commitments from the public and private sector — even if we didn't win.

All the while, this grueling process required tenacity.

"Some days I didn't think we'd pull it off," Gloria says. "Some days the arguments were too much. The suspicion and cynicism, even having City Council approve the submission of the application, because they had to sign off on it, was a challenge because they decided they wanted to divvy up some money. I really had to fight to preserve the vision that the mayor wanted for this application."

Likewise, Nettie says she became Gloria's "enforcer" to make sure those who made promises, kept them.

"At one meeting with the banks," Nettie says, "Gloria said she was having a problem with them putting their money where their mouth was, and coming through with the program. So I called a meeting with all the banks. I walked in, and the fact that I was there put them on edge. I read the riot act to them. I said, 'This is not what you promised to do. This is what we need you to do, and this is what we expect you to do.' I was not smiling when I said it. People may have thought, 'Here's this little old lady...' and tried to blow me off. But they only did that once. I wasn't playing, and I knew what I was doing. They came through."

As a result of our exemplary teamwork, President Clinton, Vice President Gore and Secretary Cisneros announced that Detroit won the Empowerment Zone on December 21, 1994.

First, they broke the news to us during a conference call with myself, Nettie, Gloria, and her two community committee co-chairs.

"You had the absolute best application, bar none, by any city or cities," President Clinton told us. That was especially exciting because Detroit — along with Atlanta, Baltimore, Chicago, New York City, and a joint effort between Philadelphia and Camden, New Jersey — were selected as winners from about 500 communities that applied. (The rural communities were in Kentucky, Mississippi, and Texas.)

"You went above and beyond in terms of community participation, with more than any other city," Vice President Gore said.

Secretary Cisneros praised that we had more promised public and private investment. The city even committed a block grant fund to the Empowerment Zone area, which was unprecedented for city council to do that.

"Everybody was so excited," Gloria says. "It was like a rebirth for the city."

David Smydra agreed. "We had been in office for almost a whole year. We were fighting one major fire after another, trying to show some accomplishments. We'd made some progress with the downtown initiative, the philanthropic outreach, and the initial stages of Goal Based Governance. The Empowerment Zone gave us a big victory for neighborhoods that led to other successes that really put Dennis on the map."

That was powerful! It could not have been more exciting to conclude my first year in office with a huge celebration that our hard work had resulted in this crowning victory for the city of Detroit.

"On behalf of the city of Detroit, I would like to thank the President of the United States, HUD Secretary Henry Cisneros, and the Community Enterprise Board, led by Vice President Al Gore, for their faith in the people of Detroit," I said during a press conference announcing the award.

"We have put forward our vision and our strategic plan to revitalize our city, and they have given us an extraordinary opportunity to implement that plan, and realize our vision. We are also grateful to our state's representatives in Washington for their bipartisan support, and in particular Senators Carl Levin and Donald Riegle, and Representatives John Conyers, Barbara-Rose Collins, and John Dingell, for their tireless efforts on our application's behalf. I would like to thank Governor Engler for his leadership through his departments and his personal commitment to Detroit's efforts."

I explained, and the media subsequently published and broadcast detailed reports, that Detroit's Empowerment Zone Strategic

Plan encompassed 80 different projects, 49 of which would receive federal funds.

"The projects are designed to do three things," I said. "Create economic opportunity; sustain competent, healthy, safe families; and restore and upgrade neighborhoods." We shared more good news that private commitments were made to invest $1.9 billion in the zone, led by local banks and industry leaders.

"The Empowerment Zone designation is a significant step in our march toward economic development and revitalization for Detroit," we announced. "Our city is a great place to live and a great place to do business, and with the Empowerment Zone, we are making Detroit even better."

"WHEN WILL WE SEE THE EMPOWERMENT ZONE?"

In early 1995, as I embarked upon my second year of being mayor, newspaper reporters began to pepper me with questions about when businesses would start moving back into the city. We had an answer for them soon enough; Chrysler Motors Chairman Robert Eaton called from Argentina.

"Mr. Mayor," he asked, "how would you like to have a $750 million engine plant in your city?"

"YES!" I shouted with a fist pump.

The Chrysler Jeep plant was built at Mack and Conner, about a 10-minute drive east from downtown.

Chrysler then followed with an announcement of a second engine plant.

With that, Chrysler became the largest corporate investor in the Empowerment Zone and had stimulated supplier investment. The Engine complex investment totaled $1.65 billion in the Empowerment Zone.

RENAISSANCE ZONES

Later, Governor Engler conceived the idea for Renaissance Zones, to spur business development in Michigan cities. General Motors tore down the Fleetwood Cadillac plant and the Hispanic Manufacturing Center was built. Former Detroit Pistons champion Vinnie Johnson opened a company. My Western Michigan University classmate Ron Hall opened Bridgewater Interiors, and John James opened James Group International, a supply chain management company. Many more businesses started coming in.

Meanwhile, newspapers nationwide were publishing critical stories that empowerment zones and cities weren't doing much, but Detroit was different. It was coming together so quickly, people doubted how much we'd raised.

"Here's how much we have now," I reported repeatedly, with our tallies continuously rising.

Our upward trajectory kept Detroit in the lead of the six Empowerment Zone cities in terms of the dollars and businesses we were attracting. Vice President Gore, who was responsible for reporting updates on the Empowerment Zones, frequently invited us to Washington, DC, to share the successes that we were cultivating in Detroit.

I suggested to the vice president that he come to Detroit to see what he had caused to happen. He agreed.

The local papers ran stories with maps of the Empowerment Zone, notating how much had been invested where. This was the confirmation for all those who thought we were telling a fib: people saw for themselves that what was occurring was huge.

Within just a few years, by 1997, the Empowerment Zone Development Corporation had implemented more than 80 major developments in the city.

One of the most exciting Empowerment Zone linkages involved the rehabilitation of an abandoned public library from the World War I era. By combining the investment commitment of the Kellogg Foundation with Empowerment Zone funding, we turned a symbol of urban blight and decay into a state-of-the-art child care and family-support center. The new family center's integration into the revitalization of the surrounding community is a powerful testimonial to the capacity of Detroit organizations working together when given the opportunity.

The impact of the Empowerment Zone and its $1.9 billion commitment in private investment make it one of America's great urban success stories.

In fact, our combined "sweat equity" of corporate, community, and governmental partnerships enabled Detroit to host the White

House Economic Zone conference featuring Vice President Al Gore on April 14th through 16th in 1997. This was the first time the conference was held outside of Washington, DC, and it provided a golden opportunity for Detroit to showcase our hard work to other Empowerment Zone cities.

"The Empowerment Zone conference with the Vice President put Detroit on the main stage in ways that we had not experienced in some time," Judith says. "It also signaled that Mayor Archer had worked really hard and would continue to foster a great relationship with our leaders in federal government and help Detroit get the resources it needed. Having the G7 and Empowerment Zone come to Detroit was Washington's confidence in the new leadership in the city."

Graphic Credit: Comerica Bank

Please see the Appendix for a larger version of this map and a complete list of development projects.

"The federal dollars came and went," says David Smydra, "but our greatest success was the private investment coming back into the city."

The success of the Empowerment Zone far exceeded our expectations and helped the city of Detroit create thousands of new jobs. Every year, Brenda made maps detailing all the new development, and she compiled all the data summarizing the Empowerment Zone's annual success in an outstanding report.

"It's been unbelievable," Brenda said in 1999. "We've met our 10-year lending goals in less than five years."

Meetings Continue with Governor Engler

Continuous meetings with Governor Engler and his staff enabled us to maintain the momentum of a positive working relationship that benefited Detroit and the state.

I'd bring my staff on a bus and sometimes it was just cars with six, eight, or 10 people and we'd sit in his conference room and talk about issues related to the city. Beth, CEO of the Detroit Economic Growth Corporation, was there. Each city and state appointee who had responsibilities with the subject matter would work together to resolve the issue.

"One of the smarter things we did during that period was to get a number of our different state agencies involved with the city," Governor Engler said. "Because of the cooperative nature of the Archer administration, we established regular sessions where members of the heads of agencies would meet with counterparts in Detroit to talk through certain issues."

Governor Engler agrees that teamwork was the key to our success. "Because Mayor Archer brought some good people into government and we could work with those people there were times when Dennis and I did not have to meet because our key lieutenants were actually deep in conversation about how to resolve it and take care of the needs we might have."

At the same time, Trudy and I had the opportunity to socialize with Governor Engler and his wife Michelle at various events. The state declared 1994 as The Year of the Family. Michelle Engler and Trudy co-chaired the year's events.

"As a couple, Dennis and Trudy Archer were exceptional representatives of the city and its leadership," Governor Engler said. "Their personal integrity and responsibility made it a positive experience for anyone who dealt with them. Dennis was a good and able representative of what you'd like to see in leadership in terms of personal qualities, integrity, and demeanor. On social occasions, he was always very charming."

Revenue Sharing

Paul Hillegonds, a Republican member of the Michigan House of Representatives, recalls, "They had their frustrations and some disagreements, but the revenue-sharing agreement is a great example of a tough issue where Mayor Archer worked with the governor to get a bipartisan solution."

David Smydra recalls on the subject of revenue sharing between the state and the city of Detroit, "There was a handshake agreement that if the city reduced income tax on residents and nonresidents, then the state would continue providing revenue sharing at the same level for eight years."

The revenue-sharing formula for the state was going to expire and had to be rewritten in Lansing. There was a great fear that what had been a very large amount to the city of Detroit based upon the povery rate would be reduced by a new formula. Detroit did benefit — about a third of the state's discretionary revenue sharing went to the city, which amounted to $334 million annually. That level of support was in jeopardy with a new formula.

I worked with Governor Engler and succeeded in grandfathering or retaining the $334 million level of support if the city would start to reduce the city income tax level by a tenth of a percent annually. At that time, the city income tax was a real deterrent to residents and to businesses wanting to invest, so it made sense to reduce that level but only if the state retained its share of revenue sharing for the city.

That was the partnership.

That policy was adopted by the legislature. Sadly, when the recession hit, the state started to reduce the amount of revenue sharing to the city and the city was forced to stop reducing the city income tax.

This reduction in revenue sharing was an important factor that over time contributed to driving the city to file for bankruptcy.

Residency Requirement for
Detroit Police Officers & Firefighters

Legislation was pending to repeal the city residence requirement for police and firefighters, and all city employees. I fought like hell trying to point out to Governor Engler why it was so important for Detroit and 83 other municipalities to keep its residency programs. We negotiated and paid more in union contracts because that's what a Michigan Supreme Court case mandated. You had to be willing to pay more if you wanted residency. We did. The police wanted its officers to be able to live outside Detroit. When Governor Engler abolished residency, the police unions supported George W. Bush for president in 2000.

Change in the School District

One of the most challenging issues was the Detroit school board, their deficit, and our schools failing our children. The legislature adopted legislation that created an appointed school board for five years with the ability of the residents to decide by vote to keep the new system or do away with it after five years. The school district was losing student population rapidly and was in financial trouble.

It was in March of 1999 that Governor Engler signed legislation giving me 30 days to name six of seven members of a reform board. Governor Engler appointed the other member and his appointee had veto power over any decision of the appointed board. I appointed Freman as Chair.

Detroit Recorder's Court

The city's criminal court was under attack in Lansing. The Republican-controlled House of Representatives, following the Malice Green trial in which two white police officers were convicted of fatally beating Green, who was black — voted to eliminate the court and move its judges to Wayne County Circuit Court.

I vigorously opposed the legislation.

I wanted to maintain Recorder's Court. Judges of Recorder's Court had to be city residents and jury members chosen to decide the fates of defendants were city residents. This issue was racially charged. Dissolving Recorder's Court would put black defendants in front of juries from white suburban communities.

Governor Engler signed the legislation abolishing Recorder's Court by merging it into Wayne County Circuit Court.

10

CONTINUING PROGRESS:
SECONDING PRESIDENT CLINTON'S NOMINATION AND CONTINUING DETROIT'S PROGRESS

WHILE WE WERE WORKING hard to transform Detroit into a thriving city, I carried our positive momentum and innovative ideas onto the national stage, through participation in several organizations and events.

First, on January 24, 1996, The National Conference of Democratic Mayors (NCDM) elected me to a two-year term as its president. This happened at the 64th annual winter meeting of the U.S. Conference of Mayors, a bipartisan organization that enables about 1,400 mayors from American cities whose populations surpass 30,000 to work together to advocate for policies that affect urban areas.

"Mayors," I said during election remarks, "we must come together and speak with a strong voice in the 1996 federal elections on how to rebuild America."

In this capacity, I had the honor and pleasure of working with Mayor Wellington Webb of Denver, Colorado, vice president for communications; Mayor Susan Hammer of San Jose, California, vice president of policy; Mayor Joe Ganim of Bridgeport, Connecticut, vice president of fundraising; Mayor Marc Morial of New Orleans, Louisiana, treasurer; and Mayor Sharon Sayles Belton of Minneapolis, Minnesota, secretary.

"Dennis had the immediate respect and admiration of all of his peers," says Marc Morial, now president of the National Urban League. "He was seen as a statesman. I looked up to him because he was a seasoned, experienced operator with a tremendous degree of confidence."

Also at this time, I served on the board of directors of the National Conference of Black Mayors and was appointed co-chair on the Intergovernmental Policy Advisory Committee of the U.S. Trade Representative's office.

"Dennis was not only the mayor of Detroit, he was a considerable national figure," Marc adds.

Vice President Al Gore referenced me and the hard work we were doing to improve Detroit at the U.S. Conference of Mayors meeting at the White House.

"I hope Dennis Archer won't mind if I cite the example of Detroit," he said the day after I became president of the National Conference of Democratic Mayors. "The Empowerment Zone there is 18 square miles, largely made up of vacant lots and abandoned buildings, many of which are brownfields. But that is changing. Now $2 billion of private investment has been targeted on that empowerment zone — a fast-growing housing market and hundreds of new jobs. And with the bipartisan support that all the empowerment zones are garnering, that is just the beginning."

Vice President Gore then elaborated on President Clinton's commitment to helping America's cities through innovative policies. My frequent trips to Washington to work with lobbyists and legislators enabled me to advocate for resources for Detroit, and I did the same for people across America through my work with the mayors' organizations.

"Dennis was a strong voice and part of a collective group of mayors who were black, white, mostly Democratic with a few Republicans," Marc recalls. "We were always meeting with the president and cabinet officers to present our concerns and our needs."

One example of this occurred when I vehemently opposed the Republican Congress' harsh, mean-spirited solution for welfare reform. While I agreed that the system needed major updating, no viable solutions had yet to be presented. In fact, President Clinton had already vetoed two welfare reform bills, and was poised to sign into law the Personal Responsibility and Work Opportunity Reconciliation Act of 1996.

Prior to that, other Democratic mayors and I lobbied President Clinton because we believed that cancelling people's benefits without providing a safety net or jobs would place the burden on cities to cope with thousands of people lacking financial support.

"Our point was that if you reform welfare and people lose their benefits," Marc recalls, "and they are kicked off the rolls with no jobs, we'll be responsible for the social ills. Dennis was with a group of us who challenged President Clinton when he wanted to sign the Welfare Reform Bill. We were opposed to it. The president convened a meeting with Henry Cisneros with the mayors of big cities in Chicago to talk through the Welfare to Work job training program where we'd control the money to allow us to assist people coming off welfare and getting into employment. Dennis delivered tough messages in diplomatic terms. He had a judicial temperament; he was assertive and measured at the same time. You never saw him hesitate to take the initiative to speak on what was best for the residents and city of Detroit. That passion came through."

Fortunately, our efforts were successful.

"Knowing the president would sign the bill," Marc says, "we were able to secure a commitment in helping our people secure jobs if they came off the welfare rolls. As a big collective group of mayors, we were trying to shape national public policy."

After President Clinton signed PRWORA into law on August 22, 1996, I appreciated that he pledged to do his best to change elements of the bill that were inappropriate. That inspired me to encourage a huge voter turnout in the fall and to vote in more Democratic support for the president in Congress.

One way that I had the honor of doing this occurred on Wednesday, August 28, 1996, when I was selected to second President Clinton's nomination for re-election at the Democratic National Convention in Chicago. My prepared speech included mention of my roots on Detroit's east side, changes in the city since I took office, and the many ways that the Clinton Administration was benefitting the city of Detroit. Among them the Empowerment Zone, which attracted $1.9 billion in new commitments from Detroit businesses and banks, and the President's Crime Bill, which put 96 new police officers on Detroit's streets with 120 more to come.

My heart was pounding as I took the podium before the world media. It was over in a flash, but it was one of the most exhilarating honors.

"This speech was less important for Dennis Archer, than it was for Detroit," David Axelrod recalls. "The image of the city had been suffering. Here was this splendid guy, a really uplifting presence, giving a very robust speech. In a sense, it wasn't just him seconding the nomination of the president, but it was also him signaling that Detroit was coming back."

President Bill Clinton was re-elected in November of 1996. After the election, Trudy and I traveled to San Francisco, where I was to give a speech to the members of the California Bar Association who helped to start the California Minority Counsel Demonstration Program. As I was getting dressed, I received a telephone call from a member of President Clinton's cabinet, who discussed two cabinet positions with me. I respectfully declined, because I had not completed my first term as mayor, and I wanted to finish what I started and did not want to let down the citizens of Detroit.

My work on a national level continued throughout our administration, and I was president of the National League of Cities in 2001. In July of that year, Detroit hosted the U.S. Conference of Mayors. *Jet* magazine published a photo of me shaking President George W. Bush's hand as we were surrounded by Philadelphia Mayor John Street, Washington, DC Mayor Anthony Williams, and New Orleans Mayor Marc Morial, who had just been elected president of the U.S. Conference of Mayors.

WORLD'S LARGEST AUTOMAKER
JUMPSTARTS DETROIT'S FUTURE

Creating a world-class city required rebuilding a solid economic base for downtown Detroit that included businesses, restaurants, sports stadiums, and gathering places, both indoors and outdoors, where people felt safe.

Yet the reality when I took office was anything but.

The Renaissance Center — the riverfront office and hotel complex built in partnership with Henry Ford II, Max Fisher, and Albert Taubman as a symbol of the city's rebirth, also known as the RenCen — was for sale. The right ownership could be a powerful catalyst to jumpstart downtown development. At the time, Ford Motor Company was using it for office space.

Meanwhile, General Motors was looking for a new home. The world's largest automaker at the time was headquartered in the 1920's Albert Khan-designed building on West Grand Boulevard in Detroit's New Center Area. GM wanted to consolidate its many satellite offices around the state, as well as evolve into a more integrated workplace that inspired face-to-face interaction between the leadership and their staff.

GM could have easily abandoned Detroit for the suburbs, where Ford Motor Company had long been operating out of world headquarters in Dearborn, and Chrysler Corporation had recently moved to Auburn Hills.

I would soon learn that Harry Pearce, GM's General Counsel who had been instrumental in the success of "The Harry Peace Letter" with the ABA, would play a starring role in making the first move in what many businesses viewed as an extremely high-stakes chess game — investing in the city of Detroit because they believed in the possibility of a true turnaround on every level.

One day, Harry was sitting in his office in the GM Building, when Matt Cullen, who headed the company's worldwide real estate operations, entered and said:

"Harry, I've got an idea, but it's really out of the box."

"Well I like out-of-the-box ideas," Harry responded. "What do you have in mind?"

"We have a shot at buying the Renaissance Center at a pretty reasonable price," Matt said. Though it had cost $350 million to build, its sale price was $125 million.

For a moment, Harry reflected on his impression of Detroit when he first came here in 1985, when he drove down Woodward Avenue to GM's legal offices in the New Center Area.

"It was pretty bleak," he says. "I had never seen anything quite like it, growing up in North Dakota. We didn't have devastated areas like that."

At the same time, Harry had known me for many years as an attorney committed to pioneering change in the legal industry across America. Likewise, Matt was aware of my judicial background, as well as my success at building bridges during my campaign and first two years, thus far, of my administration.

With a shared faith in my leadership, they discussed Matt's innovative ideas for financing the purchase, as well as the urgency because other investors were looking at the property. It was a desirable investment, due to the depressed real estate market.

"Wow, if we could get the Renaissance Center at a fair price," Harry said, "that would truly be a statement with respect to the auto industry, the city of Detroit, and the state of Michigan. For GM to have its world headquarters in the middle of a town that clearly needed to be revitalized, would be very positive."

So inspired, Harry asked Matt to join him in sharing the idea with GM Chairman Jack Smith.

Intrigued, Jack launched an immediate structural and financial analysis of the building. He and GM's leaders walked the building. Its interior was notorious for being confusing to navigate; GM's design team would need to make the building more user-friendly. The exterior felt like "a well-guarded prison" due to huge cement berms between the building and Jefferson Avenue. GM's designers decided to remove the bunker-like cement structures and replace them with a glass façade and circular driveway. That would offer a welcoming entryway for GM's world headquarters. In addition, the riverside wasteland behind the Renaissance Center was downright grim and gritty.

"When we looked out and down from the window from the 39th floor in the towers," Harry recalls, "we saw vacant lots and piles of gravel and debris. Here was one of the most potentially beautiful riverwalks on one of the busiest waterways in the country, so why don't we make an investment and transform this area?"

That could include maximizing riverfront access with a promenade, parks, concerts, outdoor restaurants, and more.

Jack, Harry, and GM leadership realized that the Renaissance Center was the ultimate diamond in the rough. It would take millions to polish it into the gleaming corporate palace that it deserved to be as global headquarters for the world's largest automaker. But that investment, they believed, could sparkle back in immeasurable dividends for both GM and the city of Detroit.

"We made the decision to buy it," Harry says. "We made an offer, and it was accepted. We sat down with Dennis and said, 'You know, we will make major contributions financially if the state will make its own commitment.'"

Specifically, when looking east down the Detroit River from the glass towers of the RenCen, Belle Isle park looked like a beautiful emerald oasis. The up-close reality, however, was that this city-run property was trash-strewn, neglected due to financial strife, and some believed, overrun with unruly teenagers and even criminals.

"We need someone else running Belle Isle, which is turning into a disaster area," Harry said.

Peter Stroh had already visited with the Detroit Economic Growth Corporation and its Downtown Development Authority to pitch a riverfront promenade that would stretch from the Belle Isle Bridge to the Ambassador Bridge. In fact, Peter, Matt Cullen, and Beth DunCombe visited Toronto, Ontario, to see its riverfront, and how its layout might inspire a similar design for Detroit. Then, thanks to Edsel B. Ford II and his work as the leader and champion of the 300th anniversary of the founding of Detroit, which was celebrated on July 24, 2001, the riverfront was transformed. A new walkway was paved with bricks bearing donors' names, and a statue was erected, as what became the Riverfront Conservancy transformed the riverfront from Joe Louis Arena to the rear of what was Ford Auditorium.

With all that said, GM laid out a plan that included the creation of a riverside promenade stretching from the Ambassador Bridge to the Belle Isle Bridge, as well as having the state of Michigan manage Belle Isle after fixing the infrastructure and cleaning it up.

"Again I give Matt Cullen a lot of credit for getting right into that and putting together an organization with the state of Michigan and GM," Harry says. "Matt, Dennis, and I also give a lot of credit to Jack Smith because he signed off to agree to buy the Renaissance Center, which he did very quickly. He could see the same vision that Dennis could see, and off we went."

Another benefit? The state of Michigan moved its Detroit offices into the former GM building, renamed Cadillac Place to celebrate Detroit's founder, Antoine Laumet de La Mothe, sieur de Cadillac, who arrived via the Detroit River in a canoe.

"The positive momentum that Dennis was creating for the city was more important to GM's decision to purchase the Renaissance Center than the actual transaction," says Matt Cullen, who now plays a leadership role in downtown Detroit's continued revitalization as Chair, Detroit RiverFront Conservancy and Principal of Rock Ventures LLC.

"We would not have made a decision to do that if it were not for the confidence that we had in Dennis Archer and the change of culture in the city. Dennis coming in and creating a foundation of trust and capacity and passion for the city that caused a lot of us to be willing to take a second look at it and say maybe the decline of the city is not inevitable, and maybe working together we could turn it around. That was definitely part of the calculus when we talked about it internally. At the time, GM made a profoundly courageous move to downtown Detroit and tying its future so inextricably to the city of Detroit."

Once the deal was made for GM to purchase the RenCen for about $70 million, Harry and I began meeting regularly.

"I sat down with Dennis," he recalls. "He thought it was clearly a move to revitalize the business community to cause other companies to come downtown. And once you could establish a larger workforce and companies residing in the city, that would lead to other things like restaurants and sports arenas. We went public and announced in the middle of May 1996, and we were off and running."

The national media covered the story. During many interviews, I expressed gratitude and excitement that the world's biggest corporation deemed downtown Detroit worthy of housing its global headquarters.

This seismic shift for Detroit's economy and morale would occur as General Motors moved 5,400 workers from Cadillac Place, and about 5,000 additional employees from its offices across Michigan. GM's purchase, ironically, made number-two automaker Ford Motor Company a tenant because its offices occupied a whole tower at the RenCen.

Meanwhile, the Detroit City Council had to approve the action of removing the cement berms. City Councilwoman Sheila Cockrel was horrified by the way GM's representatives were interrogated by some City Councilmembers, who viewed everything through a racial lens that perceived white businesses as a threat of losing black power in the city.

"I will never forget," Sheila says, "seeing Matt Cullen and a string of other people representing GM and this $500 million project to revitalize our downtown, coming before City Council and being subjected to this mentality that had hurt the city for so many years."

When Matt testified, a City Councilmember demanded, "Where do you live?"

Sheila says the question was motivated by fear that white, non-Detroiters were going to come in and "take over" the city, displacing black people.

"Why do we care where somebody lives?" Sheila asks now. "I wanted them to understand that Detroit needed a viable safety net to help people in abject poverty, by creating a tax base."

Sheila says she diffused the tension at the City Council hearings by telling Matt and others: "I'm appreciative of the $500 million investment that you're making to change the face of the Renaissance Center. And I don't care where you live!"

The City Council ultimately approved GM's plans. The automaker's designers got to work on creating a spectacular vehicle display on the ground floor, as well as the Winter Garden atrium overlooking the river and plaza leading down to a waterside promenade. The interior was reconfigured with a lighted, green walkway, and the hotel began a $100 million renovation. GM's $500 million facelift would not be completed until 2003.

But, in the meantime, the world's top automaker had given Detroit the jumpstart it needed for downtown development.

"It's very, very rewarding to see what has come of it," says Harry Pearce today. "We're not solely responsible for this. Many other companies had a similar vision, but somebody had to make a major move first. Once GM made the move, a lot of smaller companies had confidence in Detroit's future."

My appreciation for GM's support was immeasurable.

"Mayor Archer was so grateful that General Motors came downtown, that the mayor's official car was a GM vehicle," says Greg Bowens. "It was understood that he was a GM guy, and he'd say that openly to the automotive press. He said GM's commitment to Detroit deserved our loyalty."

COMPUWARE COMES TO TOWN: "WELCOME TO DETROIT, MY BROTHER"

General Motors' decision to purchase the Renaissance Center and relocate downtown Detroit sparked momentum for other businesses to do the same.

One morning I was in a car on my way at the request of Michigan Congressman Fred Upton to give a speech in St. Joseph, Michigan, when I read a column by *Detroit News* Business Columnist Jon Pepper. He had recently met with Peter Karmanos Jr., Chairman and Chief Executive Officer of Compuware, a computer technology company located in Farmington Hills, a Detroit suburb.

In the article, Peter Karmanos expressed a desire to move his company's 4,000 employees to downtown Detroit because it had outgrown its offices in Farmington Hills. This was exactly what I needed to hear! We arrived in St. Joseph early, and because we did not yet have cell phones, I used a pay phone to call Peter Karmanos to introduce myself.

"I read this article by Jon Pepper," I said, "and I'd very much like to talk with you. I'd like to invite you to come downtown."

"Yes," he said, "I'd be interested in coming downtown."

I was elated! "I have just the spot in mind for you," I told him. "It's the gateway to the city."

I envisioned Compuware in a new office building that would serve as the anchor for Campus Martius. The idea of office buildings around a park was conceived by Bob Larsen and his Land Use Task Force; they envisioned a vibrant, park-like gathering place at the center of downtown. I wanted people from everywhere to enjoy food, recreation, music, and people-watching in an attractive, safe space surrounded by office buildings bustling with businesses, restaurants, and boutiques. And I wanted this dream of Campus Martius Park to be so spectacular that people would return to their homes in Detroit, our surrounding communities, and the rest of the world, with their hearts and minds etched with unforgettable memories of their time here.

To make this happen, I called GM Chairman Jack Smith to ask, "Jack, will you please call Peter Karmanos and encourage him to come downtown?"

I was unaware at the time that GM was doing business with Compuware, an internationally recognized leader in the computer industry, as a highly competitive potential supplier of computer products, consulting, and training services. As we worked out the details of having this world-class company — whose 1998 revenues were $1.5 billion — relocate downtown, I kept the deal top secret.

"He would leave hints," Anthony Neely recalls, "such as, 'I think we're going to get a big tenant in the Campus Martius site.' Finally, he shared that we're going to have Compuware coming on board and he gave me all the details."

In April of 1999, we gave the story to reporter John Gallagher, who wrote a page-one story for the *Detroit Free Press* the day of our announcement, which gave us extra bang. Then, the press conference was televised in the mayor's office, and Peter Karmanos came in.

"Welcome to Detroit, my brother," I said, shaking his hand. That became the next day's headlines, and the excitement in the media, among business leaders and among my staff was electrifying. It jumpstarted everyone's new vision of a different downtown Detroit.

And it all began with a vision.

"I want people to be blown away and feel that Campus Martius is a special place that's unlike anywhere else they've ever been," I told the design team during a series of meetings. "I want them to say, 'I went to such and such restaurant and it was real nice, but you have to see this park!'"

Anthony says, "I witnessed the mayor's very impressive and persuasive presentation to the design team. He was impassioned with this very clear vision of what downtown Detroit should be."

The plan was for Campus Martius to include midrise office towers, stores, restaurants, and possibly a hotel centered by the new Compuware headquarters. With that, the work of the Detroit

Economic Growth Corporation, the city's Building Authority, and the Downtown Partnership proceeded to bring this vision to fruition.

In late 1999, ground was broken for Campus Martius Park, starting with the construction of the parking garage underneath it, and an additional underground parking garage on the site of the Hudson's department store. In 2000, construction began for the sleek, 17-floor, $550 million Compuware building, featuring a façade of glass, granite, and limestone. Architects designed a spectacular indoor waterfall in the airy atrium, which opened onto restaurants and shops, including Borders Bookstore. While Compuware would not move its headquarters there until 2003, the momentum of the deal and construction symbolized a true renaissance for downtown Detroit that magnetized other businesses to relocate as well.

The construction process inspired a reflection back on my childhood as I shopped downtown with my mother and grandmother.

"I'll meet you at the Kern Clock," people often said, referring to a large clock on Woodward Avenue marking the Kern Block in front of the Kern Department store. Now, cranes and construction crews were reviving that historic parcel of downtown Detroit, and I could not have been more proud. The Kern Clock is back at its original spot.

However, the entire block northeast of it — where the Hudson's department store tower had risen — had become vacant. After years of discussions about what to do with the historic landmark after the store closed in 1983 — the 29-floor building was demolished on October 24, 1998. Thousands of people throughout downtown and in Windsor gathered to watch the implosion of the tallest building to meet such a fate. It was quite a spectacle as a huge dust cloud engulfed the building and rolled through the city streets. That cleared space to continue the rebuilding of downtown Detroit, and the Compuware deal was a major boost for that momentum.

Wayne County Executive Edward H. McNamara was extremely proud of this progress. "This agreement is the result of a real team effort," he said. "It took both the City of Detroit and Wayne County working together to bring a new major corporate headquarters into Detroit. Compuware and the new jobs they bring will be a tremendous boost to the revitalization of downtown Detroit. This agreement also demonstrates our competitiveness in attracting businesses into the City and the County. With a downtown Detroit Compuware headquarters, the City, the County, and our area businesses will have local access to a world-renowned technology and computer services company. It's great to have this kind of high-caliber resource right here in our own business community."

Governor John Engler was also pleased: "What a vote of confidence this is for the rebirth of Detroit, and how appropriate this is coming from a business on the leading edge of technology. Peter Karmanos, a native son of Detroit, has built a world-class, Michigan-based company that has become a tremendous success story. What the 20th century was for manufacturing, the 21st century will be for technology. This announcement is important for state government because it keeps close at hand a strategic partner who will be invaluable as we plan our work and service delivery for the 21st century."

A Home Run and a Touchdown for Detroit: Side-By-Side Stadiums

My vision to transform downtown Detroit into a world-renowned destination for sports and entertainment hinged on building new stadiums for our professional sports teams.

"If you revitalize the center city, the progress radiates out into the community, and he recognized that," recalls David Axelrod, who spearheaded research on how to accomplish this. "I remember doing interviews with Detroiters about what Detroit was like in the past. We wanted to find out what it was like to come downtown to the stores and theaters. And I realized that Dennis' vision was very much about rekindling that sense of community with a downtown hub."

Detroit had lost that, and the sports teams were a significant factor. In fact, the departure of the Detroit Lions for the Silverdome in Pontiac — 30 miles north of Detroit — was perceived as another nail in our city's economic coffin when the team moved in 1975. Likewise, the Detroit Pistons had stopped playing at Cobo Hall and made The Palace of Auburn Hills — 35 miles north of Detroit — their home in 1988. Meanwhile, the Detroit Tigers were playing in a historic and beloved but extremely antiquated stadium. And the

Detroit Red Wings were stable in their downtown home at Joe Louis Arena, winning numerous Division and Conference Championships in the 1980's and 1990's as well as the Stanley Cup in 1997 and 1998.

Shortly after I became mayor, I began orchestrating discussions about how to bring new sports stadiums to downtown Detroit. This was a significant aspect of economic development for the city, and I wanted it executed with impeccable integrity and success.

I had appointed Bob Larson as chair of the Detroit Economic Growth Corporation, a nonprofit organization created during the Young administration to nurture existing businesses as well as generate and facilitate new economic development in Detroit. Bob shared my vision for the city's future, but he needed excellent leadership for the DEGC.

"Bob Larson offered me a job as president and CEO of DEGC," says Beth. "I was a partner at Dickinson Wright, and I had to ponder the offer; I even cried a few times, wondering, 'I've been at the firm for 22 years. Should I leave?' Obviously, I did. Everybody thinks I was hired by Dennis. I was not hired by Dennis. I was not part of the administration; I was hired by the 50 people on the DEGC board of directors. I later learned that they had called and asked for Dennis' approval."

Beth became CEO of the DEGC in February of 1996. The position enabled her to spearhead the biggest economic development initiatives in Detroit. At the top of the agenda? Meetings about bringing the Detroit Lions back downtown.

"When I arrived, the baseball stadium was already negotiated and done," Beth says. "We had a Memorandum of Understanding (MOU) — on how it could be put together and where to locate it."

At the time, the location being discussed was behind the Fox Theatre. One question that arose at these meetings was: "Is it possible to have the Lions and the Tigers play in the same stadium?" The answer was no.

Fortunately, voters approved side-by-side stadiums, which enabled us to focus on making that happen. We created the Stadium Authority, co-chaired by Beth, who led the discussion on behalf of the city, and Mike Duggan, who represented Wayne County. The Stadium Authority propelled the deal to completion.

Negotiations were spirited, as Detroit Tigers owner Mike Ilitch, Detroit Lions owner William Clay Ford, Beth, and Mike hashed out an agreement.

"It was not an easy agreement," Beth says, "because we had to satisfy four different interests."

Comerica Bank stepped forward for naming rights on the baseball stadium, which became Comerica Park. The NFL donated $100 million for the football stadium, while the Ilitches and the Fords also made significant investments. One point of contention was that I wanted a domed football stadium that could be used year-round for concerts and other events. However, the Lions insisted that their fans preferred the ruggedness of open-air stadiums, even during cold weather.

"The deal was," Beth recalls, "that if the mayor wanted a dome, the city would have to pay for it. The Downtown Development Authority issued bonds, and Ford Field had a dome."

And finally, a completed deal was reached.

I flew in from Martha's Vineyard. After months and months of tough negotiations, it was time to tell the world some of the most exciting news in Detroit's history. On August 20, 1996, I stood alongside William Clay Ford Sr., Bill Ford Jr., Mike Ilitch, and Wayne County Executive Ed McNamara, as we faced a cluster of TV cameras, print photographers, and reporters, none of whom had "broken" the story about our surprise announcement that morning.

The media did not know why we were gathered in the vicinity of the Detroit College of Law, an older hotel, and brick office buildings that had seen more lustrous days.

Despite our surroundings that reflected the battering that economic downturns and business abandonment had inflicted on our city, I was overwhelmed by the vision of an illustrious downtown filled with people, traffic jams, restaurants that required reservations weeks in advance, and world-class sporting events and entertainment attracting people from everywhere to the city of Detroit.

I couldn't have been more thrilled to reveal that the extraordinary teamwork between the city, the county, the Lions, and the Tigers was about to score a combined economic home run and touchdown that would catapult Detroit into a proverbial world series of thriving urban centers.

I was confident that two new sports stadiums in downtown Detroit would lay the foundation to truly let the future begin for our beloved city.

We announced that the Detroit Tigers baseball team and the Detroit Lions football team would each build a new stadium in downtown Detroit. They would sit side-by-side, serving as a catalyst for downtown development.

I explained that the stadiums would be built just east of Woodward Avenue, across from the Fox Theatre, and owned by the newly formed Detroit Wayne County Stadium Authority, run by six individuals: three members selected by myself; and other three members selected by the Wayne County Executive. After signing 35-year leases, the teams would manage their own facilities. The Lions had been playing home games at the Pontiac Silverdome since 1975; now they would be returning home.

During this announcement, prominent in my mind was the following week's trip to the Democratic National Convention in vibrant, cosmopolitan Chicago. Its sports stadiums, hotels, restaurants, cultural attractions, and waterfront created a highly desirable venue for conventions. I was confident that our two downtown sports stadiums and the subsequent surrounding restaurants would elevate the Motor City so that it was on par with the Windy City to attract the Democratic or Republican national conventions to Detroit in 2004.

Likewise, as I stood with Mr. Ford and Mr. Ilitch, and Wayne County Executive McNamara, we represented one of the greatest examples ever of public-private cooperation in Southeast Michigan. The $505 million project included $240 million for Tiger Stadium and $225 million for the Lions' Stadium, as well as $20 million for parking and $20 million for the Lions' headquarters and practice facility in Allen Park.

This magnanimous deal epitomized the spirit of bridge-building via private and public collaborations; the teamwork of my office; the Detroit Economic Growth Corporation; the Wayne County Executive's Office; the state of Michigan; and the city of Detroit's Legal Department. Dickinson Wright did all of the legal work and there was also outside bond counsel.

"We needed a signal sent that people were willing to invest in Detroit," recalls Governor Engler. "That kind of new investment was really significant. What we saw at the end of very complicated negotiations was the real commitment on the part of the Ilitch family and the Ford family and very creative work being done by the county, the city, and the state."

At the time of the announcement, backers of the deal faced three challenges. First, I needed to work with the Lions and Wayne County Executive Ed McNamara to obtain commitments for $50 million in corporate contributions. Second, we needed to nail down a reasonable purchase price for the land where the stadiums would be built, so we could ensure doing so within budget. Third, Wayne County voters would have to approve a November 5th ballot initiative imposing a one percent hotel tax and two percent rental car tax to raise $80 million for the Lions' stadium.

I returned to Martha's Vineyard later that day, and a second announcement was made in my office.

"Mike Duggan," observed press secretary Anthony Neely, "was McNamara's right hand man, and was there speaking for the county while I spoke for the mayor. It was a big day for the city and the media coverage was pretty tremendous because it talked about how the two stadiums would benefit downtown."

EXECUTIVE ORDER 4 ENSURES
INCLUSIVE CONSTRUCTION

It was imperative that new development in Detroit be inclusive of minority contractors and jobs for people of color. This issue had a long and controversial history in our city. So I consulted with Detroit Corporation Counsel Phyllis James about crafting a long-term solution that could be utilized in the major development projects that we were bringing to Detroit.

"Executive Order 4 is what we put in place for use in the city procurement process," she says. "In private development deals with private entities, we asked for commitments using Executive Order 4 which would not have a racial preference, and I feel we were very successful. We did not have any problems in court. We used the language that this was a 'small-business set-aside,' replacing the old 'sheltered-market' language."

A federal judge had ruled in 1993 that the Market Share Approach, an affirmative action program created by Mayor Young's administration, could no longer be used. The decision cited the 1989 U.S. Supreme Court ruling in the *City of Richmond v. J. A. Croson Co.*, which concluded that the Fourteenth Amendment's Equal Protection Clause was being violated by a program that gave preference to minority-owned businesses when awarding municipal contracts.

The similarity to our situation in Detroit was that the Richmond case said that in order to have an African American program, you must show how the city administration, by its action, had a disparate impact upon minorities. We had a black mayor. We had a majority black city council, and more than 50 percent of city departments were run by a person of color or a woman. It was impossible to show disparate impact.

Shortly after my election, I reached out to a number of folks, including some who hadn't supported me, such as Detroit NAACP President Wendell Anthony, his NAACP Executive Director Joann Watson, and leaders at the Shrine of the Black Madonna. I invited them to a meeting in my office and asked, "What are we going to do about creating opportunities for businesses of color to do work in this city? Do you have any suggestions?"

Former Young appointee Charlie Beckham was at the table representing black contractors.

As Architects Harold Varner and Howard Sims spoke, I listened carefully, intent on finding solutions.

In November of 1994, I invited the business community to a meeting at Cobo Hall. I implored them: "I would appreciate it immensely if you all would start doing business with our minority-owned businesses and in joint ventures, not only in Detroit but outside in our suburban communities as well. Here's what I want you to envision: Every time a business of color comes to you for hire or joint venture, as these businesses grow I want you to envision children seeing their friends whose fathers' or mothers' businesses have grown, other children now see their buddies have new clothes, their homes have been upgraded, or somebody's going to work for a company who has been out of work. All of a sudden families have a nicer car. You create an environment where kids can see that if they get an education, they don't have to sell drugs or be an athlete or entertainer. They can do well and support themselves locally."

What I learned was that we didn't have the requisite number of people trained in the construction trades required for the projects we were starting. We needed brick masons and other building trades, but we didn't have them.

I went to the unions and contractors very quietly, and said, "We have to work together."

The building trades supported me. I told them, "Since the riot in 1967, you all have been talking about making a commitment to train people. You did train people, but then they had to find their way to cities outside Detroit for the trainings. And with our transportation system being so poor, requiring two or three buses to get places, very few from the city were trained." We had to bring the training classes into Detroit or we would not have any contracts. Little by little, we started seeing the change we had hoped for.

"Dennis in his administration had more minority contracts implemented and a higher number of city residents go into the building trades than at any period prior to or since," says my advisor David Smydra. We had about 2,000 city workers involved in the building of Comerica Park. That was unheard of. The unions and contractors wanted to use their people and were arguing that their people were trained and certified, and that they couldn't go through the delay of selecting, certifying, and using inexperienced people to build a project of this nature. We spent a long, long time working through all that, so there was a team approach of new people and experienced people. That was a major achievement for the city."

This achievement was not without growing pains.

"I remember meeting extensively with the president of the Detroit Tigers," David says, "who was getting lambasted regularly by Detroit City Council on the building of Comerica Park for not having a sufficient number of minority contractors or minority workers. He wanted to do right, so Regina Simmons, head of the city's Civil Rights Department, met routinely with him and guided him through the City Council process."

As a result of that teamwork, more minority contractors and workers were hired.

When all the work was done, the 40,000-seat Comerica Park opened on Tuesday, April 11, 2000. A 15-foot stone tiger greets fans at the front gate, which faces the Fox Theatre. Inside, restaurants, suites, a carnival-type area, and entertainment spaces create a wondrous, vibrant experience for children and adults alike. Opening Day was electric with excitement, despite the cold and snow, and we had 39,168 fans in our spectacular new stadium as the Tigers defeated the Seattle Mariners, 5-2.

All the while, construction crews worked on the 70,000-seat Ford Field, which was completed in 2002. The $500 million complex — whose illuminated white dome redefined Detroit's nighttime skyline — includes restaurants, office space, shops, food courts, and private suites on four levels. As planned, Ford Field attracted

A celebratory photograph in 2000 after the NFL's announcement in Atlanta that Detroit's Ford Field would host the Super Bowl in 2006. From left: Bill Ford, Jr., then President and CEO of Ford Motor Company; Roger Penske, Penske Corporation Founder who served as chairman of Super Bowl XL; and Larry Alexander, president and CEO of the Detroit Metro Convention & Visitors Bureau.   Photo Credit: Tom Albert

events year-round, sporting events, concerts, conventions, banquets, and trade shows.

We were extremely proud when Roger Penske, Bill Ford Jr., Larry Alexander, and I traveled to Atlanta to appear before the NFL owners and were successful in winning the bid for Detroit to host the Super Bowl in 2006.

DETROIT TAKES A GAMBLE ON CASINOS — AND WINS

Starting in May of 1994, I could look out the window of my offices on the 11th floor of the City-County Building, and watch a river of cars flood Jefferson Avenue, all attempting to take the tunnel to Windsor. A quick glance down the river to my right revealed cars backed up on the Ambassador Bridge, waiting to enter Ontario.

From my office, I looked across the Detroit River, where Casino Windsor was operating temporarily in the city's art museum and was luring Detroiters and other Americans to enjoy Las Vegas-style gambling.

Groups that supported casino gaming in Detroit launched an advertising campaign showing dollar signs floating through the air over the river, leaving Detroit and fluttering into Windsor. A collaboration of Caesars World, Circus Circus Enterprises, and Hilton Hotels, the temporary casino lured millions of people from the United States and Canada.

Casino Windsor's permanent casino — a gleaming, blue-and-white glass tower directly across from the Renaissance Center — was to open in July of 1998 with Las Vegas-style glamour, celebrities, and a James Bond 007 theme. A hotel, restaurants, boutiques, and an indoor waterfall created a fantasy atmosphere. The temporary Windsor Casino became the highest grossing casino in North America. Its allure proved irresistible for Detroiters, and they let their voices be heard on August 3, 1994, by voting to approve an advisory plan for casino gambling.

While campaigning, I made it very clear that I did not favor casino gambling for Detroit because the voters had rejected the idea — by wide margins — between 1976 and 1988.

My opposition was rooted in concern that casinos might introduce an unsavory element of crime, gambling addictions, seediness, and a plethora of other scurrilous activities. I focused upon making the city attractive to business while creating good-paying jobs, reducing crime, and improving our education system. During my campaign, many ministers had asked me to oppose casino gaming in Detroit. However, once the voters had spoken, it was my obligation to heed the wish of the majority voters by pursuing casino gambling in Detroit.

"Our Detroit casinos will be the best in the country," I promised. I also made a personal vow to myself that the process would be overwhelmingly successful, void of scandal, or fraud of any kind. Thus began a long, oftentimes rocky road to bringing the voters' vision to fruition.

Governor Engler appointed a panel to study the issue; the panel approved having casino gaming in Detroit. However, a few months later, in June of 1995, the governor rejected their conclusion, saying that a statewide vote should decide. It did. In November of 1996, Michigan voters said yes to a ballot proposal to have three casinos in Detroit.

"I was not favorable toward the casinos," recalls Governor Engler, "although we had negotiated with the Indian tribes because they were operating 17 casinos across Michigan. Against all odds, voters were successful in getting casinos approved for Detroit. Once passed, we felt an obligation to make sure it was implemented properly to set up the gaming office and the law that Michigan continues to have to this day. That issue was very much a tribute to Mayor Archer's involvement, convincing people in the rest of the state that casinos and the jobs they would create would reduce Detroit's dependency on the state."

Beth, who was then president and CEO of the Detroit Economic Growth Corp., a quasipublic economic agency, recalls that "Many people believed that the statewide vote passed because Michigan voters held Dennis in high esteem and trusted him to establish casinos in Detroit with the utmost integrity."

As we embarked on bringing casinos to Detroit, I appointed Beth to chair the Detroit Casino Advisory Committee. The committee included business people, urban planner Kate Beebe, and Nelson Westrin, who had been appointed by Governor Engler as the Executive Director of the Michigan Gaming Control Board. Immediately after the vote, the committee traveled to cities to study the positive and negative impact of casino gaming.

"Our first stop was Atlantic City," Beth says, "and we learned a lot from their regulators. They were having real issues because the Trump casino ultimately went into bankruptcy. Another problem was the lack of community investment or spin-off investment such as restaurants and other businesses around the casinos."

Next, the committee visited New Orleans, where casino gaming had led to corruption, indictments, and high-ranking officials going to prison.

"We learned more from casino developers when we invited them into our hotel suite," Beth says. "During the course of that, we heard a lot of gossip and blame about the scandal there, and took notes on what to avoid."

After that, the committee visited riverboat casinos in Biloxi, Mississippi, and casinos in Las Vegas. The committee also met with gaming experts, including professors at the University of Nevada, Las Vegas.

"We really went to school," Beth says. "Then we compiled our findings in a report called the Detroit Casino Advisory Report, which we released to the public in the spring of 1997. After that, the mayor dismissed the committee and assigned me, the corporation counsel, and the finance director to put out a Request for Proposals for legal, financial, and urban planning experts who would take us through the casino process."

We worked with a terrific Chicago law firm that specialized in the gaming industry, as well as the gaming division of a Wall Street firm, and urban planners.

Interestingly, neither the board of directors of the Detroit Economic Growth Corporation nor the business community liked the idea of casinos.

"Some thought it would change the image of Detroit," Beth says. "The automotive companies wanted Detroit to remain an automotive city, not a gaming city." And some business leaders publicly opposed casinos, she adds, while secretly supporting them and vying for the potential business that they would generate. "I had a tough time, because I was the face of casinos to them. Someone was always mad at me, because they wanted me to report to them about what was going on with the casinos. But a lot of what I was doing, I couldn't report to anyone except the mayor."

Meanwhile, excitement was building for casinos. Data presented to me suggested that the three casinos, which would operate 24 hours every day, would employ 11,300 full-time workers with an annual payroll of $249 million. The numbers computed to suggest that one out of every 100 city residents could potentially be employed by a casino. And according to Wall Street analysts at Bear Stearns, Detroit's three casinos could generate $1.2 billion in annual gross revenue.

As we prepared to receive proposals, I worked with many advisors and experts to identify the best location to build them. I opposed anywhere near the stadiums, believing that would suggest a nexus between sports and betting, which I viewed as unsavory and unacceptable. The casinos did not want to be located on the river, nor did I want them there. Locations on land would afford the opportunity for 360-degrees of development around the casinos for restaurants, hotels, stores, and other businesses to open, thrive, and provide jobs and revenue. On August 1, 1997, 11 bids for casino licenses were submitted, including from Donald Trump.

As with my first election campaign, race became a major factor in Detroit's quest for casino gaming. I felt it was very important that people of color be solidly represented in the ownership privileges of the casinos. However, I determined from the outset that my approach to selecting the three winning bids would require the same objective, judicious consideration that I had applied to decisions as a Michigan Supreme Court Justice.

The facts — not emotion, not public sentiment, not racial bullying — would determine the winners. Therefore, when 11 casino proposals were received, I read every word of each document, as well as the mountains of legal and financial documentation supporting each. A multitude of boxes containing the proposals was delivered from city hall to the Manoogian Mansion, so I could read and study them well into the night. I discussed my findings and conclusions with no one.

"With casinos, the threat of corruption or conflict of interest was so great that he wanted to handle the whole process and make sure it was above board and carried no hint of impropriety," recalls my press secretary, Anthony Neely. "He didn't talk about that with us at all. This was a diversion from his usual way of doing things as a collaborative effort with input from his team. I think he was also trying to avoid any leaks or accusations of any kind."

Meanwhile, local businessman Don Barden launched a very vocal campaign for a successful casino bid, that included 25 supporters chanting "Barden for Detroit!" and "Mayor, pick Barden!" and "We need a black casino!" during an event that I hosted at Cobo Hall for all of the casino contenders to showcase their presentations for the public.

"This is quite a show today, Don," I said as I made the rounds to greet each group.

"I had no idea they were going to do all this," Don said.

"I know better than that," I said.

Shortly after the public display, I announced the seven best proposals to narrow the selection process, then I selected the top four contenders.

"Don Barden did not make the cut of four," Beth says. "That's when things got really ugly."

My decision galvanized Don Barden and his supporters to launch a relentless attack, using racial rhetoric, personal insults, and even pickets in front of the Manoogian Mansion. They initiated a recall campaign by gathering signatures and disseminating literature that said, RECALL MAYOR ARCHER. I was undaunted, proceeding as planned to announce the three winners on the heels of my landslide re-election as mayor of Detroit.

The day before I announced the winners, the *Detroit Free Press* ran a front-page article analyzing several proposals. The consultants gave Barden a weak score, saying he was undercapitalized and lacked the clout to pull it off.

"Barden was furious!" Anthony recalls. "He was doing media interviews and said the evaluation of his proposal in the paper was totally wrong, and that he had more than enough capital financing to do the deal. The paper gave the nod to MGM and the Atwater group, which had Circus Circus with them, along with another Las Vegas organization."

The week that I was re-elected to my second term as mayor, we held a press conference. The local TV and radio outlets broadcast my announcement live, and many print reporters were on hand with their photographers.

"The decisions were clear-cut and not difficult to make," I said. "The three winning proposals were obvious to me." Then I announced the casino winners:

- Detroit Entertainment LLC, a partnership of Atwater Casino Group LLC and Circus Circus Michigan Inc.;

- Greektown Casino LLC/Sault Ste. Marie Band of Chippewa Indians; and

- MGM Grand Detroit LLC

Detroit Entertainment was comprised of a large number of African American investors/owners; Greektown was largely minority-owned by Native American and African American investors; and MGM had African American investors/owners.

These winners and their teams were elated. As I continued to speak about the advantages that casinos would bring to Detroit in terms of jobs, visitors, and revenue, Don Barden's supporters interrupted by shouting:

"Recall!" and "Uncle Tom!"

That evening I returned to the City-County Building. A group of reporters with TV cameras were waiting for me, as was an older, black gentleman leaning against the building.

"Bad decision, Mayor," he said.

I nodded and responded, "I'm sorry you feel that way."

The man's quote ran in the newspaper.

11

THE SECOND INAUGURATION:
CELEBRATING THE CITY'S PAST, PRESENT, & FUTURE

O N ELECTION DAY IN November of 1997, I was re-elected as Mayor of Detroit with 83 percent of the vote, defeating former Michigan State Representative Ed Vaughn. The Inaugural festivities were modest compared to 1994, as I wanted to invest our time and resources into continuing our city's momentum. The swearing-in ceremony on January 2, 1998, was held in the Detroit Opera House, which opened in 1922, originally as a movie theater, and underwent a magnificent renovation that culminated with a 1996 gala featuring Luciano Pavarotti.

Family, friends, supporters, and dignitaries packed the Opera House's 2,700 seats as Michigan Court of Appeals Judge Myron H. Wahls emceed the swearing-in ceremony for the City Council. After that, Judge Wahls and Judge Damon Keith administered my oath of office.

Vincent, who was 25, stepped to the podium and made remarks. I stood behind him, extremely proud of how he addressed our

Our son Vincent DunCombe Archer delivered a rousing speech entitled, "My Father, My Friend" at my 1998 Inauguration ceremony at the newly restored Detroit Opera House.
Photo Credit: Bill Sanders

supporters as live television cameras captured his message, which is italicized here in its entirety:

> *There are certain times in a person's life when they reflect on the past, people, events, and things that have affected their lives in one way or another. Holidays usually bring this moment out for me. And with the addition of this auspicious occasion, it is only natural for me to take the time to reflect on the events that have helped shape my life.*
>
> *I believe I'm a lucky person. You see, I've had many events in my life, many good, some not so good. But through these many events I've had one constant, and this one constant has always been at my side. This constant is Mayor Dennis Wayne Archer. Like you I'm proud to have him for my mayor. But unlike you, I'm also blessed to have him as my father.*
>
> *I feel most fortunate to have him as my best friend. The man you call Mayor — my father, my friend.*

APPLAUSE.

Most of you know him for his vision. I know him for helping me create my vision. Most of you know him for his dream for our city. I know him for showing me how to dream. Most of you know him for the goals he has set for our community. I know him for helping me reach my goals. The man you call Mayor — my father, my friend.

As mayor, he has the baton that Mayor Coleman Alexander Young received when he became mayor, and Dad has run with it. As mayor, his administration has brought businesses into Detroit to invest in our city, and to invest in our people.

As mayor, he has helped break ground on more new developments than our city has seen in past decades. As mayor, he has instilled within us a new hope and desire for Detroit to be the world-class city of the new millennium. The man you call Mayor — my father, my friend.

My father —

Vincent became emotional and said, "Time out," which sparked soft laughter from the audience.

As my father, he was there for me in those young years, to teach me that wealth is not defined by money, but rather by a person's morals and integrity.

APPLAUSE.

As my father, he was there for me during my adolescence, helping me shape my views and understanding of the world. As my father, he has shown me the importance of family and friends, that accomplishments and sweet successes can never be totally enjoyed without someone special to share them with.

The man you call Mayor — my father, my friend.

As a friend, he has always been at my side through those personal problems that I thought could never be resolved. But somehow with him at my side, we seemed to resolve them together.

As a friend, he was at my side when I made my first career change, leaving law, somewhat of a family tradition, and going into corporate finance.

Television cameras captured Trudy smiling and wiping tears with a tissue.

As a friend, he gives me great satisfaction knowing he will always be at my side through all of my successes, as well as my setbacks. I'm proud to have a friend as good as my father and as good as our mayor. The man you call Mayor — my father, my friend, Mayor Dennis Wayne Archer!

HUGE APPLAUSE.

I hugged Vincent, as did Denny and Trudy. Then I delivered my second Inaugural Address, thanking the city council, the city clerk, employees of city government, distinguished public officials of local, state, and national government, reverend clergy, leaders from the community, business, labor, nonprofit, and foundation sectors, my wife Trudy, our sons, our family, fellow Detroiters, and friends. Here are my remarks, italicized:

"Except the LORD build the house, they labour in vain that build it: except the LORD keep the city, the watchman waketh but in vain."
*   With those words from Psalms 127:1, I began my journey with you four years ago. It is a journey that owes a deep gratitude and respect to Mayor Coleman Young for his extraordinary leadership in blazing a trail that we now follow.*

APPLAUSE

It is a journey that demands all of our mayors to match the standard set by Mayor Young. Four years ago, we started with a vision. A vision of a safer city, a stronger city, a prouder city, a united city. A vision that Detroit was poised to lead past the cruel remnants of decline and despair, and burst into a bright new day of hope and prosperity.
*   A vision built upon a belief in our people. A belief in our spirit, our courage, our discipline — and our faith. A vision for a new city which would lead us into a new century. Now after four years of working together, we are about to feel, touch, see, and experience the translation of our vision into the reality of new jobs, new businesses, new housing, new vitality in our neighborhoods, a new downtown, and new hope, all across the city. Four years ago, who would have believed that Detroit would be selected as an Empowerment Zone city that would lead the nation in the quality of its plan and the extent*

of its commitment; a commitment that has meant more than 30 new businesses, 3,000 new jobs and nearly $3.9 billion in new investment.

Who would have believed that both the Tigers and the Lions would commit to a new, long-term presence in the heart of Detroit by proposing two side-by side stadiums. Who would have believed that we would see $5.8 billion in new financial commitment for development all across the city, along with 33 new residential projects. New retail in the form of large projects like Kmart and dozens of small businesses throughout our neighborhoods, and new industrial and manufacturing companies in our empowerment and renaissance zones, offering new jobs for our citizens and new vitality for the city. New cultural gems like the museum of African American history, the recently opened Orchestra Place, and the beautifully restored facility we share today, the Detroit Opera House.

Who would have believed that we are now designing a new downtown for our great city? A downtown anchored by a new waterfront, a new General Motors World Headquarters in the Renaissance Center, three new casinos, a new business and retail and office district in the historical Campus Martius area, and new housing and loft-style apartments in the center of downtown, and a new Woodward Corridor that stretches from the river to the New Center.

Four years ago, who would have believed that the unemployment rate would be cut by more than half? That balanced budgets would be an annual occurrence. And that all three bond rating agencies would upgrade our ratings to very good levels. That city contracts to minority and women companies would total over $350 million and that we would be looking at an economic horizon with nearly 30,000 new jobs in manufacturing service, construction, hospitality, technology, and industry.

Who would have believed that thousands of residents, neighbors, business owners, and friends of the city would work hand in hand in the spring during our Clean Sweep days to give Detroit a good sprucing up, proving how Detroiters cherish our neighborhoods and how thousands of angels took the madness out of Devil's Night and gave Halloween back to our children.

APPLAUSE

Who would have believed that after more than 15 years, Detroit would finally come off HUD's *public housing list because of our efforts to give dignity and hope to the people who live in public housing?*

Who would have believed that Detroit's continuum of care, designed to help our homeless population get back on their feet would receive a national award? Who would have believed that the health coverage for people without the ability to buy health insurance would improve, rather than decline, because of the other Big Three: the Detroit Medical Center, Henry Ford Health Systems, St. John Hospital, who are willing to help people who need help most, despite the strains of funding cuts and increased competition? Who would have believed that local and national foundations would join with government and business to bring nearly $300 million in new funding to nonprofit organizations in government services across the city?

Who would have believed that the labor unions and contractors in the construction industry would be working with us through organizations like Detroit Works and the funding and heating industry to improve access to apprenticeship programs and make commitments to good jobs instead of creating excuses for years of barring the doors to our people?

Who would have believed all of this could happen? WE! Believed. Yes, we believed, and together we did it!

APPLAUSE

People from our neighborhoods. People who work downtown. People who own businesses. People who are active in our faith communities. People who invest in our city. People who enjoy our priceless recreational and cultural jewels. People who kept the spirit alive by living and working and paying taxes and supporting Detroit through difficult days. People from our suburbs who believe that Detroit's future is their future. And the people who came back to Detroit because home and roots and good neighbors are what matter. We are the people who believe. We are the people who did it. We are the people of Detroit. **We gave Detroit the new and beautiful future we see today.** *Give yourself a hand, Detroit! Give yourself a hand!*

HUGE, LONG APPLAUSE.

Yes, we have made great progress in building a new future for the city of Detroit. As we look forward to a new term, a new millennium, we have made a new beginning. Let us recognize that it is just a new beginning. We made Detroit safer, but we are still threatened. We cut unemployment, yet too many of our people need work. We're investing billions in new development, but we remain underdeveloped. We improved city services, yet services are still lacking. We provided more opportunity for our children, but our children are still at risk. Because of our hard work together, we should feel good about the road we have traveled, but we are not at our destination.

We can celebrate the progress we've made, but we cannot rest. We have much yet to do. Because you've blessed me with the challenge of leading this great city, allow me to point the direction to where I believe we must go. Let me be clear. This is the direction that challenges all of us. It will take every friend who believes in Detroit to work even harder with me, if we are to reach our destination.

And here is what we must do. First, we must complete what we started. We need to build the stadiums. We need to build the casinos. We need to build the housing. We need to build the office centers. We need to build the retail and supplier businesses. We need to build all the projects that have been committed to and financed and we need to do it on time and on budget.

For the next four or more years the symbol of Detroit will be the crane. The construction crane. We will be able to look at every corner of the city and see visible tangible products of our efforts emerging from the ground. Yes, we will experience the temporary inconvenience of construction traffic and the rerouting of our daily routines wherever we go. But in spite of the inconvenience, we should smile and say, "That's our new city going up. That's our future appearing in front of us."

Make no mistake. Transforming Detroit from financial commitments and construction plans into steel, wood, concrete, and brick will not be easy work. To all who are involved in this great transformation, please hear this commitment from me. I will do everything I can to help you.

City government is your partner, not your adversary. We will not abdicate our responsibility to assure that safety, health, zoning, and building standards are maintained. We will streamline our steps, shorten our times, and increase our service in every feasible, effective, and legal way. Quite simply, city government will not be an obstacle to safe, sensible, and lasting development in the city of Detroit. Allow me to make another point. Another firm commitment regarding this great transformation of Detroit. The last four years we have seen more reinvestment in Detroit than we have seen in any period since World War II. All this investment translates into jobs. Construction jobs, manufacturing jobs, service jobs, professional jobs, convention jobs, casino jobs, and entertainment and industry jobs. Experts predict that nearly 30,000 new jobs, both temporary and permanent, are on the horizon for Detroit. By any measure, that is good news for Detroit. Detroit is the largest city in America with a majority African American population of at least 76 percent. We have a Latino population of at least 1 to 2 percent. And an Arab, Chaldean, Asian, and Other of one to two percent.

We are unique, but we are also America's future. Our future will be bright if our children can see their neighbors and their friends expanding or starting new businesses; leaving for work for good jobs and returning home with good paychecks; and if our children can see, wherever they go in the city, workers at our construction sites and in our stadiums and in our stores and shops who look like Detroiters, who are Detroiters. The more our children see dads, moms, uncles, cousins, and aunts from our homes and neighborhoods with good businesses and good jobs in Detroit, the more they'll develop into caring and productive adults themselves.

APPLAUSE

The way to really reduce crime, and really reduce welfare, and really drive out the lack of hope that creates troubled children who then become troubled adults. Let's be clear about one thing. If I am to be charged with transforming the economic base of our city and leading it into the 21st century, then I must have help in expanding and creating new businesses and putting the citizens of Detroit to work.

This point is especially true, given that we are the largest region in America without a regional transportation system. The lack of such a system means that Detroit citizens are simply unable to travel in a dependable and efficient way to where the jobs currently exist in our suburban communities. Therefore, the owners, developers, contractors, business leaders, and labor unions who are building and managing our new stadiums, our new casinos, our new housing projects, our new office and retail centers, and our new industrial parks, must commit to placing Detroiters in Detroit jobs or we will not truly succeed. To revitalize Detroit, we have to invest in the human capital of Detroit.

That is what will build a solid future for the city and for the region. That is the real foundation that supports the new towers of steel and concrete, and new homes of brick and wood. Good jobs and good pay are what allow people to support families, educate children, own homes, buy goods and services. Without jobs for Detroit, we are really creating a grand illusion of prosperity which will soon evaporate like so many wistful images of smoke.

Those jobs, industries, and businesses will have lasting value in Detroit only if the people in those jobs are Detroiters. So work with me business, work with me labor, work with me owners and contractors and developers. Help me put our people to work. Help make Detroit what we want it to be. Help make this the city of the future. The city with the greatest combination of color of any large city in America. Help me make this city the pride of America. Let's show them what real and true empowerment can do. Let's make Detroit a great productive community known everywhere for the excellence of its people. Let's take advantage of the opportunity that exists today. Not tomorrow or next year or a generation from now. So I ask for your help. I reach out in a genuine spirit of good faith and cooperation. We cannot have a strong city without a strong economic base for our citizens. Similarly, we cannot have a world-class city without strong neighborhoods. We must do more in the next four years to strengthen our neighborhoods.

APPLAUSE

Neighborhoods are where our children learn. Neighborhoods are where they gain their values and get their start in life. Neighborhoods are where we plant our roots, start our families, build our dreams. Neighborhoods are where our seniors deserve to live in dignity and independence. Without strong neighborhoods, businesses will not survive. Without strong neighborhoods, our children will not stay and build their futures. Our neighborhoods must be safe, they must be clean, they must be well-lighted, there must be good, affordable housing for families and recreational opportunities for our children. There must be thriving retail businesses to serve the people who live there.

If we work together — government, community, schools, churches, and businesses — we can build neighborhoods in Detroit that are the envy of this nation. APPLAUSE. We can reduce crime on our neighborhoods. APPLAUSE. We can drive the dope man from our corners and the gangs away from our children, and we will.

To that end, I have committed to a specific goal of ridding our neighborhoods of their worst enemy. The blighted and abandoned buildings that serve as magnets for crime and symbols of decay. Beginning immediately, we will embark on a $60 million demolition and restoration project which will remove our abandoned buildings and rehabilitate our old, but still usable houses. This unprecedented, once-in-a lifetime project will enable our neighborhoods to get out from under the grasp of decay and plant new seeds of hope and growth.

Also, once and for all, I want to solve the streetlight problems that have plagued our city for too long. APPLAUSE. Good reliable lighting in our neighborhoods is at the core of safety and security. We've made progress in reducing the time it takes to get the streetlights repaired. Fewer streets are in the dark for shorter periods of time than they were four years ago. But we have not done enough. I'm prepared within the first year of this new term to make the changes and the investment necessary to keep our streetlights burning brightly on every corner and in every neighborhood of Detroit.

APPLAUSE.

Providing safe neighborhoods, ridding our city of blighted buildings, and keeping streetlights burning on every block, are key elements of local government. This is what we do. We provide essential services. Government does not make things.

We do not build cars and computers. We don't sell products. Rather, we enable others to come in and do those things. Our job is to provide efficient and cost-effective services. So our city is attractive to people and businesses. We've made great strides in providing better services, but we are not doing enough. There are still too many examples of our being too slow, too cumbersome, too inconvenient, and too expensive. We must do better.

That is why I'm dedicated to focusing this next term on simplifying, streamlining, and enhancing our services while staying within our budget limitations. That is why I'm committed to making the services we deliver in Detroit, not just as good as other cities, but better. That's why I'm initiating the joint labor management effort on benchmarking and best practices wherein we will learn from other cities the very best methods for delivering services. Then we will match or exceed them. If Boston can issue a permit in three hours, we'll match it or better. If Philadelphia can schedule and complete an inspection within two days, we'll match it or better. If Cleveland can process a purchase order and receive delivery in 30 days, we'll match it or better. If Phoenix can assure that no citizen stands in a service line longer than 10 minutes, we will match it or better it. Those are ambitious objectives. And they will not happen overnight. But let's be clear. If service is what we sell, then let's do it right. Improving services will be tough work. Practices and habits have accumulated over generations. Changing them will require changes in how all of us in government think, and about how we work. One change I will not make is to expand services by increasing taxes. I am absolutely opposed to increasing the tax burden on our citizens and our businesses.

APPLAUSE.

We are already taxed at a level six times greater than our surrounding communities. Indeed, our present tax burden stands as a major obstacle in bringing new businesses to our city and our neighborhoods. Instead I commit to the goal of increasing services while we work to reduce taxes. That is why next week I will be announcing a special task force to examine how we can lower our tax burden. They will be looking at every kind of tax we levy, whether on property, income or business, whether on residents or nonresidents. They will be assisted by staff and experts from many fields and sectors, including the leadership staff of City Council. The task force will make specific recommendations which I can then assess and turn into proposals for City Council consideration. This past budget year we made a symbolic reduction in two of our Detroit taxes, the first such reduction in more than 40 years. Now it's time to move past symbols and get into real substance.

Finally and intentionally, I placed this last point at the conclusion of my remarks. Detroit simply must do a better job of educating its children. APPLAUSE. I fully support the fiscal changes recommended by New Detroit and I also fully support the anniversary of the 21st Century Initiative. However, we must do more. When all is said and done, there is absolutely no way Detroit can be a world-class city if we do not have a world-class public education system. APPLAUSE.

It must begin with parents accepting the responsibility for teaching morals, values, and discipline. APPLAUSE. Teaching those morals, values, and discipline in the home before their children go to school. Parents also have to become more engaged in the everyday school experiences of their children. Schools are not institutional day care centers where children are simply dropped off. APPLAUSE. Schools will work well only if parents work well and become partners with teachers and principals. Businesses must become actively involved in schools on a much wider basis. They are the customers of the school system. They hire the graduates to help their companies make a profit. It is in their self-interest to define what kind of workforce is needed in 10 to 15 years.

Business needs to identify the skills that our graduates need for good paying jobs and then work with the schools to see that the skills are developed. Our colleges and universities must weigh in with commitment and resources to help all public schools, city and suburban, provide the quality of education necessary to reduce or eliminate the use of remedial classes when our students get to college. It is really a case of "invest a little now, or pay a lot later."

Public school educators must be allowed to build a new educational system for the 21st century. Our public school system was designed to help people on farms and in rural areas to make the transition to the industrial jobs of the early 20th century. That model simply doesn't work anymore. We need a new urban model that prepares our children for the information and technology jobs for the 21st century. Europe understands that. Asia understands that. Australia understands that. Why don't we get it? It is time to catch up with our competition or we'll be left behind. Our board of education and our superintendent of schools must do a better job of matching the learning skills taught in our public schools to the market needs of today and tomorrow. Right now the job is simply not getting done.

I have never suggested that anybody should take over the Detroit Public Schools. I firmly believe that Detroiters are the best people suited to educate Detroit's children. But we are at the 11th hour and the clock is ticking toward the end of the day. We do not have much time left. The board of education needs to step up aggressively to solve our education problem now. The board of education needs to move our public school system to a new model built upon the best practices found throughout the country for successfully educating children right now.

APPLAUSE

Ladies and gentlemen, you have honored me by re-electing me as your mayor. Receiving your honor, I am mindful of the Book of Proverbs that tells us, before honor is humility. I am indeed humbled by your confidence and dedicate myself to be worthy of it for however long you ask me to serve. Proverbs also tells us in Chapter Three, Verses Five and Six: "Trust in the Lord with all thine heart; and lean not unto thine own understanding. In all thy ways acknowledge him, and he shall direct thy paths."

You've given me a challenge, and I've responded by challenging you to join me. Join me because no man, no woman, no mayor, no one group would take us to our destination alone. Join me because when we work together, we multiply our strength tenfold. Join me, city and suburb, neighborhoods and downtown, rich and poor, Christian and Jew, Muslim and people of all faiths, black and white, red and brown, all beautiful shades of color. Join me because we are community. We *are Detroit. Join me in this struggle to remake our city. Join me so that we can take Detroit higher than it's ever gone before. Join me so we can build a greater future for our children, your children, my children, our children. Join me, and together we will prevail. God bless you, and God bless Detroit! Thank you!*

CASINO PROCESS CONTINUES

The casino presentations were made to the City Council, which approved them on April 9, 1998. Next, they were sent for approval by the Michigan Gaming Control Board.

Don Barden was unrelenting. He brought Michael Jackson to town on July 7, 1998, to announce their plans to build a billion-dollar casino and entertainment complex on Detroit's riverfront. Reporters asked what I thought about it.

"Well, that's politics," I said. "I'm not surprised by anything that was said. I made a decision based on the facts presented to me and asked City Council to approve."

But Don Barden continued his protest in the form of getting a proposal for the August 5, 1998 ballot asking Detroiters to overturn my casino selection. It was defeated. Then he filed a federal lawsuit on May 25, 1999, alleging that his constitutional rights were violated by the casino selection process.

Meanwhile, his people were gathering signatures to get on an August 4, 1999 ballot to recall me. I called a press conference to address this head-on. Here's what I said:

> *Let's understand what this petition drive is really all about. It's not about educating our children. It's not about strengthening our neighborhoods, creating jobs and opportunity for our people. It's not about making our streets, our schools, and our neighborhoods safer. It's not about building a brighter future for all Detroit.*
>
> *This petition drive is about a decision I made not to grant a casino license to one particular individual. That's all this recall issue is about.*
>
> *I make all my decisions as mayor based on what's best for the entire City of Detroit. Now a small group of people is attempting to hold our city hostage over those decisions. They would block our progress in reforming our schools, attracting new jobs, rebuilding*

our neighborhoods — all to seek revenge for decisions that didn't go the way they wanted.

The vast majority of Detroiters want to move forward — not backward. They don't want to refight battles that were decided months and years ago. They don't have time for endless protests and made-for-TV histrionics. They are too busy doing constructive things to keep our city's comeback on track. And those of us who are working so hard to move Detroit forward aren't going to let a few naysayers turn us around.

We're going to look at every signature on those petitions and make sure they're real and legitimate and fully comport with the law. And, frankly, I hope this whole business will end right there. But if they manage to qualify for the ballot, we're going to contest this measure with every resource at our disposal. Because it's really a choice about two directions for Detroit's future:

We can let one, spurned, casino bidder and friends throw a monkey wrench in our progress, or we can keep Detroit moving forward for all of its residents. We can go back to the politics of hate and division, or we can continue building partnerships for progress and reform. We can be held hostage by those who scream and shout the loudest, or we can listen to each other with toleration and respect. We can be diverted by the electoral equivalent of a temper tantrum, or we can focus on the challenges that will define the very future of Detroit.

I love our city, and I'm deeply grateful for the opportunity to serve as mayor. I sought this job knowing that it would be a tough one — that stones would be thrown and names would be called. It just comes with the territory.

But I've always believed that the vast majority of Detroiters share my vision for our families, neighborhoods, and communities — an inclusive vision that looks beyond the differences among us to focus on the dream we all share for Detroit: better schools to provide a quality public education for our children, economic opportunities for entrepreneurs and job seekers, safer streets and real opportunity for our people.

That dream lives today — and we are much closer to its fulfillment — because of the hard work and good faith of people and families all across our city. The heart of our city's ongoing renaissance is Detroiters from all walks of life joining together to overcome our common challenges. A handful of people preaching hate and division will never turn us around.

Thank you.

Anthony Neely recalls that period, italicized to show his words:

Mayor Archer stayed cool and steady under fire. In public, he was unruffled, focused on the facts, in control. Although he was con- sistently well-dressed — even fashionable — he was understated in just about every way. When he talked issues, he got worked up only when discussing the virtues of the city and the fact that his administration had built a new, positive image about Detroit and a momentum for reinvestment and new development that really couldn't be reversed. (And two decades later, I believe that fact has stood the test of time.)

Many of the mayor's allies, inside and outside the administra- tion, wished that we would go toe-to-toe with the "haters" more often. But much of what the rabble-rousers said about him was ignored and went unanswered. We had our talking points down regarding the accomplishments of the administration and the basic point that Mayor Archer was trying to rebuild a city that would clearly benefit all Detroiters, who were obviously mostly African American.

RECALL PETITION FAILS

The majority of signatures on the petitions gathered by Don Barden's recall campaign were bogus and therefore invalid. That was the conclusion of Wayne County Clerk Teola Hunter, City Clerk Jackie Currie, and the FBI handwriting experts who examined the signatures. Many were names copied from the phone book, and they had me signing it, too.

"I saw with my own eyes a petition allegedly signed by Bill Clinton, Mickey Mouse, and Daisy Duck," says Detroit City Councilmember Sheila Cockrel, who helped examine signatures and worked hard to stop the recall. "I wish he would've prosecuted the people who had forged the signatures."

In July of 1999, the recall effort was shut down, and U.S. District Judge Gerald Rosen dismissed Barden's lawsuit requesting the court to order the city to grant him a casino deal.

With the recall behind us and the lawsuit dismissed, the city's approval of MGM Grand, Atwater/Circus, and Greektown/Chippewa Indians could move forward.

Still, I felt a need to bring everyone back together, heal from the divisiveness, and get back to the work the city of Detroit needed. So I called a press conference and delivered the following words to bring closure:

I am gratified, though not surprised, by the county clerk's ruling today that the petitions filed lack sufficient signatures to warrant a recall election. I'm gratified because Detroiters now will be spared a divisive and unnecessary campaign.

But I'm not surprised at today's ruling, because our own review of the petitions showed them to be rife with ineligible names, errors, and outright forgeries, which now should be the subject of a criminal review.

Our analysis showed that fewer than one-in-ten names submitted were the authentic signatures of eligible voters on properly circulated petitions.

Though more than 120,000 signatures were filed, in our view, less than 11,000 were valid — far fewer than the 57,000 the law requires.

When you build your effort on an unstable foundation, it stands to reason that it will collapse.

Now it's time to turn the page on this failed campaign of political retribution and rededicate ourselves to the betterment of our city.

We will continue our efforts to bring jobs and economic growth to Detroit because these efforts are the key to a better future for all of our people.

We will continue our efforts to make our communities safer and stronger, to strengthen services in every neighborhood, and redeem our public schools for every child.

We have not solved all of Detroit's problems. But by working together, we have made a new beginning that offers hope and opportunity.

I know this is the preferred direction for the vast majority of Detroiters.

And it's the one I will pursue with all my heart in the years to come.

Finally, I want to thank the thousands of Detroiters who called, wrote, and for those who volunteered their time and support during this period, determined to be of help to me personally and to keep our city on track.

Together we will continue to move our city forward.

After that, casinos were permitted to continue as planned.

All the while, identifying the best location for the casinos presented a huge challenge. The casinos did not want waterfront venues, and it was cheaper to build them inside existing buildings. As plans proceeded and sites were selected for temporary and permanent casinos, Executive Order 4 ensured that significant numbers of Detroiters were included in the hiring for construction and other services. We used it as a model for the development deals that we did, including the stadium development project. For that, we established a target of 30 percent of utilization for Detroit-based and local businesses.

All of this culminated with glittering, black-tie openings for the three temporary casinos.

First, the MGM Grand opened on July 29, 1999, followed by The Motor City Casino on December 14, 1999, and finally the Greektown Casino on November 10, 2000.

STATE OF THE CITY: DETROIT IS ON THE MOVE!

It was with utter euphoria that I stepped to the podium to deliver my State of the City Address in 1997, because I had so much good news to report. So I started with a few lines from a popular 1962 song about a guy, once sad and rejected, who rebounds on the dance floor with impressive new skills.

Laughter roared from the audience, packed with leaders from government, business, the community, and a small army of media. Then I proceeded to list all the great news that showed Detroit was doing better than it had done in decades, and was fast on its way to becoming one of the most dramatic, urban-turnaround stories in modern history:

The city's jobless rate — which was 16 percent three years earlier in 1994 — was now below 10 percent. Detroit won the Empowerment Zone, using the $100 million federal grant to leverage another $2 billion in private investment. General Motors was moving its world headquarters downtown to the Renaissance Center. Plans were in the works to build three downtown casinos. Side-by-side stadiums would be built downtown for the Detroit Tigers and the Detroit Lions. Crime was going down, and events such as Angels' Night and Detroit Clean Sweep were mobilizing tens of thousands of volunteers to take ownership for the city's well-being.

This was my third State of the City Address, an annual tradition conceived by Freman Hendrix as we were driving back from the airport after a trip to Washington.

"You know, Mr. Mayor," Freman said, "it's State of the Union time for the country. Clinton is doing his State of the Union address soon. How about if you give the city's first State of the City address?"

I looked at him and smiled.

"That's a hell of an idea, Fre. Put that together."

"Mr. Mayor, we can do it on the 13th floor in the auditorium and have the City Council flanking you on the stage. We can invite the Friends of Archer and big supporters. We can have 300 to 400 people. We'll get the media in there, and it'll be great. Everybody in Michigan will be tuned in to your State of the City."

After that, I gave Anthony Neely and David Axelrod my thoughts on how to organize the speech. We brought teleprompters, flags, and honor guard, so that our event would resemble the president's State of the Union Address. As a result, the demand for tickets was overwhelming. We did not have enough seats.

"Mayor Archer began this important tradition for the city," Freman says, "and there's been a State of the City address every year since."

Detroit was on a major come-back and the national media was shining a bright spotlight on our successes. We harnessed this excitement by compiling excerpts from articles published in some of America's most prominent and influential newspapers and magazines.

The headlines, photographs, and articles, which all touted Detroit's astounding progress with quotations and statistics, were splashed across the glossy pages of a four-page pamphlet that we used to showcase Detroit's increasing success. This brochure became an important marketing tool that we shared with the business community, visitors from across America and the world, as well as with people whom we met while promoting Detroit in other states and countries.

INTERNATIONAL TRAVEL

The Detroit Regional Chamber of Commerce provided funding for international trade missions with representatives from Wayne, Oakland, and Macomb counties, as well as the city of Detroit and businesses. This resulted from Al Lucarelli approaching the Chamber's leader, Dick Blouse, who endorsed the idea of going around the world to encourage investment in our tricounty region. As a result, $12 million was raised to finance these trade missions designed to lure people back to the region.

Trudy and I, along with a security person and other members of our staff, traveled with Oakland County Executive L. Brooks Patterson, Wayne County Executive Ed McNamara, and a member of the Macomb County Board of Commissioners. One memorable trip was to Germany and Great Britain. We went to Hamburg, Frankfurt, Stuttgart, including visits to the Porsche automotive headquarters, Mercedes headquarters, and to Jaguar in England.

At Mercedes, I met with Dr. Luck, who was responsible for cars and trucks in South Africa. I was trying to encourage Mercedes to think about opening up a research and development facility in Michigan.

"I'll have to think about that," Dr. Luck said with a straight face.

I took a test drive with Mercedes, as I did with Porsche and Jaguar.

A few weeks later, after I returned to the United States, businessman Heinz Prechter called me. His invention was transforming cars into convertibles.

"Mayor Archer, the Auto Show is coming up," he said. "I'd like for you to meet the head of Mercedes. You're going to learn — but you cannot talk about it — that there's a merger of equals between Chrysler and Mercedes."

I said to myself, *Well, I will be just be blankety-blank. Here I went over there to sell them on a little facility, and it turns out they merged the whole company!*

On another occasion, in April of 1998, we traveled to Turin, Italy, to attend a ceremony to become "Sister Cities." At the time, we were there for the international auto show at Fiat, an eight-story building. As I rode in a car around their rooftop test track, I thought, *If this thing goes off the roof—*

They had good drivers, fortunately.

The mayor of Turin invited us to his office and we officially signed memorandums creating our sister city relationship. Then we went up the mountains to a restaurant. The aromas were decadent, and the wonderful lunch was unlike anything Trudy and I had experienced. The food was outstanding, as was the wine.

Turin Mayor Valentino Castellani and I participated in a signing ceremony in the Red Room of Town Hall. Our cities shared illustrious histories of being major automobile manufacturers, only to have car production facilities dramatically decline, along with our respective populations. As a result, Mayor Castellani and I discussed how to promote our cities that were plagued by lots left polluted by the industry. That evening, Trudy and I dined with the mayor and his wife. Our sightseeing included a visit to the Cathedral of Saint John the Baptist, where we saw the Shroud of Turin, which many believe was wrapped around Jesus after he was crucified. We also attended an airport dedication ceremony, and enjoyed breakfast with business leaders.

One morning, Dick Blouse, Sgt. Ralph Godbee, and I got up early to go for a run. We were going to run by the building with the shroud — about a three-mile run in about 25 minutes. But we got lost, and we kept running, thinking we would go back to the hotel. We tried to stop people to ask, but they couldn't speak English, and we couldn't speak Italian. Finally, after about an hour of running, I discovered a book of matches in my pocket; it was printed with our hotel address, which I showed to someone, and they flagged a taxi. At the hotel, I had to go upstairs and get my wallet to pay for the taxi.

Detroit's relationship with Turin remains vibrant and symbiotic today.

The trips were successful in attracting a lot of businesses. Those businesses were documented through the Chamber.

Trudy's Recollections of Our International Travel

Trudy and I took many international trips, not at city expense, on behalf of the city of Detroit. Here, she recalls those travels, italicized to indicate in her own words:

Several trips are worth mentioning. Toyota City, Japan, is one of Detroit's sister cities. In 1995, they opened a fine arts museum, and the city of Detroit — through the DIA — loaned them a million dollars' worth of art to put on exhibit when they opened their museum.

Dennis and I went with a delegation from Detroit. City Council President Maryann Mahaffey, DIA Director Sam Sachs, and several others traveled for the museum opening.

I have a picture of all the dignitaries lined up to cut the ribbon. They all wore white gloves. It was just a beautiful museum, but what was so heartwarming was the fact that the DIA had loaned them so much art. It was a very close relationship.

That was my first trip to Japan. Dennis had been before. We were received very well. We went to the mayor of Toyota's home for dinner, which was so lovely.

Another time, the FAA had approved Northwest Airlines to open a gate directly to Shanghai. Dennis and Governor Engler were involved in that negotiation. Northwest invited them to fly to Shanghai. We flew the inaugural trip, just our group, and that was special, from Detroit to Shanghai.

Everyone was so happy. This was the beginning of an all-new, direct destination. It was a wonderful experience. At the airport that morning here in Detroit there was a big celebration for us before we left for the 13-hour flight.

When we arrived, Dennis and I were going to attend a dinner, but his suitcase had not yet been delivered to the hotel. Unfortunately, his business suit was in the suitcase, and his travel outfit would be inappropriate to wear. Rod Gillum, a GM executive who is a little taller than Dennis, had received his luggage at the hotel. Thankfully, he had an extra suit and loaned it to Dennis. I wish we had taken pictures.

That's how we began our trip to Shanghai. Eventually, he did get his luggage later that evening. Northwest Airlines was sorry that this had occurred. They sent a tailor who measured Dennis and Rod, and they were given new, tailor-made suits.

Shanghai itself was fascinating, old and new. I had never seen so many cranes in the air. Each developer was trying to outdo the last as far as architectural design goes. The buildings are just fabulous: new, very contemporary, sharp-edge modern design.

The trade missions were wonderful overall with the last one in England. A highlight was the Detroit Symphony Orchestra performing at the Manchester Symphony Hall. The whole experience of seeing our orchestra made us very proud. The previous year, we saw the DSO in Toyota, Japan.

Each time we saw our orchestra abroad, whether in Toyota or Manchester, just to have the mayor of Detroit there watching them perform was thrilling for the members of the orchestra and for us.

In 2000, we visited Paris and visited with the president and his wife, who came to celebrate Detroit 300 in 2001.

MEETING NELSON MANDELA

I heard Nelson Mandela speak at the State Department in Washington in the fall of 1994, just months after he became President of South Africa. I had the honor of meeting him when I traveled to South Africa as part of President Clinton's delegation during his six-nation tour of the African continent.

I was one of about 20 people invited to accompany President Clinton as he and his family were to meet President Mandela in Cape Town. We paid our own way, flying on the recently decommissioned Air Force One plane that had been used to transport Presidents Kennedy and Johnson. This plane had also flown President Kennedy's body back from Texas. During our trip, the plane stopped for fuel at Cape Verde, about 350 miles off the Western coast of Africa. We finally arrived in Cape Town with enough time to change clothes, and to hear President Mandela introduce

President Clinton before he spoke at the joint parliament, which is similar to when a leader from another country addresses both houses of Congress.

After the president's speech, the delegation met President Mandela. Although our visit was brief, due to our delayed arrival, it was outstanding and very memorable. That night, President Mandela invited us to a state dinner in the wine country in honor of President Clinton and his family. Our truly unique experience also included having lunch with the Cape Town chamber of commerce, and attending a reception at the home of the United States Ambassador to South Africa.

The stark reality of South Africa was everywhere: barbed wire and glass on cement walls of houses dominated the scenery. The tops of cement walls were structured so that if people jumped up, their hands would be cut. This was to keep people from breaking into homes and businesses.

We flew to Johannesburg and enjoyed dinner in a downtown restaurant. Johannesburg was nice, but different from Cape Town, where the more upbeat atmosphere reminded me of San Diego. The entire trip was fascinating.

In 1999 and 2000, I made several trips on behalf of the President of the United States, each time paying my own way. This included traveling to Ghana with 20 colleagues to attend Reverend Leon Sullivan's Africa-African American conference, and going to Abuja, Nigeria with the president when he went to praise their efforts for democracy.

I also took several international trips as president of the National League of Cities.

DETROIT 300 — CELEBRATING OUR CITY'S TRICENTENNIAL

When Detroit celebrated its 300th birthday, we threw a huge party that attracted people from around the world. In July of 2001, we celebrated the many magnificent facets of our city that began in 1701 when French explorer Antoine de la Mothe Cadillac built a fort along the banks of the waterway between Lake St. Clair and Lake Erie. Since the river was narrow, he selected the French word for that as the settlement's name. Little did he know that the place where he arrived by canoe would become the world's automobile manufacturing mecca.

I selected Henry Ford's great grandson, Edsel Ford II, as Chairman of our Tricentennial, which he organized with the help of Maud Lyon, William Beckham, and later, Larry Givens. Also assisting was the Detroit 300 Commission, comprised of prominent male and female leaders who reflected our city's ethnic demographics.

Detroit 300, thanks to Edsel Ford's leadership, raised $30 million that was used for many development projects, including those that expanded Campus Martius. The Riverfront Promenade was dedicated during the city's 300th anniversary with a statue and commemorative bricks. The Riverfront Promenade was built from Joe Louis Arena to behind the Ford Auditorium by the Downtown Development Authority. The Authority's project manager was Ben Smith, who was also in the Reserves of the U.S. Coast Guard.

Now known as the Detroit RiverWalk, and managed by the non-profit Detroit RiverFront Conservancy, the RiverWalk has become a crown jewel of the city, attracting a virtual cornucopia of thousands of people every day to enjoy fountains, a carousel, bike rentals, nature walks, special events, and concerts. This waterside park was a hub of activity during the week-long Detroit 300 festivities, which included touring the historic Tall Ships, which were docked along the Riverfront Promenade behind Cobo Hall.

The Detroit Metro Convention & Visitors Bureau estimated that 5.7 million people participated in events such as the diversity-themed Concert of Colors, the Tigers Game, events in Windsor, programs at the Detroit Science Center, and ceremonies marking Cadillac's Landing. Film star Arnold Schwarzenegger also came to town to participate in athletic events for thousands of local kids in events sponsored by hundreds of nonprofit organizations.

The week exemplified the exciting, vibrant atmosphere that we had described in *Thoughts for a Greater DETROIT*. With bricks, cranes, people, investment dollars, and hard work, we were bringing to life the words that we had written in that document nearly a decade before. Yes, we had so much more work to do. But many, many people from every sector of our community shared with me an intense feeling of satisfaction and gratitude that our eight years of the bridge-building, collaboration, faith, and belief in our city's infinite potential, were manifesting in this new reality that was propelling Detroit toward the world-class city that we desired.

As such, the Detroit 300 ceremonies celebrated Detroit's richly diverse history. Millions of people across America and the world witnessed the excitement that was covered on CNN, *The Today Show* on NBC, and *Good Morning America* on ABC.

Very importantly, we worked with Windsor Mayor Mike Hurst to host simultaneous celebrations in Windsor, Ontario, Canada. Our cities share the international waterway of the Detroit River, and the Windsor Tunnel and Ambassador Bridge enable our residents to enjoy easy access to visit and work in our respective cities.

Windsor was also a stop on the Underground Railroad, as black people escaped slavery in the South, made it to Detroit, and crossed the river on boats to live freely in Canada. That powerful piece of history inspired the selection of African American sculptor Ed Dwight to create two statues — one for Detroit, one for Windsor — commemorating Detroit 300 with a tribute to our roots in the Underground Railroad. Dwight's website describes the Detroit sculpture as featuring two gateway pillars bracketing a 10-foot by 12-foot sculpture with nine slaves and a railroad conductor who is looking and pointing toward Canada in anticipation of boarding the boat to safety across the Detroit River. The sculpture in Windsor, as described on the artist's website, has a 20-foot-high granite tower that represents a candle; it shows a male slave giving thanks to a female slave who is holding a baby. A female conductor is welcoming them to safety. The sculpture includes a little girl who is glancing back at America with nostalgia.

"That statue shows the promise and the shame of Detroit at the same time," Greg Bowens said, "and it's a reminder that it took people of all colors, white and black, to fulfill the promise of freedom. The Underground Railroad monuments on both sides of the river, and created by a black artist, are a testament to Mayor Archer's commitment to building bridges between people and regions. The monuments are a manifestation of the kind of cooperation that he was famously known for."

Similarly, I opened a time capsule that had been buried in Campus Martius 100 years ago by the mayor, the police chief, and a businessman, just after midnight on January 1st as part of the Detroit Opera tribute. It was an amusing testament to our technological advances to read that the then-mayor asked if the telephones worked well. We created our own time capsule that will be opened in 2101.

"The Detroit 300 Festival was an experience that brought people in Detroit together, celebrating 300 years of the contributions from diverse people," said Detroit 300 Chairman Edsel Ford II. "This is our heritage. The greatest legacy of Detroit 300 is the sense of unity. It is my hope that the working relationships that have been built will have a lasting impact as we create the future of our great city."

On December 15, 2001, General Motors Corporation presented the black-tie Detroit 300 Gala, hosted by GM's President and CEO, G. Richard Wagoner Jr., Edsel Ford II and me. The event at GM world headquarters featured a performance by the Temptations. It raised money that was used for downtown development as well as the care of 1,701 trees in Detroit neighborhoods.

"The Detroit 300 celebration demonstrated that we are at our best as a region when we come together in peace and harmony to honor and value the contributions everyone has made to help make our city great," I told the media. "Clearly, the events surrounding our city's birthday are strong evidence Detroit remains an epicenter of importance to our region and our state. The estimated 5.7 million people who attended Detroit 300 events should remind everyone that we are all in this thing together."

SEPTEMBER 11, 2001
PRIMARY ELECTION DAY FOR MY SUCCESSOR — A DISASTER

I got up early to exercise, then dressed and prepared to go vote. Curious about voter turnout, I turned on the television. Reporters were talking about a plane that had flown into one of the World Trade Center buildings in New York City. As the TV screen was coming into focus, I expected to see a very cloudy day. When the picture on the television came into focus, it showed flames and smoke streaming from upper floors. I could not understand how that could have happened, because the sky was sunny, bright and clear.

Then, as I watched, another plane flew into the second World Trade Center building. Whatever was occurring, was on! Moving by instinct, and attempting to process what I saw on TV and heard on the radio, I rushed to the office. Everyone was glued to any TV in any office. The feeling was surreal.

I was briefed: the FAA ordered all aircraft to land, but about 200 planes were still flying. An airplane struck the Pentagon near Washington, DC, and another plane crashed in Pennsylvania. Meanwhile, Renaissance Center security was advising everyone to leave the buildings. My thoughts raced. Could a plane be heading toward any of our Detroit buildings? Or toward the nuclear power plant in Monroe, about 40 miles south of Detroit? I called Windsor Mayor Mike Hurst. He was closing the Ambassador Bridge and the Windsor Tunnel.

Suddenly, I stopped dead in my tracks, thinking about the loss of so many people in those buildings, the family members who would never see their loved ones again, the innocent people who reported for work on the floors above and below where the planes struck in the World Trade Center. Could they possibly escape? Those who worked in the Pentagon where the plane struck, and all their families, would be impacted for the rest of their lives. My mind whirled with thoughts about the passengers on the planes en route to destinations for various reasons, what was happening, why, by whom… and then on live TV the World Trade Center buildings collapsed and crumbled before our very eyes. All those people in the buildings trying to escape, the people below, on the streets, killed, or injured by falling debris.

Then it hit me personally. Our son Vincent was living and working in New York. Might he have been in the area for business or personal reasons? I stepped away quietly and tried to call him on his cell phone. No answer; cell phone towers in New York were down. Please God, not Vincent, too! Trudy and Denny were calling Vincent as well. I remained as calm as possible while working to assess whether our city and our people were safe from harm. Finally, Vincent called. He was safe.

We were fortunate. Those who would never be able to see, hold, or talk to those who were lost that day. Not to mention those severely injured, their lives affected forever. My heart was heavy as we learned more about the people on the four planes had purposefully directed their paths that attacked America, and how there would be a steep price to pay.

As the day progressed and it was clear that Detroit and the state were free from attack and safe from the devastation that hit others that day, my thoughts went to our Middle Eastern community. I wanted to ensure that everyone acted with civility. I talked to Dearborn Mayor Mike Guido and we shared a message for everyone: do not racially profile any of our Middle Eastern community citizens.

I was very proud how that day, as if there had been a "table top exercise" how to respond, and going forward and how members of the African American and Jewish communities, and all Detroiters spoke with one voice: do not disrespect or racially profile our Middle Eastern community brothers and sisters.

In the meantime, voters in our local primary chose Council President Gil Hill and State Representative Minority Leader Kwame Kilpatrick as the two candidates who would face off in the November 2001 General Election for mayor of the city of Detroit.

RECAP OF THE ARCHER ADMINISTRATION

My decision not to run for a third term surprised many people who believed I could continue the momentum of improving Detroit. However, I wanted to leave at the top of my service, and I did.

I was succeeded by Democratic State Representative Kwame Kilpatrick. As I prepared to leave office, I instructed my staff to create transition books for each department.

I reflected on the tremendous transformation that I had overseen as Mayor of Detroit over the past eight years, and what we had accomplished as a city. Here is a summary:

- A 2000 Census report revealed that Detroit dropped its 1990 Census designation as the city leading the nation with the highest percentage of people living below poverty to number 16.

- The total number of serious crimes committed in the city, as tracked by the FBI ("Part I Serious Crimes"), dropped from 122,329 in 1993 to 95,759 in 2000, a reduction of more than 22 percent and the lowest number of serious crimes committed in Detroit in 30 years.

- The number of homicides decreased 32 percent — from 579 in 1993 to a seven-year low of 396 in 2000.

- Fatal fire deaths declined to a 10-year low of 43 in 2000.

- Collaboration between city government, the private sector, foundations, and citizens was essential to the improvement of nearly 400 city parks and 6,000 acres of park land in the City of Detroit.

- Local foundations and corporations contributed $12 million to upgrade 33 Detroit playgrounds and to create an endowment fund for repairs.

- The City demolished nearly 18,000 abandoned homes in Detroit neighborhoods.

- More than 2,500 new and rehabilitated residential units were added to Detroit's housing stock with approximately 60 percent for low- to moderate-income families and senior citizens.

- Major supermarket, drugstore, and discount chains such as Kmart, Kroger, Rite Aid, and CVS returned to the city.

- Detroit's Empowerment Zone led the nation in attracting new development to the most distressed industrial areas and neighborhoods, and created more than 10,000 new jobs and 1,500 new residential units.

- Some 348 new buses were purchased, reducing the average age of the fleet from 12 to five years.

- Comerica Park, Ford Field, DaimlerChrysler's Mack I and II engine plants, renovation of General Motors World Headquarters at Renaissance Center, the ongoing construction of Compuware World Headquarters, and the opening of three interim casinos were some of the development highlights. The 2006 Super Bowl was scheduled to be played in Detroit at Ford Field.

- Personal income taxes in the city were reduced from 3 percent to 2 percent for Detroit residents, and from 1.5 percent to 1 percent for nonresidents. The corporate income tax was eliminated.

- Detroit's bond ratings on Wall Street improved 11 times since 1994 with A ratings from Standard & Poors and Fitch and a high-B rating from Moody's.

- We had a balanced budget every year with a modest surplus and rainy day fund.

- It was also reported that at one point during the eight years, our two pension funds — police and fire, and the general — were overfunded by $921 million.

- We generated $20.2 billion in new investments for the City of Detroit during the eight years of our administration.

With that, I moved forward with indescribable pride that our administration had truly LET THE FUTURE BEGIN.

Epilogue

Life After Elective Office, 2002 to Present

O N January 1, 2002, a new chapter of my life began, and I continued to promote the city of Detroit. This included encouraging existing businesses to expand their presence and convincing new businesses to start their futures within the city. Both endeavors would create new job prospects for Detroiters. Moreover, I sought new opportunities to inspire corporate America to cultivate supplier diversity and inclusion, as well as to utilize lawyers of color.

In the legal arena, I advocated for the appointment of more judges of color to state and federal benches. At the same time, new doors opened that broadened my influence to increase the number of African Americans, people of color, and women serving on the boards of directors of publicly traded companies.

Also in January of 2002, I became the first person of color to serve as chairman of Dickinson Wright law firm. The law firm has since grown to 450 lawyers with 40 practice areas and 18 offices nationwide. (In 2010, I started Dennis W. Archer PLLC and serve as Chairman and CEO, and also became Chairman Emeritus of Dickinson Wright PLLC.)

Much to my delight, life after elective office has enabled me to enjoy more time with my family. It has also provided the opportunity to enhance the Dennis W. Archer Foundation, which has given more than $1 million to students earning undergraduate degrees at Western Michigan University and Wayne State University.

MAKING HISTORY AS THE FIRST PERSON OF COLOR TO LEAD THE AMERICAN BAR ASSOCIATION

At our midyear meeting in February of 2002 in Washington, DC, the American Bar Association nominated me to become President-Elect. During this pinnacle moment, I walked down the aisle to accept the nomination accompanied by United States Senator, and future Secretary of State and United States presidential candidate, Hillary Rodham Clinton, as well as the wife of late United States Supreme Court Justice Thurgood Marshall, Mrs. Cecilia "Sissy" Suyat Marshall.

"I am extremely proud to be here," I said, delivering remarks in acceptance of the nomination, and feeling overwhelmed with honor and humility. I was the first person of color to become President-Elect of one of the world's largest voluntary, professional membership organizations, which has nearly 400,000 members.

"I am also keenly aware of those who came before me," I continued, "those who were not able to contribute to the great debates in the ABA House of Delegates on public policy and legal issues. I think of the tremendous contributions these lawyers, judges, and others could have made to this association, had they been allowed to join. I am here because of the hard work of others. Others who were denied the opportunities that I have had. People who broke barriers and opened doors, who paved the way for me... William Hastie, Damon Keith, Charles Hamilton Houston, Constance Baker Motley, Otis Smith, Wade McCree, and Justice Thurgood Marshall."

I was excited to spend the coming year preparing to lead the ABA, which serves as "the national voice of the legal profession" and "works to improve the administration of justice, promotes programs that assist lawyers and judges in their work, accredits law schools, provides continuing legal education, and works to build public understanding around the world of the importance of the rule of law."

United States Senator Hillary Clinton and Cecilia "Cissy" Marshall, widow of U.S.
Supreme Court Justice Thurgood Marshall, escorted me down the aisle at the ABA Annual
Meeting in Washington, DC, when I was elected President-Elect of the American Bar
Association in 2002. Photo Credit: Rob Crandall

Not slowing down a bit upon returning to Detroit, I became for the first time a member of two publicly traded corporate boards: Compuware Corporation and Johnson Controls, Inc., in rapid succession.

Meanwhile, my year as President-Elect of the ABA was absolutely exhausting, yet exhilarating. Extensive travels consumed my time, as I spoke at 40 national, state, local, and specialty bar associations. I delivered 10 commencement and commemoration speeches at law schools; testified before the Senate Judiciary Committee about asbestos litigation; and addressed corporations, law firms, legal aid societies, and judicial conferences. Many of the issues that I worked on for the ABA had been relevant to my work as an active participant with the U.S. Conference of Mayors and the National League of Cities. One example of this involved testifying before Congress in support of an initiative to examine racial profiling.

Traveling throughout the country gave me an even greater appreciation of lawyers' and judges' commitment to helping their communities through volunteer public service and *pro bono* work. I was especially proud to witness lawyers serving people in legal services and public defenders' offices. I visited one firm in New Orleans that contributed $150,000 every year to support local entities and provide matching funds for others.

Meeting lawyers and judges across America further deepened my already strong faith in my peers and our profession. These encounters created a platform to promote the ABA, emphasizing that our formidable organization was working on legal issues that were relevant to society. The positive momentum of this interaction with the legal community across America enhanced my extensive preparation at ABA headquarters in Chicago as I prepared to become the organization's President.

Finally, the year's extremely gratifying and impactful travels as President-Elect culminated on Monday, August 11, 2003, during the ABA's Annual Meeting in San Francisco, when I officially became the first person of color to serve as President of the American Bar Association. The formal "passing of the gavel" ceremony occurred during the House of Delegates meeting at Moscone Center.

"Today is a new beginning, a new chapter in the history of the world's largest voluntary professional organization," I said during my acceptance speech before an audience that included my family, my Dickinson Wright family, friends, colleagues, and dignitaries from around the world. "We sweep aside the past... to officially and emphatically declare that our association's leadership is open to every lawyer, regardless of race or color. I am deeply honored to have the privilege to serve as president of our American Bar Association."

I announced my major initiatives for the coming year. I made clear that the ABA would be at the forefront of the national dialogue about justice and diversity, and that my initiatives would put action and substance behind this crucial conversation.

I explained that the timing of my ABA leadership was important because it came in the wake of the ACLU suing the federal government, arguing that the USA Patriot Act was unconstitutional. And two months prior, the U.S. Supreme Court decided that the University of Michigan could continue to consider diversity in admissions.

"U.S. Supreme Court Justice Sandra Day O'Connor wrote in her opinion in the Michigan (affirmative action) case that she hoped that after 25 more years we may not need to use race as a factor," I said during my speech. "To assure we work hard on that time table, I respectfully ask that the ABA, NBA, HNBC, NAPABA, and other bar associations that care deeply about affirmative action and diversity to be at our annual meeting 10 years from now. There, as part of our respective annual meetings, we should come together during one or more occasions to collectively review what we have accomplished during the intervening 10 years and determine what we all must do to reach the goal of a colorblind society."

I also criticized U.S. Attorney General John Ashcroft for "attacking judicial independence" by issuing a memo requesting the names of federal judges who were reportedly light on crime.

"Our work matters," I said. "It matters to the profession, to our clients, to the justice system, to our communities, and to America. Therefore, we accept the request of U.S. Supreme Court Justice Anthony Kennedy, made at our Opening Assembly, to evaluate the mandatory sentences federal and state judges are required to impose without the ability to exercise their discretion."

My priorities during my one-year term as ABA President included:

- Increasing diversity in the legal profession, especially in corporate law.

- Reviewing the prison population. I said, "We will seek to determine why a disproportionate number of inmates — at least 60 percent of the prison population — are African American and Hispanic. We will work with the federal and state departments of corrections to assess the conditions of prisons and what positive rehabilitation options are available to reduce the likelihood of recidivism."

- Examining how new lawyers who served in the military or practiced public-interest law amassed debt.

- Appointing a Commission on the Celebration of the 50th Anniversary of *Brown v. Board of Education.* Headed by Harvard Professor Charles Ogletree Jr., the commission would review *Brown's* goals and its effect on civil rights, while honoring the heroes of the landmark decision.

- Hosting out-of-the-box summits that included a diversity conference in October 2003 in Washington, DC, as well as the National Women's Summit of General Counsels and Managing Partners in May 2004.

In my acceptance speech, I was also proud to acknowledge my successor: Robert J. Grey Jr., President-Elect, who had held the ABA's second-highest ranking office in 1998 as the first person of color to serve as Chair of the House of Delegates.

My remarks before the House of Delegates were part of a huge, six-day event attended by 7,700 lawyers, plus 3,300 spouses and family members. The 1,700 meetings and events included: a welcome reception by San Francisco Mayor Willie Brown at City Hall; 240 continuing education programs; and 500 speakers. Supreme Court Justice Anthony Kennedy, who delivered the keynote address at the Opening Assembly, and former San Francisco 49ers quarterback Joe Montana, spoke about celebrities' right to privacy.

The awesome responsibility of serving as ABA president consumed a large percent of my time as I maintained an active practice along with serving as chairman of our law firm. I balanced this duty by spending a good part of each day communicating with clients as well as staff in our ABA headquarters in our Chicago office.

Each month, I shared a pertinent message on the President's Page in the ABA JOURNAL. My first column in the September 2003 edition read: "Times Have Changed: Join My Family, Our ABA Family in Improving the Justice System and the World." The article included a photo of Trudy, Denny, Vincent, Bogie, and myself.

My next column emphasized diversity and inclusion. "A Diverse Directive: We Need More Lawyers of Color to Help Promote the Rule of Law" read the headline in the October 2003 President's Message, which featured a photo of Supreme Court Justice Thurgood Marshall with the caption: "The student you encourage could become the next Justice Thurgood Marshall."

"The American Bar Association estimates that there are 1.05 million licensed lawyers in the United States," I wrote. "Slightly more than 89 percent of them are white. Lawyers of color are woefully underrepresented when compared to our population." I mentioned how corporations understood that "the browning of America" required hiring and promoting people of color whose perspectives help companies retain and attract customers who reflect America's changing demographics. My message continued: "The ABA strongly believes that full participation of all racial and ethnic groups in the profession preserves the legitimacy of our legal system and safeguards the integrity of our democratic government."

I reiterated this message when speaking to bar associations and while representing the ABA at meetings, ceremonies, and legal events across America and around the world. Each time, the person introducing me to the audience would laud my presence as an honor and privilege, as he or she cited my experience as a former Michigan Supreme Court Justice and Mayor of Detroit, a chairman of a major law firm, and ABA President.

A poignant moment of surprise usually followed as I stood up and the audience saw, for the first time, a person of color as ABA President. This reaction was especially palpable when I spoke abroad. On each occasion, my remarks were always sharp, to the point, and humorous; I really enjoyed this aspect of serving as ABA President. On each occasion, I exuded humility and respect; my example set the tone for a warm reception for my successor, Robert Grey Jr.

MAKING AN IMPACT DURING INTERNATIONAL TRIPS

As President, I had the honor of representing the American Bar Association at events in the Virgin Islands, Europe, Russia, Asia, and Africa. Trudy and I met many outstanding lawyers from around the world, and I was often invited to speak or participate in a panel discussion.

My first international trip as President was to attend the annual meeting of the Union Internationale des Avocats, which met in the beautiful city of Lisbon, Portugal.

Perhaps the most memorable trip was the opening of the Inns of Court in London, England. As invited guests, we followed the traditional protocol of wearing top hats and tails. Trudy enjoyed special seating as we took in the pomp and circumstance, and the history, which included lawyers and judges wearing robes and wigs. It was unforgettable.

An equally ceremonious event followed in Paris, France.

When we visited Moscow, Vladimir Putin had just changed the law to allow jury trials in criminal cases. We attended formal meetings with lawyers and Trudy and I met with law students to discuss domestic abuse. Trudy was also given a private tour of the beautiful Bolshoi Theatre, and later that evening, we saw a most spectacular performance of *Swan Lake*.

Another memorable trip took us to Abuja, Nigeria, to celebrate the fifth anniversary of the country's new constitution. I spoke before the President and a 2,500-person audience while my remarks were broadcast live on national television and radio.

Trudy and I still laugh about my watery mishap in the Cambodian capital of Phnom Penh. We were escorted from the plane into a private airport room, where we were graciously greeted and I was draped with leis made of fresh flowers. I spoke at a press conference with dignitaries and leaders in the legal community about the purpose of my visit on behalf of the ABA, which was to sign a Mutual Operating Agreement between the United States, Japan, Canada, and Cambodia. The MOA promised that legal organizations in our countries would work with Cambodian law school graduates during their first year of practice to help them quickly grasp the practice of law in all the relevant areas that interested them.

"Boy," I wondered as I addressed the media. "What's that damp feeling around my lap?" Little did I know, the lei was filled with water, which had drained onto my clothes during the press conference! A watery mishap, indeed.

At the time of our visit, only 439 lawyers existed in a nation of 12 to 13 million citizens. Former totalitarian dictator Pol Pot had ordered the execution of every lawyer in the country during the Khmer Rouge genocide from 1976 to 1979. This grave history made my visit and remarks at the press conference very meaningful.

Later, while running on a treadmill in the exercise room in our hotel, I marveled at a view across the Mekong Delta River into Vietnam. I was fascinated by that region's history, and proud to serve in the capacity of helping to cultivate democratic ideals of justice and equality for attorneys there. That evening, Trudy and I attended a ceremony with representatives from our U.S. Embassy and others from Canada and Japan to celebrate the signing of the MOA.

When we went to Nairobi, Kenya, I participated in a panel discussion on the importance of avoiding governmental corruption. In Brussels, Belgium, I participated with the ABA International Law Section and we met with elected officials of the European Union.

Our international travels were extraordinary, and deeply humbling, as I always took a moment to reflect on how far life had brought me since my early years in Cassopolis, Michigan.

Celebrating My Successor

Blazing a trail for another person of color to succeed me as ABA President was extremely gratifying. When my term ended, I passed the gavel to Robert Grey Jr., who served with distinction.

Ushering him into this role and witnessing his success epitomized a driving force of my life and career: using my left arm (my weakest) to pull myself up into positions where I could make a difference, then using my stronger right arm to reach behind to pull people up, and swing them out in front, to bypass me, where they could take advantage of opportunities. Many people have done this for me. We all need people to open doors, to give back, and we should all serve as that person for others.

ABA Center on Racial and Ethnic Diversity

The national economic downturn during the mid-2000's triggered a dip in membership dues and sponsorship dollars for the ABA. This coincided with the "Scope and Correlation" committee's responsibility every five years to analyze existing committees to determine if they should be continued. The goal is to pinpoint any extraneous or redundant efforts to cultivate the most streamlined and efficient organization possible.

The committees that were born of the ABA Commission on Opportunities for Minorities in the Profession back in 1986 were having such a powerful impact on diversifying the ABA's endeavors, that some wondered if those committees were still necessary. This prompted the question: "Does the ABA have too many committees for affirmative action, diversity, and inclusion?" To find answers, incoming ABA President Mike Greco (2005–2006) from Boston appointed me Chair of the ABA Center on Racial and Ethnic Diversity from 2005 to 2006. Our task was to examine every ABA entity that dealt with diversity and inclusion, and evaluate its usefulness.

Our outcome was influenced by the action of Tom Mars, General Counsel for Walmart Stores. He encouraged law firms to diversify their staff by hiring female and minority lawyers. Walmart made it very clear that it wanted to hire lawyers who reflected the changing demographics of America, and that it was important to include women and people of color in making its legal decisions. When a number of law firms ignored his advice, Tom noted that he withdrew $60 million worth of legal work from these law firms and awarded that work to law firms that actively made diversity and inclusion a priority.

This powerful statement inspired the realization that the ABA needed a separate entity to examine our five diversity and inclusion committees. As a result, DuPont attorney Thomas L. Sager (who was second to DuPont's General Counsel Stacey Mobley, who is African American) arranged for DuPont to pay for an outside consulting group to evaluate whether the ABA's diversity and inclusion committees remained relevant and worthy of maintaining. The group concluded that the committees should continue to operate independently. We presented their report, and the Board of Governors approved it. The committees would continue to be funded.

In 2009, ABA President Carolyn Lamm asked me to serve as Representative to the United Nations to explore whether the ABA was having the desired, relevant impact within the U.N. During this one-year assignment, I was granted access to the U.N. in New York, which was a heady experience. My research included consulting with the ABA's International Law Section to determine how the ABA would be better served — and heard — within the United Nations. I reported my findings to the Board of Governors, which accepted them.

TASK FORCE ON PRESERVATION
OF THE JUSTICE SYSTEM

The recession also devastated funding for court systems across America. Chief judges were forced to reduce staff, and some civil dockets were backed up for a year. As cases went unresolved, corporations suffered. The criminal dockets were also negatively impacted.

Justice was not being served, so the ABA's Task Force on Preservation of the Justice System held hearings across the country to assess the problem and identify solutions that could be implemented quickly. ABA President Steve Zak (2010–2011) appointed me to serve on this task force from 2010 to 2011. Our assessment resulted in providing solutions that made a positive impact on funding for state and federal courts.

TASK FORCE ON THE FINANCING OF
LEGAL EDUCATION

In 2014, under ABA President James R. Silkenat (2013–2014), I chaired the Task Force on the Financing of Legal Education, which addressed the rising cost of law school. Students were graduating with crippling student-loan debt, only to face a job market that was so stunted by the sluggish economy that law firms had stopped hiring summer associates.

The goal was to determine why legal education costs were rising, and what options could be implemented to help students pay down debt and secure jobs. We produced a report and recommendations about how best to help the students, then submitted a resolution to the House of Delegates, which approved our resolution.

HONORARY CO-CHAIR OF THE 360 COMMISSION

In August of 2016, I concluded an assignment from ABA President Paulette Brown (2015-2016) to serve as honorary co-chair of the 360 Commission with Mark Roellig, Executive Vice President and General Counsel at Massachusetts Mutual Life Insurance Company.

She had tasked us with examining the impact of the recession between 2008 to 2014, when lawyers were laid off as law firms downsized. African American attorneys and lawyers of color were the hardest hit. She wanted us to investigate what happened, make suggestions, and present our findings to the ABA House of Delegates within one year.

"Dennis, I just want to use your name," President Brown said.

I smiled and said, "Of course."

"Sure enough," recalls former President Brown now, "Dennis worked in the trenches like a regular member. He participated in the quarterly meetings in San Diego and New Jersey, staying for the entire two full days of work."

This assignment echoed the concerns that, about 30 years prior, had inspired the ABA to appoint the Task Force on Opportunities for Minorities in the Legal Profession, which produced Goal 9, a program that promoted diversity and inclusion for women and people of color.

We called our new endeavor a "freshening" of former Goal 9 (now Goal 3), with the mission of encouraging general counsels to utilize the services of lawyers of color and women in large law firms and in minority- and women-owned law firms. We created a survey for corporations to give to law firms to ascertain how many lawyers of color and women they employed, and whether those individuals were working on the corporations' files. We presented our report in Resolution 113 before the ABA House of Delegates, and received an overwhelming vote of support.

In September 2016, 22 corporate general counsels signed a letter that was sent to the Fortune 1000 general counsels, asking them to embrace ABA Resolution 113. Attached to the letter was the survey, along with a request to use it. This endeavor reiterated the message that Harry Pearce had expressed three decades earlier.

It's more important than ever to advocate for diversity and inclusion of lawyers because American demographics, according to the Census, project that by 2019, the majority of people age 18 or younger living in the United States will be people of color. Likewise, the Census Bureau predicts that between 2035 and 2042, the majority of people living in the U.S. will be people of color. Advocating for diversity and inclusion of lawyers of color matters to corporations because this emerging population will have discretionary income, and will choose to spend it with companies that respect and represent them.

That is a major tenet of the Billion Dollar Roundtable (BDR). According to its website, the BDR "was created in 2001 to recognize and celebrate corporations that achieved spending at least one billion dollars with minority- and woman-owned suppliers. The BDR promotes and shares best practices in supply-chain diversity excellence through the production of white papers. In discussions, the members review common issues, opportunities, and strategies. The BDR encourages corporate entities to continue growing their supplier diversity programs by increasing commitment and spending levels each year."

The same philosophy inspired the Ilitch family and Olympia Entertainment to utilize a historic number of minority contractors to construct the new Little Caesars Arena, which will house our Detroit Red Wings and our Detroit Pistons beginning in the fall of 2017. They accomplished this by using a system (Executive Order 4), which was created and used during my administration for construction of the Compuware Building, Comerica Park, Ford Field, and the three casinos.

THE OBAMA YEARS

In 2003, both Vincent and Denny became intrigued with, and began to fundraise for, a state senator from Illinois who was running for United States Senate. His name was Barack Obama. His political consultant was David Axelrod.

By happenstance, while attending an ABA meeting in Boston at the same time as the Democratic National Convention, I had the good fortune of meeting State Senator Barack Obama and his wife, Michelle. I enjoyed a conversation with them, and was extremely impressed.

At the time, John Kerry was running for president and had asked the U.S. Senatorial candidate to give a keynote address. When Barack Obama took the stage, he spoke of one America, not a black America or a white America, and his senatorial campaign skyrocketed into high gear. State Senator Obama ran without any real opposition, traveling America to help other Democrats. I saw him a second time in Denver while there for another ABA meeting.

In 2004, he won the election and became U.S. Senator Barack Obama. Several years later, both Denny and Vincent again became involved in fundraising for Senator Obama's campaign for president. At the time, Hillary Clinton had also announced that she was running for president, and sought support of U.S. Congresswoman Carolyn Cheeks Kilpatrick, the incoming president of the Congressional Black Caucus, and her son, Detroit Mayor Kwame Kilpatrick.

Hillary did not ask me to participate in her campaign, but U.S. Senator Barack Obama did. We hosted a significant fundraiser for Senator Obama in Detroit. Interestingly, loyalty to the Clintons made some folks hesitant to support his campaign. However, my involvement in his campaign intensified after Senator Obama invited me to the Democratic National Convention in Denver. I joined monthly, then biweekly, then weekly telephone conference calls with soon-to-be presidential advisor Valerie Jarrett, and Eric Holder, who would become the first African American to serve as U.S. Attorney General.

What a proud moment when Barack Obama was elected in November of 2008 as America's first African American president! Watching him run the country was a delight, and I loved how he helped Detroit and the auto industry. I also admired that he filled his administration with respected, like-minded people.

During his first term, when President Obama's advisors asked me on two different occasions to consider taking a post in his

We are extremely proud to enjoy a friendship with former First Lady Michelle Obama and former President Barack Obama.

administration, I respectfully passed; I wanted to position myself in a way that could help facilitate his re-election. I did accept an invitation to serve as an at-large member on the Democratic National Committee (DNC). I later was elected to the Executive Committee, and was appointed to the DNC's Rules and Bylaws Committee.

I am proud to call President Barack Obama and First Lady Michelle Obama friends. He did so much for all of America and for the city of Detroit. He was a master of grace under pressure.

In 2016, when Hillary Clinton ran for president, I accepted the invitation to participate in her campaign. I joined mayors, DNC members, and Congressional Black Caucus (CBC) representatives on a bus tour through Florida. I boarded in Tallahassee. In Jacksonville, we visited 16 churches on a Sunday. Next, in Miami, we stopped at a few early voting places and a college campus where Senator Tim Kaine, the vice-presidential candidate, was speaking. We also met with U.S. Senator Bill Nelson at the rally.

Shortly thereafter, I joined mayors, CBC members, and leaders such as former U.S. Trade Representative and former Mayor of Dallas, Ron Kirk, who had served under President Obama, at a rally in Columbus, Ohio. I enjoyed visiting with President Clinton, when he spoke at the rally in Columbus, and when we walked during Detroit's Labor Day parade.

It was a delight to campaign for Hillary. It was important for America that she become our next United States President. Much to my surprise, we lost the election.

Work on Corporate Boards Continues

As mentioned earlier, I was invited in 2002 to serve on the corporate boards of Compuware and Johnson Controls, Inc. Two years later, I was elected to the MASCO board of directors.

This work was fascinating and tremendously rewarding, because it enriched my understanding of the inner-workings of the business world, while also providing new opportunities to promote diversity and inclusion in corporate America.

I was inspired to serve on corporate boards by former National Urban League President Vernon Jordan, a brilliant lawyer and a partner in a Washington, DC law firm. I had read about his influential work on different boards of directors that enabled him to promote diversity and inclusion in corporate America by opening doors for people of color and women to become employed and promoted in our nation's largest corporations. This concept intrigued me. He became a voice for us in a society where very few people of color rise to the ranks of executive leadership and CEOs.

My roles with Compuware, Johnson Controls, and MASCO taught me firsthand that serving on corporate boards provides a responsibility to help a company grow, enhance shareholder value, and impact how the corporation operates. Furthermore, the responsibility of being a board member inspired a deep desire to do my very best, cultivating the skills required to better contribute and keep abreast of issues and trends that could affect my service.

I achieved this, in part, by becoming active in the Black Corporate Directors Conference. I attended my first meeting in Chicago and later the meetings that now take place in Laguna Beach, California. I also joined the National Association of Corporate Directors, attended their conferences, and became a Fellow. That association provides professional publications that prepared me to better serve on the boards of directors.

In 2004, I became Chair of the National Advisory Board for The InfiLaw System, which owned Florida Coastal Law School in Jacksonville, Florida. They wanted to start two other law schools: Phoenix School of Law (now Summit); and Charlotte School of Law. Our Advisory Board helped them secure ABA accreditation.

In 2008, I served as Co-Chair of the National Transportation Policy Project for the Bipartisan Policy Center (BPC), a 501(c)(3) entity. As a result, I was invited to serve on the BPC Board of Directors. Under the outstanding leadership of BPC Founder Jason Grumet, this great board provided excellent guidance to both sides of the aisle in Congress.

In 2011, I was asked to join the board of Progressus Therapy, a for-profit company that worked with K-12 schools by providing substitute or full-time physical therapists, speech therapists, and occupational therapists. Several years later, the board of directors followed management's recommendation and voted to sell Progressus Therapy.

In 2011 and for several years, I served on the Jefferies Global Senior Advisory Board. I worked with a seven-member board, which included two CEOs from France, one from the United Kingdom, and three former CEOs from the United States, including former GM Chairman Rick Wagoner. This unique opportunity enabled me to invest significant time for several years, learning more about municipal finance, and observing the impressive way that Jefferies' two remarkable leaders ran the firm, where many talented men and women exhibited a great commitment to their clients.

My work on corporate boards began to taper in 2014, when I concluded 12 years of service with Johnson Controls and Compuware, followed by MASCO. Then, after a dozen years with InfiLaw, I resigned. On July 1, 2015, MASCO spun off a new company called TopBuild, an insulation business for housing and commercial buildings, and it went public. I was elected for a one-year term on the board of TopBuild. In May of 2016, I was re-elected to the board for a three-year term.

Chairing the Board of Directors for the Detroit Regional Chamber

While mayor, I cultivated good relationships with Detroit Renaissance and the Detroit Regional Chamber, both of which played crucial roles in fostering cohesion and cooperation in the business community. Working with both organizations was mutually beneficial, as their objectives aligned with my vision for the city of Detroit.

After I stepped down as mayor, I joined the Detroit Regional Chamber board, which led to my becoming chair of the annual Mackinac Policy Conference in 2005 to 2006. Then in 2006, I became chair of the board of directors until 2007. During that period, the Detroit Regional Chamber was the country's largest metropolitan chamber. I worked closely with CEO Richard Blouse and Executive Vice President Tammy J. Carnrike, who was lead staff for the Mackinac Policy Conference, and her direct reports.

"One of the things that stood out when Dennis was the Mackinac Conference chair, was that we give out gift bags that are stuffed with all kinds of things from sponsors, and they were very heavy and really big," recalls Tammy, who has been Chief Operating Officer at the Detroit Regional Chamber since 2006. "The staff would literally stuff 1,500 bags, walking around the room, putting in all the pieces. Dennis came early to the island, took his jacket off, rolled up his sleeves, and stood side by side with the staff for hours, working to fill the bags. That made such an impression on the staff to have a leader like that. That's his character. He'll do anything. It doesn't matter what the level is. He'll treat you the same as the person at the top of the company. He's not above anybody else, and he's there to support the staff as much as the staff supports him."

Tammy also noted that it is unusual for someone in the legal profession to become so business-focused and excel at being part of that Chamber board. My enthusiastic participation included speaking at their national association meeting in Cleveland, which was having trouble finding a speaker who could talk about the importance of diversity.

"He did it at his own expense," Tammy says. "Everyone was glued to his words. When you talk about diversity, you can hear about it in seminars, but with Dennis, you get the passion. He includes not only minority and race; he includes females and tends to open up minds in that way."

I also talked about diversity at another Chamber meeting in Durham, North Carolina.

"Here's this African American politician and businessman in Detroit going down to a country club to do a luncheon speech on diversity," Tammy says. "They were overwhelmed and loved it. He finds a way to cross over. I also have always called him a pied piper. Just about anything he does, you can see people naturally following him, whether it's in politics or his legal work or diversity or his bar associations, he's just the kind of person who others naturally follow."

At two chamber events in Cleveland, between 2006 and 2010, I talked about the often-overlooked buying power of women and their impact in the economy.

I continued to participate as an emeritus board member and serve on committees appointed by Detroit Regional Chamber President and CEO Sandy Baruah.

I watched with pride as our son Denny served as Chair of the Mackinac Policy Conference (2015–2016), an extremely successful gathering of 1500 business, foundation, and major non-profit leaders, as well as local, state, and federal elected officials. The event included Denny conducting a high-energy interview with Detroit business leader Dan Gilbert. After that, Denny served a very successful year as Chairman of the Board of Directors of the Detroit Regional Chamber (2016–2017).

GIVING BACK AS A TRUSTEE AT WESTERN MICHIGAN UNIVERSITY

When Michigan Governor Jennifer Granholm appointed me to serve on the Western Michigan University Board of Trustees, I was delighted. This position enabled me to encourage the administration to consider diversity and inclusion in all aspects of the university. I served from 2005 to 2012, and as chair of the board from 2011 until 2012.

Serving on the board was a tremendous learning experience about how our public, state-supported colleges and universities operate. I earned how the state had significantly decreased funding for state-supported colleges and universities, compared to 15 years before that. My service also included bearing witness to the opening of The Western Michigan University Homer Stryker MD School of Medicine.

Western Michigan University and Wayne State University are the two schools to which the Dennis W. Archer Foundation provides scholarships for students who graduate from Detroit high schools and Cassopolis' only high school. In September of 2015, we held a press conference to announce that we had awarded more than $1 million in scholarships. Whenever I speak in Cassopolis, I encourage young people to consider attending these two universities.

My participation at Western Michigan University included the thrill of watching the game at Ford Field in December 2016, when the WMU football team experienced its first undefeated season since the university was established in 1903! They played in the Cotton Bowl on January 2, 2017; we lost to Wisconsin, 24–16.

Most recently, I was awed and humbled when WMU announced that two new residence halls were named *Hall-Archer-Pickard Hall East* and *Hall-Archer-Pickard Hall West,* and a conference room in Heritage Hall would be called the *Hall-Archer-Pickard Conference Room.* This honor is occurring thanks to a $3.05 million donation by William "Bill" Pickard, in celebration of the 50-year friendship enjoyed by

William F. Pickard, Ann Hall, the widow of Ronald Hall, and I celebrate on September 27, 2017 after the naming of the dorms by the President of WMU, approved by the Board of Trustees.

Bill, Ron Hall — who died June 1, 2016, mid-way through his eight-year term as a WMU Trustee — and myself.

I am exceedingly proud of Western Michigan University, and very pleased with how it has grown. I always eagerly accept invitations to speak to a class or participate in fraternity events or in business programs, and I do so with great pride and enthusiasm. It's called giving back, and paying it forward.

From Cassopolis, Michigan, to Harvard University

In the Fall of 2009, I was sitting in my office at Dickinson Wright when Stephen Strong called. He was attending Harvard, and suggested that I become a Resident Fellow for the Harvard University Institute of Politics in the John F. Kennedy School of Government.

My immediate thought was, *Yeah, right! From Cassopolis to Harvard? Are you kidding me?*

So, I told him, "Thank you very much. I appreciate your call, but I doubt if they want anybody like me." Back in November 1993, I had attended a four-day, New Mayor's School at the John F. Kennedy School of Government, along with 20-plus mayors, before we took office. Several Michigan mayors attended, and our teachers included Philadelphia Mayor Ed Rendell.

That program had introduced me to Americorps, which "engages more than 75,000 Americans in intensive service each year at non-profits, schools, public agencies, and community and faith-based groups across the country," according to its website.

I brought Americorps to Detroit with the help of Henry Ford Hospital CEO Gail Warden and Penny Bailer, who became Executive Director of City Year Detroit, which enabled young people to work in our city schools for two years in exchange for free college tuition.

Stephen called again in the spring of 2010, and urged me to participate in the Resident Fellow program. The beneficial impact of my first Harvard visit caused me to rethink the prospect of returning. I was asked to spend a day interviewing. Later, they invited me to participate as a Resident Fellow during the Fall of 2010, from September until December. I stayed in a condo, and loved being on the beautiful campus, learning how to use the Boston subway system, and watching the rowing team practice on the Charles River.

At the same time, the learning experience was exhilarating. The Resident Fellows were prominent individuals who worked in government, media, and business, including a former member of the Israeli Parliament, and a former leader of Haiti. We were able to invite guest speakers, so I arranged for visits by: former ABA President and Boston lawyer Mike Greco; Michigan Governor Jennifer Granholm; Mona Sutphen, who was number two under President Obama's Chief of Staff, Rahm Emanuel; and Jason Grumet, CEO of the Bipartisan Policy Center in Washington, DC.

Gordon Brown, the former Prime Minister of the United Kingdom, and former Florida Governor Jeb Bush, were Visiting Fellows during our service, and we interacted with them, learning invaluable lessons and information from both leaders.

While on campus, I met with African American scholar Dr. Henry Louis Gates, and enjoyed visits with several friends: Harvard Law Professors Charles Ogletree; David Wilkins; and Lani Guinier, President Clinton's nominee for Assistant Attorney General for Civil Rights who became the first woman of color appointed as a tenured professor at Harvard University Law School. Her husband, Nolan Bowie, is a Lecturer in Public Policy at Harvard University's Kennedy School of Government. I attended many events, including a lecture by U.S. Supreme Court Justice Steven Breyer, who spoke about his new book, and anniversary celebrations of John F. Kennedy being elected president.

At the end of the program, the Resident Fellows were invited to participate in the "New Members of Congress School," as newly elected lawmakers went through the same process that I did as a new mayor. Our discussions explored ways they could have a positive impact.

My time at Harvard was outstanding. It was only made better when Trudy visited for a month. To this day, I maintain contact with colleagues and students whom I met during that fellowship.

Consulting Work

Whenever opportunities arise for me to share my expertise and experience to help corporations improve their work with diversity and inclusion, I eagerly accept the chance to serve. This was especially true when I participated on Walmart's Employment Practices Advisory Panel (EPAP) with attorney Vilma Martinez, who sat on several corporate boards and was a partner at Munger Tolles in Los Angeles, and Claudia Kennedy, a former three-star general in the U.S. Army.

Tom Mars, Walmart's Vice President and General Counsel, asked us to serve as consultants to examine the company's policies and practices relating to diversity and inclusion, and to make recommendations. Near the conclusion of our work, President Obama appointed Vilma as Ambassador to Argentina.

During the last several years, I have been honored to serve as a Salary Arbitrator for Major League Baseball and the Major League Baseball Player's Association.

Awards & Honors
Receiving the American Bar Association's Highest Honor: The ABA Medal

Each year at the ABA's annual meeting, I watched legal giants receive our organization's highest honor, the ABA Medal. This award, according to the American Bar Association, "recognizes exceptionally distinguished service by a lawyer or lawyers to the cause of American jurisprudence and is given only in years when the ABA Board of Governors determines a nominee has provided exceptional and distinguished service to the law and the legal profession."

With that understanding, while sitting in the annual awards ceremony year after year, I always wondered whether I might someday be found worthy of mere consideration of this award. Past winners

My family and I posing proudly after I received the American Bar Association's highest honor, the ABA Medal. Pictured standing from left: our son, Dennis Archer Jr.; our grandson, Chase Archer; our son, Vincent Archer; our grandson, Dennis Archer III (Trey); Trudy; our daughter-in-law, Roberta Archer, and my sister-in-law, Beth DunCombe Brown.

included: U.S. Supreme Court Justice Thurgood Marshall; civil rights attorney Oliver White Hill; U.S. Supreme Court Justice Ruth Bader Ginsberg; U.S. Supreme Court Justice Oliver Wendell Holmes; U.S. Supreme Court Justice Felix Frankfurter; U.S. Supreme Court Justice Louis F. Powell, Jr.; former ABA President Chesterfield Smith; former ABA President William Reece Smith; and Hillary Rodham Clinton.

So, in June of 2016, when ABA President Paulette Brown informed me that I would receive the award, I was overwhelmed with humility and gratitude for such a unique and high honor.

"Dennis, you are exactly who this award was created for," President Brown said as she introduced me during the General Assembly of the ABA Annual Meeting in San Francisco on August 6, 2016. "It is all of us in this room and in the legal community who need to question whether we will ever be able to accomplish enough to be considered worthy to be in your company."

I was overjoyed to experience this moment surrounded by Trudy, Denny, Vincent, Robbie, Trey, Chase, Beth, John Krsul, W. Anthony "Tony" Jenkins, Reggie Turner, and many other friends and supporters.

Trudy and I enjoy spending time with Robbie, Denny, Chase (left), and Trey.

"Dennis Archer's professional accomplishments are unparalleled, and he is held in the highest regard by his peers," President Brown said. "On a personal level, Dennis has been a wise and encouraging mentor and role model to me as well as ABA leaders. I hear so many people tell me how Dennis has whispered in their ears and has encouraged them to do great things. He truly exemplifies the 'conspicuous service to the cause of American jurisprudence' the ABA Medal recognizes."

The moment that I stood at the podium to accept this honor was both surreal and profound, with high emotions surging through me during my remarks.

"When you drive by a fence post and you see a turtle sitting on top of it, you know the turtle did not get there by itself," I said to begin a 15-minute speech. "It had to have meaningful help to get to the top. My meaningful help came from the person who first urged me, then encouraged me, to go to law school before she became my wife, 49 years ago, my wife, Trudy DunCombe Archer."

I continued, "To me, the practice of law has been a calling. Thanks to the American Bar Association, it has given myself and others a chance to participate in, or be an advocate for, what we believe are the right and proper things that will make America even stronger."

That statement roused applause, as did my heartfelt conclusion: "Finally, as Erma Bombeck has observed, *When I stand before God at the end of my life, I would hope that I would not have a single bit of talent left, and I can say, 'I used everything you [I glanced upward] gave me.'* Thank you!"

Back in Detroit, my dear friends Dr. Lorna Thomas, William "Bill" Pickard, PhD, and Roy Roberts hosted a party at the Detroit Athletic Club to celebrate my receipt of the ABA Medal. I used that opportunity to ask guests who were general counsels to join the ABA House of Delegates and implement a policy to utilize the services of lawyers of color through ABA Resolution 113.

The honor of receiving the ABA Medal inspired accolades from friends and colleagues across America and around the world. Lillian Gaskin, a Legislative Consultant for the Federal Administrative Law Judges Conference in Washington, DC, emailed this: "Like them, I want to let you know how great it is that you have received this

The Detroit Public Library's Main Branch, located in the Cultural Center, featured an exhibit about my life. Pictured standing from left, my brother-in-law, Joe Brown; our son, Vincent Archer; Trudy; me; and our son, Dennis Archer Jr. Seated from left: my sister-in-law, Beth DunCombe Brown; my mother-in-law, Eleanor DunCombe; and my father-in-law, James DunCombe. Photo Credit: John Meir Photography

honor. Truly, my hand is on my heart; I am so touched. To use your words, you are a lawyer who has gone out of his way to heal that which needs healing. In addition to all you do for the ABA in your leadership positions, I have watched you be so kind and so gracious with staff and with everyday ABA members. What can I say? I am very proud of the ABA for selecting you to receive the medal. I wish you luck as you continue to use your power to heal."

Another thrilling accolade for my life's work occurred when I received an award that was first presented to Vernon Jordan. A red-carpet event at the Lincoln Center for the Performing Arts in New York City set the stage for the Lifetime Achievement Award from the Minority Corporate Counsel Association (MCCA). Attending the Diversity Honors Gala with me were: Trudy; Denny; several partners from Dickinson Wright; members of Compuware, MASCO, and Johnson Controls; and friends.

MCCA President and CEO Joe West said I was honored for "making important and lasting contributions to advancing a society that fully appreciates, celebrates, and recognizes the value of diversity" and for having "worked tirelessly in law, politics, business, and education to create opportunities and improve the lives of countless Americans." He added that my "remarkable record of service and achievement has won… acclaim not only in Michigan but also across the nation."

This honor inspired the same awe as when, in December of 2016, I received an honorary degree from Michigan State University. I could never have imagined, while attending Cassopolis High School, that I would receive 25 Honorary Degrees from outstanding colleges and universities.

While all the honors bestowed on me have been outstanding, the American Lawyer Lifetime Achievement Award from *The American Lawyer* magazine in October of 2009 was particularly memorable. As was another in May of 2008, when I was honored in New York City along with Eric Holder and 48 other outstanding minority lawyers with the *National Law Journal's* designation as one of the "50 Most Influential Minority Lawyers in America."

RECEIVING A HIGH HONOR FROM JAPAN

The Japanese government usually gives it prestigious award known as "The Order of the Rising Sun, Gold Rays with Neck Ribbon" to a private Japanese citizen who is living abroad and working to enhance international trade for Japan.

I was extremely honored to receive this award after I successfully advocated for Japanese people living in Michigan who wanted to renew their driver's licenses. The Secretary of State, Terry Lynn Land, believed that Japanese people could obtain driver's licenses here in Michigan. However, Attorney General Michael Cox disagreed, saying they should return to Japan to get a driver's license. To resolve this, United States Congresswoman Candice Miller and I joined Secretary of State Land and testified before a Michigan State Senate Committee in opposition to Attorney General Cox's point of view. Fortunately, the attorney general changed his mind.

During the awards ceremony at the Detroit Athletic Club in June of 2013, I received the gold-and-red medallion and lapel pin

Judge Damon Keith speaks with our grandsons, Dennis Wayne Archer III (Trey) and Chase Alexander Archer. Photo Credit: Roberta C. Archer

that depicts the energy of the rising sun. There to witness the occasion were Trudy, Denny, Vincent, Robbie, Trey, Chase, Judge Keith, friends, members of Dickinson Wright, and many people from the business community.

Enjoying Family Time

One of the greatest joys of my life has been spending time with our grandsons, Dennis W. Archer III (Trey) and Chase Alexander Archer, who were born after I left office. Trudy and I enjoy traveling with the boys, as well as taking them to museums and events. On June 7, 2016, 11-year-old Trey stood at a podium before hundreds of people at Cobo Center and introduced me as the American Diabetes Association's Father of the Year.

On another occasion that year, Chase, then eight years old, recited a poem he had written about his grandparents at a Grandparents' Day event at Detroit Country Day School. We are so proud of our grandsons!

In addition, I cherish spending time with Trudy. We visit Vincent in Los Angeles, where he is consulting, utilizing his marketing skills, and also pursuing his dream as a producer of television and film projects.

"I went to law school for a year, and it was not me," Vincent says. "I was stressed out about it. But my parents told me, 'You have to find your passion. Don't stress. Everybody is different. You don't have to be a lawyer. Law school is not for everybody.' That helped me a lot."

Vincent worked first for Deloitte in Detroit. Later, he was employed by PricewaterhouseCoopers (PwC) in New York City. After some time, he was hired by The New York Empowerment Zone. He enjoyed several promotions, one of which made him responsible for working with new businesses within the Empowerment Zone and with President Clinton's staff to relocate his office to Harlem. Vincent, who lived in Harlem at the time, invited me to attend the opening celebration of President Clinton's office. He even arranged for me to be on stage during the ceremony.

Vincent was later recruited and motivated to join a marketing and advertising firm that marketed Chrysler cars to 18- to 34-year-olds. Wouldn't you know it, six months later, Chrysler changed advertising executives; the marketing firm lost its contract.

Vincent attended New York University Film School. Trudy, Beth, Joe, and I traveled to New York for a screening of his film project, which was shown along with his classmates' productions. Vincent's film was phenomenal, and we remain extremely proud that he is pursuing a career that is meaningful to him. In doing so, Vincent feels inspired to serve as a trailblazer for diversity and inclusion in the entertainment industry.

"My dad taught my brother and me that you should always try to reach back with your strongest arm to pull people forward with you," Vincent says. "He had done that forever in all facets. We grew up watching him be a mentor to many people, just as Judge Keith has mentored him. My father's ability to break ground in so many ways has given me courage to come out to Los Angeles to make an impact on the entertainment industry, then reach back with my strongest arm to help others succeed here."

Detroit's Future Has Begun

During the time that I was mayor, the city experienced excitement, an enormous sense of hope, and a positive outlook toward the future.

"An inflection point in history occurred when Dennis Archer was elected mayor," says David Axelrod. "It was clearly an election about turning the page to project hope on the future while attacking the problems that had beset the city. We wanted to make voting for Dennis Archer a vote for what the future could be. So, when we said, 'Let the Future Begin' it was really not about him. It was about Detroit. And it was about what the city and community could do together to build a better future."

David, who has witnessed Detroit's revival, adds, "Now the future has truly begun in Detroit, and it's an exciting story!"

Today, I am overwhelmed with pride as I step onto Woodward Avenue from Ally Detroit Center (formerly One Detroit Center), the 41-story building that houses Dickinson Wright's Detroit offices. The sidewalk is a river of people representing every race and ethnicity, age, and religion. I join this sea of humanity as it flows past construction cranes, traffic jams, vibrant new restaurants, and tall buildings whose office space, loft apartments, and condos are filled to capacity by the recent influx of young professionals, Detroiters, and those moving to Detroit from Brooklyn, Los Angeles, Chicago, and suburban Detroit. New cafés serving coffee are vibrant with people conversing and working on laptop computers.

On any given day, throngs of people wearing jerseys for the Detroit Tigers, Detroit Lions, and Detroit Red Wings walk in clusters from restaurants and bars toward Comerica Park, Ford Field, and Joe Louis Arena. If I were to walk farther north, I would see the nearly complete Little Caesars Arena where the Red Wings and Detroit Pistons will soon play, and where concerts and other world-class events will be held.

Looking straight ahead, I am dazzled by the color, movement, and sound in Campus Martius Park. I stare in near disbelief at the fruition of what we envisioned so many years ago. Campus Martius has become the ultimate gathering place at the core of our downtown, surrounded by new and updated office buildings. During the winter, an enormous Christmas tree towers over the ice rink that's packed with families, couples, and tourists. In spring, summer, and fall, Campus Martius pulsates with live music from a band shell, two restaurants with outdoor seating, a "beach" with lounge chairs on real sand, a beautiful fountain, and café style chairs where people gather, eat, enjoy life, and watch movies in an atmosphere that's joyous, safe, and cosmopolitan. Seeing this inspires me to pause and reflect upon the contributions of Robert Larsen, Beth DunCombe, Phyllis James, Gloria Robinson, Edsel Ford, and many others.

As I walk through the park, I am awed by the cornucopia of humanity reflected in faces of every hue, and attire that suggests that they may be lawyers, judges, janitors, teachers, students, young professionals, ministers, and tourists from around the world. All have come to Detroit to experience this electrifying rebirth.

"Mayor Archer," someone says to me daily as I marvel at how Detroit is becoming a world-class city. "Thank you for everything you did for Detroit."

"You are quite welcome," I respond, glancing up at the Compuware Building, which has since become One Campus Martius, world headquarters for Quicken Loans, founded by Dan Gilbert, whose investment in downtown Detroit has played a major role in its revitalization. His companies, including Rock Ventures, employ more than 14,000 people in downtown Detroit.

When I look to the southeast corner of Campus Martius, I am overwhelmed with pride at the sight of the diverse people filling the outdoor seating area and chic interior of Central Kitchen + Bar. Denny and his business partners opened the restaurant in August of 2015 on the ground floor of the First National Building. Its stylish, comfortable interior, distinctly Detroit vibe, and American food ranked it as one of the *Detroit Free Press'* Best Restaurants of 2016.

"Central looks as Detroit should look," Denny says, "as one of the most truly diverse places in terms of clientele, the people who opened the restaurant, and the 50-plus people we employ on our staff. We're really proud of that."

Central Kitchen + Bar also overlooks Cadillac Square, which at lunchtime is jammed with food trucks, live bands, and a playground. During the evenings and weekends, the square is alive with bands, gala party tents, and events such as the Winter Blast festival and the Detroit International Jazz Festival every Labor Day weekend.

"Unfortunately, because of the time lapse between Dad leaving and Mayor Mike Duggan getting into office," Denny says, "a lot of people forget the tremendous start that we had as it relates to development in Detroit, particularly downtown. During my father's tenure, GM moved into the Renaissance Center, the three casinos were built, the two stadiums were built, Compuware was being built, and that subsequently led to Campus Martius Park evolving into the central point of downtown now."

Denny, who is developing more businesses in historic Paradise Valley, also played an integral role in building a Meijer store in Detroit on a 28-acre plot.

"Had we had more continuity," he says, "we'd have more attribution to the contribution of his years in office. The problem is that between then and now, you had public corruption, and three different mayors, so some people forget. But it always happens on a weekly basis that someone will say, 'Hey, your dad is really the one who got this started.' That is refreshing to hear."

Former GM Vice Chairman Harry Pearce, who was instrumental in bringing GM downtown, also appreciates this point: "It's very rewarding to know that even if you played only a small role, GM got the ball rolling and started attracting people like Dan Gilbert, Peter Karmanos, and Roger Penske, who made commitments to get the city rolling again. Dennis Archer was front and center of all that in the early days before anyone had a lot of confidence that it could be done. All the sports stadiums, the restaurants, the new condos, the M1 Rail streetcar line, all this comes from bringing people like Dan Gilbert into the city. He has a similar vision and obviously put his money where his mouth is and invested in dozens of major buildings, many of which have been renovated."

Matt Cullen, a principal of Rock Ventures LLC, which continues to spearhead downtown development, agrees. "Mayor Archer came in as this incredibly accomplished guy who had all this historic success from a career standpoint," he says, "and made the decision that he was going to invest all that he had created on a personal basis from a personal capacity standpoint into the future of the city. And he took on a lot of political noise in the process. He was a real bridge between a primarily African American community that was going through a lot of challenges in the city and the business community that had its own challenges, unsure how to engage with the city. He mended a lot of fences and created a lot of opportunities for people to connect. He was a great connector. He was a very talented, charismatic guy who played that role in bringing people together."

Former Corporation Counsel Phyllis James, who now lives in Las Vegas, wonders, "Is Dennis Archer getting enough credit in terms of changing the landscape for the trajectory of Detroit? Without his work, a lot would not be happening as quickly as it is now. Obviously, I applaud mega investment in the city, but we must give credit where credit is due, which is Dennis Archer's compassion and tireless commitment to get the job done by surrounding himself with brilliant people to transform the city of Detroit with innovation and excellence."

Many of those individuals celebrated at my 70th birthday party, along with friends, family members, and colleagues. Among them was James Turnbull, a friend of more than 40 years, whom I met when we both worked on Ed Bell's campaign for mayor and who wound up being a valued member of my administration. He wrote this for me:

Dennis Archer at 70!

He wasn't from money
Or a mighty metropolis.
If memory serves,
He came from Cassopolis!

He titled himself
A poor country lawyer.
Some thought of Huck Finn.
The wise thought Tom Sawyer.

When he prayed for God's guidance,
God's answer was swift:
"Take Trudy," said God.
"Consider her My gift!"

And while I'm in the mood
(and gift-giving's the onus)
Take younger sister Beth.
We'll call it a bonus.

Dennis moved through chairs,
Made partner and such,
But he still wanted more
And he now had the touch.

Then on to '86,
Where the height of his dreams
Was to boogie to Lansing
To join the Supremes.

Could Dennis top that?
(We pause for the tension)
If he stayed, we couldn't blame him.
Have you seen the pension?

He wanted another challenge
He wasn't an old man.
But could he really be serious
Could he take on Coleman?

You all know the answer.
The Old Man was a goner.
Starting in '93,
We called Dennis, Your Honor!

The City gave him loyalty.
He gave Detroit class.
And he was still taking names
And he was still kickin' ass.

You may see some judges
In the shadows tonight.
Ed Bell and Sam Gardner
Who taught wrong from right.

Thank God Damon Keith
Is still hale and hearty.
So on with the merriment.
Proceed with the party.

You'll hear it all tonight,
Jokes, legends, what have you?
But, Dennis, let's 'fess up,
We're here 'cos we love you!

I am immensely grateful that the citizens of Detroit blessed me with the opportunity to serve in a capacity that enabled me to invest my talents to help the city that I love. Now, as I walk down the street, I can humbly and proudly declare that the future is now, and Detroit is truly becoming world-class.

In closing, allow me to repeat the Erma Bombeck quote that concluded my remarks when receiving the ABA Medal:

"When I stand before God at the end of my life, I would hope that I would not have a single bit of talent left, and could say, 'I used everything you gave me.'"

It's not the end, but what's next?

Trudy and I cherish our grandsons, Chase (left) and Trey (right).

Photo credit: Stills by Stinson

APPENDIX

● RESIDENTIAL/ MIXED-USE

HOUSING - ○

1. **Addison Apartments/ Addison Hotel**
$3.5 million project involves the renovation of a vacant hotel into 42 loft apartments.

2. **Alberta W. King Village**
$10 million investment developed 121 garden-style apartments located in the Empowerment Zone.

3. **Alexander Court Apartments**
Rehabilitation of 36 units completed in late 1999.

4. **Algonquin Apartments**
Rehabilitation of 12 units completed in 1998.

5. **Architects Building**
$6.2 million renovation in 1998 of the historic building into 27 apartments and 24 units.

6. **Ariel Square**
$4.2 million development housing 28 units, 16 have been built in the New Center area.

7. **Averhill Park**
216 vacant city-owned lots and 46 abandoned city owned homes have been renovated.

8. **Bagley Housing Association**
22 homes in Phase I & II for low and moderate income families and 6 market rate townhouses.

9. **Bethany Presbyterian Villages**
$3.5 million three story development, 52 subsidized units for senior citizens.

10. **Bicentennial Towers**
Renovation of 300 apartments to be completed in 2001.

11. **Boydell House**
$380,000 renovation of the historic building into 4 residential units and 2 commercial units.

12. **Bradby Homes**
$19.7 million 111 condominium project developed by Grayhaven L.L.C. expected completion date 2002.

13. **Brainard Street Housing**
Construction is planned for 130 new units of 2-3 story garden style apartments

14. **Brightmoor Homes**
$6.8 million 50 affordable lease to own sites developed by Northwest Detroit Neighborhood, Local Initiative Support Corporation, First Federal of Michigan, City of Detroit HOME funds, and MSHDA.

15. **Brush Park Manor Paradise Valley**
113 unit three story senior housing facility developed by Lutheran Village of Michigan and Joint Fraternal Development. Brush Park Manor is scheduled for occumancy the summer of 2001.

16. **Burroughs Avenue, 41-47**
Renovating building into loft style apartments part of Phase One of the New Amsterdam Development.

17. **Campau Farms Condominiums**
$20 million, 180 unit condo project developed by Crosswinds Communities, Inc.

18. **Canfield Lofts**
$5.5 million renovation of a former printing company into 35 for sale condominiums.

19. **Cass Avenue Building, 623**
The building will be converted into residential lofts developed by The Sterling Group and DIF.

20. **Cass Corridor Neighborhood Development, Inc.**
$6 million renovation of 51 apartments in 2 separate buildings.

21. **Castle II Homes**
Joseph Berry single family homes were constructed in the $300,000 to $500,000 price range.

22. **Chalmers Apartments**
Renovation of 76 units completed in 1998.

23. **Charles Terrace**
$21 million in improvements by the Detroit Housing Commission.

24. **Charlotte Street Redevelopment**
$1.6 million conversion of three structures into ten rental units.

25. **Chesterfield Building**
$2.4 million historic rehabilitation into 26 affordable housing units.

26. **City Homes Development**
Proposed 400 single family development lead by Pulte Home Corporation.

27. **Clairpointe Woods.Clairpointe at Victoria Park**
$10 million investment along a 15.8 acre strip resulting in 41 single family homes.

28. **Corktown Condominiums**
$2.0 million project development of 10 townhouses in Phase I. Phase I consists of 8 units and 3 single family homes to be completed in 2001.

29. **Corktown Estates**
$640,000 six unit townhouse development.

30. **Courtyard by Marriott**
Renovation of the hotel will be completed in 2001.

31. **Days Inn, Rivertown**
Renovation of the hotel was completed in 1998.

32. **Detroit Central Cities Community Mental Health, Inc.**
$5 million rehabilitation of a partially vacant building into a health clinic and apartments.

33. **Detroit Veteran Center**
104 new apartments were completed in 1998.

34. **Diggs Homes**
$6.4 million in site improvements.

35. **Downtown Loft Housing Developments**
$250,000 pre-development loan pool to assist loft housing developers between Grand Circus Park and Campus Martius.

36. **East Ferry Street, 295**
Renovation 1893 building into nine rental units for low and moderate income tenants.

37. **Eden Manor**
65 new apartments were completed in 1996.

38. **Edmon Apartments**
$700,000 renovation resulting in 6 new 2 bedroom, 1 bath apartments.

39. **Ellis Manor**
89 new units of apartments completed in 1994.

40. **Elmwood III Vision**
$5.7 million investment resulting in 97 apartments.

41. **Elmwood Park Plaza**
202 apartments were renovated in 1995.

42. **Emmanuel Community Housing**
$1.2 million Phase I is the construction of 11 single-family homes.

43. **E. English Village**
$16 million project for 70-100 condominiums starting at $160,000.

44. **Euclid Square Condominiumns**
$2.5 million 28 unit three story condo development. 16 have already been built.

45. **Evergreen Manor**
Rehabilitation of 75 exiting residences completed in1998.

46. **Faith Manor**
56 new apartments were completed in 1995.

47. **Fellowship Homes**
$3 million joint venture Phase I will construct 28 in-fill single family homes.

48. **Field Street I & II**
49 new duplexes were completed in 1998.

49. **Forest Park II**
150 new apartment project began in 2000.

50. **Forest Park III**
$7.8 million 100 senior citizen units.

51. **Fourth/Willis Historic Development and Weber Block**
Large rehabilitation project of 250 homes to begin construction in 2001.

52. **Frederick Douglass Apartments**
$5.6 million renovation to be completed in 2001.

53. **Friendship Meadows II and III**
53 units were completed in 1995. Phase III of construction began in 1999 and will include an additional 100 units.

54. **Garfield Block**
Phase on renovation of two apartment buildings into 60 rental units. The project will eventually have 151 housing units.

55. **Garfield Building**
$6.5 millioin renovation into 56 units of loft housing and a Rite Aid on the ground floor.

56. **Genesis Villa at Medbury Park Phase II**
$11.5 million Phase I building of 89 units along Harper near John R. Construction scheduled for completion in Fall of 2001. $16 million Phase II represents 105 units scheduled to begin in Spring of 2002. Developed by Genesis Community Development Corporation.

57. **Ghandi McMahon Building**
24 new apartments were completed in 1998.

58. **Gramont Manor**
50 unit residential structure completed in 2000.

59. **Grand River Plaza Hotel**
$37 million 20 story hotel with 220 rooms being developed by MSG Development Ltd. LLC.

60. **Greyhaven Marina Village/ Greyhaven Estate Limited LLC**
$21 million development consisted of 127 condominiums. $25 million for 57 single family homes is in the planning.

61. **Grinnell Place Lofts**
40 unit residential lot development scheduled for completion in late Summer 2002.

62. **Habitat for Humanity**
$425,000 total for 25 units West and 30 units East.

63. **Habitat for Humanity Blitz Build**
$795,000 construction of 15 new homes in 1995. 20 more homes were built in the same community in 1997.

64. **Hancock Square**
$1.7 million construction of 12 units.

65. **Helen Odean Butler Apartments**
97 new apartments were completed in 1995.

66. **Herman Gardens**
$92 million demolition and renovation of the Herman Gardens Homes with construction slated for 2001.

67. **Holiday Inn**
$25 million six-story hotel with 200 rooms being developed by Icon Development LLC.

68. **Hotel St. Regis**
$2.5 million renovation of St. Regis Hotel into Holiday Inn St. Regis. Project completed in May 2000.

69. **Howard Johnson Hotel**
$3.2 million renovation of an abandoned hotel into a moderately priced hotel.

70. **Hubbell Group**
$2.6 million development of sixteen new condominiums.

71. **Ida Young Housing**
$3.4 million 56 unit apartment complex.

72. **Indian Village Manor Condominium Conversion**
Restored 7 story, 87 units of luxury condominium.

73. **Islandview Village**
$3.2 million Phase I of 22 single family homes, Phase II features 28 new townhomes.

74. **Jefferson Avenue Housing**
$98 million redevelopment of an entire neighborhood including 380 housing units.

75. **Jeffries Homes**
$80 million in demolition and renovation of the Jeffries homes to be completed in 2001.

76. **Joseph Berry Park Estates**
20 new waterfront luxury homes at a project cost of $5 million.

77. **Judith & Angeline Apartment Buildings**
Renovation of two apartment buildings into 7 units each.

78. **Junction Avenue Duplex Development (SWAN)**
$700,000 development of 4 duplex units.

79. **Knights Inn**
Renovation to the motel was completed in 1998.

80. **Lakewood Manor**
30 new apartments were completed in 1996.

81. **Landsberg Lofts**
$1.3 million development of ten loft condominiums.

82. **Lenton Development**
$706,500 Phase I restoration of an abandoned building into six for-sale residential units.

83. **Liberty Construction Corporation**
$4.5 million each for two 75 unit senior housing facilities.

84. **McGivney-Bethune Apartments**
80 new apartments were completed in 1995.

85. **Mahatawa Apartments**
$1.7 million project will result in at least 12 residential units.

86. **Mariner's Inn**
21,000 square feet addition.

87. **Marketplace Court Apartments**
$8 million, six-buildings, 120-unit housing development, 1996.

88. **Marriott Detroit Hotel**
$100 million renovation to be completed in 2001.

89. **Medbury Park/Genisis Villa Townhouses**
$20 million 14-block redevelopment of 194-townhouse units $11 million Phase 1 construction in 2000.

90. **Meyers Court Townhouses I & II**
$11 milliioin 15-unit townhouse concepts.

91. **Meyers Plaza Cooperative**
75 new apartments completed in 1998.

92. **Mid-City Residential Redevelopment**
New residential ancillary commercial. Detroit is currently seeking developers.

93. **Mildred Smith Manor**
52 single-family units. Phase I was 28 units, has been completed. Phase II will cost $2.5 million.

94. **Milner Arms Apartments**
Renovation of 150 apartments completed in 1999.

95. **Morningside Commons**
$30 million construction and rehabilitation of 500 single & multifamily units. 40 new homes were constructed in 1999.

96. **Motor City Blight Busters**
Scattered project that is the acquisition and rehabilitation of 15 homes.

97. **Nailah LLC**
$3.8 million renovation of historic buildings into 50-60 apartments.

98. **Newberry Estates**
$7.7 million, 60 in-fill single family homes for lease.

99. **New Center Loft Condominiums**
Residential project of 250 attached condominiums.

100. **New Hope Non-Profit Housing Corporation**
$1.35 million single family housing development consisting of 10 units in Phase I.

101. **NHT Housing, Inc. & Eastside Emergency Center**
$3.2 million for 30 units of transitional housing for homeless women and children.

102. **Northwest Detroit Neighborhood Development, Inc.**
$6 million renovation of 10 homes and construction of 56 new homes.

103. **Oak Village Square**
75 new apartments were completed in 1998.

104. **Omni River Place Hotel**
Renovation of the building was completed in 1999.

105. **Pablo Davis**
$7.7 million for 81 new apartments.

106. **Palmer Court Townhomes**
$18 million for 172 new 2-3 bedroom townhomes.

107. **Palmer Street Redevelopment**
$10 million to rehab 85 apartments and to build 44 new townhouses.

108. **Pania Development**
120 unit housing development completed in 1999.

109. **People United as One**
50 new residential units to begin in 2001.

110. **Petoskey Place**
$9.5 million development of 96 low-income housing units sold to individual homeowners.

111. **Pilgrim Village Apartments**
$2.2 million 22 unit complex developed in 1997.

112. **Presbyterian Villages of Michigan**
$4 million, 52 unit three story subsidized apartments for senior citizens.

113. **Prevost Gardens**
$3.7 million project of 40 affordble homes being developed by West Detroit Interfaith Community Organization (WDIFCO).

114. **Rehoboth Apartments**
The renovation of 31 apartments was completed in 1999.

115. **Savannah Apartments**
Historic rehabilitation of 20 apartments finished construction in 1999.

116. **Second Avenue, 6200**
Phase I of the New Amsterdam Development Building will be renovated into loft style apartments. Interior demolition will begin in Spring 2001.

117. **Sheridan Place**
$4 million renovation of Sheridan Place.

118. **Sixth Avenue Lofts**
$600,000 renovation of a warehouse into residential lofts and indoor parking is underway.

119. **Smith Homes**
$12 million renovation of Smith Homes.

120. **St. Anne's Gate Senior Housing**
$5 million, in all 65 unit senior rental housing will be constructed.

121. **Sticks and Bricks**
4 new homes on Phillip Street.

122. **University Club Apartments**
120 new apartments were completed in 1994.

123. **University of Detroit Mercy Manor**
Conversion of an apartment building to 28 for-sale condominiums.

124. **University Towers**
$25 million investment resulting in 300 new apartments, completed in 1995.

125. **Uptown Row**
47 new apartments were completed in 2000.

126. **Van Dyke Apartments**
$1.5 million renovation, 16-units of low and moderate-income apartments.

127. **Van Vilet Condominiums**
$2.25 million development of sixteen condominiums. Construction is to begin in the fall of 2001.

128. **Venn Apartments**
$483,000 historic renovation project resulted 6 new 3 bedroom, 2 bath apartments.

129. **Victor Attar Court**
$15 million rehabilitation project featuring 29 units.

130. **Victoria Park II**
157 single-family homes have been built in two phases. Phase II will include 100 more new homes.

131. **Villages of Parkside**
$90 million demolition and repairment of a public housing complex with a 570-unit to townhouse development.

132. **Virginia Park, 600**
4 new townhouses to sell at $175,000.

133. **Virginia Park Estates**
$7.5 million single-family subdivision of 45 homes.

134. **Wabash Homes in Historic Corktown**
Five new single-family homes completed in 1998.

135. **Waldof Lofts**
Renovation of an abandoned property into a four-unit condominium complex.

136. **Warren West Apartments**
$6 million in upgrades to this apartment complex.

137. **We Care Non-Profit Housing Corporation**
$696,000 renovation project will result in 6 homes.

138. **Westwill Apartments**
Renovation of a 60-unit complex into low income housing completed in 1998.

139. **Wilshire Apartments**
$1.75 million historic rehabilitation of a 20 unit building, originally built in 1926.

140. **Woodbridge Historic District Homes**
$786,000 renovation of six homes and apartment buildings.

141. **Woodward Lofts**
$25.5 million construction of 168 new loft town homes on Woodward just north of West Grand Boulevard to be developed by Crosswinds Communities. Construction began in the spring of 2001.

142. **Woodward Place at Brush Park**
$90 million development of more than 400 single-family condominiums and for-sale housing units.

MIXED USED - ○

143. **Beck Building**
Renovation into office, residential lofts, with ground-floor shops and restaurants.

144. **Broadway, 1521**
DIF has partnered with the Larson Realty Group to purchase and co-develop 12,500 square feet of office and retail space. The $3 million project will provide four 1,800 square foot loft apartments. Project completion and full occupancy is expected in 2001. DIF closed this $510, 000 land acquisition transaction on December 29, 2000.

145. **Campus Martius Development**
$1 million restoration of downtown

into a tree-lined office, shopping, and entertainment district.

146. **Care Village**
Multi-use new construction building was completed in 1999.

147. **Caribbean Cultural Center & Residential Development/East Ferry Housing**
$3 million renovation of five historic homes into 11 new residential units and a Caribbean Cultural Center.

148. **Cornice and Slate Building**
Expansion of the mixed-use building for the Metro Times was completed in 1999.

149. **Detroit Science and Technology Park**
Preliminary master plan for the park builds on potential of the sites two principle assets, the Woodward Avenue Corridor and the New Center's medical and manufacturing base.

150. **Detroit Virtual Reality Center**
$3 million commercial virtual reality showroom.

151. **Farwell Building**
Mixed-use building will include 50 residential lofts.

152. **Ferguson Building**
Renovated by Farbman Group into office and residential lofts with ground floor shops and restaurants.

153. **Ferry Street Bed and Breakfast Inn**
$6.5 million renovation of four historic homes and three carriage barns into a 42-room, bed and breakfast inn.

154. **Fisher Taubman Development**
A riverfront project with direct access to the Detroit River.

155. **Furniture Factory**
$600,000 renovaiton of the historic Weber Furniture Factory and warehouse into a furniture factory, theater, performance space and rehearsal studio.

156. **Harmonic Park Development**
$20 million loft, office, restaurant/entertainment project.

157. **Harper Hospital/Detroit Medical Center**
$10.5 million deck provides 1,550 parking spaces.

158. **Healy Building**
The building will be renovated into office and residential lofts with ground floor shops and restaurants.

159. **Kales Building**
The 18-story Kales building was rennovated into office and residential lofts with commercial space in the first two floor.

160. **Kresge Building/Cass Lofts Building**
$3.6 million conversion into seven lofts. 32 patient kidney dialysis and Veterans' Administration Services Office.

161. **Library Lofts**
Mixed-use project includes 10 residential lofts.

162. **Madison Madison International (MMI)**
$3 million rennovation of a 7-story abandoned building into the MMI headquarters and commercial space.

163. **Majestic Theater and Cafe**
Rennovation of restaurant, pool hall, and performance venue.

164. **Martin Luther King, Jr. Development Plan**
This multi-million 300 acre project consists of several phases of residential, commercial, and light industry.

165. **Metropole Building Redevelopment**
Rehabilitation of this building into office space and a new cajun restaurant.

166. **Mexicantown Welcome Center**
$8 million international Welcome Center and retail center.

167. **Michigan Ave. Lofts**
Renovation included 8 residential lofts.

168. **Motown/Sanders Building**
Mixed-use building rehabilitation will contain 20 residential lofts.

169. **Mueller Building**
Rennovated office building completed in 1994.

170. **New Amsterdam Development Project**
$57 million development of a district located in southern New Center between the CN railroad tracks and Burroughs Avenue will be redeveloped into a mixed-use community consisting of residential loft, office and retail uses.

171. **North Village Project**
The large mixed-use venture will contain 250 lofts.

172. **Northwest Institutional Leadership Action Counsil (NILAC)**
$750,000 transformation of property into a health care organization, restaurant, and other various businesses.

173. **Orchestra Place**
$80 million performing arts, education and office center of Orchestra Hall.

174. **Parker Webb Building**
Rehabilitation of the existing structure was completed in 1998.

175. **River Park Lofts**
Rehabilitation of 25 lofts, completed in 2000

176. **Rose Building**
Rehabilitation was completed in 1997, including 7 residential lofts.

177. **Stuber-Stone Building**
$2.6 million building renovation with health care facility and 13 residential loft units.

178. **Talon Gratiot Avenue Development**
Retail & commercial project to be built in phases.

179. **Tech Villas**
$33.8 million residential learning and conference center, hotel and 100 seat virtual reality area.

180. **The Family Place**
$4 million library rehabilitation for a family center.

181. **Wayne State Technology Park**
The city of Detroit, Wayne State University, Henry Ford Health System and GM are jointly developing a Tech Park between Woodward, Third, Amsterdam and Antoinette anchored by the 140,000 square foot building at 440 Borroughs. Phase I will feature a 45,000 square foot business incubation center and offices and will complement the New

Amsterdam development project.

182. **Whitney Building Improvements**
$37 million conversion into a suite hotel.

183. **Woodward Building Purchase, 1425**
Conversion of building into 28 residential lofts with commercial space on the first floor. Development lead by Sterling Group and DIF.

184. **Woodward Gladstone Townhouse Restoration**
Mixed-use project containing 12 residential units.

185. **Woodward Millenium Partners Professional Plaza**
$100 million investment. Phase I consists of a 150-unit apartment complex and a five-story parking deck. Phase II will build a 10-story office building and either a hotel or congregate-care facility. At Woodward & Garfield, a 22,000 s.f. former warehouse will become an Art gallery.

186. **Wright Kay Building**
Mixed-use development includes residential lofts and the nightclub Pure Detroit.

▲ COMMERCIAL -

BANKS - △

1. **Bank One**
$2 million renovation of its Michigan headquarters.

2. **Detroit Commerce Bank**
The new offices was completed in 1998.

3. **Omni Bank Building**
$1.9 million four story banking headquarters.

ENTERTAINMENT - △

4. **Bleu**
$1 million conversion of the former Telnews Theater on Woodward into an upscale techno sound and lighting dance club featuring a video wall.

5. **Belle Isle Park**
$5.6 million improvements including water slides, pool, canal system, and other repairs.

6. **Century Theater & Gem Theatre**
$2 million relocation and renovation.

7. **Chandler Park Aquatic Center**
The new waterpark was completed in 1998 on Detroit's east side.

8. **Columbia Street Entertainment Center**
$10 million project including sports bars, themed restaurants, micro-breweries, and coffee houses.

9. **DAC (Detroit Athletic Club)**
$15 million renovation to existing building The expansion of the parking structure is scheduled for completion in 2001.

10. **Detroit Institute of the Arts**
The renovation of the DIA was completed in 1998.

11. **Detroit Academy of Arts and Sciences**
The new building completed construction in 1999.

12. **Detroit Golf Club**
$5 million renovation completed in 1999.

13. **Detroit Science Center**
$80 million development of new exhibition space.

14. **Elwood Bar and Grill**
Located near the new Comerica Park, it opened in 2000.

15. **Fine Arts Building**
$450,000 renovation of a vintage facility into a 350-seat dinner/ performance club.

16. **Greektown Casino (Interim & Permanent)**
This structure built a $147 million two-story building behind Trappers Alley for a temporary casino. A permanent Casino Hotel with 800 rooms is to be built one block west of the temporary casion location.

17. **MGM Grand Detroit Casino (Interim and Permanent)**
MGM turned the old IRS building into a $230 million temporary casino creating gaming space of 84,160 sq. ft., restaurants, retail, and offices.

18. **Michigan Opera Theatre**
$41 million development renovation, restoration, and expanding of the Detroit Opera House.

19. **Michigan State Fairgrounds**
$80 million development plan on the 206 acre fairgrounds at Woodward and Eight Mile will include 438,000 sq. ft. of new and renovated convention space, an equestrian center, renovated Amphitheatre, Crystal Colosseum and onsite parking for 10,000 acres.

20. **Motor City Casino (Interim/ Formerly Circus Circus and Permanent)**
This $160 million temporary casino is four stories and 188,000 sq. ft. The first two floors are for gaming, the third and fourth floors are for customers and employee dining.

21. **Music Hall**
$6 million renovation of the hall built in the 1920's.

22. **Post on Broadway**
$8 million entertainment project on the site of the former five-story 50,000 sq. ft. Madison Theater. Construction is to begin in summer of 2001.

23. **Pure Detroit**
The new nightclub opened in 1990.

24. **Riverbend Plaza Phase III**
Home Depot will anchor the eastern edge of the Jefferson East Commercial District.

25. **River East**
$1.5 billion development is both a private and public venture along the Detroit River for a new district of shops, lofts, offices, and restaurants.

26. **Stadium Complexes**
$600 million sports entertainment complex includes Comerica Park and Ford Field in the new homes for the Detroit Tigers and Detroit Lions.

27. **YMCA of Metropolitan Detroit**
$12 million project for a new facility in Detroit.

FOOD - △

28. **Bennigans**
The new restaurunt located at 105 Brush was completed in 1997.

29. **Blimpies**
Renovation completed in 1998, plus new stores.

30. **Blue Moon Jazz Cafe**
The former Finney's restaurant is being renovated into a new restaurant and entertainment spot.

31. **Burger King**
$14 million invested to open 16 Burger Kings in the city of Detroit.

32. **Cass Cafe**
The popular Cass Cafe was renovated in 1997.

33. **Docks Great Fish**
Three new locations in 1995 and one in 1998.

34. **Duet Restaurant/Unique Deli**
$2.3 million restaurant opened in 1998.

35. **International House of Pancakes**
$500,000 restaurant opened in 1996.

36. **KFC**
Two new restaurants opened in 1995.

37. **McDonald's Restaurant**
New McDonalds at Davison & Linwood resulted in 50 new jobs.

38. **Milano Bakery**
$3.85 million expansion of a wholesale bakery building & new equipment in the Eastern Market.

39. **Papa Romanos**
Four new locations opened in Detroit.

40. **Pizza Hut**
Renovation on five locations around Detroit.

41. **Rivertown Bagel**
New restaurant opened for business on E. Jefferson.

42. **Twingo's**
A French cafe on the Wayne State Campus. Plans for expansion into the adjacent storefront were completed in 2000.

43. **White Castle**
Six new locations throughout Detroit.

44. **Woodward Bagel Bakery Coffee House**
Two storefronts renovated for this bagel shop, bakery, and coffee house with an outdoor cafe.

MISCELLANEOUS - △

45. **Ameritech**
$30 million in upgraded cable, electronic equipment, and telecommunications infrastructure improvements in Detroit.

46. **Downtown Gateway BID**
Funds raised from district propery owners are being expended on Jefferson Avenue for district improvements.

47. **Eagle Way Full Gospel Ministries**
$2 million new church dedicated in 1998.

48. **Eastlake Missionary Baptist Church**
Multipurpose facility which houses a Headstart Program, gym, and 2,000 seat auditorium was completed in 1997.

49. **Grand Circus Park**
$2.4 million renovation of Grand Circus Park and the historic Edison Fountain.

50. **Greater Grace Temple**
Construction if a new Apostolic

church has resumed and will feature a 4,000 seat mail sanctuary, banquet hall with in-house catering services, offices, classrooms, meeting rooms, media sales office center, credit union, travel agency, and parking.

51. House of Prayer and Praise
$700,000 new church dedicated on December 26, 1998.

52. Hudson's Project Imagine Art Park
Hudson's Project Imagine has funded the enhancement of the green space at the corner of Farnsworth and John R. The new art park includes flowering trees, flower beds, seating and a commissioned sculpture at the center of the plaza. The park was completed in 1996.

53. Jefferson Veterinary Clinic
$330,000 construction of a veterinary clinic and boarding facility was completed in 1996.

54. Kingdom Hall of Jehovah Witness
Throughout Detroit from 1994-1999, 7 new halls were constructed and renovated.

55. L.S.C. Holdings, Inc.
$12 million investment in headquarters to aquire funeral homes in African-American communities throughout the United States.

56. Mack and Warren Median Flowerbeds
Wayne State University, Detroit Medical Center and the University Cultural Center Association have collaborated to increase the size and number of flower beds on Mack, Warren, Anthony Wayne and St. Antoine Avenues. Sponsorship of the beds will be solicited and other funding will come from the Hudson-Webber foundation. The flowerbeds will be installed in 2000-2001. The project cost is approximately $300,000.

57. Mascotech-Braun
$1.4 million in building improvements.

58. Michigan Re-Packing & Produce Company
$1.5 million facility expansion.

59. New Center Woodward Gateway
A streetscape enhancement project has been initiated by the New Center Council. The project will include the removal of an existing metal canopy that obscures store signage and the historic building facades. Plans also call for new decorative sidewalk paving, lighting, landscaping and street furniture.

60. Prentice Building
Rehabilitation was completed in 1998.

61. Providence Baptist Church
$2.9 million multi-phased project conducted to meet the needs of the growing congregation.

62. R Hirt Jr. Company
$2 million for a new facility in the Eastern Market.

63. Riverfront Promenade
The Detroit Downtown Development Authority awarded a $5 million contract to build a 3500

ft riverfront walkway between Joe Louis and the western edge of the Renaissance Center property. Construction will be completed in the spring of 2001. The project is being financed with a $6.2 million waterfront reclamation grant from the state's Clean Michigan Initiative. The Promenade will feature a twelve to twenty-two foot wide walkway bordered by a serpentine wall with recessed lighting, built in benches, and landscaping. Detroit Renaissance provided $50,000 for the development of the design plan.

64. Rose of Sharon Church of God in Christ
Phase I of the expansion of the church on State Fair will provide 8,000 sq. ft. for office space, a fellowship hall, and an elevator. The expansion also added 300 seats to the sanctuary. The $1 million project was completed in 1999. Phase II will include additional expansion and renovations.

65. Spin Cycle
Seven new facilities throughout Detroit in 1998.

66. Stroh's Ice Cream Company
$600,000 acquisition and relocation.

67. United House of Prayer
The new Joy Road church was dedicated in July 1998. The red brick building features twin steeples, gold exterior trim, and on-site parking. The church can accommodate more than 1000 in the main sanctuary.

68. West Detroit Interfaith Community Organization
$3.4 million investment for 26 single-family homes.

69. Wolverine Packing
$3 million expansion of warehouse and office space in the Eastern Market.

70. Victory Plaza
New commercial project completed in 1998.

OFFICE - ◬

71. Albert Kahn Building
Albert Kahn Association, Inc., a 400-person planning, design and management firm of the built environment, has completed a $4.5 million, 3 1/2 year renovation of its offices in the historic Albert Kahn Building. The Virtual Reality Center, located in this building, includes some of the world's most advanced computer technologies from 30 companies.

72. Alpha Data Services
Office renovation completed in 1997.

73. A-Mac Builders Building
Office renovation completed in 1997.

74. American Society of Employers
Office renovation completed in 1997.

75. Ameritech Corporation
$16 million in building renovations and improvements.

76. Arab American & Chaldean Council
Renovation was completed in 1998.

77. Book Building
$25 million in renovations.

78. Buhl Building Renovation
$5 million in renovations.

79. Cadillac Tower Building Renovation
Renovation completed in 1998.

80. Children's Center
$6 million Program Services Building for programs for at-risk children.

81. Compuware
$1.2 billion initiative to move its headquarters downtown at Campus Martius by 2000.

82. Contract Interiors, Inc.
$2 million renovation of a warehouse for storage and other operations.

83. Detroit Manufacturing Training Center
$4 million work force training center opened in 2000.

84. Detroit Neighborhood Housing Services (DNHS)
A non-profit housing corporation purchased and renovated the former Kuhlman building.

85. Detroit News Building
$10 million headquarters renovation.

86. First National Building
Renovation completed in 1999.

87. General Motors/UAW Training Facility & Human Resources
A new seven story 398,000 sq. ft. training facility is being built by GM and UAW.

88. Guardian Building Renovation
Renovation of the existing office space was completed in 1999.

89. Honeywell Building
Renovation is expected to be completed in 2001.

90. Jefferson Centre
New commercial venue completed in 1999.

91. Kingsway Building
The rehabilitation is currently under way, to be completed in 2001.

92. Lason Systems, Inc.
Renovation of the existing offices was completed in 1998.

93. Michigan Federation of Teachers
$1.8 million new headquarters.

94. Mueller Building
Renovation of this existing offices completed in 1994.

95. One Kennedy Square/Griswold Place
$35 million to be invested to renovate the 23-story office building.

96. One Woodward Avenue Building
The renovation of the offices currently under construction, scheduled for completion in 2001.

97. Penobscot Building Renovation
The renovation of the building was completed in 2000.

98. Rebert Building Renovation
$1.3 million commercial renovation into new offices for the Southwest Detroit Business Association and visiting tenants.

99. Renaissance Center Renovation
$72 million purchase by General Motors to relocate world headquarters. Additional $500 million in renovations began.

100. Reiver Park Lofts
Rehabilitation of 25 residential lofts.

101. Silver's Building/Savoyard Centre
Renovation of the Fort Street building was completed in 2000.

102. TelePlanet Data Center
HDC partners announces the purchase of a large industrial site on Detroit's west side and is converting it into a $20 million data center; 363,000 sq. ft. complex called TelePlanet will open 2001.

103. UAW Local 7
The new office is under construction.

104. UAW-Chrysler National Training Center
$2.8 million in office building renovations.

105. UAW-Ford National Programs Center
$25.6 million center design by SHG, is scheduled for completion in the spring of 2001.

106. Veterans Memorial Building
$10 million renovation of the riverfront Veterans' Memorial Building into an Employee Development and Training Center.

107. West Adams Street, 28
David Howell, asset manager for Capozzoli Advisory for Pensions, Inc. (CAP) announced purchase of 20-story tower building-former Michigan Mutual Building-and will spend $7 million in its renovations.

108. West Fort Street, 211
$30 million reconstruction and ADA renovation.

109. West Fort Renovation, 333
Office renovation (153,000 sq. ft.) development by the Sterling Group. Expected completion is in 2001.

110. West Fort Renovation, 455
$12 million renovation developed by the Sterling Group. Expected completion is to be in 2001.

111. West Shelby Building, 607
The building in the new home of Hawkins Food Group. The nine-story building underwent a $2 million renovation in 1998 and now features Class A office space. Each floor contains 5,200 sq. ft. of office space.

112. West Willis Business Center
Renovated to house the Associated Medical Services.

RETAIL - ◬

113. Arbor Drugs/CVS
13 new Detroit locations have been built since 1997.

114. AutoZone
5 new Detroit locations have been added throughout Detroit from late 1997-1998.

115. Blockbuster
4 new Detroit locations have been built since 1997.

116. Chene Square
$7.2 million retail complex with tenants includes Fuddruckers Restaurant, Hollywood Video, a bank branch, Heritage Optical, Sports Essential, Dock's Great Fish, and Lucky Dragon Restaurant.

117. College Park Commons
$30 million retail and medical services facilities.

118. C-Pop Gallery
Specializing in underground art,

the C-Pop Gallery moved from Royal Oak to the southeast corner of Willis and Woodward. Gallery owners invested over $1 million to restore a three-story, 9,600 sq. ft. building. Completed in 1999, the building incorporates exhibit space, studio and roof deck. Future plans include a coffee house and sculpture garden.

119. Detroit Artists' Market
The Detroit Artists' Market has comleted renovation of their new gallery space at the corner of Forest and Woodward. Estimated cost of the project is $370,000.

120. Detroit Discount Distributors
$1 million new bulk food distribution center.

121. Farmer Jack
Two new stores were added to the Detroit area.

122. Gratiot Central Market
$3 million reconstruction of the Eastern Market.

123. Harbortown
$4.5 million project. Phase II includes the addition of 22 new townhouses.

124. Hartford Kmart Retail Center
$15 million new retail center.

125. Livernois Square Shopping Plaza
$11.2 million Phase I & II, strip mall and professional offices.

126. Movie Mania
One new store is opened and three others are planned for the city of Detroit.

127. Murray's Discount Auto Parts
From 1994-1998, five new locations have opened in Detroit.

128. Pep Boys
20-30 new automotive part stores throughout the city over the next three to five years.

129. R.A.C. Detroit
A new $4.17 million retail center is being built at Grand River and Greenfield. The 22,680 sq. ft. center will be anchored by Rite Aid. Standard Federal Bank provided a $1.75 million mortgage on the property.

130. Rite Aid Drug Stores
$8 million in Detroit for five new drug stores.

131. Riverbend Plaza Shopping Center
$2.2 million expansion. Phase II of The Jefferson-Chalmers shopping center has been completed.

132. The Shops at Northeast Village
$3 million retail center that will feature a 54,000 sq. ft. Kroger and other commercial stores.

133. University Center
$7.5 million retail center includes a 40,000 sq. ft. University Foods and other tenants.

134. Walgreens Drug Stores
$14 million for seven new locations planned throughout the city.

■ **INSTITUTIONAL & MANUFACTURING**

EDUCATION - ▢

1. African Heritage Culture Center (DPS)
The renovation to the center is expected to be completed in 2001.

2. Center for Creative Studies
Renovation of the public institution is scheduled for completion in 2001.

3. Cesar Chavez Acadamy
Expansion of the building was completed in 1998.

4. Cornerstone Schools
The school was renovated in 1998.

5. Cultural Center Parking
Parking facility constructed to the east of the DIA, in conjunction with the City of Detroit.

6. Detroit Public Schools
$1.5 billion investment locations throughout the country for repairs and new construction.

7. Detroit School for Fine and Performing Arts
School construction along with the 50,000 sq. ft. expansion on the north side of Orchestra Hall for a new facility and locker facilities for the musicians.

8. Edison Schools/YMCA Service Learning Academy
This $3.2 million project involves the construction of a new YMCA Service Learning Academy near Lahser and Seven Mile Road. Standard Federal Bank and Bank One are providing project financing.

9. Focus: HOPE
$3.5 million, two-story addition for classrooms.

10. Hutchinson Elementary School
Rehabilitation completed in 1999.

11. Jefferson School
The former public school has been renovated into a charter school.

12. Museum of African-American History (Charles H. Wright Museum)
$35 million museum is the largest African-American museum in the country.

13. Manufacturing Engineering Building
$4.5 million new building project suppliments the Wayne State University campus.

14. Sankore Marine Immerson Academy
The renovation was completed in 1998.

15. Ser Casa Academy
$2.4 million renovation of Saint Anne's School into a 250 student, 6-12 grade Charter School.

16. University of Detroit Jesuit High School and Academy
$25 million new building to house the cafeteria and classrooms.

17. University of Detroit Mercy
$11 million new School of Dentistry.

18. Wayne State University Capital Expansion
$64 million new home for the College of Pharmacy and Allied Professionals and over $245 million in renovations and expansions.

19. Woodward Academy
$2 million renovation of the existing vacant building into a 600 student, 2-8 grade Charter School.

GOVERNMENT - ▢

20. City of Detroit Civic Center; Waterfront
The project will link the Renaissance Center to the Joe Louis Arena.

21. City of Detroit Recreation Department (Bishop Playfield)
The renovation of this field was completed in 1990.

22. City of Detroit Department of Public Works
The City Department constructed a new 15,000 sq. ft. three story glass and brick building at its vehicle storage site on Michigan Avenue. The new facility includes a lobby, offics, meeting and conference rooms, kitchen, elevators and parking lot. The building will house all administrative offices for the Street Maintenance/Construction Division and Traffic Engineering. A total of $3.3 million was invested in the development, which was completed in 1999.

23. City of Detroit Recreation Department (Detroit River Link Parks)
This development includes area from the Renaissance Center East to the Belle Isle Bridge.

24. City of Detroit Water and Sewerage Department
$300 million in improvements to the system.

25. Considine Center
The rehabilitation of the public institution was completed in 1997.

26. Department of Social Services Building
$4.5 million new construction of a 50,000 sq. ft. DSS Building.

27. Detroit Recreation Department
$3.6 million to re-develop Mt. Elliott Park.

28. Federal Drug Enforcement Agency
$13 million new regional headquarters completed in 1996.

29. IRS Computer Center
$100.5 million IRS computing center completed in 1995.

30. Michigan Family Independence Agency
The 32,000 sq. ft. facility was renovated and expanded to accomodate more offices. A total of $1.3 million was invested in the northwest Detroit facility. The State of Michigan facility provides social services to area residents.

31. Millennium Garage
$20 million structure to serve Cobo Hall and W. Fort Street completed in 1999.

32. One Stop Capital Shop
The Empowerment Zone's One Stop Capital Shop opened in 1996.

33. Southwest Detroit Contaminated Sites Project
$7.8 million to clean up six contaminated sites in the Empowerment Zone.

34. State of Michigan Building
The state of Michigan will soon have a new home in the General Motors Building. All state approvals have been completed to consolidate state services for Greater Detroit into 1.3 million sq. ft. of this landmark building. 300 employees are scheduled to relocate in summer of 2001 and completion of the renovations is

scheduled for spring of 2002.

35. Wayne County Buildings Division
$40 million juvenile detention center.

HEALTH CARE - ▣

36. Adult Well Being Administrative Offices
The administrative offices completed construction in 1999.

37. Afton Dialysis Center
$1.2 million renovation of a vacant building, which will house 20 dialysis machines.

38. Alexander J. Walt Comprehensive Breast Center
New building project that is currently under construction with completion scheduled for 2001.

39. American Red Cross
$7 million construction of a new blood testing lab.

40. Blue Cross and Blue Shield of Michigan Development
$32 million expansion of the Blue Cross Blue Shield downtown Detroit headquarters.

41. Children's Hospital
$16.5 million renovation of Children's Hospital was completed in 1998.

42. Complete Health Services/Wellness Place
$6.5 million new facility.

43. Comprehensive Health Services
$10 million full-service health center.

44. Detroit Community Health Connection
$2 million new non-profit community health center.

45. Detroit Medical Center
$12.4 million renovation of their ER and of the Primary Care Access Facility.

46. Detroit Receiving Hospital
$10.5 million in renovations to their operating rooms.

47. DMC Sinai/Grace Hospital
The expansion was completed in 2000.

48. Gateway Clinic
This new medical clinic was recently constructed by the wellness plan.

49. Henry Ford Health System
$27 million three-story medical clinic in Northeast Detroit was completed in 1995.

50. Henry Ford Health System/GM Health and Fitness Center
$10 million health and fitness center.

51. Henry Ford Hospital
$87 million expansion and renovation of Henry Ford Hospital.

52. Holy Cross Hospital
$3.5 million in renovations.

53. Hospice of Southeast Michigan
$7.5 million 81 bed hospice and offices.

54. Hudson-Webber Cancer Research Center
$23.2 million has been sponsored by the Karmanos Cancer Institute.

55. Hutzel Hospital
Expansion of the existing institution was completed in 1996.

56. Karmanos Cancer Institute
$5 million renovation of bone marrow unit.

57. Mercy Hospital
$2.7 million renovation and

addition to upgrade the existing building.

58. St. John Hospital
$19.1 million addition to its facilities and a new birthing center.

59. United Community Hospital
The renovation was completed in 1999.

60. Veterans' Administration Hospital
$250 million new 432-bed VA hospital built in 1996.

61. Wertz Clinical Cancer Center
$16 million expansion by the Karmanos Cancer Institutes.

62. William Clay Ford II Athletic Medicine Center
The new public institution was completed in 1996.

63. Woodward Corridor Family Medical Center
$2 million primary health care facility.

MANUFACTURING - □

64. Ace-Tex Corporation
$5.5 million 100,000 sq. ft. expansion of the facility.

65. Ad Mail Services
Renovation of a 68,000 sq. ft. facility.

66. Advance Steel Company
The manufacturing center was completed in 1995.

67. Aguirre Collins & Airman Plastics, L.L.C.
New building completed construction in 1998.

68. Allied Supply Company
$500,000 renovation of two vacant buildings into a headquarters, warehouse, and workshop.

69. American Axle & Manufacturing Co.
$350 million investment in plant restoration and new equipment.

70. Arbor Research
$2 million to relocate and expand its operations from Ann Arbor to Detroit.

71. Arrow Cold Storage
Construction is complete on a $4 million, 60,000 sq. ft. refrigerated storage center near the Eastern Market. A total of 20 new jobs were created.

72. Arvin Meritor Building
Arvin Meritor, formed following the merger of Meritor Automotive from Troy with Arvin Industries from Indiana, is relocating to southwest Detroit. This Light Vehicle Systems Company is building a new 150,000 sq. ft. facility to accommodate sunroof assembly operations as well as sub-manufacturing for its new encapsulated glass product line. The project, located near West Fort Street and Rademacher, will accomodate 400 employees.

73. Better-Made Potato Chips
The Detroit Potato Chip Company expanded its 100,000 sq. ft. facility on East Gratiot by 20,000 sq. ft. in December 1998. The $500,000 expansion created 15 new jobs.

74. Bing Group at North Industrial Park
$7.5 million to build two new facilities.

75. Blue Circle Cement Co.
This cement manufacturing

company is reinvesting $14,234,000 in its southwest Detroit facility.

76. Bridgewater Interiors
$5 million facility to produce interior components for GM.

77. Broad, Vogt, & Conant, Inc.
$1.1 million on renovations to relocate the company in a vacant three-story building.

78. Budd Company
$20 million in renovations and plant improvements.

79. Canvas Products Company
$1 million purchase of q 65,000 sq. ft. factory, improvements, new equipment, and company relocation.

80. Caramagno Foods
$300,000 company expansion.

81. Cattlemans, Inc.
Expansion was complete in 1996.

82. Chrysler Corporation
$2.1 billion for new engine plant & expansion throughout the city.

83. Clark Street Technology Park
$125 million redeveloping a technology park in southwest Detroit on the grounds of the former Cadillac Plant.

84. Commonwealth Industries
This Metal heat-treating plant, located on 5900 Commonwealth is reinvesting $3.9 million in its facilities. Commonwealth Industries, incorporated in 1919, is one of the largest and most efficient high production heat treating and metal finishing operations in the United States.

85. Connolly-Ervins
A joint venture for a new 75,000 sq. ft. facility is to produce automotive interior prototype components.

86. D & C Industries, Inc.
$3.5 million new plant for prototype tools and parts.

87. Dana Container Corporation
$2.2 million warehouse expansion.

88. Detroit Automotive Interiors
$3.7 million (plus an additional $1.5 million in equipment) joint venture auto interiors plant.

89. Detroit Axle Plant
$300 million addition by Chrysler for sport utility manufacturing facility.

90. Detroit Bagel Factory/Patch Bagel
The company will construct a new $15 million facility on Detroit's West side. The company will use the 65,000 sq. ft. facility to distribute bagels to the Detroit Medical Center. Patch Bagel will serve as the organization's wholesaler.

91. Detroit Edison Testing Center
$1.3 million for new office and testing center, additional 32,000 sq. ft.

92. Detroit Heading/Textron Automotive
This joint venture is a project between a minority-controlled manufacturer of standard and cold headed products and a major automotive fastener and bold manufacturer. This $16 million project is located in the Lynch Road Renaissance Zone, and consists of a distribution and state of the art manufacturing facility, servicing two of the Big 3 automotive companies. The DEGC was

instrumental in successfully attracting Detroit Heading to the Renaissance Zone site.

93. Detroit Salt Company
New company created 57 new jobs in SW Detroit.

94. Detroit Technologies, Inc.
Renovated an abandoned warehouse into interior systems and components.

95. Dinverno, Inc.
$1.6 million to construct a one-story steel recycling facility.

96. Dos Manos
The new building was completed in 1998.

97. Eagle Steel Products, Inc.
$800,000 investment to modernize and expand the operations.

98. F.X. Coughlin/Ace Paper
Coughlin has opened a 107,000 sq. ft. facility.

99. General Motors Detroit/Hamtramck Assembly Plant
$250 million expansion of its Detroit/Hamtramck assembly complex.

100. Global Titanium
Expansion of the existing manufacturing building was completed in 1998.

101. Hispanic Manufacturing
$10 million development by three Hispanic owned manufacturing companies.

102. H.S. Automotive
This automotive supplier has initiated expansion plans within the city of Detroit.

103. Ideal Shield
$6 million expansion for this manufacturer of protective plastic components for buildings. The company broke ground on their expansion in August of 2000. President Loren Venegas said they have two more expanions in the pipeline.

104. JBS Co.
$500,000 upgrade for the former Westside Chevrolet site.

105. Kirlin Electric Company
$2.5 million expansion to this 100 year old lighting company.

106. Lafayette Steel & Processing/Olympic Steel Corporation
$7 million plant expansion.

107. Leatherworks
The first minority leather-cutting facility to be located in the heart of Detroit's Renaissance Zone, the company will introduce a new, innovative concept in leather cutting and auto seat production. Leatherworks will occupy 40,000 sq. ft. in its new, one-story building.

108. Mark IV Automotive
$1,575,000 renovation for this manufacturer of fuel filler pipes.

109. Mt. Elliot, 6600
The owner of 6600 Mt. Elliot is investing some $3 million to improve his 300,000 sq. ft. building in Detroit's I-94 Renaissance Zone. With the assistance of the DEGC, owner Mike Freedland already has two major tenants: Prestressed Systems, Inc., a Canadian manufacturer of structural concrete products, opened a 33,000 sq. ft. facility, creating 20 new jobs that are expected to grow to 100, and

Pulte Homes which leased 100,000 sq. ft. for production of prefabricated housing components. The Pulte facility will employ 65-75 plant workers and another 20 in office.

110. MNP Corporation
The expansion of the existing structure was completed in 1997.

111. Mexican Industries of Michigan
The new office is under construction.

112. Midwest Steel
$2 million investment in a new 32,000 sq. ft. office and warehouse.

113. MPS & Soave Enterprises Joint Venture
A joint venture 27,000 sq. ft. facility provides cleanup, transport, and meditation services for hazardous waste.

114. New Wave Material Handling
$1 million-plus automotive metal fabricating facility.

115. NYX Inc.
$5 million investment for a molding plant, which employs 50 people.

116. O.J. Group
$8.9 million private investment for mahchinery and equipment for this trucking distribution facility.

117. Perstorp Xytec
$10 million plant to produce plastic material-handling containers used by automakers and other industries.

118. Piston Automotive
Built warehouse facility for the sub-assembly of struts, sequencing of finished material to support Just In Time shipments to GM and other major customers.

119. Piston Packaging
$3.3 million supplies of corrugated pallets and boxes.

120. Pre-Stressed Systems, Inc.
The new building was completed in 1998.

121. Renaissance Global Logistics
$16.7 million joint venture 450,000 sq. ft. facility to produce vehicle kits for Ford Motor.

122. Richmond Steel Erectors
Minority Contractor just moved into their new 35,000 sq. ft. facility.

123. Ronart Industries
The expansion of the existing buildig was completed in 1996.

124. SBF Automotive, Inc.
$700,000 restoration in the Renaissance Zone of a joint venture. SBF was the first manufacturer.

125. Strong Steel Products LLC.
$14.5 million was invested to build a new steel-shredding facility.

126. Superb Manufacturing
$500,000 steel processing and automotive stamping complex expansion.

127. Thermo Tech
Thermo Technologies has broken ground on a $25 million plant and U.S. headquarters at 1601 E. Grand Boulevard in Detroit.

128. Thorn Apple Valley Foods Distribution Facility
$25 million processing plant renovation and expansion.

129. Thyssen Steel/Ken-Mac Metals
$100 million expansion of steel processing center.

130. Trim Tech LLC.
$4 million joint venture to make

foam products for auto suppliers.

131. TruMack Assembly
$8 million MEGA Credits provided by the state for a 210,000 sq. ft. new manufacturing building.

132. Unitog/Mechanics Rental Uniform Company
$5.6 million expansion for manufacturer of tack rags and industrial linens.

133. USL City Management
The new building was completed in 1996.

134. VITEC
$50 million new plastic automotive components manufacturing plant, located in the Clark Street Technology Park.

135. Winston Morrow
$5.3 million new equipment and improvements to scrap metal

TRANSPORTATION - ▢

136. Ambassador Bridge Facelift
The Ambassador Bridge is undergoing its first facelift in more than 68 years. The bridge is being stripped and repainted teal green. The project is a milestone, marking the first time in its history that the Ambassador Bridge will be painted a color other than black. The project will cost $25 million and is expected to be completed by 2004.

137. Ambassador Bridge West Expansion
The existing bridge is expected to reach capacity during the first decade of the new millenium; therefore preparations for a second span of the Ambassador Bridge are underway. The proposed project may cost as much as $300 million. The expansion project may be completed by 2012.

138. Detroit City Airport
$4 million rehabilitation completed in 1998.

139. Detroit Freight Terminal
The terminal is in the planning stages.

140. Detroit/Wayne County Port Authority Cruise Ship Dock & Terminal
The new project is in the planning stages.

141. MDOT I-375
$100 million expansion, new ramps, and interchanges for improved access is downtown.

142. MDOT Gateway Project
$100 million public project is in the planning stages, stated for completion in 2003.

143. New Center Train Station
The new station construction is stated to begin in 2001.

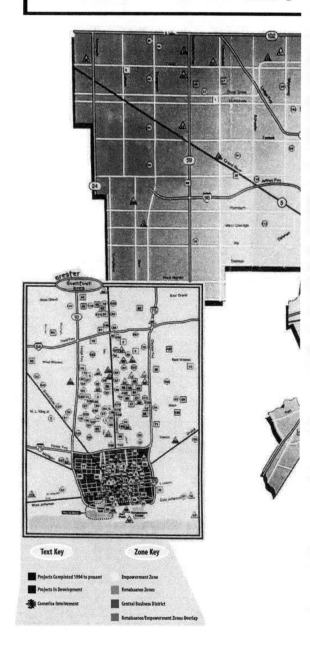

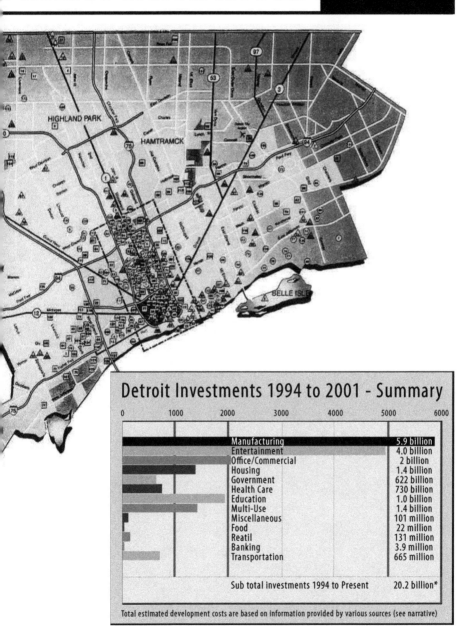

PMENT INITIATIVES 2001

Detroit Investments 1994 to 2001 - Summary

	0	1000	2000	3000	4000	5000	6000	
Manufacturing								5.9 billion
Entertainment								4.0 billion
Office/Commercial								2 billion
Housing								1.4 billion
Government								622 billion
Health Care								730 billion
Education								1.0 billion
Multi-Use								1.4 billion
Miscellaneous								101 million
Food								22 million
Reatil								131 million
Banking								3.9 million
Transportation								665 million

Sub total investments 1994 to Present	20.2 billion*

Total estimated development costs are based on information provided by various sources (see narrative)

INDEX

CPSIA information can be obtained
at www.ICGtesting.com
Printed in the USA
LVHW04s1511010618
579263LV00001B/182/P